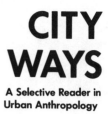

CITY
WAYS
A Selective Reader in
Urban Anthropology

CITY WAYS

A Selective Reader in Urban Anthropology

Edited by

JOHN FRIEDL
Ohio State University

and

NOEL J. CHRISMAN
University of Washington

Thomas Y. Crowell
HARPER & ROW, PUBLISHERS
New York   Hagerstown   San Francisco   London

CITY WAYS
A Selective Reader in Urban Anthropology

Copyright © 1975 by John Friedl & Noel J. Chrisman

Library of Congress Cataloging in Publication Data

Friedl, John, comp.
    City ways.

    Includes bibliographical references.
    CONTENTS: Introduction: Friedl, J. and Chris-
man, N. J. Continuity and adaptation as themes in urban
anthropology.—The city as a unit of analysis: Wirth, L.
Urbanism as a way of life. Fox. R. G. Rationale and
romance in urban anthropology. Price, J. A. Reno,
Nevada; the city as a unit of study. [etc.]
    1. Urban anthropology—Addresses, essays, lectures.
2. Cities and towns—Addresses, essays, lectures.
I. Chrisman, Noel J., 1940–   joint comp. II. Title.
GN505.F74   301.36   74-23254
ISBN 0-690-00152-5

Typography and cover design by Elliot Epstein

Foreword

The popular image of an anthropological study, and one to which many professional anthropologists themselves subscribe, is the very antithesis of an examination of a modern American suburb or the busy market place of a foreign metropolis. It connotes the cloistered calm of remote islands, of deep forests, or the exotic spells of magical practices rather than the all too familiar and prosaic day-to-day activities in modern cities. The excitement of anthropology, however, lies not in the strangeness of its subject material but in the way in which an analysis made in terms of principles developed in a very different cultural context may throw intriguing light upon formerly very matter-of-fact and familiar features of everyday life. Anthropological theory is general and not specific to strange and exotic societies.

It is for this reason that the recent emergence in anthropology of a field of specialization devoted to the study of urban phenomena is particularly to be welcomed. But the development of urban anthropology has been hampered by a paucity of published material and by the fact that many of the studies germane to the subject have appeared in sources not easily accessible. With the appearance of several collections since Eddy's *Urban Anthropology: Research Perspectives and Strategies* (1968) the position is being rectified. But as yet we lack a single source which is not a set of papers given to a seminar by a small set of specialists but is a careful selection of papers chosen for their contribution to urban anthropology and that a reader may turn to for quick reference. This collection by Professors Friedl and Chrisman is, as far as I know, the first attempt at such a volume.

The particular papers published here have been selected on several criteria. Firstly, each essay does not simply provide a description of some urban phenomenon but also makes explicit a theoretical orientation which the writer has found useful in looking at that phenomenon. Not unexpectedly these orientations are varied: quite correctly they draw from most of the approaches of the larger subject of which urban anthropology is only a part. And not surprisingly, sharp differences of

v

88807

opinion crop up on the same topic from one contribution to another: this is characteristic of a vigorous and expanding new specialization. Secondly, the essays have been chosen to cover the topics that normally fall within the province of the urban anthropologist. The complexity of urban life being what it is, the anthropologist usually limits his analysis to some aspect of the whole: an extensive city ethnography is a daunting prospect even if there are some brave souls who are prepared to attempt one. For the present we must be satisfied with selections covering major topics. Thirdly, the selections have been made to cover as varied a range of cultural areas as possible since one of the richnesses of anthropology is its comparative perspective. This provides a salutary correction to those specializations that are rooted in only one cultural milieu.

Happily Professors Friedl and Chrisman play Ariadne to the Theseuses amongst us by providing a linking thread of introductions to the various Parts in the collection. Students taking advanced courses in anthropology, specialists in urban studies in other disciplines, and, of course, anthropologists working in other fields should all find this collection an invaluable guide to an expanding and exciting branch of modern anthropology.

Nuffield College
OXFORD
England
1 November 1974

J. Clyde Mitchell

Preface

City Ways is a collection of previously published articles that describe and conceptualize ways of life in urban environments. The title, one of the last elements of the book to be completed, reflects much of what we hope to express in publishing this volume. In the words "city ways" we see a continuity and a parallel with such traditional notions as "life-ways" or "folkways" and an acceptance of the proposition that city ways are another human adaptation to a specialized physical and sociocultural environment. These themes of continuity and adaptation are dealt with at some length in the introductory essay.

Our initial motivation for the project was to gather significant readings into one volume for courses in urban anthropology. None of the existing readers fit our needs and our students were spending excessive time in the library completing assignments using material placed on reserve; as a result, the selections made at that time included articles we were accustomed to assigning as necessary historical background to our lectures on current research issues. Although these articles answered our needs to some extent, other ingredients were missing. We wanted to capture the ferment and change within urban anthropology and describe the theoretical and methodological challenges which we and our colleagues were working on.

Recognizing the amount of variation in approach among urban-oriented anthropologists, we decided that the volume could be organized to make a statement about emerging directions within the flux and redefinition of urban anthropology. This proved to be an enjoyable task, for to our amazement, we, the editors, were in substantial agreement about past influences and exciting developments. These joint understandings became the basis for the six part headings and we began the painful chore of reducing the number of articles we had collected to a manageable size.

The articles ultimately selected and their positioning throughout the book conform to several principles. Mentioning these might be useful to the reader. In our view, the selections are arranged in a logical sequence from raising issues in the initial three articles, through consideration of method and technique, to assessing specific contributions to anthropology by urban anthropologists. Most of the selections deal in some fashion with one or more of the traditional issues in anthropology: family and kinship, the holistic perspective, and participant-observation, for example. We included articles approaching issues from various points of view: e.g., Louis Wirth and the responses of Herbert Gans and William Bascom; Lawrence Crissman and Gerald Berreman on ethnic identity; Oscar Lewis and the critique by Nathan Glazer of the culture of poverty. As our concept of the book developed, we discovered that numerous more specialized theoretical points surfaced again and again. Some of these are identified in the Part introductions, but there was neither time nor space to identify all of them. Undoubtedly other readers of the book will see points that we missed.

Our hope is that this volume, either as a statement by the editors or as a collection of articles to be read for their intrinsic merit, will stimulate our colleagues and their students to explore the city ways that surround and encompass them. Perhaps some of the questions posed by authors included here will be answered or elaborated on as a result of these explorations.

Finally, we would like to thank Robert Carola, formerly anthropology editor at Thomas Y. Crowell, and several anonymous reviewers for their helpful suggestions which guided us in arriving at the final product represented in this volume.

November 1974

John Friedl
The Ohio State University

Noel J. Chrisman
University of Washington

Contents

CITY
WAYS
A Selective Reader in
Urban Anthropology

1

Continuity and Adaptation as Themes in Urban Anthropology[*]

John Friedl and Noel J. Chrisman

INTRODUCTION

Until recently anthropology had been concerned almost exclusively with the study of so-called primitive societies, nonliterate peoples living in non-Western countries with a low level of technological advancement. During the nineteenth and early twentieth centuries, the city was the province of sociology, and few anthropologists dared to stray into that unknown territory. Traditional boundaries between the two disciplines were established during their formative years, and were maintained, by practice more than by design, for the better part of a century. Early anthropologists concerned with comparative questions in the areas of kinship, religion, and the like, studied simple societies in isolated rural settlements, preferably untouched by Western influences. At the same time, such European sociologists as Max Weber, Georg Simmel, and Émile Durkheim were grappling with problems grounded in the social organization of Western society, or the complex civilizations of the world (for a detailed analysis of this period, see White and Weaver 1972).

From these European roots grew an increased and more formalized interest in the city on the part of American sociologists, centered at the University of Chicago during the 1920's. The theoretical approach arising out of this interest, known as the *ecological* school, was led by Robert E. Park, Ernest W. Burgess and Roderick D. McKenzie, who were primarily concerned with the relationship between the individual and the physical and social environment in which he found himself, particularly the urban environment. Park concentrated on the competition he saw arising in the city, coupled with the necessary cooperation

[*] This essay has been especially written for this volume.

1

among city dwellers for their mutual survival (recalling Durkheim's essay on the division of labor [1893]). Burgess proposed a theory of urban development based on concentric zones, ranging from the central business district through lower class and then middle class residential areas to a zone of commuter dwellings. McKenzie outlined the process of urbanization, by which people first concentrate in cities, then centralize in areas within the city according to specific social and economic criteria, thus segregating themselves at the same time, and finally invade new areas of the city. Thus he viewed urbanization as a continual process within an urban area (Park, Burgess *et al.* 1925).

Followers of the Chicago school had a profound impact upon early anthropological interest in cities. One such man was Louis Wirth, who in his study *The Ghetto* (1928) had followed the ecological approach in analyzing an urban subgroup. Wirth's important article "Urbanism as a Way of Life," the following selection in this volume, was a major step in moving beyond the ecological approach and seeking out the social characteristics of the city as well, or what he calls a *sociological definition* of the city. Picking up the thread of Simmel's work, Wirth formed a link between the ecological school and what Martindale (1966:30) has called *the social-psychological theory* of the city. Wirth called for a social as well as a physical definition of the city, to discover social institutions and their forms as they emerge in the urban center. Thus he was able to carry out what Park had tried to accomplish earlier, namely a concentration on the moral order rather than the technological order of the city (White and Weaver 1972:101).

The significance of the Chicago school and its followers for anthropology is found chiefly in the work of Robert Redfield, who in one sense can be said to be the first social/cultural anthropologist to delve into urban anthropology. (Archaeologists, of course, had been studying prehistoric urban centers for quite some time.) At Chicago during the development of the ecological approach, Redfield was profoundly influenced by the work of Wirth and others. Trained as an anthropologist, he brought a new perspective to the study of urbanism.

In its concentration on primitive, nonliterate societies, anthropology had developed a number of unique techniques of research and reporting which distinguished it from sociology. Because the people anthropologists studied did not provide written records of their past, the time depth of anthropological investigations was relatively shallow. Missionary accounts, travel diaries, and the like did fill the gap in a few cases, but for the most part the anthropologist was limited in the historical depth of his analysis to the extent of the memories of the oldest members of the society. Sociologists who concentrated on Western societies, however, were blessed with historical records dating back to the earliest literate peoples. For urban sociology in particular, this proved to be an important distinction, allowing Max Weber to document the growth of cities in the East and West and to contrast the patterns of development in these areas centuries earlier (Weber 1966—orig. 1921). Clearly the anthropologists of Weber's day did not share these interests, for "primitives" did not live in cities, nor was there any chance of reconstructing their history through written records. Rather, cultural evolutionists at the turn of the century were primarily interested in reconstructing the history of mankind through the evidence available in contemporary primitive societies, which supposedly represented lower or "earlier" stages of development. This so-called conjectural history, based on the comparative method of nineteenth-century anthropology, necessarily avoided reliance upon written historical records.

Another distinction in the anthropological approach was based upon the investigative method anthropologists adopted. Ever since the work of Lewis Henry Morgan, first-hand personal contact with the subject group had been a characteristic of anthropological research. A lawyer and naturalist as well as a student of American Indian culture, Morgan's field trips combined these interests. He studied Indian culture, not from the point of view of an outsider, but as a participant. His biographers note the eagerness with which he established a secret society that engaged in practices he had seen or heard about among Indian tribes in the nearby countryside (Stern 1931; Resek 1960). Morgan's active participation in field research was not shared by his European contemporaries, and it was not until Bronislaw Malinowski's fieldwork among the Trobriand Islanders in the Pacific that Europeans began to adopt this practice (witness Durkheim's book *The Elementary Forms of Religious Life* [1912], based on the Australian Aborigines whom he never studied first-hand). Yet the tradition of participant observation had long since become the established method of fieldwork in the United States, due largely to the influence of Franz Boas and his students. Boas was a stickler for empirical verification of even the most minute generalization, and he demanded that the anthropologist thoroughly investigate his facts. Living with the people, learning to speak their language and documenting it from field experience, and observing the native culture in its own context were the trademarks of the Boasian school in American anthropology in the generation preceding Redfield. Thus it is not surprising that Wirth's influence upon Redfield should be tempered by this long-standing anthropological tradition.

The scope of analysis has been another important distinction between anthropology and sociology. Because they had studied small, relatively isolated primitive communities, anthropologists had come to look upon the unit of analysis as a closed system, one which could be described and analyzed as if it were uninfluenced by the outside world. Thus the anthropologist who lived in a community could describe it as a self-contained unit logically consistent within itself, that is, whose parts were all interrelated and interdependent. This *holistic* approach, as it has been called, is a major feature of the anthropological approach which has distinguished it as a discipline. But holism was based upon the community study method, in which a single community was taken as a unit of analysis and treated as if it could be separated from its surroundings and described in and of itself. It was this background that Redfield brought into the interaction of anthropology and sociology at Chicago which led to the distinctively anthropological approach to urban studies that followed his work.

Redfield accepted Wirth's hypothesis that the city was characterized by disorganization, impersonal relationships, alienation, and the predominance of nonkinship bonds between individuals. Moreover, he accepted the implication that the community most isolated from the city was most unlike it. He set out to document this hypothesis through first-hand investigations in the field, selecting the Yucatan peninsula for his research. In *The Folk Culture of Yucatan* (1941), Redfield offered a comparative analysis of four different communities, in which he introduced the notion that has come to be known as the *folk-urban continuum*. The folk-urban continuum was designed not only as a descriptive paradigm contrasting cities with rural communities, but also as an indicator of cultural change as rural communities came into increasing contact with urban influences. Thus, in Redfield's model of the urban community, influenced by Wirth's negative perception of the city, the urban pole of the continuum was characterized by a socially heterogeneous population in which individuality was dominant over adherence to group norms. Institutions of control in urban society were primarily secular rather than familial or religious. The city had a high degree of division of labor and specialization, a money economy, and business for profit. Relations between members of the society were generally impersonal, and the primary structure of interpersonal interaction was based upon voluntary associations rather than the more personal kin-based ties characteristic of village communities.

In contrast, the typical folk society was characterized by the opposite features. The population of a rural community was homogeneous and shared a large basis of commonality, much more so than urbanites. Face-to-face personal interaction promoted homogeneity and group solidarity, and there was no complex division of labor in the folk community. The family was the primary social institution, acting together and serving as the identifying unit for the individual. Sanctions governing behavior were sacred rather than secular, and religion was more pervasive, directing the community's entire way of life. Piety was emphasized and ritual was highly developed. The strong force of custom and tradition which governed behavior made the folk community highly resistant to change, and this conservatism was manifested in the technological as well as the social aspects of village life.

It is clear from this rural-urban contrast that Redfield, Wirth, and others considered the influence of urban life upon the folk culture as leading to the breakdown of the basic foundation of human society—the family and the shared values of a tightly knit, socially and economically homogeneous community. The strong Rousseauean sentiments behind these notions about the city were to have a lasting impact upon the early urban studies in anthropology, not surprising considering the proclivity of anthropologists for the relatively simple life styles of the rural populations they had traditionally studied.

In *The Folk Culture of Yucatan*, Redfield contrasted four communities: Mérida, a city of about 100,000 inhabitants on the coast of the Gulf of Mexico; Dzitas, a town of about 1,200 with a number of smaller villages and hamlets adding about as many to the total population; Chan Kom, about thirty kilometers south of Dzitas, containing about 250 people; and Tusik, a three-day ride on mule-back from Chan Kom, inhabited by 106 people. In analyzing these four communities he was particularly interested in documenting the existence of folk and urban characteristics in each, and correlating the degree of "folkness" or "urbanness" with the amount and type of contact each had with the urban centers and the Spanish heritage and literate culture of post-conquest Mexico, or what Redfield called the Great Tradition. His descriptions predictably placed Mérida far to the urban side of the continuum, with Dzitas next to it, being relatively less urban and more folk than Mérida, but less folk and more urban than the other two. Chan Kom, the peasant village, was still more like the folk model, and Tusik, the isolated tribal village, was far to the folk side of the continuum, exhibiting almost no urban characteristics.

But Redfield did not stop here. To say that an isolated village is less urban than a large city does not tell us much. He went on to postulate a law of cultural change, suggesting that as the isolation of a community decreases and the contact with the surrounding urban centers increases through transportation and communication advances, changes in the culture of the community would follow the folk-urban continuum. That is, the face-to-face, personalistic relations of the small community would yield to the impersonal bureaucratic behavior demanded by the dense concentration of people in the city; the sacred and pious character of the village would be replaced by the secular and commercially competitive nature of the city; specialization would make the people less like one another; and perhaps most important, the family would lose its importance, giving way to voluntary associations, with the nuclear or conjugal family replacing the larger extended family typical of the rural community.

In making the folk-urban continuum a dynamic model rather than purely descriptive, Redfield stimulated a great deal of research, much of which did not support his conclusions. In response to Redfield's predictions about the direction of change in the process of urbanization, Oscar Lewis investigated the changes that occurred among a number of migrants to Mexico City from the peasant village of Tepoztlán, which he had studied earlier. In "Urbanization without Breakdown: A Case Study," Selection 15 in this volume, Lewis presents evidence that refutes Redfield's claims. As the title of the article indicates, Lewis showed how migrants to the city do not suffer from the disorganization and breakdown of rural culture that was expected along the lines of the folk-urban continuum.

> We found very little evidence of family disorganization in the city. There were no cases of abandoned mothers and children among our 69 families studied nor was there a history of separation or divorce in more than a few families. Families remain strong; in fact, there is some evidence that family cohesiveness increases in the city in the face of the difficulties of city life. In Tepoztlán the extended family shows solidarity only in times of crisis or emergency. Although there is more freedom for young people in the city, the authority of parents shows little sign of weakening, and the phenomenon of rebellion against parental authority hardly exists. Nor are the second-generation children ashamed of their parents. Perhaps this can be explained by the general cultural emphasis upon respect for age, authority, and parenthood. Similarly, we found no sharp generation cleavages in values and general outlook on life (Lewis 1952:36).

It is important to recognize a basic difference in the level of analysis which distinguishes Lewis' work with Tepoztlán migrants from Redfield's exposition of the folk-urban continuum. Lewis focused upon individuals and families, whereas Redfield was concerned with differences in types of communities, and secondarily with the nature of life within them. Thus the more urban type contained heterogeneity, lack of isolation, literacy, and the like. Although it is clear that the individuals as an aggregate within the city exhibit these characteristics, it is a much different proposition to expect that individual units (persons, families, extended families, neighborhoods) will exhibit the same characteristics. Lewis made a significant contribution in showing that migrant families were not disorganized; however, he stopped short of pointing out the difference in *level* of analysis.

This problem is not ignored in this volume. The issue Richard Fox raises in Selection 3 is relevant: he asks whether we are really engaged in urban anthropology, the anthropological study of cities, or whether we are doing rural or tribal anthropology in cities. Leeds (1968a) poses the same problem when he suggests that we must study the "cityness" of urban kinship, rather than kinship in the city. What seems to exist is an unresolved tension in approach between the city as macrocosm and the microcosmic elements that constitute and populate the city. Many of the writers included here have examined the microcosm in various ways. The most influential—and to date the most comprehensive—statement outlining the nature of the urban macrocosm is Wirth's "Urbanism as a Way of Life," first published in 1938. Fox argues for another kind of macrodata—perhaps "urban character studies" is a way of expressing his position. However, we are not much closer to a conceptual, theoretical position regarding the structural and cultural properties of cities than we were in 1938.

Obviously "folk" characteristics may be discovered in the city. Yet we must distinguish between two related meanings of this term: the first in Redfield's sense of homogeneity, nonliteracy, isolation, and the like; the second referring to the traditions activated by migrants to the city. The former is a more abstract, structural statement; the latter refers to specific cultural traits. Lewis' discussion in "Urbanization without Breakdown" relates to the maintenance of family ties in a setting supposedly conducive to their dissolution, that is, the retention of the "folk" in the city. Although this is unexpected, given the properties of urban life as suggested by the folk-urban continuum, we should not be surprised to see variation in familial organization in a social form as complex and variable as the city. Scott Greer, for example, suggests that life styles in the city range between "familistic" and "urban" poles on a continuum (1962). Thus, sets of urban relationships exhibiting characteristics of cultural homogeneity, intimacy, and the like need not be called "folk," evoking images of tribal folk society. Instead, no matter what the social field—family, voluntary association, or neighborhood—these relationships may be characterized as familistic, reducing (but not removing) confusion as to urban or rural influence. The cause of familistic (folklike) relationships within the city continues to be problematic in urban studies. To some extent, these relationships are related to the traditional cultural backgrounds of migrants, or to the class, ethnic, or life-cycle position of the group.

Lewis' work in Mexico City was in many ways typical of the wave of anthropological interest in cities that followed upon Redfield's Yucatan study. During the 1930's and 1940's, anthropologists had moved away from the exclusive concentration on isolated, tribal, "primitive" societies into the broader area of peasant societies, dealing not only with the internal culture of the village community but also with the relationships on many different levels between the peasant village and the wider society. Market institutions, political and economic controls exerted by outside forces, and the interaction of religious and secular customs and traditions on the village and statewide levels—these became topics of anthropological investigation. In an era of rapid economic and social change in which peasant villages were rapidly incorporated into national economies and cultures, the anthropologist no longer could be content to study a single community in isolation, without considering that community's relationships with the outside world. Moreover, with the increasing migration of peasants from their natal villages to the cities to find work and seek the new life style about which they had heard so much, it was tempting for the anthropologist to follow the migrants into the city and study them in their new environment. Having earlier acquired a thorough understanding of their native customs and practices, the anthropologist could then make comparisons in the urban setting that were most inviting. Lewis was one of many anthropologists who followed the migrants from village to city, expecting to find the breakdown Redfield predicted; instead, he was surprised to find that it did not occur.

At the same time, anthropologists who had studied "primitive" tribal societies were moving to the cities. As colonial policies shifted from the exploitation of natural resources to the exploitation of human labor, tribesmen were lured away from their homes by the economic promise and fascination of the city. More and more countrymen left their homes to seek their fortunes in the city, and as news of their success reached back to their villages, the process of migration accelerated. Thus, the anthropologist in Africa was left with much the same alternative as the peasant specialist in Latin America—to study a rapidly changing culture on the village scene, or to follow the migrants into the cities and trace the impact of urbanism upon traditional patterns of behavior. Selection 17 by J. Cyde Mitchell offers an excellent example of this trend in social anthropology in Africa. Choosing specific customs traditionally found in the village, Mitchell shows how the impact of the city is not enough to alter the way of life completely, and that many more of the old ways are retained than we might expect, reinterpreted to fit the particular circumstances.

One of the most interesting studies of the transition in moving to the city is found in Philip Mayer's *Townsmen or Tribesmen* (1961), in which Mayer describes a Bantu-speaking area of the city of East London, South Africa, where there is little tribal diversity and almost all of the labor force originates from the same region. Here he finds that social opposition arises between those natives who consider themselves urban (townsmen) and those who still regard themselves as countrymen (tribesmen). Among the tribesmen there is a further split between those who feel it is desirable to adopt the white man's ways and those who do not. Mayer claims that since all natives act "urban" in their formal life at work, the place to look for the cleavages is in their informal life and leisure activities. Mobility also takes on a new dimension, since the social categories are determined by choice, not by any firm criteria such as race, language, or tribal background. Mayer's study is particularly important because it documents the transition from rural to urban, whereas many of the earlier efforts dealt more with either supporting the contention of the Chicago school and Redfield that there would be breakdown or refuting that contention by emphasizing the lack of breakdown.

The Chicago school had an impact on another early venture into urban anthropology, namely, Horace Miner's *The Primitive City of Timbuctoo* (1953). Miner accepts Wirth's definition of a city as a relatively large, dense, permanent settlement of socially heterogeneous individuals, and applies this definition to the North African settlement of Timbuctoo. He finds that although the population is relatively small, only 6,000 inhabitants, it fits this definition in all other respects. The density of the population is high, the economy of the settlement is based upon a profit-oriented market system, and the city fulfills a number of quite varied functions for its residents. Furthermore, since the population of Timbuctoo is composed of three distinct ethnic groups, the Songhoi, Arabs, and Tuaregs, each with its own language, it fits the definition of social heterogeneity offered by Wirth. Miner concludes that in fact Timbuctoo must be considered a city, despite its size.

Turning from Wirth's definition to Redfield's folk-urban continuum, Miner claims that Timbuctoo lies somewhere in the middle between the two opposite poles. He makes the important observation that the continuum must be applied within the city as well as among different settlements. Within the primitive city, because of its heterogeneity he found a wide range of behavior patterns and life styles ranging from folk to urban. Thus the degree of "folkness" increases as the unit of observation changes from the community to the family. Where traditional norms apply, within the ethnic group, the existence of culturally shared meanings leads to a deeper and more intimate, folklike interaction. Where this knowledge is not shared, between ethnic groups, individuals must rely upon the more superficial role relationships derived from citywide institutions.

Finally, Miner compares Timbuctoo to the older, more traditional African cities such as those found among the Yoruba of Nigeria. This rather unique urban phenomenon is described by William Bascom in Selection 10 in this volume. Among the Yoruba, urbanism existed before the penetration of Europeans, and these urban centers were not based upon industry, but served as ceremonial centers. Early urbanism was based on farming, craft specialization, and trade. However, because these cities often contained very large populations, Bascom claims that they cannot be denied the status of city, even though they were primarily agricultural in nature. He therefore calls for a revision of the traditional definition of a city, in which density or heterogeneity of population would not be the most important factor; rather, the economic dependence of individuals upon the city would be the defining criterion.

Miner claims that Timbuctoo is more urban (in Redfield's usage of the term) than are the cities Bascom describes, size notwithstanding. It is more heterogeneous, and the interethnic interaction is much more characteristic of the urban model noted by Wirth and Redfield than is the intraethnic behavior of the Yoruba. The division of labor is greater in Timbuctoo, the impersonality of interpersonal relations is more advanced, and in general Miner makes a case for considering Timbuctoo as a city in many respects.

The significance of the early work of anthropologists, particularly those mentioned above, is that anthropology did indeed have much to contribute to the debate among sociologists as to the important defining characteristics of a city. Wirth and others of the Chicago school were not looking beyond their own society, and one can recognize in their discussions of disorganization, crime, and, violence the influence of Chicago itself, a rather atypical city in the Prohibition era. Redfield, Bascom, Lewis, Miner, and others were trained in the comparative approach of anthropology, and brought their experience in non-Western cities to bear upon the problems being considered by urban sociologists. Nor was the criticism of the Chicago school limited to anthropology. Herbert Gans, a sociologist by training, disagreed with the ecological approach to the understanding of human behavior in the city. In his article "Urbanism and Suburbanism as Ways of Life," Selection 8 in this volume, Gans argues that life styles are determined more by economic and social conditions than by place of residence. He points out that the generalizations Wirth made about the inner city cannot be extended to cover the entire metropolitan area. After contrasting the life style of the suburb with that of the inner city, he concludes that if these ways of life do not coincide with settlement patterns, and if they are instead functions of class and life-cycle stage, then a sociological definition of the city such as that proposed by Wirth cannot be formulated.

Gans was also influential in a growing area of concern of both sociologists and anthropologists, namely the study of ethnic subcommunities within the city. In *The Urban Villagers* (1962), based upon fieldwork in an Italian section of Boston, Gans again offers a contrasting point of view to Wirth's general notion of urban disorganization, claiming that such communities are not really slums, but urban villages, made up of European ethnic minority groups who have retained a great deal of their traditional culture. Earlier studies such as William Foote Whyte's *Street Corner Society* (1955) had led to similar conclusions regarding the relatively organized and successful adaptation of the life style of the urban ghetto. The urban village offers its inhabitants cultural continuity in their transition from a rural or foreign urban setting to the American city ways of life. The conclusions of most of these studies followed a similar line, as summarized by White and Weaver:

> It is logically unsound to deduce, as Wirth does, that since people in cities are less likely to know everyone else on a face-to-face basis, that primary groups will necessarily be disrupted, relationships will be impersonal, groups and personalities disorganized, anomie, suicide, crime and insecurity will increase, or that people will be forced to seek voluntary associations as the only effective means of social action in the face of loss of control over the technological apparatus of the city (1972:101).

THE ANTHROPOLOGICAL APPROACH IN URBAN STUDIES

In the preceding section we discussed briefly the methodological distinction between anthropology and sociology which served as the cornerstone for the development of urban anthropology as a separate field of study. The holistic approach to a culture, the community-study method, and the consideration of the subject group as an isolate have led to a particular style of fieldwork and reporting in anthropology. Even studies in large metropolitan centers, such as Whyte's analysis in *Street Corner Society,* have proposed the artificial isolate of the urban village as a valid unit. Peter Marris' article, "Slum Clearance and Family Life in Lagos" (Selection 14), points out how even within a large, relatively heterogeneous city an artificially isolated subsection of that city can be taken as the unit of anlysis. While Marris' work is a beautifully detailed description of the internal dynamics of an urban neighborhood, it also indicates the style of research prevalent until recently in urban anthropology. Epstein's article, "The Genesis and Function of Squatter Settlements in Brasilia" (Selection 11), also considers a subsection of a large urban center. Epstein's work, however, is more typical of some recent trends in anthropological investigations of cities, for he is aware of the interplay between the urban village and the wider society to a much greater degree than most of his predecessors.

Several reasons combine to explain the retention of traditional anthropological techniques and methods in urban studies in the early work in the field. Looking at Redfield's work or Lewis' study of migrants to the city, we might well expect that traditional anthropological methods would be carried out, for at the time they were a radical departure from the conventional sociological analysis so prevalent in urban studies. In some of his later works such as *Five Families: Mexican Case Studies in the Culture of Poverty* (1959), *The Children of Sanchez* (1961), and *La Vida: A Puerto Rican Family in the Culture of Poverty—San Juan and New York* (1965), Lewis adopts the rare and insightful approach of studying urban phenomena through the members of a single family unit, rather than an entire community. Tracing the various members of the family through their migrations and their daily routines in the city and the village, he portrays a vivid picture of the life style of the urban dweller without relying upon the more traditional community-study approach. But for the most part, the early work in urban anthropology retained the same techniques used to study tribal societies and peasant villages.

One of the reasons for this methodological conservatism can be traced to the way in which anthropologists were introduced to the city. Anthropologist W. Lloyd Warner, in the introduction to *The Social Life of a Modern Community* (1941), the first volume of the "Yankee City Series," notes that although his earlier research had been among the Australian Aborigines, he intended to be able to apply his work there to complex societies as well.

> . . . my objective in studying them was not simply to understand how they organized their own social relations, but also to obtain a better understanding of how men in all groups, regardless of place or time, solve the problems which confront them. The more simple

types of communities—with their smaller populations, less numerous social institutions, less complex ideational and technical systems—provide the social anthropologist with the equivalent of a laboratory wherein to test his ideas and research techniques. By investigations of these simple societies he is able to equip himself better for the analysis of more complex forms of human society. An obvious analogy here suggests itself between the social anthropologist and the biologist who examines the physiology of more simply constructed organisms to arm himself for his scientific attack on the problems of the human organism. (Warner and Lunt 1941:3)

Located in a village, an anthropologist who found that a large proportion of the population was migrating to urban centers was tempted to follow them. But in studying urban immigrants, the anthropologist already had a preconceived notion of what he would find, based upon his experience in the rural hinterland. His research usually was designed to explain why he did or did not find a breakdown in rural culture, but in either case the research plan was set up in terms of that rural culture. There was little rephrasing of questions about rural traditions to fit the new urban context; as a result, many of the early works appear to be extensions of village studies rather than separate urban studies with their own methodology and theoretical approach.

Another reason for the maintenance of the more traditional approach can be seen in the nature of the change experienced by migrants. Generally it was found that the city did not cause an immediate transformation of rural culture to fit the urban mold. Rural patterns persisted, and were fostered by tightly knit groups within the city. For the anthropologist this meant that he was describing similar phenomena, and there was therefore little incentive to devise new methods, or to put the old questions in a new context. The buffer groups that existed in the city to ease the transition of migrants were viewed as replicas of the village communities, and it was natural that they be studied in the same way. Therefore, the intensive holistic approach was applied to segments of the urban center just as it had been applied to isolated village communities, but with different results. Instead of describing the urban subgroup in its totality, anthropologists found that they had to concentrate upon specific areas of analysis, for despite the attempt to set off the ethnic enclave as an isolate, the enclave's residents had too many ties with the outside world. Contact between urban villagers and the rest of the city, through economic enterprises extending into the ghetto or drawing its residents outside, and through mass communication, led to a broad range of problems that had not existed in the small rural community, and which the community-study method was therefore not able to cope with. As Weaver and White note, "Anthropological holism flounders when it attempts to capture a differentiated and heterogeneous civilization within the simplified formula and ethnographic style used for small-scale societies" (1972:111).

One of the principal areas where this problem was seen was in the study of kinship. As Anthony Leeds notes, in a recent comment on the methodology of urban anthropology,

> [urban anthropology] has dealt with social phenomena which, like kinship, are not restricted to the city or even to urban society. . . . In such studies, the question asked has generally been, 'How is kinship operating in this city?', not, 'What is the effect of cityness on the operation of kinship?', i.e., what systemic and characteristic aspects of kinship—if any—are elicited or forced into being in the city, and only in the city, as a function of specifiable features, or variables if you will, characteristic of the city. They have been studies of kinship in the city, not of the city in kinship (1968a:31).

More recent studies have reacted to this problem, seeking out new ways of dealing with the city as an entity in itself, separate from the village or the tribal settlement. Elizabeth Bott, in her study of kinship in London (Selection 7), found it necessary to introduce the concept of *social network* into her analysis in order to make sense out of the interrelationships of the members of the kin group. To treat kinship in the traditional anthropological way ignores the structural differences imposed upon it by the very nature of the city, and it is through the use of network analysis that Bott illustrates this new approach to an old problem. Her article draws upon an earlier discussion by J. A. Barnes, "Class and Committees in a Norwegian Island Parish" (1954), the pioneer work in network analysis by an anthropologist. Barnes found that even in a relatively small rural community, ties to the outside made it impossible to consider the community as a closed isolate. Rather, to understand the behavior of its inhabitants it was necessary to look at them in terms of what he called "social fields," or cultural contexts of interaction. He recognized a territorially based network, an economic network, and a social network, all of which existed as distinct fields of interaction for the individual.

Anthropological studies of urban kinship are particularly interesting because of their relationship to findings from rural tribal areas, and because bonds among kin are those most likely to exhibit familistic characteristics. As we have seen above, the initial supposition about family and kin relations was that they would tend to break down. Their persistence in an urban setting raised new questions, especially whether these were rural traits transplanted or whether early conceptions of urban social structure were in error. As Gluckman (1961) points out, African migrants to the city are in a new context which influences their behavior. However, people do not lose their needs and desires for companionship. Rural kinship patterns into which the individual was well integrated in a tribal setting are not forgotten in the new setting; but in the absence of large numbers of kin, the full set of relationships cannot be activated in the city. Kinsmen become important contacts from whom the migrant can expect limited hospitality when he first arrives and with whom he may continue a relationship if interaction is rewarding. This element of greater *choice* is critical in urban kinship. With alternative means of making a living, finding housing or a spouse, and creating friendships, kin relationships are not as obligatory in the city as in the village. They are, however, an important social and economic resource to the migrant or the established city dweller.

Kinship is an excellent medium through which to express relationships, perhaps serving to intensify them as well. In describing the social relationships of an individual (Chanda) in the city, Epstein explains how Chanda's friendship tie with Crawford was enhanced through their discovery of a classificatory father-son bond. Crawford exclaims: "Now it is good that our relationship is revealed today. That is why we get on so well together. It is the blood of kinship. Very fine indeed" (Epstein 1969:87). The "blood of kinship" leads the urban dweller to hearken back to another, related social system, but more importantly to the primordial bonds uniting those people with shared ancestors. That kin terms, and their related obligations to some extent, may be used to cement even fleeting relationships is documented by Liebow (1967), and discussed by Jacobson in this volume in Selection 16.

Documenting the longevity and flexibility of kinship as a means of expressing social relationships is an important contribution of urban anthropology. That relationships thought to be characteristically rural are retained or regained within a complex urban social system suggests that this favorite anthropological research topic is an important focus in the city. It is of particular significance that individuals may use kin relationships in an adaptive manner. Relying upon the never-ending nature of kin ties, individuals may move in and out of such relationships.

Kinship studies have played an important role in the anthropological investigation of cities in understanding the process of migrant adjustment to the urban environment, and the broader process of urbanization in general. Urbanization has variously been defined as the movement of people from the countryside to cities, the growth in number and size of cities, the growth in the percentage of urban dwellers, the diffusion of urban culture to rural areas, and the adjustment of migrants to city life and their adoption of urban cultural patterns. An important distinction has been made by J. Clyde Mitchell between the processes of *urbanization, detribalization,* and *stabilization* (1956a). He points out that despite the fact that these three terms are frequently used interchangeably in the literature on urbanization in Africa, they do not have the same meaning. For Mitchell, urbanization implies participation in social relations in the city, while detribalization implies rejection of tribal behavior and social relations with former relatives and friends or tribesmen in rural areas. The third process, stabilization, refers specifically to the cessation of labor migration, which in the case of urbanization implies permanent urban residence. Mitchell derives a formula to measure stabilization based upon the factors of age, number of years away from home, marital status, attitudes toward labor migration, education, occupation, and the like.

Mitchell's contribution through this set of distinctions is particularly important in light of Hilda Kuper's warning (1965:13) of the danger in considering urbanization as both a process and a measure. She notes that by viewing urbanization as a series of uniform consequential changes, we overlook the complex differences which attend to this process in different instances. For example, stratification, associated with economic and political pluralism, is based upon overt racism backed by force in the southern parts of Africa, while in West Africa this was not the case to nearly the same degree.

Many anthropologists have commented on the role of kinship in the process of urbanization and migrant adjustment. People who migrate to cities tend to go where they have relatives, or where someone from their village is already established. Once in the city, residence is taken up along these same lines, ultimately leading to a close alliance on the basis of kinship and village affiliation, sometimes even closer than that existing in the village itself due to the pressures exerted upon the migrants within the city. Where kinship or village ties cannot insure adequate security, voluntary associations based upon tribal or ethnic identity are created.

Voluntary associations are one of the most characteristic urban institutions. Wirth saw them as a major mode of organization, replacing the disappearing family and close-knit neighborhood groups as focal points for personal interaction and urban integration. The critical advantage of these associations in the city is their *adaptability.* Frequently developing a formal bureaucratic organizational structure, they may become corporate groups capable of sustained concerted action. Although the formal aims of such bodies vary, they may be organized around such goals as mutual aid, recreation, regional, national, or tribal origins, religious experiences, or governmental action (see Little 1965b).

Urban dwellers with few other institutional resources may join together on the basis of common interest or common identity to create an association to further the accomplishment of their felt needs. In Selection 13 in this volume, Abner Cohen describes how the Freemasons in Sierra Leone share a common interest and similar class background, and Lawrence Crissman, in Selection 12, notes that the overseas Chinese associations also reflect a shared identity. One of the most frequently found types of association is organized for mutual aid. A group may meet weekly or monthly, donating a small amount of money to a common fund to be drawn upon by one of their number at specified times, and then repaid at a later date. A popular type of mutual aid society in nineteenth- and early twentieth-century America was the ethnically based health and/or life insurance association. Immigrants could thus gain some security in rapidly urbanizing areas without turning to outsiders for charity. At the same time, the associations provided a context in which immigrants could gather with their own kind, away from the hustle and bustle of the city, to engage in congenial social interaction.

The adapative significance of voluntary associations is related to their dual nature: providing real economic or political benefits in addition to pleasant sociability. Individuals who join initially for pragmatic gain may become closely integrated with other members, forming important social ties which can be of value in finding a job, a house, or other necessities. In addition, such sustained interpersonal ties aid in integrating the association as a viable unit better able to accomplish its instrumental goals.

The pragmatic aspects of voluntary associations are important in individual and group adaptation because they make usually unavailable services accessible. Knowledge that capital for business ventures, money for health expenditures, or unusual recreational opportunities are readily available may set the member more at ease as he negotiates the urban environment. Even in associations organized to maintain tribal or ethnic identity, individuals become skilled in behavior patterns enabling them to deal with impersonal bureaucracies and their rules (Little 1965b; Broom and Kitsuse 1955). Thus, while cultural continuity is being fostered in a folklike context, maintaining the heterogeneity of the urban scene, members of voluntary associations become better able to cope with the wider society.

Cultural pluralism has always been of major interest to anthropology, due to the importance of the concept of culture for the investigations of behavior. Cities, as Wirth noted, are by definition culturally heterogeneous, and a great deal of investigation of the interplay of different cultures in contact in the urban milieu has been conducted. Miner's study of Timbuctoo, mentioned earlier, is an excellent example, where three quite distinct cultures were found to be operating in the city, and the nature of that interaction was documented in great detail. Gerald Berreman's article "Social Categories and Social Interaction" (Selection 9) offers a more recent example of this type of investigation, using a somewhat different methodological approach to the problem of cultural pluralism and the interaction of diverse groups in the city.

As many different approaches to the study of the city exist as there are problems to be solved. Anthropologists have been increasingly willing to adapt their methods and goals to the particular urban situation under study, and in recent years this has led to a major new direction in urban anthropology which is primarily responsible for the long overdue recognition of this branch of anthropology as a valid subfield within the discipline. This new direction will be discussed below in a summary of recent trends in the field.

RECENT TRENDS IN URBAN ANTHROPOLOGY

Several years ago Hutchinson (1968) noted three reasons why anthropology was so late in moving into the realm of urban studies, based upon justifications given by Redfield and Wirth for concentrating upon the rural areas. First was the interest in studying the effects of innovations upon rural dwellers, as these innovations diffused outward from the urban centers. The acceptance of this notion is implicit in Redfield's folk-urban continuum. Second was the consensus view of the city as the scene of breakdown and disorganization; thus if the anthropologist were to study a pure form of the culture, he would not find it in the city, but rather in the place farthest removed from the city, where breakdown had not occurred. Third was the feeling that the holistic approach was impossible in a complex urban society comprised of such a large and culturally diverse group of people.

Recent trends in urban anthropology have broken through these barriers and directly confronted the problems raised by Redfield and Wirth. The notion that innovation was confined to urban centers was challenged many years later by Redfield himself. In *Peasant Society and Culture* (1956), Redfield discusses what he calls the "social organization of tradition." He finds that not only are new ideas and cultural practices invented in the city and diffused to the countryside through a process he calls "parochialization," but the opposite pattern occurs as well. In a process he terms "universalization," innovations in the peasant culture arise on the village level, gain wider acceptance regionally, and ultimately some of them are adopted by the urban culture, or the Great Tradition, to be diffused to outlying areas of the realm.

We discussed the notion of the breakdown of "pure" culture in the city in the two preceding sections, citing the refutations of this claim. However, Hutchinson's third point, the insufficiency of the holistic approach for the study of the city, has until recently posed a serious obstacle to anthropological researchers who would attempt to apply their knowledge and methods to urban centers. Of course, social scientists in other disciplines have dealt with cities as units in themselves without this problem, and anthropologists who have been concerned with typologies of cities rather than life styles within the context of the city environment have followed suit. Urban typologies have contributed important understanding to the ways in which a city interacts with other urban centers and with its surrounding countryside. An early but vitally important distinction was made by Mark Jefferson in his article "The Law of the Primate City" (1939). This "law," briefly stated, is that a country's leading city is frequently disproportionately large and exceptionally expressive of national capacity and feeling. This valuable concept contributes much to the understanding of the *primate* city's function within and relationship to its national environment; and it has been of particular importance to anthropologists, for primate cities tend to be found primarily in underdeveloped nations of the world. The fact that the importance of a city leads to its potential for increasing its importance, much as wealth breeds greater wealth, is certainly relevant to an understanding of the demography and mobility of a region or a nation, and contributes to other questions as well.

Robert Redfield and Milton B. Singer, in "The Cultural Role of Cities" (1954), offer another typology of cities. Concerned specifically with the concept of culture as a basis for typological distinction among cities, the authors make an important distinction between what they call *orthogenetic* and *heterogenetic* cities. The orthogenetic city is an administrative-cultural center that has grown out of the indigenous cultural tradition; its major role is to carry forward the local culture or civilization. The heterogenetic city, on the other hand, does not derive from the indigenous tradition, but includes new commercial, modern administrative, and metropolitan centers. Such cities generate new ideas and innovations which conflict with the values of the old culture.

The formulation of urban typologies, however, should not be confused with the application of the holistic approach in anthropology to the study of cities. Redfield and Singer's typology, for example, is not based upon an intensive study of a particular city. While typologies did lead the way for subsequent anthropological interest in cities as single units capable of analysis as wholes, they did not in themselves offer the type of analysis sought by urban anthropologists. Rather, it is in many ways a partial return to the methods and viewpoints of the Chicago school that has enabled modern anthropology to overcome the methodological barrier which kept it out of urban studies for so long. In "Urbanism as a Way of Life," Wirth saw the city as a total community, where urbanites are not enclosed in slowly changing, close-knit traditional sets of social relations as are tribal peoples in their villages. His suggestions as to the characteristics of cities viewed from this perspective have been the springboard from which contemporary anthropologists have jumped into particular social problems.

In recent years anthropologists have begun to describe entire urban centers in terms of their providing a living environment for residents, as well as their interaction with other cities, surrounding suburbs, and rural areas. One such example of this recent trend toward holism is seen in Fox's article (Selection 3) in this volume. He points out the need for anthropologists to avoid engaging in tribal anthropology in an urban setting, and argues that the tradition of holism should be applied to the city as well as the hinterland. His demonstration of the utility of the approach using two cities in the eastern United States stands as a major argument for this point of view within urban anthropology. Along similar lines, John Price, in Selection 4, not only familiarizes us with the nature of a whole city but demonstrates the utility of a team approach to the study of the city as well. The reader gains a feeling for the heterogeneity of urban life as it is molded within a specific historical stream of development. The use of a set of investigators, each with his or her own problem, merges the holistic approach with the more problem-oriented strategy frequently appearing in the literature today.

Needless to say, the search for relevance has not left anthropologists standing idly by. As anthropology has moved into the cities, it has brought with it a fresh outlook on urban problems and a new perspective from which to attack them. Long an applied science with its American roots in studies of Indian assimilation and urbanization, anthropology has turned quickly to address the contemporary ills of urban society in America and throughout the world. Peter Marris, in Selection 14, deals with the problem of slum clearance and rehousing. David Epstein also is concerned with the problem of dwelling in slum communities in his article (Selection 11) on squatter settlements in Brasilia.

But the social issue of major concern within the Western hemisphere in recent years has been the problem of poverty, and in particular the approach to understanding the life style and solving the problems faced by poor people. Oscar Lewis, in a move that was sharply attacked from all sides, set forth the notion that poverty can in some instances actually become a way of life in itself, a self-perpetuating system of values and patterns of behavior, which he summarized under the term "The Culture of Poverty." His article on that topic (Selection 18) is a refinement of his earlier discussion, in the introduction to his book *Five Families: Mexican Case Studies in the Culture of Poverty* (1959). Accompanying this article are two others on the subject of poverty, one of the more popular problems open for investigation by urban anthropologists. Nathan Glazer, in Selection 19, offers specific criticism of Lewis' concept of a poverty culture based on indications from two major cities (New York and Hong Kong) that the data do not support the contentions made by Lewis. And Edward Spicer, in Selection 20, describes a specific case in which those individuals who live in a poverty culture are exploited by members outside of the community.

Other problem-oriented approaches have become popular in recent anthropological literature, as a greater understanding of the varied urban subgroups within our society is sought. Migrant groups to the cities have been studied in an attempt to understand why they migrate, how they adjust, and what problems they face. Perhaps one of the most spectacular areas of interest has been the urban street gang. Recent books on black ghettoes, such as Elliot Liebow's *Tally's Corner* (1967), R. Lincoln Keiser's *The Vice Lords: Warriors of the Street* (1969), and Ulf Hannerz's *Soulside: Inquiries into Ghetto Culture* (1969), have popularized urban anthropology perhaps as much as any other efforts in the discipline.

One of the bright spots in the future of urban anthropology is precisely the facility with which it has moved into the area of applied science and proposed solutions to some of the major social problems facing our country—indeed the entire world—today. It is true that some damage has been done by the pronouncements of prominent social scientists such as Oscar Lewis, Daniel Patrick Moynihan, and Edward Banfield, not only in terms of changing the course of government policies toward social welfare programs aimed at alleviating the poverty of the ghetto, but also through the alienation of a great many people and the creation of a distrust of social science in general. On the other hand, however, works such as those by Liebow and Hannerz mentioned above and the Valentines (Selection 5) are opening the way for a greater understanding of ghetto life and its problems. In many cases we find that the issues we have been so vigorously attacking have been straw men all along, and instead we ought to turn our attention to other areas of ghetto life. Nor has interest centered solely on blacks. James Spradley, in Selection 6, focuses upon urban nomads, or tramps, a subculture relatively ignored by anthropologists. Recent interest in the plight of other urban groups—American Indians, Mexican-Americans, Appalachians—offers additional hope for significant contributions to understanding some of the major social problems of society today.

As the title of this essay indicates, the theme of continuity of tradition with adaptive change underlies the articles selected for this volume. Like migrants from nonurban areas and rooted urbanites, the anthropologists represented here have drawn from an established tradition of appropriate questions and explanations, means of dealing with social situations, and interpersonal relationships. These have been adapted in the course of urban research, but much of the traditional core remains. Urban anthropologists are investigating the social and cultural behavior of humans in an historically new context and in a field setting only recently entered by members of the discipline. Although there is a continuing interest in describing and explaining social relationships and cultural meanings among individuals in groups, groups in the urban setting are not as simply related to each other as they are in villages. And the urban dwellers who are studied tend to be members of a great many more and more varied groups simultaneously than is the case in rural, tribal areas.

Urban inhabitants must adapt family, group, or cultural traditions to city ways. It is virtually impossible to reside in an urban area without being touched by elements of the macrocosmic whole. The basic needs of life are influenced, if not regulated, by the major institutional complexes. In most cases these needs must be met through interactions with strangers, some of whom will be ethnically or culturally unrelated. Strategies for dealing with outsiders must be adopted whether by individuals or by groups acting for numbers of individuals.

The question for anthoropology remains, in both urban and nonurban situations, what is human variability and why does it occur? In this collection, we have attempted to select both past and present approaches to these questions, hoping to highlight some of the trends in urban anthropological research. The first part contains articles suggesting the nature of the city as a whole; the second includes discussions of methodology and research technique for studies within that whole. With these parts setting the stage, the following four reflect specific research interests, but ones that are broadly representative of the current investigations being conducted by anthropologists in cities. In addition to their importance in communicating issues in urban research, these articles should also stimulate the reader to formulate his or her own questions about urban social life, and provide some of the knowledge and the impetus to seek the answers.

Part One

THE CITY AS A
UNIT OF ANALYSIS

The three selections that comprise this part are introductory in that many of the issues considered in the remainder of the collection are implied, suggested, or discussed. Wirth's contribution, for example, has been the starting point for many contemporary anthropologists' research. In addition to outlining the characteristics of the urban pole of the folk-urban continuum, Wirth's discussion of urban social process remains a significant stimulus for urban anthropological research. In particular, the following two fragments of his argument speak directly to the more "folk"-oriented anthropologist:

> The bonds of kinship, of neighborliness, and the sentiments arising out of living together for generations under a common folk tradition are likely to be absent or, at best, relatively weak in an aggregate the members of which have such diverse origins and backgrounds. Under such circumstances competition and formal control mechanisms furnish the substitutes for the bonds of solidarity that are relied upon to hold a folk society together (1938:11).

> The contacts of the city may indeed be face to face, but they are nevertheless impersonal, superficial, transitory, and segmental. The reserve, the indifference, and the blasé outlook which urbanites manifest in their relationships may thus be regarded as devices for immunizing themselves against the personal claims and expectations of others (1938:12).

In pointing out that urbanites are not enclosed in slowly changing, close-knit, traditional sets of social relations as are tribals in their villages, Wirth identifies an issue susceptible to comparative anthropological research: what kinds of social relationships do exist in cities and how do these compare or contrast with those found in villages?

Wirth's level of analysis here is the city as community and the
population as an aggregate, two concerns similar to those of traditional
anthropology, but ones which are difficult for anthropologists studying
the city to work with. Yet the city as a unit of analysis cannot be ignored,
for "the influences which cities exert upon the social life of man are
greater than the ratio of the urban populations would indicate. . . ."
(Wirth 1938:2) Wirth must be considered to be clearly within the
mainstream of anthropological holism in his call for understanding the
city as a whole. However, as Gans (see Selection 8) suggests, there is
an ever-present difficulty in defining the boundaries of such a complex
analytical unit.

In his recent and succinct statement, Richard Fox scores anthropologists
for searching for bounded, isolable units within the city by pursuing
"the exotic and marginal within urban locales. . . ." He suggests they
are guilty of "the psychological and sociological reductionism implicit
in studying city men, families, and associations on urban streets and
corners." In his purposely controversial argument, Fox points to the
tradition of anthropological holism, to the need to view the city as part
of "the political and economic order in which it exists." Such holistic
studies need not be typological and static; adding the concept of
adaptation, one can see the city in a dynamic relationship to its external
and internal environments. Fox's demonstration of the utility of his
approach using two cities in the eastern United States strongly supports
his argument for this point of view within urban anthropology.

Price, too, touts a holistic approach to urban studies. Yet his work is
only partly the kind of "urban character" study proposed by Fox; it is
also a result of collating nine smaller, more personal studies completed
by seminar participants and merging these with three integrating studies.
The pressure of tradition upon seminar leaders and students is evident
from the fact that three students focused upon ethnic minority groups,
"although we knew that ethnicity played only a small role in Reno
culture."

This article not only familiarizes us with the nature of a whole city
but also demonstrates the utility of a team approach to the study of the
city. The reader gains a feeling of the heterogeneity of urban life as it
is molded within a specific historical stream of development. The use of
a set of investigators, each with his or her own problem, merges the
holistic approach with the more problem- or population-oriented strategy
found in other articles in this volume.

The ethnographic results of the Reno project are necessarily slim,
owing to the short period of time the researchers spent in the field.
However, the methodological and technical suggestions arising from this

team approach experiment are instructive. Price states the need for more variable representation of social science disciplines and for an 18- to 24-month duration of the investigation. Team collaboration, it was found, reduced inaccuracies in approach and promoted exchanges of data and perspective. Central accumulation of published local information, of survey research results, and of individual hypotheses greatly benefited each investigator and highlighted both the complexity and the unity of Reno.

2
Urbanism as
a Way of Life

Louis Wirth

I. THE CITY AND CONTEMPORARY CIVILIZATION

Just as the beginning of Western civilization is marked by the permanent settlement of formerly nomadic peoples in the Mediterranean basin, so the beginning of what is distinctively modern in our civilization is best signalized by the growth of great cities. Nowhere has mankind been farther removed from organic nature than under the conditions of life characteristic of great cities. The contemporary world no longer presents a picture of small isolated groups of human beings scattered over a vast territory, as Sumner described primitive society (1906:12). The distinctive feature of the mode of living of man in the modern age is his concentration into gigantic aggregations around which cluster lesser centers and from which radiate the ideas and practices that we call civilization.

The degree to which the contemporary world may be said to be "urban" is not fully or accurately measured by the proportion of the total population living in cities. The influences which cities exert upon the social life of man are greater than the ratio of the urban population would indicate, for the city is not only in ever larger degrees the dwelling-place and the workshop of modern man, but it is the initiating and controlling center of economic, political, and cultural life that has drawn the most remote parts of the world into its orbit and woven diverse areas, peoples, and activities into a cosmos.

The growth of cities and the urbanization of the world is one of the most impressive facts of modern times. Although it is impossible to state precisely what proportion of the estimated total world-population is

SOURCE: *American Journal of Sociology* 44 (July 1938): 1–24. Copyright © 1938 by the University of Chicago. Reprinted by permission of the University of Chicago Press.

urban, 69.2 per cent of the total population of those countries that do distinguish between urban and rural areas is urban (Pearson 1935:211). Considering the fact, moreover, that the world's population is very unevenly distributed and that the growth of cities is not very far advanced in some of the countries that have only recently been touched by industrialism, this average understates the extent to which urban concentration has proceeded in those countries where the impact of the industrial revolution has been more forceful and of less recent date. This shift from a rural to a predominantly urban society, which has taken place within the span of a single generation in such industrialized areas as the United States and Japan, has been accompanied by profound changes in virtually every phase of social life. It is these changes and their ramifications that invite the attention of the sociologist to the study of the differences between the rural and the urban mode of living. The pursuit of this interest is an indispensable prerequisite for the comprehension and possible mastery of some of the most crucial contemporary problems of social life since it is likely to furnish one of the most revealing perspectives for the understanding of the ongoing changes in human nature and the social order.[1]

Since the city is the product of growth rather than of instantaneous creation, it is to be expected that the influences which it exerts upon the modes of life should not be able to wipe out completely the previously dominant modes of human association. To a greater or lesser degree, therefore, our social life bears the imprint of an earlier folk society, the characteristic modes of settlement of which were the farm, the manor, and the village. This historic influence is reinforced by the circumstance that the population of the city itself is in large measure recruited from the countryside, where a mode of life reminiscent of this earlier form of existence persists. Hence we should not expect to find abrupt and discontinuous variation between urban and rural types of personality. The city and the country may be regarded as two poles in reference to one or the other of which all human settlements tend to arrange themselves. In viewing urban-industrial and rural-folk society as ideal types of communities, we may obtain a perspective for the analysis of the basic models of human association as they appear in contemporary civilization.

[1] Whereas rural life in the United States has for a long time been a subject of considerable interest on the part of governmental bureaus, the most notable case of a comprehensive report being that submitted by the Country Life Commission to President Theodore Roosevelt in 1909, it is worthy of note that no equally comprehensive official inquiry into urban life was undertaken until the establishment of a Research Committee on Urbanism of the National Resources Committee. (Cf. *Our Cities: Their Role in the National Economy* [Washington: Government Printing Office, 1937].)

II. A SOCIOLOGICAL DEFINITION OF THE CITY

Despite the preponderant significance of the city in our civilization, however, our knowledge of the nature of urbanism and the process of urbanization is meager. Many attempts have indeed been made to isolate the distinguishing characteristics of urban life. Geographers, historians, economists, and political scientists have incorporated the points of view of their respective disciplines into diverse definitions of the city. While in no sense intended to supersede these, the formulation of a sociological approach to the city may incidentally serve to call attention to the interrelations between them by emphasizing the peculiar characteristics of the city as a particular form of human association. A sociologically significant definition of the city seeks to select those elements of urbanism which mark it as a distinctive mode of human group life.

The characterization of a community as urban on the basis of size alone is obviously arbitrary. It is difficult to defend the present census definition which designates a community of 2,500 and above as urban and all others as rural. The situation would be the same if the criterion were 4,000, 8,000, 10,000, 25,000, or 100,000 population, for although in the latter case we might feel that we were more nearly dealing with an urban aggregate than would be the case in communities of lesser size no definition of urbanism can hope to be completely satisfying as long as numbers are regarded as the sole criterion. Moreover, it is not difficult to demonstrate that communities of less than the arbitrarily set number of inhabitants lying within the range of influence of metropolitan centers have greater claim to recognition as urban communities than do larger ones leading a more isolated existence in a predominantly rural area. Finally, it should be recognized that census definitions are unduly influenced by the fact that the city, statistically speaking, is always an administrative concept in that the corporate limits play a decisive role in delineating the urban area. Nowhere is this more clearly apparent than in the concentrations of population on the peripheries of great metropolitan centers which cross arbitrary administrative boundaries of city, county, state, and nation.

As long as we identify urbanism with the physical entity of the city, viewing it merely as rigidly delimited in space, and proceed as if urban attributes abruptly ceased to be manifested beyond an arbitrary boundary line, we are not likely to arrive at any adequate conception of urbanism as a mode of life. The technological developments in transportation and communication which virtually mark a new epoch in human history have accentuated the role of cities as dominant elements in our civilization and have enormously extended the urban mode of living beyond the confines of the city itself. The dominance of the city, especially of the great city, may be regarded as a consequence of the concentration in cities of industrial and commercial, financial and administrative facilities and activities, transportation and communication lines, and cultural and recreational equipment such as the press, radio stations, theaters, libraries, museums, concert halls, operas, hospitals, higher educational institutions, research and publishing centers, professional organizations, and religious and welfare institutions. Were it not for the attraction and suggestions that the city exerts through these instrumentalities upon the rural population, the differences between the rural and the urban modes of life would be even greater than they are. Urbanization no longer denotes merely the process by which persons are attracted to a place called the city and incorporated into its system of life. It refers also to that cumulative accentuation of the characteristics distinctive of the mode of life which is associated with the growth of cities, and finally to the changes in the direction of modes of life recognized as urban which are apparent among people, wherever they may be, who have come under the spell of the influences which the city exerts by virtue of the power of its institutions and personalities operating through the means of communication and transportation.

The shortcomings which attach to number of inhabitants as a criterion of urbanism apply for the most part to density of population as well. Whether we accept the density of 10,000 persons per square mile as Mark Jefferson (1909:537–566) proposed, or 1,000, which Willcox (1926:119) preferred to regard as the criterion of urban settlements, it is clear that unless density is correlated with significant social characteristics it can furnish only an arbitrary basis for differentiating urban from rural communities. Since our census enumerates the night rather than the day population of an area, the locale of the most intensive urban life—the city center—generally has low population density, and the industrial and commercial areas of the city, which contain the most characteristic economic activities underlying urban society, would scarcely anywhere be truly urban if density were literally interpreted as a mark of urbanism. Nevertheless, the fact that the urban community is distinguished by a large aggregation and relatively dense concentration of population can scarcely be left out of account in a definition of the city. But these criteria must be seen as relative to the general cultural context in which cities arise and exist and are sociologically relevant only in so far as they operate as conditioning factors in social life.

The same criticisms apply to such criteria as the occupation of the inhabitants, the existence of certain physical facilities, institutions, and forms of political organization. The question is not whether cities in our civilization or in others do exhibit these distinctive traits, but how potent they are in molding the character of social life into its specifically urban form. Nor in formulating a fertile definition can we afford to overlook the great variations between cities. By means of a typology of cities based upon size, location, age, and function, such as we have undertaken to establish in our recent report to the National Resources Committee (1937:8), we have found it feasible to array and classify urban communities ranging from struggling small towns to thriving world-metropolitan centers; from isolated trading-centers in the midst of agricultural regions to thriving world-ports and commercial and industrial conurbations. Such differences as these appear crucial because the social characteristics and influences of these different "cities" vary widely.

A serviceable definition of urbanism should not only denote the essential characteristics which all cities—at least those in our culture—have in common, but should lend itself to the discovery of their variations. An industrial city will differ significantly in social respects from a commercial, mining, fishing, resort, university, and capital city. A one-industry city will present different sets of social characteristics from a multi-industry city, as will an industrially balanced from an imbalanced city, a suburb from a satellite, a residential suburb from an industrial suburb, a city within a metropolitan region from one lying outside, an old city from a new one, a southern city from a New England, a middle-western from a Pacific Coast city, a growing from a stable and from a dying city.

A sociological definition must obviously be inclusive enough to comprise whatever essential characteristics these different types of cities have in common as social entities, but it obviously cannot be so detailed as to take account of all the variations implicit in the manifold classes sketched above. Presumably some of the characteristics of cities are more significant in conditioning the nature of urban life than others, and we may expect the outstanding features of the urban-social scene to vary in accordance with size, density, and differences in the functional type of cities. Moreover, we may infer that rural life will bear the imprint of urbanism in the measure that through contact and communication it comes under the influence of cities. It may contribute to the clarity of the statements that follow to repeat that while the locus of urbanism as a mode of life is, of course, to be found characteristically in places which fulfil the requirements we shall set up as a definition of the city, urbanism is not confined to such localities but is manifest in varying degrees wherever the influences of the city reach.

While urbanism, or that complex of traits which makes up the characteristic mode of life in cities, and urbanization, which denotes the development and extensions of these factors, are thus not exclusively found in settlements which are cities in the physical and demographic sense, they do, nevertheless, find their most pronounced expression in such areas, especially in metropolitan cities. In formulating a definition of the city it is necessary to exercise caution in order to avoid identifying urbanism as a way of life with any specific locally or historically conditioned cultural influences which, while they may significantly affect the specific character of the community, are not the essential determinants of its character as a city.

It is particularly important to call attention to the danger of confusing urbanism with industrialism and modern capitalism. The rise of cities in the modern world is undoubtedly not independent of the emergence of modern power-driven machine technology, mass production, and capitalistic enterprise. But different as the cities of earlier epochs may have been by virtue of their development in a preindustrial and precapitalistic order from the great cities of today, they were, nevertheless, cities.

For sociological purposes a city may be defined as a relatively large, dense, and permanent settlement of socially heterogeneous individuals. On the basis of the postulates which this minimal definition suggests, a theory of urbanism may be formulated in the light of existing knowledge concerning social groups.

III. A THEORY OF URBANISM

In the rich literature on the city we look in vain for a theory of urbanism presenting in a systematic fashion the available knowledge concerning the city as a social entity. We do indeed have excellent formulations of theories on such special problems as the growth of the city viewed as a historical trend and as a recurrent process,[2] and we have a wealth of literature presenting insights of sociological relevance and empirical studies offering detailed information on a variety of particular aspects of urban life. But despite the multiplication of research and textbooks on the city, we do not as yet have a comprehensive body of compendent hypotheses which may be derived from a set of postulates implicitly contained in a sociological definition of the city, and from our general sociological knowledge which may be substantiated through empirical research. The closest approximations to a systematic theory of urbanism that we have are to be found in a penetrating essay, "Die Stadt," by Max

[2] See Robert E. Park, Ernest W. Burgess, et al., The City (Chicago, 1925), esp. chaps. ii and iii; Werner Sombart, "Städtische Siedlung, Stadt," Handwörterbuch der Soziologie, ed. Alfred Vierkandt (Stuttgart, 1931).

Weber (1925:514), and a memorable paper by Robert E. Park on "The City: Suggestions for the Investigation of Human Behavior in the Urban Environment" (Park, Burgess, *et al.* 1925). But even these excellent contributions are far from constituting an ordered and coherent framework of theory upon which research might profitably proceed.

In the pages that follow we shall seek to set forth a limited number of identifying characteristics of the city. Given these characteristics we shall then indicate what consequences or further characteristics follow from them in the light of general sociological theory and empirical research. We hope in this manner to arrive at the essential propositions comprising a theory of urbanism. Some of these propositions can be supported by a considerable body of already available research materials; others may be accepted as hypotheses for which a certain amount of presumptive evidence exists, but for which more ample and exact verification would be required. At least such a procedure will, it is hoped, show what in the way of systematic knowledge of the city we now have and what are the crucial and fruitful hypotheses for future research.

The central problem of the sociologist of the city is to discover the forms of social action and organization that typically emerge in relatively permanent, compact settlements of large numbers of heterogeneous individuals. We must also infer that urbanism will assume its most characteristic and extreme form in the measure in which the conditions with which it is congruent are present. Thus the larger, the more densely populated, and the more heterogeneous a community, the more accentuated the characteristics associated with urbanism will be. It should be recognized, however, that in the social world institutions and practices may be accepted and continued for reasons other than those that originally brought them into existence, and that accordingly the urban mode of life may be perpetuated under conditions quite foreign to those necessary for its origin.

Some justification may be in order for the choice of the principal terms comprising our definition of the city. The attempt has been made to make it as inclusive and at the same time as denotative as possible without loading it with unnecessary assumptions. To say that large numbers are necessary to constitute a city means, of course, large numbers in relation to a restricted area or high density of settlement. There are, nevertheless, good reasons for treating large numbers and density as separate factors, since each may be connected with significantly different social consequences. Similarly the need for adding heterogeneity to numbers of population as a necessary and distinct criterion of urbanism might be questioned, since we should expect the range of differences to increase with numbers. In defense, it may be said that the city shows a kind and degree of heterogeneity of population which cannot be wholly accounted for by the law of large numbers or adequately represented by means of a normal distribution curve. Since the population of the city does not reproduce itself, it must recruit its migrants from other cities, the countryside, and—in this country until recently—from other countries. The city has thus historically been the melting-pot of races, peoples, and cultures, and a most favorable breeding-ground of new biological and cultural hybrids. It has not only tolerated but rewarded individual differences. It has brought together people from the ends of the earth *because* they are different and thus useful to one another, rather than because they are homogeneous and like-minded.[3]

There are a number of sociological propositions concerning the relationship between (a) numbers of population, (b) density of settlement, (c) heterogeneity of inhabitants and group life, which can be formulated on the basis of observation and research.

Size of the Population Aggregate

Ever since Aristotle's *Politics*[4] it has been recognized that increasing the number of inhabitants in a settlement beyond a certain limit will

[3] The justification for including the term "permanent" in the definition may appear necessary. Our failure to give an extensive justification for this qualifying mark of the urban rests on the obvious fact that unless human settlements take a fairly permanent root in a locality the characteristics of urban life cannot arise, and conversely the living together of large numbers of heterogeneous individuals under dense conditions is not possible without the development of a more or less technological structure.

[4] See esp. vii. 4. 4–14. Translated by B. Jowett, from which the following may be quoted:

"To the size of states there is a limit, as there is to other things, plants, animals, implements; for none of these retain their natural power when they are too large or too small, but they either wholly lose their nature, or are spoiled. . . . [A] state when composed of too few is not as a state ought to be, self-sufficing; when of too many, though self-sufficing in all mere necessaries, it is a nation and not a state, being almost incapable of constitutional government. For who can be the general of such a vast multitude, or who the herald, unless he have the voice of a Stentor?

"A state then only begins to exist when it has attained a population sufficient for a good life in the political community: it may indeed somewhat exceed this number. But, as I was saying, there must be a limit. What should be the limit will be easily ascertained by experience. For both governors and governed have duties to perform; the special functions of a governor are to command and to judge. But if the citizens of a state are to judge and to distribute offices according to merit, then they must know each other's characters; where they do not possess this knowledge, both the election to offices and the decision of lawsuits will go wrong. When the population is very large they are manifestly settled at haphazard, which clearly ought not affect the relationships between them and the character of the city. Large numbers involve, as has been pointed out, a greater range of individual variation. Furthermore, the greater the number of individuals participating in a process of interaction, the greater is the *potential* differentiation between them. The personal traits, the occupations, the cultural life, and the ideas of the members of an urban community may, therefore, be expected to range between more widely separated poles than those of rural inhabitants.

That such variations should give rise to the spatial segregation of individuals according to color, ethnic heritage, economic and social status, tastes and preferences, may readily be inferred. The bonds of kinship, of neighborliness, and the sentiments arising out of living together for generations under a common folk tradition are likely to be absent or, at best, relatively weak in an aggregate the members of which have such diverse origins and backgrounds. Under such circumstances competition and formal control mechanisms furnish the substitutes for the bonds of solidarity that are relied upon to hold a folk society together.

Increase in the number of inhabitants of a community beyond a few hundred is bound to limit the possibility of each member of the community knowing all the others personally. Max Weber, in recognizing the social significance of this fact, pointed out that from a sociological point of view large numbers of inhabitants and density of settlement mean that the personal mutual acquaintanceship between the inhabitants which ordinarily inheres in a neighborhood is lacking (1925:514). The increase in numbers thus involves a changed character of the social relationships. As Simmel points out:

> [If] the unceasing external contact of numbers of persons in the city should be met by the same number of inner reactions as in the small town, in which one knows almost every person he meets and to each of whom he has a positive relationship, one would be completely atomized internally and would fall into an unthinkable mental condition. (Simmel 1903:187–206)

The multiplication of persons in a state of interaction under conditions which make their contact as full personalities impossible produces that segmentalization of human relationships which has sometimes been seized upon by students of the mental life of the cities as an explanation

---

to be. Besides, in an overpopulous state foreigners and metics will readily acquire the rights of citizens, for who will find them out? Clearly, then, the best limit of the population of a state is the largest number which suffices for the purpose of life, and can be taken in at a single view. Enough concerning the size of a city."

for the "schizoid" character of urban personality. This is not to say that the urban inhabitants have fewer acquaintances than rural inhabitants, for the reverse may actually be true; it means rather that in relation to the number of people whom they see and with whom they rub elbows in the course of daily life, they know a smaller proportion, and of these they have less intensive knowledge.

Characteristically, urbanites meet one another in highly segmental roles. They are, to be sure, dependent upon more people for the satisfactions of their life-needs than are rural people and thus are associated with a greater number of organized groups, but they are less dependent upon particular persons, and their dependence upon others is confined to a highly fractionalized aspect of the other's round of activity. This is essentially what is meant by saying that the city is characterized by secondary rather than primary contacts. The contacts of the city may indeed be face to face, but they are nevertheless impersonal, superficial, transitory, and segmental. The reserve, the indifference, and the blasé outlook which urbanites manifest in their relationships may thus be regarded as devices for immunizing themselves against the personal claims and expectations of others.

The superficiality, the anonymity, and the transitory character of urban-social relations make intelligible, also, the sophistication and the rationality generally ascribed to city-dwellers. Our acquaintances tend to stand in a relationship of utility to us in the sense that the role which each one plays in our life is overwhelmingly regarded as a means for the achievement of our own ends. Whereas, therefore, the individual gains, on the one hand, a certain degree of emancipation or freedom from the personal and emotional controls of intimate groups, he loses, on the other hand, the spontaneous self-expression, the morale, and the sense of participation that comes with living in an integrated society. This constitutes essentially the state of *anomie* or the social void to which Durkheim alludes in attempting to account for the various forms of social disorganization in technological society.

The segmental character and utilitarian accent of interpersonal relations in the city find their institutional expression in the proliferation of specialized tasks which we see in their most developed form in the professions. The operations of the pecuniary nexus leads to predatory relationships, which tend to obstruct the efficient functioning of the social order unless checked by professional codes and occupational etiquette. The premium put upon utility and efficiency suggests the adaptability of the corporate device for the organization of enterprises in which individuals can engage only in groups. The advantage that the corporation has over the individual entrepreneur and the partnership in the urban-industrial world derives not only from the possibility it affords of centralizing the resources of thousands of individuals or from the legal privilege of limited liability and perpetual succession, but from the fact that the corporation has no soul.

The specialization of individuals, particularly in their occupations, can proceed only, as Adam Smith pointed out, upon the basis of an enlarged market, which in turn accentuates the division of labor. This enlarged market is only in part supplied by the city's hinterland; in large measure it is found among the large numbers that the city itself contains. The dominance of the city over the surrounding hinterland becomes explicable in terms of the division of labor which urban life occasions and promotes. The extreme degree of interdependence and unstable equilibrium of urban life are closely associated with the division of labor and the specialization of occupations. This interdependence and instability is increased by the tendency of each city to specialize in those functions in which it has the greatest advantage.

In a community composed of a larger number of individuals than can know one another intimately and can be assembled in one spot, it becomes necessary to communicate through indirect mediums and to articulate individual interests by a process of delegation. Typically in the city, interests are made effective through representation. The individual counts for little, but the voice of the representative is heard with a deference roughly proportional to the numbers for whom he speaks.

While this characterization of urbanism, in so far as it derives from large numbers, does not by any means exhaust the sociological inferences that might be drawn from our knowledge of the relationship of the size of a group to the characteristic behavior of the members, for the sake of brevity the assertions made may serve to exemplify the sort of propositions that might be developed.

Density

As in the case of numbers, so in the case of concentration in limited space, certain consequences of relevance in sociological analysis of the city emerge. Of these only a few can be indicated.

As Darwin pointed out for flora and fauna and as Durkheim (1932: 248) noted in the case of human societies, an increase in numbers when area is held constant (i.e., an increase in density) tends to produce differentiation and specialization, since only in this way can the area support increased numbers. Density thus reinforces the effect of numbers in diversifying men and their activities and in increasing the complexity of the social structure.

On the subjective side, as Simmel has suggested, the close physical contact of numerous individuals necessarily produces a shift in the mediums through which we orient ourselves to the urban milieu, especially to our fellow-men. Typically, our physical contacts are close but our social contacts are distant. The urban world puts a premium on visual recognition. We see the uniform which denotes the role of the functionaries and are oblivious to the personal eccentricities that are hidden behind the uniform. We tend to acquire and develop a sensitivity to a world of artifacts and become progressively farther removed from the world of nature.

We are exposed to glaring contrasts between splendor and squalor, between riches and poverty, intelligence and ignorance, order and chaos. The competition for space is great, so that each area generally tends to be put to the use which yields the greatest economic return. Place of work tends to become dissociated from place of residence, for the proximity of industrial and commercial establishments makes an area both economically and socially undesirable for residential purposes.

Density, land values, rentals, accessibility, healthfulness, prestige, aesthetic consideration, absence of nuisances such as noise, smoke, and dirt determine the desirability of various areas of the city as places of settlement for different sections of the population. Place and nature of work, income, racial and ethnic characteristics, social status, custom, habit, taste, preference, and prejudice are among the significant factors in accordance with which the urban population is selected and distributed into more or less distinct settlements. Diverse population elements inhabiting a compact settlement thus tend to become segregated from one another in the degree in which their requirements and modes of life are incompatible with one another and in the measure in which they are antagonistic to one another. Similarly, persons of homogeneous status and needs unwittingly drift into, consciously select, or are forced by circumstances into, the same area. The different parts of the city thus acquire specialized functions. The city consequently tends to resemble a mosaic of social worlds in which the transition from one to the other is abrupt. The juxtaposition of divergent personalities and modes of life tends to produce a relativistic perspective and a sense of toleration of differences which may be regarded as prerequisites for rationality and which lead toward the secularization of life.[5]

The close living together and working together of individuals who

---

[5] The extent to which the segregation of the population into distinct ecological and cultural areas and the resulting social attitude of tolerance, rationality, and secular mentality are functions of density as distinguished from heterogeneity is difficult to determine. Most likely we are dealing here with phenomena which are consequences of the simultaneous operation of both factors.

have no sentimental and emotional ties foster a spirit of competition, aggrandizement, and mutual exploitation. To counteract irresponsibility and potential disorder, formal controls tend to be resorted to. Without rigid adherence to predictable routines a large compact society would scarcely be able to maintain itself. The clock and the traffic signal are symbolic of the basis of our social order in the urban world. Frequent close physical contact, coupled with great social distance, accentuates the reserve of unattached individuals toward one another and, unless compensated for by other opportunities for response, gives rise to loneliness. The necessary frequent movement of great numbers of individuals in a congested habitat gives occasion to friction and irritation. Nervous tensions which derive from such personal frustrations are accentuated by the rapid tempo and the complicated technology under which life in dense areas must be lived.

Heterogeneity

The social interaction among such a variety of personality types in the urban milieu tends to break down the rigidity of caste lines and to complicate the class structure, and thus induces a more ramified and differentiated framework of social stratification than is found in more integrated societies. The heightened mobility of the individual, which brings him within the range of stimulation by a great number of diverse individuals and subjects him to fluctuating status in the differentiated social groups that compose the social structure of the city, tends toward the acceptance of instability and insecurity in the world at large as a norm. This fact helps to account, too, for the sophistication and cosmopolitanism of the urbanite. No single group has the undivided allegiance of the individual. The groups with which he is affiliated do not lend themselves readily to a simple hierarchical arrangement. By virtue of his different interests arising out of different aspects of social life, the individual acquires membership in widely divergent groups, each of which functions only with reference to a single segment of his personality. Nor do these groups easily permit of a concentric arrangement so that the narrower ones fall within the circumference of the more inclusive ones, as is more likely to be the case in the rural community or in primitive societies. Rather the groups with which the person typically is affiliated are tangential to each other or intersect in highly variable fashion.

Partly as a result of the physical footlooseness of the population and partly as a result of their social mobility, the turnover in group membership generally is rapid. Place of residence, place and character of employment, income and interests fluctuate, and the task of holding organizations together and maintaining and promoting intimate and lasting acquaintanceship between the members is difficult. This applies strikingly to the local areas within the city into which persons become segregated more by virtue of differences in race, language, income, and social status, than through choice or positive attraction to people like themselves. Overwhelmingly the city-dweller is not a home-owner, and since a transitory habitat does not generate binding traditions and sentiments, only rarely is he truly a neighbor. There is little opportunity for the individual to obtain a conception of the city as a whole or to survey his place in the total scheme. Consequently he finds it difficult to determine what is to his own "best interests" and to decide between the issues and leaders presented to him by the agencies of mass suggestion. Individuals who are thus detached from the organized bodies which integrate society comprise the fluid masses that make collective behavior in the urban community so unpredictable and hence so problematical.

Although the city, through the recruitment of variant types to perform its diverse tasks and the accentuation of their uniqueness through competition and the premium upon eccentricity, novelty, efficient performance, and inventiveness, produces a highly differentiated population, it also exercises a leveling influence. Wherever large numbers of differently constituted individuals congregate, the process of depersonalization also enters. This leveling tendency inheres in part in the economic basis of the city. The development of large cities, at least in the modern age, was largely dependent upon the concentrative force of steam. The rise of the factory made possible mass production for an impersonal market. The fullest exploitation of the possibilities of the division of labor and mass production, however, is possible only with standardization of processes and products. A money economy goes hand in hand with such a system of production. Progressively as cities have developed upon a background of this system of production, the pecuniary nexus which implies the purchasability of services and things has displaced personal relations as the basis of association. Individuality under these circumstances must be replaced by categories. When large numbers have to make common use of facilities and institutions, an arrangement must be made to adjust the facilities and institutions to the needs of the average person rather than to those of particular individuals. The services of the public utilities, of the recreational, educational, and cultural institutions must be adjusted to mass requirements. Similarly, the cultural institutions, such as the schools, the movies, the radio, and the newspapers, by virtue of their mass clientele, must necessarily operate as leveling influences. The political process as it appears in urban life could not be understood without taking account of the mass appeals made through modern propaganda techniques. If the individual would participate at all in the social, political, and economic life of the city, he must subordinate some of his individuality to the demands of the larger community and in that measure immerse himself in mass movements.

IV. THE RELATION BETWEEN A THEORY OF URBANISM AND SOCIOLOGICAL RESEARCH

By means of a body of theory such as that illustratively sketched above, the complicated and many-sided phenomena of urbanism may be analyzed in terms of a limited number of basic categories. The sociological approach to the city thus acquires an essential unity and coherence enabling the empirical investigator not merely to focus more distinctly upon the problems and processes that properly fall in his province but also to treat his subject matter in a more integrated and systematic fashion. A few typical finds of empirical research in the field of urbanism, with special reference to the United States, may be indicated to substantiate the theoretical propositions set forth in the preceeding pages, and some of the crucial problems for further study may be outlined.

On the basis of the three variables, number, density of settlement, and degree of heterogeneity, of the urban population, it appears possible to explain the characteristics of urban life and to account for the differences between cities of various sizes and types.

Urbanism as a characteristic mode of life may be approached empirically from three interrelated perspectives: (1) as a physical structure comprising a population base, a technology, and an ecological order; (2) as a system of social organization involving a characteristic social structure, a series of social institutions, and a typical pattern of social relationships; and (3) as a set of attitudes and ideas, and a constellation of personalities engaging in typical forms of collective behavior and subject to characteristic mechanisms of social control.

Urbanism in Ecological Perspective

Since in the case of physical structure and ecological processes we are able to operate with fairly objective indices, it becomes possible to arrive at quite precise and generally quantitative results. The dominance of the city over its hinterland becomes explicable through the functional characteristics of the city which derive in large measure from the effect of numbers and density. Many of the technical facilities and the skills and organizations to which urban life gives rise can grow and prosper only in cities where the demand is sufficiently great. The nature and scope of the services rendered by these organizations and institutions and the advantage which they enjoy over the less developed facilities of smaller towns enhances the dominance of the city and the dependence of ever wider regions upon the central metropolis.

The urban-population composition shows the operation of selective and differentiating factors. Cities contain a larger proportion of persons in the prime of life than rural areas which contain more old and very young people. In this, as in so many other respects, the larger the city the more this specific characteristic of urbanism is apparent. With the exception of the largest cities, which have attracted the bulk of the foreign-born males, and a few other special types of cities, women predominate numerically over men. The heterogeneity of the urban population is further indicated along racial and ethnic lines. The foreign born and their children constitute nearly two-thirds of all the inhabitants of cities of one million and over. Their proportion in the urban population declines as the size of the city decreases, until in the rural areas they comprise only about one-sixth of the total population. The larger cities similarly have attracted more Negroes and other racial groups than have the smaller communities. Considering that age, sex, race, and ethnic origin are associated with other factors such as occupation and interest, it becomes clear that one major characteristic of the urban-dweller is his dissimilarity from his fellows. Never before have such large masses of people of diverse traits as we find in our cities been thrown together into such close physical contact as in the great cities of America. Cities generally, and American cities in particular, comprise a motley of peoples and cultures, of highly differentiated modes of life between which there often is only the faintest communication, the greatest indifference and the broadest tolerance, occasionally bitter strife, but always the sharpest contrast.

The failure of the urban population to reproduce itself appears to be a biological consequence of a combination of factors in the complex of urban life, and the decline in the birth-rate generally may be regarded as one of the most significant signs of the urbanization of the Western world. While the proportion of deaths in cities is slightly greater than in the country, the outstanding difference between the failure of present-day cities to maintain their population and that of cities of the past is that in former times it was due to the exceedingly high death-rates in cities, whereas today, since cities have become more livable from a health standpoint, it is due to low birth-rates. These biological characteristics of the urban population are significant sociologically, not merely because they reflect the urban mode of existence but also because they condition the growth and future dominance of cities and their basic social organization. Since cities are the consumers rather than the producers of men, the value of human life and the social estimation of the personality will not be unaffected by the balance between births and deaths. The pattern of land use, of land values, rentals, and ownership, the nature and functioning of the physical structures, of housing, of transportation and communication facilities, of public utilities—these and many other phases of the physical mechanism of the city are not isolated phenomena unrelated to the city as a social entity, but are affected by and affect the urban mode of life.

Urbanism as a Form of Social Organization

The distinctive features of the urban mode of life have often been described sociologically as consisting of the substitution of secondary for primary contacts, the weakening of bonds of kinship, and the declining social significance of the family, the disappearance of the neighborhood, and the undermining of the traditional basis of social solidarity. All these phenomena can be substantially verified through objective indices. Thus, for instance, the low and declining urban-reproduction rates suggest that the city is not conducive to the traditional type of family life, including the rearing of children and the maintenance of the home as the locus of a whole round of vital activities. The transfer of industrial, educational, and recreational activities to specialized institutions outside the home has deprived the family of some of its most characteristic historical functions. In cities mothers are more likely to be employed, lodgers are more frequently part of the household, marriage tends to be postponed, and the proportion of single and unattached people is greater. Families are smaller and more frequently without children than in the country. The family as a unit of social life is emancipated from the larger kinship group characteristic of the country, and the individual members pursue their own diverging interests in their vocational, educational, religious, recreational, and political life.

Such functions as the maintenance of health, the methods of alleviating the hardships associated with personal and social insecurity, the provisions for education, recreation, and cultural advancement have given rise to highly specialized institutions on a community-wide, statewide, or even national basis. The same factors which have brought about greater personal insecurity also underlie the wider contrasts between individuals to be found in the urban world. While the city has broken down the rigid caste lines of preindustrial society, it has sharpened and differentiated income and status groups. Generally, a larger proportion of the adult-urban population is gainfully employed than is the case with the adult-rural population. The white-collar class, comprising those employed in trade, in clerical, and in professional work, are proportionately more numerous in large cities and in metropolitan centers and in smaller towns than in the country.

On the whole, the city discourages an economic life in which the individual in time of crisis has a basis of subsistence to fall back upon, and it discourages self-employment. While incomes of city people are on the average higher than those of country people, the cost of living seems to be higher in the larger cities. Home ownership involves greater burdens and is rarer. Rents are higher and absorb a larger proportion of the income. Although the urban-dweller has the benefit of many communal services, he spends a large proportion of his income for such items as recreation and advancement and a smaller proportion for food. What the communal services do not furnish the urbanite must purchase, and there is virtually no human need which has remained unexploited by commercialism. Catering to thrills and furnishing means of escape from drudgery, monotony, and routine thus become one of the major functions of urban recreation, which at its best furnishes means for creative self-expression and spontaneous group association, but which more typically in the urban world results in passive spectatorism on the one hand, or sensational record-smashing feats on the other.

Being reduced to a stage of virtual impotence as an individual, the urbanite is bound to exert himself by joining with others of similar interest into organized groups to obtain his ends. This results in the enormous multiplication of voluntary organizations directed toward as great a variety of objectives as there are human needs and interests. While on the one hand the traditional ties of human association are weakened, urban existence involves a much greater degree of interdependence between man and man and a more complicated, fragile, and volatile form of mutual interrelations over many phases of which the individual as such can exert scarcely any control. Frequently there is only the most tenuous relationship between the economic position or other basic factors that determine the individual's existence in the urban world and the voluntary groups with which he is affiliated. While in a primitive and in a rural society it is generally possible to predict on the basis of a few known factors who will belong to what and who will associate with whom in almost every relationship of life, in the city we can only project the general pattern of group formation and affiliation, and this pattern will display many incongruities and contradictions.

Urban Personality and Collective Behavior

It is largely through the activities of the voluntary groups, be their objectives economic, political, educational, religious, recreational, or cultural, that the urbanite expresses and develops his personality, acquires status, and is able to carry on the round of activities that constitute his life-career. It may easily be inferred, however, that the organizational framework which these highly differentiated functions call into being does not of itself insure the consistency and integrity of the personalities whose interests it enlists. Personal disorganization, mental breakdown, suicide, delinquency, crime, corruption, and disorder might be expected under these circumstances to be more prevalent in the urban than in the rural community. This has been confirmed in so far as comparable indices are available; but the mechanisms underlying these phenomena require further analysis.

Since for most group purposes it is impossible in the city to appeal individually to the large number of discrete and differentiated individuals, and since it is only through the organizations to which men belong that their interests and resources can be enlisted for a collective cause, it may be inferred that social control in the city should typically proceed through formally organized groups. It follows, too, that the masses of men in the city are subject to manipulation by symbols and stereotypes managed by individuals working from afar or operating invisibly behind the scenes through their control of the instruments of communication. Self-government either in the economic, the political, or the cultural realm is under these circumstances reduced to a mere figure of speech or, at best, is subject to the unstable equilibrium of pressure groups. In view of the ineffectiveness of actual kinship ties we create fictional kinship groups. In the face of the disappearance of the territorial unit as a basis of social solidarity we create interest units. Meanwhile the city as a community resolves itself into a series of tenuous segmental relationships superimposed upon a territorial base with a definite center but without a definite periphery and upon a division of labor which far transcends the immediate locality and is world-wide in scope. The larger the number of persons in a state of interaction with one another the lower is the level of communication and the greater is the tendency for communication to proceed on an elementary level, i.e., on the basis of those things which are assumed to be common or to be of interest to all.

It is obviously, therefore, to the emerging trends in the communication system and to the production and distribution technology that has come into existence with modern civilization that we must look for the symptoms which will indicate the probable future development of urbanism as a mode of social life. The direction of the ongoing changes in urbanism will for good or ill transform not only the city but the world. Some of the more basic of these factors and processes and the possibilities of their direction and control invite further detailed study.

It is only in so far as the sociologist has a clear conception of the city as a social entity and a workable theory of urbanism that he can hope to develop a unified body of reliable knowledge, which what passes as "urban sociology" is certainly not at the present time. By taking his point of departure from a theory of urbanism such as that sketched in the foregoing pages to be elaborated, tested, and revised in the light of further analysis and empirical research, it is to be hoped that the criteria of relevance and validity of factual data can be determined. The miscellaneous assortment of disconnected information which has hitherto found its way into sociological treatises on the city may thus be sifted and incorporated into a coherent body of knowledge. Incidentally, only by means of some such theory will the sociologist escape the futile practice of voicing in the name of sociological science a variety of often unsupportable judgments concerning such problems as poverty, housing, city-planning, sanitation, municipal administration, policing, marketing, transportation, and other technical issues. While the sociologist cannot solve any of these practical problems—at least not by himself—he may, if he discovers his proper function, have an important contribution to make to their comprehension and solution. The prospects for doing this are brightest through a general, theoretical, rather than through an *ad hoc* approach.

3
Rationale and Romance in Urban Anthropology[1]

Richard G. Fox

"*The community with which this volume is concerned is nondescript; it is a place of unusual interest.*"

ROBERT PARK, INTRODUCTION TO *The Gold Coast and the Slum*, BY HARVEY ZORBAUGH (1929).

"*Romance—[a prose tale] dealing with the remote in time or place, the heroic, the adventurous, and often the mysterious.*"

WEBSTER'S THIRD NEW INTERNATIONAL DICTIONARY OF THE ENGLISH LANGUAGE, UNABRIDGED.

Whether urban anthropology will ever provide significant insights into urban society and city man ultimately depends on how it defines its purpose. In much contemporary urban anthropology, the city only appears as a difficult, even hostile environment for impoverished, culturally distinctive and historyless populations. Great emphasis is also placed on newly-arrived urban settlers and the process by which individuals accommodate to the urban locale. Little of the city as urban community and less of the interactional or ideological fit of the city to the larger society emerge from such studies. Justification for this approach usually comes from the supposed difficulty of transforming traditional anthropological methodology to meet the complexities of the urban sphere, as though methodology rather than conceptual framework should determine the proper arena for anthropology. What in fact often restricts the scope of urban anthropology is its pursuit of the exotic and

SOURCE: *Urban Anthropology*, 1, no. 2 (1972): 205–33. Reprinted by permission.

[1] This paper is a revision of one read at the seventieth annual meeting of the American Anthropological Association, November 19, 1971.

marginal within urban locales rather than any necessary limitations of ethnographic method or ethnological theory. Gaining an insider's view of the Outsider to the City, knowing what it means to be an urban man cultured in poverty recreates the traditional anthropological vision of the strange, the exotic, the bypassed in a modern world of industrialism, mass culture, and high-rise existence. Although pursuit of the exotic has been the basis of anthropology's strength in the past, the form it takes in contemporary urban anthropology often means that little can be said about city and society or urban organization and national culture. The primary objective of this paper is a critical examination of current research and conception in urban anthropology with the aim of indicating the limited approach to cities often adopted in such studies. But rather than purely negative scholarship, the paper also proposes a remedy for some of the ills which beset the study of urban peoples and places in anthropology. Part I of this paper suggests a reorientation of urban anthropology's purpose away from isolated ghetto studies or arbitrarily delimited urbanization networks and towards a holistic perspective on cities in their social and cultural settings. Part II illustrates this approach from the author's field research in urban America. Through a critical review of recent city studies in anthropology, Part III illustrates the contrastive microsociological approach current in much urban anthropology and explores the conceptual deficiencies which emerge from so limited a view of anthropology's role in urban research.

I. CITIES AND SOCIETIES

To see the city and its behavioral and ideological links to the larger society should be a major goal of urban anthropology (cf. Miner 1965:6 and Arensberg 1968:3.) The emphasis on the urban world as a separate social realm, with its own dynamic, and its special features of heterogeneity, ecological zones, and architectural form may be appropriate to other disciplines; it may also be an ethnocentrism derived from modern times when the city creates the political order for the society and when the urban center originates and transmits its mass culture (cf. Keyfitz 1967:275–276.) For the anthropologist interested in cross-cultural comparison or analysis of urban development, the city becomes only one of many institutions such as kinship, value systems, and subsistence activity which he has always treated as parts of a socio-cultural whole. This "super-organic" approach to urbanism absolves the anthropologist of the psychological and sociological reductionism implicit in studying city men, families, and associations on urban streets and corners.

I wish to suggest two ways in which the urban anthropologist may perceive the city in the context of the larger society. Both require a diachronic approach and a wider viewpoint than the single urban center or one of its component class or ethnic populations. One way is to focus on the ideological ties which bind the city to the countryside and vice versa, to measure how the ideological motifs of the larger society are embedded in the culture of its cities, to recognize how the urban sphere projects self-generated beliefs onto its hinterland. This approach is no great departure for anthropology. Is there any difference between studying belief systems as they affect carvings on a totem pole or as they arrange urban space and condition urban values? The other viewpoint is inter-actional: the city is a socio-economic and political factor in the organization of the society; it is both product and producer of particular political alignments, economic sectors, and social structures. Just as kinship organization stands in functional relationship to ecological factors, just as the form of the family reflects political and economic institutions, so the city relates to the political and economic order in which it exists.[2]

These two ways to a macroscopic urban anthropology are not revolutionary. They have been already partially marked out, although in many areas the road is very rough and other places are not yet reached. Studies such as those of Miner (1965), Banton (1957), Van der Berghe (1964) and Gulick (1967), which take the entire city as the unit of description, pave the way for cross-cultural comparison and necessarily do away with psychological and sociological reductionism. In one of the first essays into the ideological links of city and society, Singer and Redfield distinguished "heterogenetic" and "orthogenetic" urbanism (Singer 1960:261). Whether or not the distinction is valid, the approach is an important step which few have followed. Continuing this interest in the ideological links of city and society, Harris (1956:279–280) described the "urban ethos" of a small country town in Brazil: the passion for city life, the contempt for the country and agricultural labor. This urban ethos exists in spite of. the town's isolation and lack of great population. For Harris, it derives from a historical tradition of the Mediterranean and Latin America reinforced by the town's continuous involvement in an industrial economy. Leeds (1968:37) has recently sketched the difference in ethos between Rio and Sao Paolo and discusses how it helps explain the condition of urban migrants in either city. Another urban ethos appears in pre-British northern India, where local lineage leaders living in what were little more than mud huts emulated the image of the urban as they perceived it from the king's court (Fox 1971:170–182).

[2] Cf. Arensberg's comment (1968:13) that ". . . as we come to identify new forms of the city, perhaps we shall also identify new forms of the state;" and Miner's contention (1967:9) that ". . . societal dominance is the city's raison d'etre . . ."

Elliot Liebow's concept of a "shadow system of values" among street corner Negroes in Washington most clearly indicates what the anthropologist may come to see of city and society even from the confines of ghetto streets when he views them in relation to the larger society:

> . . . the stretched or alternative value systems [of the ghetto] are not the same order of values, either phenomenologically or operationally, as the parent or general system of values [in the larger society]: they are derivative, subsidiary in nature . . . less completely internalized, and seem to be value images reflected by forced or adaptive behavior rather than real values with a positive determining influence on behavior . . . a shadow cast by the common value system in the distorting lower-class setting (1967:213).

The interactional study of city and society is even less well developed. Pocock (1960) and Lynch (1967) indicate the continued role of caste and kin institutions of Indian society in an urban context. Another study of a North Indian market town traces the town's political and economic development and relates it to preindustrial and postcolonial types of urbanism (Fox 1969b). Although he does not believe in specifically urban studies, Cohen's work (1969) on the Hausa merchants of Nigeria indicates how economic conditions in the larger society and spatial allocations in the city "retribalized" and ghettoized this people. Geertz (1965) shows how the process of involutional change which he delineates for Java conditions the social history of a specific Indonesian town. Tiger (1967) analyzes the role of bureaucracy and the mass media in the organization of modern towns.

An ideological and interactional approach to the city is not automatically a dynamic one. The concept of "adaptation" must be added to introduce a perspective on urban development and social change in the city. Cities are and have been in a continual (and often long-standing) process of adjustment to their external socio-cultural environments and their internal economic and political conditions. To perceive the city in the setting of a society, the anthropologist must study the enduring pattern of relations between the urban sphere and the external socio-cultural fabric which conditions its existence. A similar position is articulated in Lampard's call for a "multilineal" analysis of cities:

> The great variety of urbanizing experience underlines the fact that population concentration is everywhere an *adaptive* process. Each urban tradition, like each city, represents a continuing accommodation of general societal tendencies to particular sets of demographic and environmental exigencies (1967:538–539).

"Environment" for the anthropologist need not directly involve physical circumstances affecting the city, such as water supply, soil type, or rainfall average. Rather, a city's external environment represents the sum of all social and cultural factors impinging on the city (some of which may ultimately derive from the physical environment because of those cultural rules which are technologically and ecologically determined). These social and cultural factors include political pressure, economic conditions, communication and transportation channels, and rural values which condition a city's "foreign" relations with the part of society external to it (including other urban places) and which necessarily affect the course of urban development and internal urban social arrangements. Adaptation to an external environment thus refers to the changing pattern of ideological and interactional links between city and society over time. The adjustments of cities to their external environments can be discussed as their pattern of relationship with their "hinterlands."

Another process of adaptation congruent with the pattern of hinterland relations goes on within the city. The organization of urban government, class structure, and residential arrangements reflect the city's economic functions, political power, and communication lines as they develop over time and in conjunction with or apart from those of the hinterland. This internal adaptation of cities in terms of their interactional links with the hinterland can be discussed as the "functional organization" of the city or "urban (functional) organization." Although the following section on two American cities concentrates on urban organization, hinterland relations also condition urban spatial arrangements and physical layout through the ideological links between city and larger society. The ideological arrangement of urban space as determined by the city's adaptation to external socio-cultural factors can be referred to as the "ideological form" of the city or "urban (ideological) form." The process of urban adaptation and its effects on urban organization and form convey the conceptual base for investigating the interactional and ideological settings of cities in their societies through time.

The following section applies the concepts of interaction, adaptation, hinterland relations, and urban (functional) organization to an analysis of the origins, continuities in development, and present constitution of two American cities.

II. NABOBS AND NONPARTISANS

So often in the study of cities, the magnitude and diversity of urban phenomena become overwhelming. How to deal with the multitudes of cities which exist or have existed? How to perceive the uniformities of urbanism within the particulars of a thousand cities? The concept of adaptation helps to categorize the great variability in the nature of cities. The adaptation of cities to their hinterlands can be viewed as creating both a primary and a secondary level of urban variation. Primary urban variability reflects the general or gross nature of the sociocultural environment, or hinterland. Thus, different sorts of hinterlands lead to different kinds of cities. Pre-industrial cities (e.g., cities before the advent of Western industrialization) share certain general characteristics due to their technological and economic base which differentiate them from all industrial cities. The latter similarly share certain characteristic economic and productive arrangements. The nature of the hinterland therefore provides a means of differentiating cities into general types which constitute the primary level of urban variability.

To recognize that different city types are associated with different kinds of hinterlands is not to cover the full extent of urban variation. Within any general type of hinterland and its related (primary) urban variety, a range of secondary urban variation exists because specific cities follow divergent patterns of adaptation to the larger society. For example, in terms of primary urban variability, Chicago and Charleston (South Carolina) share many common characteristics of urban organization and form because their adaptive patterns have developed within a common American industrial hinterland. But Charleston and Chicago differ in population, urban morphology, ethnic arrangements, extent of industrialization, class structure, and ideology as a result of their individual patterns of adaptation to this industrial hinterland, an individuality compounded of historic factors and location. To understand the full extent of urban variation, the anthropologist cannot be content with gross typological distinctions between, for example, preindustrial and industrial cities. He must also study the dynamics of secondary urban variability, the directions which this variability takes, and the sociocultural factors which lie behind the specific adaptive paths of individual cities.

My research on urban America set out to determine the variations in the adaptive pattern of urban settlements possible in an industrial socio-cultural environment characterized by a common industrial market economy and a modernized nation-state.[3] The research had three broad theoretical objectives: to investigate the influence of various historical adaptive patterns linking locality and larger society on the development

[3] The research in urban America is being conducted under grant # MH18336 from the Public Health Service, National Institute of Mental Health, which I gratefully acknowledge.

of urban centers; to analyze the nature and growth of urban governmental forms and urban social classes originating from such adaptive patterns; and to observe the persistence or decline of these urban adaptive patterns under the impact of a modernized society.

Two basic types of local government evolved in the English colonies of North America from the early 1600s on, and greatly influenced the subsequent pattern of urban development. The first type is found in the New England region where the town meeting developed as the method of local administration. Although scholars disagree about how democratically this system operated (cf. Lockridge 1970 and Grant 1970), the town meeting gave a great amount of independence and initiative to local civic authorities at the same time as it restricted the authority of town officers. A contrasting type of local adminisration developed in the remaining American colonies. Here the county or parish system of government obtained, and urban areas when they developed were administered within the county or parish political framework. In New York, New Jersey, and other mid-Atlantic colonies, this system was modified by the granting of urban charters which guaranteed such incorporated areas a municipal existence apart from local county organization. However, from North Carolina southward, urban charters were absent before the Revolution, and even in the mid-Atlantic region, most urban charters fell into disuse or were countermanded within a short time by colonial legislatures. Especially in the colonial South but also elsewhere outside New England, therefore, urban locales constituted administered urban places which developed as adjuncts of central government and never achieved an independent municipal identity.

The specific research objective has been to contrast the past and present of two cities which developed in these quite distinct sociopolitical environments within industrial America. Participant observation, historical research, and quantitative surveys were undertaken in the cities of Newport, Rhode Island and Charleston, South Carolina—the former representing urban growth emerging from the New England town meeting, the latter reflecting urban development out of a monolithic colonial government. Data on these cities, especially quantitative information, are not yet completely analyzed. This preliminary presentation is in illustration of a particular approach to urban anthropology.

Newport has not always been a city on the other side of a bridge from the major part of Rhode Island including the state capital, Providence. In an earlier period, transportation links for the seaport city at the southern tip of Aquidnick Island were solely by water. But the bridge provides a physical symbol of Newport's separation from the northern part of the state. For many Newporters, "anything that comes over the bridge is bad," a statement which signifies their distaste for the intrusion of the governmental power and economic supremacy which has lodged in the Providence area since the state capital was moved from Newport and since the Rhode Island economy shifted from seaport mercantilism to inland industrialism. The statement also reflects an urban image which accentuates Newport's former glory and present cosmopolitaness, as distinct from the working-class provincialism of the northern country over the bridge. This desire for autonomy, this mental and, at times in the past, physical resistance to the "other" Rhode Island has its organizational analogue in the contemporary nonpartisan city manager municipal government, which formally, and in the expectation of many residents, actually, removes Newport from (state) party politics.

Throughout the history of the town and, subsequently, city of Newport, a nonparitsan style of local government has always been the ideal of many citizens. Their advocacy is not only or even mainly based on the merits of this form of municipal organization for the internal direction of the city. Nonpartisanship for many Newporters has to do with removing them from the flow of politics in the rest of Rhode Island. Town or city government was to concern internal arrangements only; formal links of government between state and city or informal links of party were best avoided. In a recognizably American combination of political naivete with belief in the moral worth of commerce, the cry in Newport has always been that party politics has no place in a city, whose proper government, instead, must rest on business-like principles.

An ideological and behavioral tradition of autonomy lies behind this pursuit of the nonpartisan. Although the constitution of Rhode Island makes Newport an urban creation of the state, the city at present and in the past often acted as if its existence and organization were solely at local discretion. The city's political history, including the first (abortive) charter shortly after the American Revolution as well as the successful incorporation of 1853, involves a never-ending contest between state authority and local autonomy, the last installment of which occurred as recently as 1970. This contest, indicative of Newport's lack of synchronization with the state, is partially explained by its economic dependence on external sources such as the non-local wealthy elite, the so called "summer colonists," and more recently, on the United States Navy. This economic reliance on the outside explains much of Newport's "cosmopolitan" outlook, and also why its interests often diverged from the rest of Rhode Island.

A political heritage also helps explain the nonpartisan tradition. The Newport town meeting antedates the formation of the colony of Rhode

Island by several decades. It was only with reluctance and the reservation of many local powers that Newport town agreed to join Providence and other newly settled areas to form a colonial government under the royal charter of 1663. Since this time, the town form of local government has continued to play an important role in Rhode Island. Although a division into formal counties exists, these have relatively few functions and bear no relationship to the importance of the county elsewhere, especially in the South. Newport carefully guarded its prerogatives as a town, and having become a city continued to believe in its autonomy. Both in 1784 and 1847–1853, attempts at incorporation seem generated by a desire to remove Newport from state politics and policies, which in both periods were moving in a direction hostile to Newport's interests. Incorporation was resisted by a combination of those who did not want such isolation from the state and others, stauncher nonpartisans, who feared any attempt to abridge the powers of the town meeting. Over the past 125 years the sentiment for autonomy has often lost out to a more organic structure of state and city government of politics, but the nonpartisans of Newport continually reasserted themselves. In 1953, they won their greatest success by passage of a home rule charter which established a nonpartisan city manager form of local administration. However, this system is not completely secured; it has been continually challenged up to the present by those who wish to see Newport politics defined in the image of the state, and many residents feel that the next swing in a cyclical alternation between party politics and nonpartisanship (which they only perceive in its most recent form) will shortly be upon them.

The pursuit of the nonpartisan in Newport establishes the adaptive pattern of the city: a retreat from outside political domination through creation of political forms divergent from the rest of Rhode Island, a reservation of the city for its residents and their economic pursuits whether or not the "other" Rhode Island concurred—in short, a bounding of the city as an enclave within the state. No dreams of empire have ever come from Newport, as they did from Charleston. The symbol of the bridge, like the Chinese Wall, marks off what is without from what is within, a political and economic insularity which the nonpartisans of Newport have taken pains to establish or maintain throughout the city's development.

The relationship of Newport to its governmental hinterland has a reflection in the "urban organization" of the city. The shift in political power and economic pre-eminence to the Providence area not only threatened the civic autonomy Newport enjoyed as a heritage of the town meeting system. It also indirectly promoted changes in the urban class structure which over the last century reinforced the decentralized and nonpartisan spirit of city government, ultimately derived from the town meeting system. The dislocations of the Revolution, the end of the slave trade, the rise of the port of New York all eliminated Newport's prosperity and most of her resident elite. Absence of a local elite for whom the city might serve as a power base in politics at the state level, coupled with the desire of the summer colonists for "cheap and honest" government, acted against the machine politics of the ethnic minorities to maintain a decentralized and "representative" municipal government. In the early twentieth century, for example, city government consisted of over 200 elected representatives drawn from a total population of under 25,000. Just as the present class composition of the city shows no elite domination of politics, so the contemporary city manager system (which puts urban administration into the hands of an apolitical specialist) continues a former weak-mayor organization and reflects the even earlier decentralization of the town meeting.

The municipal history of Newport is thus a never-ending cycle of charter alterations and changes in the structure of city government— some times promoted by increasing intervention from Providence, at other times generated by local antipathy to external domination. The analogue of the external quest for autonomy is the pursuit of decentralized civic authority within the city. In the absence of controlling power groups within the urban area, electoral alliances with state parties or factions are minimized. Thus, the wish for local autonomy and the desire for internal decentralization intertwine and reinforce each other. Their interdependency defines the adaptive pattern of Newport as a city of nonpartisans with a characteristic view of their political hinterland as "over the bridge."

Charleston achieved municipal incorporation after the American Revolution, although an earlier charter of 1722 was in force for a year before the colonial legislature countermanded it. During almost the entire colonial period, the urban area was directly administered by the colonial legislature working through parish organization and special urban commissions. When the incorporated city did emerge in Charleston, it was a small-scale replica of the state, centralizing the same powers of social control, being staffed by the same class which controlled state government, having the same responsibility for controlling an internal population as the state had for controlling an external one.

The early history of South Carolina government (up to 1808) consisted of attempts by the minority low-country slave-owning planters to politically dominate the majority up-country small-scale farmers who disliked the slavery, aristocratic airs, and grandiose economic consumption of the coast. The colonial and early state government of South Carolina was in large measure only an agency of control over these potential dissidents in the "uncultured" hinterland to the west. Because the urban area of Charleston was the physical location of the colonial capital and because the leaders of the state legislature were also the wealthy "nabobs" who formed the elite of the city, colonial government in South Carolina was the manner in which Charleston "city-state" controlled its political hinterland (cf. Rodgers 1962:144.) Incorporation of the city of Charleston was in the same way an attempt to control another group of dissidents, in this case radical artisans who had grown vocal during the American Revolution and who became increasingly militant (and riotous) as resumption of imports from England and the use of slaves in artisan trades threatened their existence (Walsh 1959). Rather than the result of a desire for municipal autonomy as in Newport, Charleston city was chartered as a special arm of state government, charged at its outset with the maintenance of public safety (which meant, in effect, the suppression of the radical artisans). Even though city and state were organizationally separate, they were, in fact, a single structure in the sense of a continuity of centralized and elitist administration, and in the sense of an interlocking directorate of low country nabobs who controlled both city and state. The latter formed a self-conscious group linked to each other as much by unity clubs, and dance balls, or other pageants as by economic purpose and political power. Some Charlestonians compare themselves at present to the Chinese because "we eat rice and worship our ancestors." Not only a statement of cuisine and religion, this saying lays bare the economic base and elite organization which made Charleston city and South Carolina state for long inseparable in a way which Newport and Rhode Island never were.

The structure of city government replicates the organization of the state, and until very recently, few other governmental bodies intermediated between city and state government. Charleston's municipal organization has been highly centralized, with a de facto strong-mayor system even when this form was not permitted by state statute. City government has been remarkably stable in formal constitution, and characterized by severe fighting between elite factions or personal cliques rather than clashes between contesting political ideologies. The relationship of Charleston to state government has sometimes been friendly and sometimes hostile, but the city has always recognized the outside as an important constraint on its power and as further avenue for political ambition. Before the War Between the States, its links to the external world were predatory and paternalistic, as indicated above in the fact that South Carolina state was an extension of the city, and in that

Charleston provided both political resistance and cultural style to the pre-Civil War South. Even in the last 100 years, when in the aftermath of the Civil War and the populism of the late nineteenth and twentieth centuries, Charleston has ceased to dominate South Carolina, when its power and paternalism have waned, the city has not walled itself off from state politics. Rather, its formal organization seeks to limit the control of the outside by a replication of political forms at the state level. Through a strong machine politics which was often both corrupt and violent, Charleston has been able to guarantee votes to various state-wide candidates, and thus won favors at the same time that it protected local autonomy. Only in the last two decades has a burgeoning county government (see below) intervened and altered Charleston's ability to cope with the outside.

The continuity of state and city in the past and the duplication of state powers in city government has promoted in Charleston a predatory and/or repressive adaptive pattern in respect to its hinterland and to its internal organization. Charleston's urban organization represses the black population of the inner city or, in former days, the slave populace which worked the low country plantations and served in the nabobs' town houses. Their separation and removal from the body politic was symbolized in the past by legal disfranchisement; it continues up to the present in an urban organization of politics and city redistricting to render their almost-majority electoral weight ineffective and to keep them isolated from the political currents of state and city.

Throughout its history, fear of the black majority has conditioned Charleston's urban structure, internal class divisions and relations with a changing external hinterland. Electoral suppression of the upcountry white majority and physical suppression of the slaves mandated the centralization with one or another of these populations. The nabobs of early Charleston had to choose whether it would be blacks used to contain up-country whites or vice versa. After the exportation of the slave system westward in the early 18th century, Charleston compromised and allied with its hinterland, an alliance which weakened the city relative to the state (by geographically and organizationally separating the latter from city domination) and which founded the problems that now beset the urban area.

At the present, this hinterland, now having encircled Charleston in the form of post-war suburban communities inhabited by upcountry whites attracted to local industry, has disowned the city and its pattern and voted to incorporate as an independent city. Today's Charleston has reacted to this most recent threat from its hinterland in a fashion characteristic of its past: by predation and political maneuvering. The city has urged creation of a consolidated government over the whole of Charleston county, which many people see as only a device for the extension of the city's power over land which it desperately needs to counteract inner city black poverty and increasing black voting power, but which is unlike it in population origins and life style. The last Congressional elections witnessed an alliance of the sort which Charleston city has always most feared: one between city blacks and hinterland whites to circumvent the choice of the city's political leadership. Whether the final outcome will be an expanded and consolidated Charleston or the creation of a separate city in the northern suburbs which will economically strangle the old town has not yet been resolved. The methods of battle and the contesting ideologies of city and suburban hinterland reflect three hundred years of Charleston's urban organization and adaptive links with the outside.

Fear of the black majority within and the white majority without have played an important role in internal class organization in Charleston. At several points in its history, the city has been confronted with internal populist and radical activism by whites. The city elite has always feared an alliance of these people either with city blacks or with up-country whites, and consequently has moved to quickly suppress these groups or to make its own alliances up-country to undermine their potential power sources. Time and again, Charleston has reverted to a political two-class condition in which no intermediary groups exist between urban elite and urban slave/black. The radical artisans of the post-Revolutionary period were put down by electoral suppression and economic competition from blacks and also by absorption through intermarriage with the elite. After the Civil War, a new generation of radical artisans appeared, in this case Irish Catholic immigrants who came to "Little Mexico" (so named for its bloody battles rather than ethnic composition) and other urban ethnic enclaves. At first, Charleston met the threat of carpetbaggers and Reconstruction government by attempts at alliance with blacks, but later in response to Hampton's Red Shirt movement at the state level, the urban elite played ethnic politics with the immigrant white population to disfranchise the former slaves. The political power of these immigrants grew, especially after their alliance with upcountry whites, but after the First World War they were suppressed through the use of the Ku Klux Klan. Charleston again became a two-class city, a condition heightened into the present by the gradual enrichment and social acceptance of former immigrants, by the exodus of middle-class whites to the suburbs after World War II, and by the greater fertility and lack of residential mobility of the black population. In the 1960's, Charleston met this problem by incorporating some of the white suburbs, although with much opposition and only limited success. In 1971, an alliance of inner city blacks with white leadership in the suburbs threatens to unseat the ruling clique which has controlled the city since 1959. In conjunction with this internal threat comes the external problem of its unincorporated white hinterland promoting a country government which infringes the city's political ties with the state, and attempting a separate incorporation which would undermine the city's economic base. These contemporary dilemmas repeat situations which the city has often seen before in its long-standing attempts at balancing and controlling internal class organization and external hinterland. It remains to be seen whether Charleston's equally long urban adaptive pattern of absorption, predation, and suppression will be equal to these current tasks.

Utilization of the concept of interactional links between city and society, and analysis of the adaptive urban patterns and urban functional organization resulting from such links has enabled this presentation to discuss two American cities as contrastive city types within a modernized society. Although the author is well aware of the deficiencies and difficulties in the analysis of Charleston and Newport, it at least attempts to set the study of urban places in the context of a larger view of urbanism and a wider perspective on the anthropologist's role in city studies. Yet, such a macroscopic view is not commonly found in contemporary urban anthropology (with the exception of the works cited in part I). The following section indicates the limited perspective on the city current in urban anthropology and consequently, its inability to answer or even ask many significant questions about the nature of urbanism and urban development. The section also tries to explain why urban anthropologists have generally rejected a holistic, adaptive, and cross-cultural view of the settings of cities in their societies.

III. URBANIZATION STUDIES AND THE ANTHROPOLOGY OF CITY STREETS

Not all anthropology done in cities is urban anthropology, at least as it has been defined in part I of this paper and as it has been illustrated in part II. Many studies take the urban environment as a given, a mere location, a site selected for small-scale investigation of what are assumed to be (on the basis of their residence in the city) urbanized tribals or poverty-stricken industrials. This emphasis on urbanization and slum denizens has made of urban anthropology something less than it could be. It has promoted at least four major conceptual limitations: 1. Failure to undertake research which aims to define the city or cities, and in the absence of such an overview, concentration on the city as merely a location for research rather than the conceptual object of research; 2. Implicit assumption of the Western or industrial city as the model of urbanism, and lack of a cross-cultural investigation of urban adaptive patterns; 3. Absence of a holistic view of the city and its cultural and behavioral links with the larger society; and 4. Preservation of a synchronic approach originated in the ethnography of primitive society.

1. The emphasis on the city as a research locale rather than as the object of investigation has given much urban anthropology a limited theoretical perspective. This defect characterizes the two major currents of urban work in anthropology: urbanization research in Africa and slum studies in the United States and Latin America.

According to Epstein, ". . . urbanization refers to a social process involving people in social relationships within a new kind of *physical environment*" (1967:293, italics added). Mitchell similarly believes

> . . . the focus of sociological interest in African urban studies must be on the way in which the behavior of town-dwellers fits into, and is adjusted to, the social matrix created by the commercial, industrial, and administrative framework of a modern metropolis—having regard to the fact that most African town-dwellers have been born and brought up in the rural hinterland of the city in which the cultural background is markedly dissimilar from that in the city itself (1966:38).

This focus on urbanization may clarify how individuals adapt to new social environments, including urban ones, but it has only obscured anthropological investigation of the city and urban life. In the African material, the city is rarely described as such (beyond introductory demographic data and a smattering of chronological history); it only enters the study parenthetically as the unanalyzed "something" which requires acculturative behavior patterns from recent migrants or as an unexplained "ether" through which situational structures and personal networks channel.

Epstein, for example, describes the political urbanization of former tribals in a Copperbelt mining town without ever indicating why he regards the community as urban or what attributes distinguish it from what he refers to as the "rural" area. He makes occasional reference to an "urban" or "industrial milieu" (1958:236) as if all urban places were industrial or all industrial centers were urban. The appeal is to the reader's intuition. In any case, the author need not be more specific since the "urban" designation is only a convenient peg upon which to hang an analysis which deals neither with the city nor urban man, but only native locations filled with dislocated men.

Mitchell builds this nonconception of the urban into an analytic virtue. He believes that treatment of African towns as single social systems has no heuristic value. He also negatively evaluates comparative studies of African urban types, and treats investigations of processive or historical change as "of limited interest" to African urban sociology.[4] Instead, Mitchell suggests, urban studies must concentrate on social relationships and personal networks as conditioned within any particular urban location (or "framework") by external determinants. The latter (called "external imperatives" by Mitchell and "extrinsic factors" by Southall) include density of settlement, mobility, heterogeneity, demographic disproportion, economic differentation, and administrative and political limitations. These external imperatives form as much of a view of urbanism as Mitchell and his colleagues ever propound. Yet, characteristically, Mitchell (1966:48–51) believes this external backdrop needs no analysis by the anthropologist. It is a structural given upon which the ethnographer builds up his network and situational analysis.

Plotnicov continues this limited use of the city. The object of his study "is to describe and analyze the adjustments individuals make to modern conditions of urban development . . ." (1967:3). He utilizes the technique of "situational analysis" as developed by Gluckman, Mitchell, and Epstein. This methodology delimits

> . . . the urban field of inquiry—the totality of which can appear as an incomprehensible jumble of contrasts and contradictions—in order to concentrate on, and thereby to abstract, the normative patterns of behavior that associate with role and group identification (1967:10).

In this form of situational analysis or in the "network" approach favored by other British urban anthropologists (cf. the articles in Mitchell 1969b) the city appears neither as an object nor a goal of research (cf. Leeds 1968a:31). Can we put all normative patterns of role and group identity together, can we trace out the many-stranded networks which link urban individuals and see the reflection of city and society? That Plotnicov could not accomplish this will become clear below.

The pitfalls in the urbanization approach are especially transparent when its advocates leave their native locations and discuss cities in general. In a review of African town studies, Epstein recognizes that a

[4] Mitchell (1966:38ff.) distinguishes between "situational" or adaptive change by individuals or groups newly come to the urban area and "processive" or evolutionary change of the urban area and its population in response to such phenomena as modernization.

valuable urban anthropology must address other questions besides urbanization, among them, the integration of town and country and the role of urban institutions in national integration. Yet his subsequent discussion mainly concerns the effects of town *residence* on the countryside. Epstein describes the physical or demographic interaction of town and rural areas as if they stood apart from a national political order (1967:282–283). Concentration on urbanization means the scholar sees the city in its physical aspect as a receptacle of population, and leads him to overlook its position in an urban hierarchy or a chain of political power leading from rural community to state. As Bruner indicates, "Epstein's major weakness is that he . . . sees urbanization processes almost entirely as a function of factors intrinsic to the city itself" (Bruner 1967:297).

Excessive emphasis on urbanization in African studies often leads to narrow visions of the city. Sometimes the city disappears altogether from the anthropologist's enterprise—in this case, purposely defined away as a construct of limited significance. Southall differentiates type A towns which are "old, established, slowly growing" from those of type B containing "new populations of mushroom growth" (1961:6). Cities are thus distinguished solely by different sorts of acculturative space and differential quantities of migrants. Cohen values urban locales only as anthropological supermarkets that bring together divergent groups and social processes which in tribal society are too dispersed for easy study. Urban research is not significant, according to Cohen, for what it may say about urbanism or urbanization, since he does not believe special principles govern urban life. He concludes that much urban social anthropology is nothing more than human ecology, and that when an urban study is indeed sociological, it is "no longer necessarily urban" (1969:214).

Urban anthropology in the New World has often evolved little from its African genesis. Some American research duplicates the limited perspective of African urbanization studies. Mangin, Leeds, and others have described the accommodation of rural peasant to urban "tin can" cities. Such shanty towns are often viewed as communities with an internal cohesion which justifies their study as isolates within the city (cf. Leeds 1968a:31ff.). None of these studies attempts to define the city as an outgrowth of shanty town research, or primarily focuses on the involvement of tin can settlements in the larger urban sphere. Other studies go beyond the assumption of community in shanty town, and reify cultures or subcultures of poverty or homeless and migratory urban alcoholics. Spradley writes of the latter "urban nomads," "The distance between most Americans and urban nomads cannot be measured in miles; they are separated from us by cultural distance" (1970:6). Oscar Lewis has identified another urban "culture of poverty," comprehension of which is hindered by analyzing the city as a totality. In a critical summary of the work of Louis Wirth and the folk-urban concept, Lewis writes,

> The city is not the proper unit of comparison or discussion for the study of social life because the variables of number, density, and heterogeneity as used by Wirth are not the crucial determinants of social life or personality. There are many intervening variables. Social life is not a mass phenomenon. It occurs for the most part in small groups, within the family, within households, within neighborhoods, within the church, formal and informal groups, and so on. Any generalizations about the nature of social life in the city must be based on careful studies of these smaller universes rather than on a priori statements about the city as a whole (1967:497).

Lewis provides an outline of the priorities in urban research which accentuates such small-scale study of communities within the city and the collection of data on urban personality (1967:502–503). Yet, if the anthropology of tribal societies had concentrated only on family and household, on neighborhood and church, would the concept of cultures and societies as organized systems of social life have arisen? Have Lewis' descriptions of family life in Mexico, Puerto Rico, and the United States clarified the nature of the city or even elucidated his own concept of the culture of poverty? (cf. Valentine 1968:48–77.) Lewis' concentration on individual psychology and on family life is an attractive step for the anthropologist confronted with the complexities of urban society. But it is a great retreat from the traditional holistic approach of anthropology to society and culture (cf. Beals and Hoijer 1971:647–648). Lewis absolves the anthropologist of any concern with analysis of the city; he replaces Wirth's urbanism as a way of life with the altogether different concentration on the urban way of individual lives.

Even Valentine, who convincingly argues against the assumption of distinctive poverty cultures within the city, who questions whether it is "not equally important to understand how the affluent and the powerful threaten the poor," nevertheless suggests "neighborhoods and districts of the poor in our cities" as the locale for ethnographic fieldwork (1968: 90, 175). Although Valentine recognizes that the "units of study and boundaries of inquiry" should be determined by research, he seems to view their discernment as an empirical matter rather than as the result of a theoretical orientation towards the study of urban places. Mitchell (1966:60) also sees the tactics of urban research as initially an exploration of networks and fields of activity, and only afterward an "attempt to see their connection at a higher level of abstraction." This "cargo cult" view of theory-building suggests that accumulating enough powerful facts inevitably brings the anthropologist to high-level abstraction. Such beliefs rationalize the present limited horizon of urban anthropology more effectively than they hold out a future promise of theoretical rewards. Without an approach based on a conception of the city or cities, will the observer ever generate it from slum localities, impoverished families or formerly tribal peoples?

In one way the city is always visible, even to the anthropologist deep down in the ghetto. In their most material form, modern cities are always locations of concrete and glass, they comprise streets on which men live or try to live. Only in this ecological sense does the city appear in the work of many American urban anthropologists—as a *zone* of misery and penury, as an *area* "across the tracks," as a harsh *environment* which demands, as do the African towns, accommodation. In America, the equivalent of the African tribal (that is, of the stranger to the city) is fabricated from outcaste populations, culturally foreign to mainstream American life. Spradley writes, "The problems and vicissitudes of urban nomads differ from those encountered by other categories of urban dwellers and [the nomad learns] varied strategies for satisfying biological needs, achieving his goals, and adjusting to his environment" (1970:98).

To see city and society, is it not more important to know what in American (urban) culture produces urban nomads, rather than describing their conception of and coping behavior in a hostile environment? How might American, Hindu, or perhaps pan-urban notions of alcohol consumption alter or determine the circumstances of urban nomads. Although Spradley provides some very interesting data on how American courts promote the mobility of urban nomads, on how they are economically exploited as trustees in prisons, his primary concern is with delimiting the nomad's "culture" rather than analyzing that of the larger society.

For Spradley, Lewis, Mangin, and many of the African social anthropologists, the urban area is only a locale for research on men. In the case of urban nomads, this environment is summed up in the term, Skid Road. The city as a sociological or cultural institution remains unstated. Its cultural identity or qualities do not appear clearly or in central focus. We learn of city streets and city men but not about urban society or urban man.

2. The Western city is the often assumed but rarely analyzed version of urbanism which appears in the literature of urban anthropology. This

view of the city clearly lies behind Epstein's conjunction of "urban" and "industrial" cited earlier. Mitchell recognizes urbanism outside the Western model but finds the great majority of African towns to be colonial in origin. He regards traditional Yoruba urbanism as not really constituting city forms and cites the difficulty of distinguishing what was truly urban structure from what was determined by Yoruba culture. Mitchell is, therefore, content to make the colonially derived African town the single avenue for sociological research, acceptance of which neatly avoids the definitional problems inherent in a cross-cultural approach to urbanism (1966:38–50 passim). In urbanization studies, then, rural and (industrial) urban are treated as synchronic evolutionary levels similar to those found in a former (diachronic) evolutionary anthropology. The task of the anthropologist is to chart the passage from tribal rung to city level. That the sequence from rural or tribal to urban always requires family breakdown or secularization has been contested; that these distinctive types or stages are universally meaningful constructs is generally assumed. Following Gluckman, Mitchell argues that "an urban social institution is not a changed rural institution: it is a separate social phenomenon existing as part of a separate social system . . ." (1966:48; also see P. Gutkind 1969:217).

Other scholars have contested this view of rural and urban as separate social systems, at least in some areas of the world (cf. Pocock 1960:63–81, and Lynch 1967:142–158). Resolution of this problem requires a cross-cultural view of city and society much wider than the Western model implied by American urban studies. In the African case and to a smaller degree in Latin America, the assumption of a single (industrial) urban type to which migrants must accommodate is reinforced by the historical nature of the assimilation pattern. Lacking a well-developed indigenous urbanism, such societies inherit a European and industrial or capitalist form of the city as a heritage of conquest. The familiarity of such city types to the Western or capitalist anthropologist perhaps explains why he fails to analyze what he means by "urban." In this sense, even those studies fail which only wish to talk about small group social life in the city, unless they see the urban research location as purely a sociological accident (cf. Marris 1962 and Rubel 1966). Yet, most such studies at least in their titles proclaim an involvement with *urban* studies. Perhaps that is not their message, and what the author really means by politics or family or burial societies "in Urban Africa" is really merely a geographical designation, a more specific version of the "Todas of the Nilgiris" or "The Trobrianders of Melanesia." Yet some urban social anthropologists wish to be more than just geographically precise. Epstein (1969:117) notes an increasing tendency to see all urban areas as sharing common characteristics, but he does not say of what this similarity consists or how studies of urbanizing Africans pertain to this assertion of universality. Similar preconceptions of the city (or more precisely, a willingness to accept it as given) exist in American urban anthropology. Spradley hopes that increasing tolerance will root out "the separateness which now permeates *our* cities" (1970:262, italics added). What is the reference of "our" cities: American cities, industrial cities, all cities? In a geographical sense, the statement clearly refers to American cities, but in an anthropological sense, the domain of its applicability remains unspecified. Until the anthropology of the city is added to the anthropology of urban streets and migrant men, such statements will only communicate the sentiments and implicit beliefs of the urbanist, but not his knowledge.

3. The populations which urban anthropologists study often impede a recognition of the links between city and society or a holistic approach to urban organization and form. To see the city through recently detribalized peoples or newly arrived peasants is extremely difficult. Urban nomads and ghetto men also participate minimally in the city. (This may also be a reflection of the community study methods—cf. Valentine and Valentine 1970). Residentially, economically, and politically, they are often strangers to the city. Even were it true that traditional ethnographic techniques require study of small-scale urban localities or communities, what explains the lack of research on middle-class Americans or European elites in Africa? In his analysis of such influential or powerful social categories, the anthropologist could not so readily ignore the city and larger society. By choosing urbanization and ghetto men instead, anthropologists only confirm their inadequacies in the description of urban life. They thus practice a strange empiricism in which the research universe is defined by the observer's sensibilities (more on this below).

Although he recognizes the restricted scope of an urban community study, Epstein takes the "embracing politico-economic system and its events" as given. He writes ". . . the community, as conceived here, is not a microcosm, but a field of social relations the limits of which have been arbitrarily set for convenience of study" (1958:xiii–xiv). That convenience of study may be at the price of conceptual vigor is illustrated by Plotnicov's work which also arbitrarily demarcates a field of social relations in the city. From his intensive analysis of eight individuals in Jos, Nigeria, Plotnicov concludes that urban life is not disorganized: ". . . the people of Jos make up a stable urban population and the community itself continues to develop its own vitality" (1967:60). Plotnicov's approach may indicate that selected urban lives show little disorganization, in this case lives selected for high status. It cannot, however, say much about urban life which is a generalization of a rather different order. Yet Plotnicov offers more than psychological generalizations. He concludes "[the city's] institutions are viable and durable and integrate the various ethnic components" (1967:290). In an earlier footnote, the author indicates that this statement, based on fieldwork in the early 1960's, is no longer valid because of the clashes between Ibo and Hausa in Nigeria during the mid-1960's. Situational analysis based on urban lives or urban networks does not allow even short-term prediction of urban events which are a reflex of national happenings. More reliable judgments of urban viability can only be achieved by noting the relationship of tribal region to central polity and the intermediary role of the city in the larger society.[5]

4. A slice of the present is perhaps an inevitable modus operandi in societies without pasts. The anthropologist duplicates the ahistory of the primitive world by a careful selection of urban populations without pasts. But he pays dearly for this gratuitous continuity of approach. Urban anthropology cannot engage cross-cultural comparison of city development or cultural patterns of urban migration. It cannot address the problems of ethnocentric approaches to city research as raised by Sjoberg (1960), or even legitimately criticize the concept of the preindustrial city which Sjoberg proposes as a cure. (For an historian's criticism, see Thrupp 1961:60–63).[6] The anthropology of contemporary urban communities says little to those archaeologists who adopt holistic views of the city and urban development in the past (Adams 1960:153–172 passim, and the historian, Lampard 1967:519ff.), and even less to historians interested in the cross-cultural validity of Weber's distinction (1927:318) between oriental and occidental patterns of urbanism.

In what is for many urban anthropologists the most important aspect of their work (in the analysis of contemporary urban problems and in prediction and prescription for their future course), the urban anthropologist often seems as impoverished as the peoples he studies. A diachronic viewpoint coupled with a holistic approach to city and society might more analyze the malaise of American cities and the nature of an urban society which is "multicultural" and in crisis. But how do we explain the emergence of this presumed multicultural American city instead of the expected or hoped-for melting pot urbanism? And

[5] Plotnicov argues that his analysis will again hold true when national political stability returns. But if this factor is so determinative, why exclude it from the initial formulation and prediction?

[6] An exception is Arensberg's (1968) criticism of Sjoberg and Wittfogel, and his contrast between traditional "stone" and "green" cities.

what do we, as theoreticians of the city, offer as cure, beyond the palliatives of social welfare or a respect for the urban outsider which leaves him still outcaste? These fundamental problems of society and culture the urban anthropologist must evidently leave to a historian like Warner, who adopts a holistic and diachronic view of the city. In his study of Philadelphia over three centuries, Warner (1968:x) describes an American (urban) cultural tradition of "privatism" which fixes the nature of urban polity and through its limitations creates the urban crisis which Spradley, Lewis, and Valentine see in the city's poor. Whether or not Warner's analysis proves viable, it is significant as a statement of what can be done in urban research and as a reflection of what has not yet been done in urban anthropology.

Why have city streets and urban men formed the main concentration of urban anthropology? Traditional ethnographic methodology and an antiurban bias have been suggested as contributing factors (Gulick 1968:93–95). The selection and training of the anthropologist is perhaps another determinant. Gulick believes that ". . . anthropology . . . tends to attract individuals who by temperament are inspired to live among and study people about whom no one else cares" (1963:560–561). In urban areas, the poverty-stricken, often ethnically distinct slum dweller is the equivalent of the primitive about whom none care. Training in anthropology fosters a highly individual scholarly experience, and anthropologists, also individualized and isolated by their research style, perhaps overemphasize similar qualities in peasant and urban societies.

Still another factor—or perhaps a summation of all previous ones—is the anthropological quest for the romantic and foreign. Although most introductory texts proclaim an anthropology larger than the primitive world, students quickly learn that anthropologists are specialists in the arcane, the outer, and the exotic. Very early in the development of anthropology, the Seligmanns viewed with the disdain proper to ethnographers seeking the "true" culture those Veddas who donned loin cloth and hefted spears in a British-inspired image of the primitive. Such "professional primitives" garnered tips from the less sophisticated British colonial officers who only wanted photographs of the exotic, rather than a scholarly description of it (Fox 1969a:13–27). Like the Seligmanns, other anthropologists figuratively turn off the radios and phonographs which bring new waves to peasant villages and tribal settlements. Their eyes close to the cinema which etches on celluloid a different culture from the acceptably exotic sort carved on monuments or shaped into temple deities.[7] Such problems attending the pursuit of

[7] Tiger (1967) is one of the few anthropologists doing research in cities to discuss the role of the mass media.

the romantic have always hampered anthropology, but even in their most modern guise, as Whitten and Szwed (1970:17) recognize in their preface to *Afro-American Anthropology*, "Anthropologists are people who specialize in the study of the culturally exotic."

Pursuit of the romantic in anthropology is no discredit, for it has given the field a breadth and involvement with humanity which other disciplines rarely achieve. Only when the exotic is narrowly defined, as it must to be rediscovered in modern urban environments, only when the romantic grows beyond a frame of mind and materializes into city streets and urbanizing men does the problem of limited perspective arise. Gutkind notes how hesitantly African enthnographers turned to urban places. Most cities were of recent origin and populated by non-Africans, and ". . . anthropologists were not particularly interested in studying Europeans or Asians" (1969:216). A similar distaste for the unromantic and familiar explains the lack of middle class or elite studies in urban America. But pursuit of the exotic in urban anthropology has produced greater disabilities than mere avoidance of mainstream economic and ethnic categories. Ethnographers of the tribal world studied the romantic customs of family, religion, or war as reflections of the variety of human cultural experience. Only incidentally to this purpose and in recognition of world political realities did they investigate uncared for peoples in out of the way places. Yet contemporary urban anthropology gives its whole attention to fulfilling only the latter geographical or physical criterion of the exotic in its selection of what and whom to study in the urban sphere. By embracing the exotica of poverty populations, slum environments, and native locations, much urban anthropology falls into an inappropriate ahistoricism, accepts the absence of a holistic viewpoint, denies the city as the goal of research—and thus factors out what cities can say about the nature of man and his societies. A cross-cultural reflection of the varieties of urban experience, an analysis of urban familial, religious, or political institutions as aspects of the larger society, in sum, a theoretical as apart from a locational interest in the exotic remains undefined in urban anthropology.

If such is to be the approach in urban anthropology, the field has been misnamed. It would more properly earn the title of "street" anthropology from its involvement with social life found on cement sidewalks, at the bottom of high-rise buildings, or in housing clusters at the periphery of the urban core. Unfortunately, this field's comparability would be narrowly defined, for other anthropologists have yet to institute an equivalent "mountain," "rice-paddy," or "ice-float" anthropology.

Is the only defense of this urban anthropology to be that we study those for whom no other scholarly fraternity cares? Is an impoverished urban anthropology behind the "culture of poverty?" This paper has attempted to define urban anthropology as something more than the leftovers of other disciplines. It suggests a holistic approach to city and society and an investigation of patterns of adaptation by cities—thus a view of their changing ideological and behavioral linkage to the societies in which they occur. The foregoing discussion of how two American cities have evolved from distinctive urban origins, how they have adapted to external social environments, how they have organized internal class organization is hardly more than a sketch of various historical and contemporary urban patterns possible within an industrial sociocultural environment. Yet, it hopefully illustrates the wider viewpoint which urban anthropology can encompass when it adopts the interactional or ideological links between city and society as a central focus.

Many questions of the city and urban society are not resolved in the current literature of urban anthropology; many have not yet been asked. Until urban anthropologists adopt a larger view of their work, many questions will not even be recognized, and the research of other disciplines which might help both ask and answer anthropology's questions will remain unused. Such is the case for Warner's historical study of Philadelphia and the American urban ethos of privatism, previously mentioned. An urban anthropology interested in the ideological fit of city and society would benefit greatly from the work of city planners and architects, such as E. A. Gutkind's monumental *International History of City Development* (1964). An interactional urban anthropology could follow many leads in the sociology of Vidich and Bensman's *Small Town in Mass Society* (1968), or in English's (1966) geographical analysis of Kirman and its hinterland, or in the historical sociology of Muslim cities as undertaken by Lapidus (1967). Urban anthropology may justifiably plead backwardness because of the present paucity of comparative material or juniority as a field. It is quite another matter if it defaults due to conceptual poverty and thus pursuit of limited research goals.

4

Reno, Nevada: The City as a Unit of Study[1]

John A. Price

INTRODUCTION

This is a discussion of problems and perspectives involved in attempting a holistic study of a city. A team ethnography of Reno, Nevada, is described to illustrate the advantages of team work, some of the weaknesses of the project, and the need to do research on regional and national cultures to understand the cultural dynamics of cities.

We need to be able "to look at cities as wholes, to see them as objects of study in themselves . . . for crosscultural perspective on city located cultural data and problems" (Arensberg 1968:3). Gulick (1968:96) discussed the "macrocosmic" research strategy of "an institutional inventory of the city, including mapping, relevant historical materials, relationships of the city and its institutions to the larger society, and elements of ethos which seem to be outstanding." He pointed out that this is "essential raw material for comparative analysis in urban anthropology," but that many social scientists "see little value in such 'descriptive' material and disparage publications which feature it." In fact, his book on Tripoli (Gulick 1967) is a rare product in these days when so few have the audacity to try to describe a whole city.

Few anthropologists have ever focused on the city itself as a unit of study, usually working instead on an urban neighborhood or ethnic group

SOURCE: *Urban Anthropology* 1, no. 1 (1972): 14–28. Reprinted by permission.

[1] This paper is primarily based on data collected in a National Science Foundation sponsored course in ethnographic field methods. Dr. Warren L. d'Azevedo was the Program Director, I was the Field Director, and Dr. Ronald Provencher was the Associate Field Director. A 132 page manuscript report, "Twelve Doors to Reno," and a computer analysis of questionnaire returns are in the archives of the Department of Anthropology, University of Nevada, Reno, Nevada.

or a process such as migration to the city. A generation ago there were several community studies of American cities, such as Yankee City, Middletown, and Deep South, but this was never carried out in other cultural areas. West Africa has been a focus for a great amount of work in urban anthropology since around 1954 and yet that work has virtually ignored the city as a unit of holistic ethnography (Simms 1965). In looking for general descriptions on any particular city in the world the best material one can find is usually a booklet distributed by the local chamber of commerce, although there may be an abundance of dissertations on tiny cultural niches within the city. *Peasants in Cities* edited by Mangin (1970) touches the predominant themes of current urban anthropology: rural-urban networks and migrations, the establishment of slums within cities by rural people, and the continuing importance of kinship and other features of traditional culture.

Urban anthropologists tend to retain a "rural ethos," preferring rural or traditional cultures and seeing the city as a destroyer of these cultures rather than a creator of new cultures. Like many other North American ethnographers at the time, I began by studying American Indians on reservations and then several years later followed their migrations to the cities (Price 1968, 1971). My units of study were ethnic groups, not the city itself. With this frame of reference it was easy for me to be critical of the city as an environment for the future development of Indian cultures. Still, the city does, of course, have many positive features, evidenced in the simple fact that over two hundred thousand Indians elected to migrate to cities in the United States and Canada in the past few decades. The holistic study of cities and their functional roles for their inhabitants and for a wider region should promote a more sympathetic understanding of urban cultures.

The city is to some degree a natural unit to work with. It usually has a geographical unity as a multifunctional center with a high population density. It usually has strong governmental unity, although suburban and exurban growth can complicate its governmental organization. Ideologically, cities have a unity as well, in that they have stereotyped reputations that influence people's behavior toward them: pride in living there or not, pretty or ugly, safe or dangerous, and so forth.

A city, however, is conceived as a difficult thing to study. It is internally extremely complex and it is linked by external networks to a surrounding rural region and to other urban centered regions. We sometimes forget that primitive and peasant villages are also difficult to study. Perhaps in the village at least the ethnographer could have the confidence and satisfaction that comes from personally knowing a large proportion of the people of the village. It may be that it is as much our traditional methods and dispositions as the complexity of the subject matter that has led ethnographers usually to limit themselves to small scale, individual projects where they can have a personally satisfying intimate knowledge of a community. Whatever the reasons, there are several hundred holistic ethnographic studies of primitive communities, peasant villages, and small towns, but very few of cities.

Miner (1965:xvii) selected Timbuctoo for a study in part because it was small, with a population of only 6,000. "It has been found in studies of populous American cities that large staffs, working over long periods, were required. With the research facilities at my disposal, it was apparent that a man and wife could not learn much about a very large city, in less than a year and in a completely foreign tongue." Although he characterized it as an extremely heterogenous primitive city, he admitted that in terms of size it might be called a town.

THE IDEAL OF HOLISM

A traditional ideal of ethnographic methods was that through the intimate participation and study of a small nonliterate community over a long period of time a single ethnographer could acquire a fairly reliable and valid understanding of the community's cultural dynamics. That rather broad and multicausal understanding was considered a more accurate description of the way a culture worked than the understandings of other social scientists, who were seen as specialists working on small parts of more complex societies. Traditional ethnographers of course did specialize somewhat in terms of their own particular interests. And they often glossed over matters which later study demonstrated to be of crucial importance. However, that search for holism was a productive ideal behind ethnography because it sought the multicausal dynamics of cultural systems.

Turning to work in cities ethnographers have tended to persist in working with relatively small units. In fact the major interest of urban anthropology so far has not been urban life per se but how the groups like those that anthropologists studied in primitive and peasant settings are getting along in the cities. Racial groups, ethnic groups, outcaste groups, and poverty groups, the downtrodden of the earth seem to be followed around by anthropologists. We have much more description of poverty culture than middle class or upper class culture. We have little in terms of integrated understandings about the contexts of urban life that all classes live in.

The careful, small scale work on neighborhoods or ethnic groups is important. And large scale ethnography is difficult. Still, there are good reasons why some anthropologists should conduct research designed to achieve holistic understandings of large cultural units: cities, regions, and even nations. Rather than simply following the limits of traditional ethnographic methods, anthropologists need some of the audacity of the traditional discipline. We occasionally need to ask broad questions, such as "What are the crucial cultural dynamics of this city?" Then we need to work out the best methodology to answer those questions. It is in this spirit of a search for holistic understanding that we studied Reno, Nevada.

THE RENO STUDY

Reno was selected for an attempt at a holistic study of a city because it is large enough to be a challenge ·(80,000 "city," 125,000 "metropolitan" population) and the sponsoring institution is located there, so that administration would be easier. Ronald Provencher and I directed twelve graduate students in the ten week program in the summer of 1969. One advantage of team over individual ethnography was soon apparent in that the students by their differing personalities and expertise were able to do a wider variety of things than any individual ever would.

Three students handled projects of an integrating, overview character: a general questionnaire, cultural geography, and history. Three worked on cross-cutting topics about the majority society: women, religion, and mobile home courts. Three others had projects that came out of special questions about Nevada society: gambling, patterns of social deviance, and the social relations of the residents in Virginia City, a satellite tourist town. Finally, three students studied ethnic subcultures: Negroes, Indians, and Basques.

The study was different from usual ethnography in several ways. We maintained a central list of key informants, a library on local materials, and a file on newspaper clippings. Since each student's project was different, each was able to give the others unique insights into Reno as a whole. There was systematic sharing of data throughout the study through regular discussion sessions.

We prepared and sent out two thousand mail-in questionnaires. This was composed of questions submitted by the students, edited, and pretested. The students were also brought in on the statistical analysis of the survey material so that each could test his own hypotheses. Although only 19.3 percent of the questionnaires were returned in the mail, we were fairly satisfied with the representativeness of the return because several checks indicated its validity. The results were similar on comparable items (income, family size, ethnic composition, etc.) to the United States Census and other surveys. Also, we received back approximately the same proportions we sent out by area, although the areas differ greatly in average income, average education, ethnic composition, and other features. For example, 18.5 percent of all the questionnaires were mailed to people living in Sparks and 19.8 percent of those we received back were filled out by people living in Sparks. Sparks is an area with a lower average household income, a lower average education, a shorter period of occupancy, and other differences, yet its return rate was apparently not significantly affected by these differences.

One of the things that we learned was that the team as a whole could work to eliminate inaccurate biases and hypotheses much more rapidly than individuals working alone. In the team situation each member's methods, data, and hypotheses were under a relatively continuing critical appraisal by his fellow team members. This accelerated the exchange of data and the modification of inaccurate hypotheses while the data were still being gathered. Thus in only ten weeks the team was able to demonstrate many original insights into the cultural dynamics of the city.

The major weaknesses of the project were insufficient time, the limitations of working with just anthropology graduate students when a broader variety of academic backgrounds would have been more useful, and some mistakes in the research design. As for time, a professional team should be able to do an adequate ethnography of a city the size of Reno in about a year and a half to two years, approximately the same time that it takes an individual ethnographer to adequately study a primitive community. The anthropology students were not well prepared to work in geography or history and none would even attempt projects in such crucial areas as government administration, the economy of the city, the legal system, or the education system. It would be much better to start with an interdisciplinary research team.

One major mistake in our research design was that we went along with the traditions of anthropology and had three students working on ethnic minority groups, although we knew that ethnicity played only a small role in Reno culture. The three ethnic studies were concerned with very small populations to begin with, since only about 2 percent of the metropolitan population were Negroes, 1.5 percent were American Indians, and there was a similar proportion of Basques. Then these projects were allowed to focus down very narrowly on the spectacular institutions of Negro prostitution, American Indian politics, and Basque hotels. In their own right the studies were excellent, but the insights they added to a general knowledge of Reno were about only tiny cultural niches of the city. It would take hundreds of such narrow studies to cover all the significant sub-cultures of the city and even then an understanding of general integrative dynamics could still be missing.

Another weakness was that we did not spend enough time studying the broader contexts of Reno, such as its place in the economics and politics of the state and region. With a longer field session this may have been done since many questions about city-state relations emerged in the field. However, in trying to synthesize a description of the city, I have relied on three broad hypotheses that were largely untested in the field.

The first hypothesis is that Reno's special character can best be explained in terms of its geographical and historical adaptations in a symbiotic cultural network. It is an important link in an interdependent relationship between Nevada and California. The second hypothesis is that Reno is involved in a revitalization of elements from Western cowboy culture as a modern solution to such typical urban problems as the search for a satisfying personal identity, life style, and social relations. A third related hypothesis is that this "New Western" revitalization involves a politically conservative form of a philosophy of personal freedom.

NEVADA'S SYMBIOSIS

Nevada is a resource-poor area with vast reaches of almost useless arid land. Over 85 percent of Nevada belongs to the federal government, for such purposes as atomic and military testing ranges. Nevada has had a small population, currently just over half a million, although it had the highest increase rate (53 percent) of any state in the United States in the 1960's. And Nevada is next to the very populous state of California, which is currently over twenty million in population or forty times the number for Nevada. These resource-poor, large space, low population, and convenient location factors have pressured Nevada into earning a living by supplying what are usually illegal services: gambling, quick divorce, quick marriage, risque shows, and prostitution. Nevada is culturally symbiotic with the other western states and with America generally, so much so that Nevada could not feed its own population on its agricultural production. Nevada annually produces only about $100 million worth of crops and livestock and $100 million worth of minerals, but it earns over $400 million in gambling and about an equal amount in other tourist services.

While some modern semi-legal services have apparently been rejected, such as easy abortions, pornographic movies and literature, and selling drugs, Nevada has recently developed such new services as tax shelters from personal state income tax, inheritance tax, and inventory taxes on goods in interstate transit. Industry now enjoys the advantage of Nevada's Freeport Law which permits tax-free storage of goods destined for out-of-state markets. Thus goods can be placed in tax-free warehouses in Reno and quickly shipped when needed into the markets of California, Oregon, and Washington.

A new kind of conservative philosophy is apparently being developed in Nevada based on traditional concepts of individual freedom that will rationalize Nevada's way of life and attract some people to Nevada. Rather than pushing on in the development of what appears to be the mainstream of American urban evolution, Nevada is again exploring a specialization, as it did when it found a market for gambling and divorcing. That specialization is the revitalization of Western American culture and selling it to tourists and to a wave of modern pioneers from metropolitan centers who move to the country.

Las Vegas seems to be more a part of the main evolutionary trends than Reno. Las Vegas is politically more liberal, is more closely tied with Southern California, and it has had a rapid growth from shallow historical roots. The only way in which Reno seems to be more liberal is that Reno changed to women dealers in "21" while Las Vegas continues with male dealers. Reno, on the other hand, is closely tied with northern California and has been a provisioning and entertainment stop along the east-west continental route between Salt Lake City and San Francisco since 1868.

RENO

Reno is located at the base of the Sierra Nevada Mountains and at the western edge of the Nevada desert at 4,500 feet above sea level. It lies in the basin of the Truckee River which flows from Lake Tahoe, a mountain resort area, to Pyramid Lake, in an Indian reservation. The city was founded in 1868 during the building of the Central Pacific Railroad on the site of a toll bridge and named in honor of a Civil War hero, General Jesse Reno. Sparks, just east of Reno, was laid out by the Central Pacific as a division point for the railroad and was named for the Nevada governor, John Sparks. Railroading through Reno-Sparks is almost all concerned with freight now and there is a social movement on to have the tracks moved entirely out of the downtown area.

Reno looks unique in some ways. The small enclaved casino section is unique in appearance with its massive advertising displays of colored lights. There are a large number of motels and hotels in the city, with some 75 of them within a mile of the casino section. And there are commercial wedding chapels on the highways into the city. Other than these things, Reno looks like several other medium-sized cities in the Great Basin, such as Idaho Falls, Idaho, or Provo, Utah.

Reno has a lot of beautiful older houses, tree lined streets, well kept lawns, and parks along the Truckee River; a new library, convention center, coliseum, atmospherium, and historical museum; and a university. Like so many other cities, it has new outlying suburbs, new shopping centers, and an old highway through the city with motels, gas stations, restaurants, and used car lots. Reno is the commercial, educational, and entertainment center for all of western Nevada. Even Carson City, the state capital, is essentially a satellite of Reno, just as Reno can be seen as a satellite of San Francisco. Towns and cities in eastern Nevada, such as Elko, are more influenced by Salt Lake City while southern Nevada is dominated by Las Vegas.

The southwest quadrant of Reno is growing with middle and upper income people, some who are building "mini-ranches" with a house and a few horses on an acre of land. The large number of wealthy residents in Reno has shifted the averages very high so Reno had the sixth highest annual per capita income in the United States in 1969 ($4,207) according to the United States Department of Commerce. At the other end of the economic scale, a small community of Negroes and the Indian Colony are in particular areas among the predominantly lower and middle class Whites of northeast Reno and adjoining Sparks. The northwest quadrant is middle class, mostly in new suburbs, while the southeast has middle and lower class residences mixed with industries.

The Indian Colony is a 29 acre tract of land in an industrial and warehousing district on the edge of Reno with 537 residents, according to a recent survey. The survey also indicated a high unemployment rate (17.6 percent) and a low median family income for 1967 ($3,250, for the total family rather than per capita given earlier). Local tourist promotions often use the local Washo, Paiute, and Shoshone Indians in parades, at the rodeo, and county fair with Indian dances, craft displays, and athletic contests.

Mobile homes have become an important alternative for housing in Reno, more because they are inexpensive than because of their mobility. This general line of housing evolved "trailers," then "coaches," then "mobile homes," and now prefabricated "modular houses" that have been progressively less movable. Trailer courts have many problems such as zoning, being placed along noisy highways, high internal densities, and complicated rules to restrict intrusion by children, pets, and noise. However, they are useful to an area undergoing boom conditions of growth like Reno.

GAMBLING, PROSTITUTION, AND DIVORCE

Traditions of the American West are part of the advertising of the Reno casinos, from pioneer themes in visual ads to cowboy dress uniforms for the casino staff. However, the largest task of the casinos has been to promote gambling as respectable fun for the general American public. The rules and terms used in the games are explained in brochures and by the casino staffs. They also promote the casino and avoid problems with the rules of interstate commerce by advertising the restaurants, hotel accommodations, and shows, rather than the gambling. There are no advertisements that say "Come and gamble in Reno." Then, when the tourist arrives, gambling facilities dominate the ground floor areas while the restaurants are out in the back corners or up on the second floor. Gamblers are offered free drinks and cigarettes. The casino setting is designed to be bright, colorful, and informal. The new casinos have wide open fronts with just a "curtain" of air between the strolling patrons on the sidewalks and the gambling action on the inside. The heritage of contemporary gambling in Nevada comes from card games played by miners. The nineteenth century towns of Nevada typically had card playing in the bars. As part of a nationwide reform movement, gambling was outlawed or restricted at various times between 1910 and 1931. Still, illegal gambling persisted. Then, in 1931 gambling was legalized and licensed to control local corruption, to raise state and local revenues, and to boost the economy in a time of economic depression by attracting tourists from outside the state. Gambling has been fairly carefully regulated since 1945.

Gambling became an economic success for both business and government and the small population of the state and other factors have led to effective government supervision of gambling. Gambling became big business with the general expansion of tourism after World War II. However, Nevada still ranked only sixth in the nation in 1967 in gambling revenue collected by states, with $26 million in revenue taken from $366 million in gross casino winnings.

Raymond I. Smith and his son Harold launched a carnival-like advertising campaign for what was to become Harold's Club as the place for inexpensive fun. Their club started with a penny roulette table in Skid Road in 1936. William Harrah, another carnival man, started out with a small bingo parlor on Virginia Street. He now owns the most elaborate hotel-casino in Reno and one at nearby Lake Tahoe. These men and other casino operators worked on taking the sin and social pathology connotations out of gambling, in part by referring to it as "gaming." We asked a sample of Reno adults what they thought of gambling and found that 53 percent thought of it as fun, 29 percent said it was a waste of time, less than 1 percent thought of it as sinful, and the rest had other comments.

Prostitution has existed in Reno since the nineteenth century mining days. Some of the prostitutes are even important figures in history. By the 1930's a prostitution area called The Cribs was operated near the Truckee River. The Cribs employed some fifty women and was reportedly operated by a gang connected with one of the local casinos. Now the local house of prostitution operates just over the county line with, as one Reno police officer said, "Some of the prettiest girls I've ever seen, just like models or coeds." There are some sixty brothels in the state with an average charge of $20, of which the girls receive 25 to 50 percent. Prostitutes in brothels are usually licensed and required to carry identification cards by local district attorneys and sheriffs. In addition, Reno and Las Vegas usually have dozens of prostitutes working out of certain clubs and hotels and as call girls.

The liberalization of divorce laws paralleled the liberalization of gambling. In 1913 the residence requirement was one year. Then in 1927 it was lowered to three months and finally in 1931, the same year as Reno's final legalization of gambling, the state residence requirement was lowered to six weeks. The legislators considered making it even less but they felt that other states might not recognize the Nevada divorce. One of the indications that Nevada is shifting toward conservatism is that, in spite of its economic advantage in doing so, it has not further reduced this waiting period in the last four decades. In recent years other states have decreased their waiting periods and simplified the divorce proceedings to such an extent that the divorce industry in Nevada is rapidly declining. At one time the Reno area had dozens of "divorce ranches" where wealthy people spent the six-week waiting period, but now only two are left. Reno still has a large number of divorce lawyers for a city its size, but further simplification of divorce in California in 1970 was the final blow to one of Nevada's unique attractions. Quick marriage services are now more important than quick divorce services.

THE NEW WEST

To the tourists Reno means gambling and adult entertainment. However, to a wave of new residents, Reno means a freer, more personal, more leisure-oriented style of life in an increasingly restricted world. As American society becomes more impersonal, urban, and modern there are countercurrents that place increasing value on the personal, the rural, and the traditional. Thus, many people with urban backgrounds are seeking out a more satisfying mix of urban and rural by moving out of large metropolitan areas to small cities. However, by placing the rural on a pedestal, so to speak, it becomes a new kind of rural which is clean, easy, and aesthetic. The rural "Old West" is being replaced by a "New West" without mud, hard work, or horse manure.

American culture contains many diverse sub-cultures, but as part of that diversity rural western American culture is being revitalized, particularly in places like Reno. The rural West has long been idealized in novels, movies, and songs. This is more than that. The rodeo is an important community event in Reno, even though the skills of riding and roping are of decreasing commercial value. Horseback riding is a popular pastime in the suburbs. Slacks, boots, and man-tailored shirts, originally ranch wear, are common dress among the women of Reno. Associations that take people out into the country flourish in Reno: archaeological surveys of Indian sites, historical searches through ghost towns, and the amateur geology of rock hunting.

Virginia City is a ghost mining town in the hills 23 miles southeast of Reno. It capitalized on the rise of interest in western history to become a major tourist attraction. It also attracted an unusual collection of permanent residents such as artists, a clique of homosexuals, a commune, a yoga school, and many "just plain folks" who "escaped their past," "smog and the urban sprawl," and so on.

The important position of the antique automobiles in Reno reflects this regional interest in the past. Harrah's Museum, with over 1,400 cars, has the world's largest auto collection. The Reno Chamber of Commerce promotes tourism by emphasizing the historic sites along the "California Emigrant Trail" and in the old mining towns. "Explore the bonanza-land of gold, ghosts, and the rip-roarin' Old Frontier." Gray Line Tours emphasize a trip to the Ponderosa Ranch and Museum, a photographic setting of the Bonanza television series.

The large internal North American migration, our mobility and circulation, is primarily related to locating for new jobs, responding to a shifting labor market. However, people also seem to be looking for a more personally satisfying identity and life style. We found in our summer study that only 18 percent of the adults we surveyed in Reno were born in Nevada while 56 percent were born in other western states. Their backgrounds were more of the city (34 percent) or town (44 percent) than the rural (22 percent). About half said they came to Reno for employment, but a large proportion said they came for the climate, the recreation possibilities, to marry or divorce, and other "non-economic" reasons. Significantly, we found that 72 percent felt that the size of Reno should be kept the same or would be even better if it were smaller, a conservative position on urban growth. Some 85 percent said they were satisfied with life in Reno. Reno seems to have held the solution to the problems of identity and life style, for the majority of our informants.

THE VALUE OF PERSONAL FREEDOM

As a part of revitalizing the American rural West, Nevada culture places a high value on individual freedom. Thus, Nevada laws allow driving at unlimited speeds on the highways, carrying and using guns freely, easy divorce and quick marriages, no state personal income tax, tax free inheritance, and open gambling. For an additional $25 Nevadans can purchase personalized automobile license plates with their own message of letters or numbers. Prostitution is permitted in many counties in the state and operates in houses of prostitution in all counties except the large urban ones, Washoe (Reno) and Clark (Las Vegas). Nevada also has the highest per capita sale of alcoholic beverages in the nation. In the casino areas there are bars, food stores, and beauty parlors that stay open twenty-four hours a day. Nevadans sometimes rationalize that the gambling, drinking, and womanizing are done by "tourists," short term residence "transients," and long term residence "outsiders."

While a few Renoites enthusiastically support the entertainment industry and many Renoites are employed in it, the majority find it necessary to build cultural walls around it, to isolate it physically, socially, and ideologically. The local newspapers virtually ignore the news on gambling. Since 1945 there has been pressure to restrict the area of wide open gambling. At first a "gentlemen's agreement" developed to restrict the area and this was formally imposed in 1957 by the City Council creation of the Red Line area of unrestricted gambling in three adjoining city blocks. Except for two clubs with "grandfather clauses," clubs outside of the Red Line blocks are restricted to twenty slot machines and three "21" tables, unless the casino is part of a hotel with one hundred rooms or more.

The casino center has been physically restricted to a few blocks, the Red Line area, where two major highways meet. Renoites try to avoid the area when driving around town because of the difficulty of driving through the crowds of tourists there. By concentrating most of the casinos in a small area the environment of a single large entertainment area, rather than just a collection of clubs, has been created.

Gambling and womanizing are usually seen as innocuous dissipations, but "They should not be allowed to enter family, neighborhood, or business life." Thus, the elements of Reno's culture which have given it its national reputation, such as open gambling and easy divorce, play only a minor role in the everyday life of Renoites. The general Reno philosophy of personal freedom, which allowed the institutions of open gambling and easy divorce to flourish, is more important than the specific institutions. In our survey we found the reasons that residents give for going to the casino area were for dinner and shows (75 percent), to take out-of-town guests (70 percent), to gamble (46 percent), and to cash checks (15 percent).

This philosophy of personal freedom is in fact limited, traditional, and conservative. When people feel that "I made mine, now you make yours," they depress the development of welfare services, racial integration, public education, and so on. The private sector is advanced at the expense of the public sector. The search for new freedoms, such as the new sub-cultural styles of life among the youth, are repressed in Reno. We found a generally moderate racial intolerance and a high intolerance for Negroes. We found that student radicals, hippies, draft resisters, and drug addicts were much more disliked than such older style villains as criminals, prostitutes, alcoholics, and hobos. These attitudes are shown in the following scales.

Our study sampled the opinions of the heads of 386 households scattered throughout the Reno-Sparks area. Part of this survey measured the degree of trust of political agencies and the degree of acceptance of social types and "ethnic groups." The results of our survey are given below from least trust or acceptance to most trust or acceptance. Thus, 22 percent of our respondents indicated they trusted the Race Relations Center while 78 percent were either neutral about it or distrusted it. The first two scales have five points while the third has seven points from "Would accept in family (marriage)" to "Would not like in my country." I use only the first two points of each scale to indicate "trust" or "acceptance."

Trust in Political Agencies

	%
1. Race Relations Center	22
2. Regional Planning Commission	27
3. City Councilmen	30
4. Mayor	39
5. Inter-tribal Council	43
6. State Highway Department	46
7. Gaming Control Board	60
8. Governor	62
9. City Police	66
10. County Sheriff	68
11. Highway Patrol	81

Acceptance of Social Types

1. Drug Addicts	8
2. Students for a Democratic Society	9
3. Black Nationalists	9
4. Homosexuals	11
5. Marijuana Smokers	11
6. Minutemen	11
7. Draft Resisters	13
8. Hippies	14
9. John Birch Society	15
10. Hobos	17
11. Sundowners (Reactionary)	26
12. Alcoholics	33
13. Ex-convicts	35
14. Prostitutes	37
15. Civil Rights Workers	38
16. House Trailer Residents	71
17. VISTA Volunteers	79
18. Tourists	83

Acceptance of Ethnic Groups

1. Hippies	26
2. Student Radicals	28
3. Africans	56
4. Negroes	59
5. Hindus	64
6. Cubans	69
7. Washo Indians	72
8. Shoshoni Indians	73
9. Chinese	75
10. Mexicans	78
11. Jews	89
12. Basque	92
13. Italians	93
14. English	94
15. French	96

CONCLUSIONS

The city has been largely ignored as a holistic unit of study, apparently because of a retention of traditional methods and dispositions in urban anthropology. While it is financially and administratively difficult to organize an inter-disciplinary research team, this seems to be a reasonable solution to the simultaneous study of such a complex cultural entity.

There are several advantages of team over individual ethnography. The team represents a wide variety of academic skills and personalities that together produce a wider variety of ethnography than an individual does over a long period of time. Through formal and informal discussions, the team is able to create a productive information exchange. It also accelerates the generation and testing of hypotheses much more rapidly than individuals working alone.

One problem in the development of a holistic ethnography on cities is in the research design. Representative sampling and balanced coverage to discover the significant cultural dynamics of the city should take precedence in the research design over the special, spectacular, or sentimental interest of ethnographers. The research design should also explore the adaptation of the city within regional or national contexts. In the case of Reno, Nevada I hypothesize the adaptations of (1) semi-legal practices (gambling, prostitution, quick divorce, etc.) in Nevada's symbiotic relationship with California, (2) a revitalization of western cowboy culture as a solution to national urban problems of personal identity and life style, and (3) an emphasis on a value of personal freedom within this "new western" culture.

SELECTED READINGS

EPSTEIN, A. L.

1958 Politics in an Urban African Community. Manchester: Manchester University Press.

In this study of the growth of unionism and intertribal relationships in an African mining town, Epstein shows how social structure is developed in response to the actions of the mine-owning group.

MINER, HORACE

1965 The Primitive City of Timbuctoo. Revised Edition. New York: Anchor Books.

This relatively early and holistic description of a traditional African city is a good example of the use of the folk-urban continuum in urban research.

MURPHEY, RHOADS

1953 The City as a Center of Change: Western Europe and China. Annals of the Association of American Geographers 44:349–362.

Murphey contrasts the cities of Western Europe, which formed the base for an independent entrepreneurial group, with the cities of China, which promoted the unity of the political order. The implications for cultural development are discussed in terms of European cities as centers for political and economic change, as opposed to Chinese cities as centers for the maintenance of tradition.

PARK, ROBERT E., ERNEST W. BURGESS, and RODERICK D. MC KENZIE

1925 The City. Chicago: University of Chicago Press.

The classic work of the "Chicago School" in urban sociology, which presents the ecological approach to the study of the city. Much of the work of Wirth, Redfield, and later urban sociologists and anthropologists was strongly influenced by the theoretical approach developed by these three men.

REDFIELD, ROBERT, and MILTON B. SINGER

1954 The Cultural Role of Cities. Economic Development and Culture Change 3:53–73.

The authors review various attempts at constructing typologies of cities, and the present their own terms of the role of the city in the creation and spread of a cultural tradition into the surrounding region. A distinction is made between cities in which the Great Tradition is maintained (orthogenetic) and those in which new traditions are introduced (heterogenetic).

SJOBERG, GIDEON

1960 The Preindustrial City, Past and Present. Glencoe: The Free Press.

Reacting to what he saw as an overemphasis on industrial cities in the literature of urban sociology, Sjoberg clearly and concisely discusses the nature of preindustrial cities in this comparative study.

VIDICH, ARTHUR, and JOSEPH BENSMAN

1968 Small Town in Mass Society: Class, Power and Religion in a Rural Community. Revised Edition. Princeton: Princeton University Press.

The small New York town of "Springdale" provides a useful comparison to the urban studies in this book. Although rural, Springdale is subject to many of the same national political and economic pressures experienced by city dwellers.

Part Two
URBAN ANALYSIS: SCOPE AND METHOD

Another way of viewing anthropology in the city is to stress the discipline's methodological approach in constrast to the techniques frequently used by the other social sciences in the same setting. Traditionally, anthropology has been person-oriented: fieldworkers often make close friends in the field and attempt to know their research population as intimately as possible, a characteristic equally prevalent in the discipline as the holistic perspective discussed in Part One. In tribal societies, holism and personalism are not mutually exclusive. The unit of research is generally small, leading to success in merging intimate knowledge of persons with a holistic account of the culture. In cities, however, large population size precludes knowing all urban dwellers personally. Most urban anthropologists have chosen to retain the personal approach to their area of research, relegating to a minor role such mass data-gathering techniques as questionnaires or formal interview schedules administered by an army of field assistants. However, as Price shows in Selection 4, the Reno study, such techniques are not at all unimportant.

The articles that follow suggest a range of methodological approaches used by anthropologists in their study of the city. Although each of these is consonant with a goal of personal knowledge of the target group, they vary according to the research aims of the fieldworkers. The Valentines make a convincing argument for the value of participant observation as a research technique, even within the complexity of the city. Their close relationships with neighbors and friends—as their research population had become—were essential for gathering data and for the high quality of their understanding of black ghetto behavior. This article is usefully read in conjunction with the selections in Part Six on the culture of poverty, in that the Valentines' research was formulated to test hypotheses derived from that concept.

The Spradley and Bott contributions are methodologically more self-conscious, yet each relies upon the primary techniques of participant observation and in-depth interviewing emphasized by other anthropologists. *Ethnoscience* (Spradley) and *network analysis* (Bott) may be differentiated on the basis of their varying emphases: ethnoscience is more cultural, while network analysis is more structural, differences arising perhaps from the American origin of the former and the more British cast of the latter. Each is gaining in importance as more anthropologists attempt to solve the difficulties of working within the city.

Spradley's reconstruction of part of the semantic map of Skid Road inhabitants opens a window through which we are able to see significant aspects of the lives of urban nomads in Seattle. In addition to the value of this article in introducing the reader to a particular approach to urban research, it also demonstrates that similar objects and events in the city can have different meanings to culturally different groups. Thus an attempt to define the city and its boundaries from the insider's point of view might result in as many definitions as there are subculturally distinct populations.

Bott's article is included in this section because of its focus upon research technique and social networks, although it could also have been placed in Part Five for its discussion of variation in urban family structure, conjugal role relationships, and family-environment interaction. This article was one of two early statements on network analysis (see Barnes 1954). Bott found that in the absence of concrete corporate groups organizing the daily lives of urban dwellers, sets of social ties could be expressed as "networks." Although the term had been used metaphorically by Radcliffe-Brown (1940), for example, Barnes and Bott were among the first to define and use the concept. Social networks are useful as a focus for almost any research problem; but more importantly, they more faithfully reflect the segmental nature of urban social relationships. Subsequent development of the notion has taken place since the 1950's (see Mitchell 1969b), but there is a need for more ethnographic research using this technique.

Research combining the more cultural ethnoscience approach with that of network analysis could be extremely fruitful in urban studies. For example, one could investigate the extent to which meanings are shared in ever-widening circles of partial networks. In addition, such research would contribute to knowledge of the structural characteristics of urban subcultures.

5

Making the Scene, Digging the Action, and Telling It Like It Is: Anthropologists at Work in a Dark Ghetto

Charles A. Valentine and Betty Lou Valentine

MAKING THE GHETTO SCENE IN 1968: WHY AND HOW?

Why Anthropology in the Ghetto?

This is an early report on the beginnings of a research project. We are a husband-wife team attempting to carry out a well-rounded urban ethnographic study. We have the indispensable aid of a contact man and initial rapport-builder, our 18-month-old son. As this is written (November, 1968), we have been in the field for four months. The area under study is an urban enclave which is notable for its poverty and its ethnically distinct populations. Its location is in a large metropolitan area in the northeastern United States. Its inhabitants belong mainly to non-white minorities.

We feel obligated by our relationship with the people under study not to identify the community further at the present time. For readers who may have been acquainted with plans and proposals that preceded this field work, we should add that the location of our research has shifted somewhat.

The work reported here rests on two main sets of basic assumptions.

SOURCE: Norman Whitten and John Szwed, eds., *Afro-American Anthropology* (New York: The Free Press, 1970), pp. 403–18. Copyright © 1970 by The Free Press, a division of Macmillan Co., Inc. Reprinted by permission.

One is that solid and insightful knowledge of any human community is worth having. We believe this is true for humane as well as intellectual reasons. The second assumption is that such knowledge and understanding are particularly lacking for certain human categories in our society. Among these are our most disadvantaged groupings, preeminently black people of the poorer urban communities in the United States.

These deficiencies of knowledge are not a matter of quantity of information. There are vast bodies of recorded data on the least fortunate of our social groupings. The weaknesses of available knowledge have rather to do with frameworks of thought and outlook. Most of those who study and report on our darker ghettos do so from a thoroughly external viewpoint. This circumstance strongly influences the kinds of data gathered and the quality of understanding that emerges.

We have long felt that careful research by cultural anthropologists can provide a worthwhile start toward remedying these deficiencies. It has taken some time for this conviction to be translated into practical activity. We had to come to terms with considerable professional skepticism and negative advice about our plans. We also had to make the decision to go into the field without any normal research support.

These background factors make us feel that a preliminary field report is even more appropriate than might otherwise be the case. We want to let it be known that this kind of research is eminently possible. We also want to present our tentative but growing sense that this work is turning out to be very much worthwhile.

Our orientation can also be stated in slightly more formal terms of immediate objectives and long-range goals. One objective is to examine current ideas about culture patterns among low-income, urban, minority populations. A second aim is to investigate the nature of contemporary culture change among poor minority urbanites. Third, we hope to contribute to an understanding of the relationships between these populations and the wider society. While in the field a fourth aim has come to seem equally important: improving the quality of relevant public information for wide audiences.

One of our broader goals is to contribute to developing techniques and methods in urban anthropology. Second, we hope to play a part in advancing theory within the anthropology of complex societies. In both these connections we see much potential, but rather little achievement of insight thus far, from existing approaches and ideas. Finally, we are committed to an additional goal which stems directly from a value position. We believe that the fortunes and interests of the minority poor —indeed of the poor in general—should be rapidly and radically advanced. We therefore hope that whatever knowledge and understanding we may develop will contribute to present and future efforts by disadvantaged ethnic populations to promote their own advancement. We also hope that what we learn may help establish potential bases for more rational and humane public policies in our society as a whole.

Ways and Means of Making the Scene

The basis for all operations in this research is that we shall live for at least two years within the community and among the people under study. This kind of residential experience has, of course, long been a standard basis for anthropological work in small-scale societies. We believe that it is no less necessary in studying the urban sectors of a complex society. We find that a rounded perception of ongoing social life is largely impossible unless one is immersed in it day and night over a long period of time. Our first few months' experience has borne this out many times over.

We have so far found that participation in local life is the key technique for gathering data. Direct observation of behavior in its natural setting is the principal necessary supplement to participation. Indeed, these two approaches necessarily go hand in hand. No doubt interviewing and other forms of verbal elicitation will become more important as the work progresses. In the early months, when building initial rapport is vital, however, we have found that straightforward participation as neighbors and as interested citizens has been the most productive approach. We have always combined this with candid statements of our actual purpose for being in the community.

In a few months this orientation has produced rich records of immediate experience and observation. These materials are supplemented by much informant testimony in the form of largely unsolicited explanation and commentary. The topical areas of these data range from children's games, food customs, and adult entertainment patterns of associational networks, religious behavior, and infant care to non-legal traffics of various kinds and mass demonstrations under armed attack. On the other hand, we have yet to collect our first formal genealogy, record a single life history, or initiate an interaction which would be recognizable as a formal interview.

This approach has dangers as well as limitations. We have experienced many of these difficulties in a short period of time. There are, first of all, the hazards of being treated as a member of the community by powerful outsiders. Significant outsiders range from bureaucrats to policemen, and so one must be prepared for problems extending from denial of normal social services to serious physical danger. Participation, more than other modes of study, involves the risk of cutting one's self off from one community faction by associating with another. Heavy reliance on participation increases the ever-present difficulty of keeping observer effects on the object of study to a minimum.

Living in a partisan community, rather than simply viewing it from a distance, adds other special qualities to normal research problems. It greatly sharpens the general problem of maintaining intellectual integrity in relation to controversial, value-laden materials. Participation leads to stronger emotional relationships—and perhaps more compelling ethical obligations—to the community than do more detached styles of research. Our experience leads us to reject the idea that involvement in community life necessarily makes one's work only advocacy. We do not feel that a participatory basis disqualifies the work as scholarship or science. The same experience, however, is teaching us to appreciate some of the pressures and strains of intensive participant observation. We are thus aware of factors that may lead others to see an opposition between participatory involvement and research which has integrity.

In spite of all this, however, choosing participation as the dominant research mode is the key to solving a most fundamental problem. We begin our research as outsiders in a community that has many reasons to be suspicious of outsiders. Yet in order to achieve our goals we must become, in effect, insiders. We have found that this requires being credible members of the community by actual performance. Suspicions that one is a detective or a spy are not affected by verbal assurances or protestations. On the other hand, these and similar fears of false pretense *do* yield to actual experience which shows that the researchers are credible neighbors and predictable community members.

We have found that initial anxieties as to our identities and motives have given way to a high degree of openness. A few early and mild expressions of direct hostility have been similarly resolved. Our approach has already passed several tests in the present research. One kind of expression is the spontaneous remark by a neighbor that she finds it hard to believe we have only been here a few months because she feels she has known us for a long time. Another indication is that quite a number of individuals who initially suspected us of being agents for dangerous external forces have now volunteered to describe those early perceptions. More significant, however, is the fact that we now receive considerable unsolicited information which would be quite dangerous to community members if it fell into the wrong hands. All in all, we now feel confident that substantially more behavioral and organizational settings are open to us than to the average member of the community.

DIGGING THE ACTION: EARLY IMPRESSIONS AND INTERPRETATIONS

Organization of the Local Community

We call the urban district whose people we are studying *the community*. In this we have adopted the usage followed by many local residents. Our area bears the same name it was given when it first became urban over a century ago. This name is in common usage today among both residents and outsiders. The territorial extent of the community is generally clear, though there is some local uncertainty about some of its boundaries. With one exception, on the other hand, the community is not recognized as an entity by any official agency outside the local area. The one exception is the complex of metropolitan establishments which administers public anti-poverty programs.

This community is inhabited by more than 100,000 people. Nearly three-quarters of this population are English-speaking Afro-Americans. The majority of these are North Americans, but West Indians are a significant minority. The largest remaining group are Spanish-speaking Latin Americans, chiefly from Puerto Rico. Much smaller local minorities —really little more than remnants—who have nevertheless long been established in the area include American Jews of Eastern European extraction, Yemeni Arabs, and a few Italians. Both in ethnic composition and in class structure our community appears to contrast quite sharply with adjacent predominantly Black and Latin districts. Here we have a very few resident Black professionals and no owners of large and comfortable homes, nor is there any numerically substantial white minority living within the community.

Available survey data indicate that the median family income of the community is well below official poverty lines. Except for a few recent public housing projects, virtually all housing was built well before World War II. Deterioration reaches literal ruin in many blocks. Community rates approach or exceed double the corresponding citywide indices for many factors associated with poverty. These include infant mortality, tuberculosis, venereal disease, aid to dependent children, and juvenile delinquency. Drug addiction and crimes against property are recognized throughout the community as major problems. Pupil achievement in every local school stands far below standard levels. While it might be difficult to demonstrate this with certainty, it is generally believed among local administrators and professionals that 80 percent of the community's residents are dependent on the welfare system.

There are major territorial divisions within this community which appear to be significant in the local social structure. We do not understand these divisions very well as yet. We are tentatively calling them sections, again in conformity with local usage. Section lines are probably conditioned by certain externally imposed spatial factors. These factors include variations in land use apparently dictated by outside economic forces. Also apparently involved are city policies with respect to residential locations for families supported by the welfare system.

On the other hand, sections certainly do not correspond to administrative areas established by extra-community bureaucracies. Indeed it is conspicuous that the territorial units set by supra-community agencies seldom bear any resemblance to entities of the local social structure. Most externally established boundary lines cross-cut the community and chop up its sections in mutually inconsistent confusion. Among such lines are those of political and electoral districts, census tracts, police precincts, urban renewal areas, school districts, and the service areas of numerous other agencies.

The section in which we live and which we know best includes some 25 city blocks. The population here is probably somewhat less than 5,000. It displays an ethnic diversity similar to that of the community as a whole. The area is almost entirely residential or what might be better described as ex-residential: there are great stretches of abandoned tenements in advanced stages of decay or demolition. This is one of the poorest sections in the community. Public facilities are generally lacking or exist in varying states of dilapidation. Many public services are unpredictable or unobtainable.

Our own block is typical of this section, except that it has a relatively dense population. This is because comparatively few of its housing units are uninhabited. Over 600 people reside in this block. They include a somewhat higher proportion of black Americans than does the community as a whole. A large majority of our neghbors receive public assistance in various forms. Residents often refer to the block as their neighborhood. Many neighborly interactions and networks are confined —or at least focused upon—the personnel of the block. The block appears to be a more clearly established unit in the local social structure than the section.

Our investigation has proceeded at each of these three organizational levels: the block, the section, and the community. Many events occur and many organizations function in ways that anchor them clearly in one of these structural contexts. Other social entities are also emerging as promising units of study: households, kin groups, personal networks, age groupings, and numerous community institutions. At least preliminary contacts have been made and initial data have been gathered from sample units at all these levels. This whole social field also has many significant interconnections with extra-community groupings and forces. We are beginning to scrutinize these relationships as well.

The Community, Wider Scenes, and Familiar Images

At the present point in the field study, one general finding seems to be emerging. *It is proving difficult to find major community patterns that correspond to many of the sub-cultural traits often associated with poverty in learned writings about the poor.* Consider, for example, the lack of participation or disengagement from major institutions of the wider society commonly mentioned in this connection. In our community, on the contrary, there is continuous involvement with numerous public agencies and private establishments of the larger society. These include various levels of governmental institutions. They also include many types of commercial and financial enterprises. Only a few examples can be cited in this brief presentation.

Dealings with metropolitan welfare agencies are a major part of community life. Approaches to these agencies include patient acceptance of whatever is easily available, persistent group pressure for maximum benefits, and resourceful individual manipulation of the welfare system. Clinics and emergency wards of major hospitals available to the community are regularly crowded. This is true despite the fact that medical personnel feel the community people do not use medical facilities properly, while many local citizens feel the health institutions do not serve their needs either competently or equitably. Prominent among institutions of the wider society whose projections into the community receive widespread daily attention are the mass media, both printed and electronic. Community people participated heavily in the national and local elections of November, 1968. At the polling place in our section, this participation included considerable commentary, by electoral workers and voters alike. A frequent comment was that the whole exercise was undemocratic because few or none of the candidates were in any sense representative of the local community.

In spite of unemployment, under-employment, and low wages, other economic patterns do not appear as might be expected from familiar images. Few homes are bare of possessions, and most display at least minimal comforts and decorations. Durable goods such as household appliances are not rare. Some people with low incomes tell us that they own or share in ownership of land and other real property. Most of these holdings seem to be located in the southern United States or Puerto Rico. A minority of unknown proportions own the two-family city dwellings in which they presently live. Small bank accounts and other modest forms of savings are by no means unknown among our neighbors. This is especially true when such resources available through kin ties or other networks are taken into account.

Modest food reserves normally exist in most households. The predominant food-buying pattern involves a once-a-week shopping schedule. Constant indulgence in small purchases, which is often portrayed as part of a culture of poverty, is prominent here only among children and adolescents. Householders make considerable use of department stores as well as supermarkets, particularly those of the smaller type that exist in or near the community. These economic patterns are intertwined with extensive networks for obtaining and distributing resources which are quite unconventional or illicit in terms of overt middle-class values.

According to familiar models of sub-cultures among the poor, social organization beyond the household level is practically nonexistent. Within the community under study, however, there is a veritable plethora of organizations. These range from block associations to the area-wide community council. The council itself maintains both central agencies and neighborhood branches with social service functions. The council has more than 100 member organizations, though some of these exist largely on paper.

Churches and other religious institutions abound. Many of them are small and purely local, while others are large and affiliated with major national denominations. Among the more highly structured secular organizations are several varieties of youth groups, political clubs, ethnic cultural organizations, athletic associations, clubs for social entertainment, parent-teacher associations, lodges and other fraternal groups, and various categories of service organizations. Many either maintain or periodically initiate contacts outside the community.

We do not yet have sufficient information to make confident or extensive statements about many aspects of family life, cultural values, and kindred topics often dealt with in generalizations about the minority poor. Yet here too we have strong early impressions suggesting that many common expectations are not confirmed in this community. Many standards and orientations generally associated with the middle class are conspicuous among our neighbors. These cover such diverse areas as career aspirations, interpersonal etiquette, dress and grooming, expressed marital and domestic ideals, conceptions of kinship, life crisis rituals, and child-rearing patterns.

Change: Where It's At and Where It's Going

This is a heterogeneous and dynamic community. It bears little resemblance to the static uniformity often attributed to poverty ghettos. Along with the historically derived diversity of ethnic groupings, change is occurring at different rates in various segments of the populace. Many outward signs of cultural black nationalism—such as "natural" hair styles, "African" clothing, and associated speech styles—are common but by no means universal among Afro-Americans here. There is a less conspicuous, often more low-keyed cultural nationalism among some but not all Puerto Ricans. These trends appear to be much in flux and to touch many aspects of community life.

Materials for case studies in social change abound. An instance which we have followed closely emerged as developments outside the community closed down a public institution for child care located in our section. Scattered elements within a previously moribund citizens association coalesced in an effort to reopen the institution. This sectional group was aided a little by the community council and by minor connivance from a disaffected faction within an extra-community bureaucracy. However, it was mainly the local blacks and Latins who forced a physical opening of the establishment. Next they obtained the services of a skeleton staff of dissident and community-oriented professionals to re-establish the essential functions of the institution. Other necessary services, from janitorial to secretarial, were performed by a combination of citizen volunteers and personnel supplied by the community council. The citizens' group also publicized the reopening among residents of their section. Then the institution's clientele began returning and additional popular support for the whole effort developed.

All this was accomplished against active and powerful opposition from outside the community. In the process, the citizen group transformed itself, not only in personnel and leadership but also with respect to the group's goals and functions. It became a force for expression and implementation of local needs and demands in relation to public institutions heretofore entirely controlled from extra-community power centers. Central control was forcefully re-established within a few weeks, and many local activists were successfully co-opted with appointments to non-professional positions in the target institution. Nevertheless, the possibility exists that the institution itself may still undergo significant permanent changes in response to a resurgence of pressure along similar lines. In the meantime, some local people have learned from this attempt at creating change, and some have acquired new sources of income.

Many such local occurrences, in our area and elsewhere, are beginning to be viewed as a broad movement for social change. This is the movement for community control over the local operations of presently centralized public institutions. As the name indicates, the basic initiatives for change are quite local in their immediate scope. Yet there is also a growing consciousness of parallel interests and outlooks shared more widely.

When the people in our section reopened a closed public institution and pressed for changes in its operation, they did not do this in the name of community control. Since that original initiative, however, some neighborhood people, encouraged by the community council, have begun to see their accomplishment in precisely those terms. This process has begun to create a sense of identification with a larger movement, as well as some organizational links with other groups in the community. This consciousness is expanding further as people learn that similar actions are occurring in many other communities.

The movement for community control has received notoriety in the news media with respect to recent disputes about public schools in New York City. In the area of our study, however, the institutional focus is much broader. While schools may have been a catalyst, there are beginnings of a parallel approach to health institutions, social service agencies, legal services, and police forces. Initiatives in these different sectors are at different stages of development. They are often pressed under different organizational sponsorships. Yet there is also much overlap and interconnection, developing in the direction of unified effort. The basic thrust of the movement as we have seen it is a demand that the local branches of major public institutions be made accountable to local groups which represent the publics that the institutions are supposed to serve.

This movement draws strength from long-standing dissatisfactions with the quality and relevance of local public institutions. Along with this goes a widespread conviction that the same types of institutions in affluent white communities are of a higher quality, more relevant to local needs, and more responsive to the popular will. Moreover, there are many memories of unavailing attempts by low-income minority groups to gain access to these putatively superior public facilities. These memories relate particularly to various schemes for integration.

Among the assumptions underlying all these perceptions and the resulting efforts for change are a number of value orientations common to dominant American culture. One such assumption is the belief that quality education is a principal key to achieving a comfortable and respected place in society. Another is the assumption that adequate health care is an essential to which everyone is entitled. A third is that police agencies should serve and protect the community rather than prey on it. Such ideals persist in the face of long-standing conditions to the contrary. For example, it is well known throughout the community that the city police are deeply involved in payoffs and other forms of corruption that contribute directly to many forms of unlawful behavior and non-enforcement of criminal statutes. A very common reflection of local experience is that the same policemen who are so zealous in violently breaking up political demonstrations generally fail to protect householders, prevent muggings, or control the drug racket.

The movement for community control often combines a stress on ethnic identity with much emphasis on intergroup unity within the community. This is a combination which obviously involves the tension of potential contradiction. Moreover, opposition outside the community has had some success in cultivating pre-existing hostilities and suspicions between the community's ethnic segments.

A favorite tactic of this kind is for the external (generally white) opposition to suggest to Puerto Ricans the spectre of an oppressive Black Power under community control. Nevertheless, the movement as we have seen it does manage to unite individuals and groups representing a great range of ethnic, organizational, and ideological affiliations. Conservative clergymen and declared revolutionaries, black nationalists and Latin matrons, young militants and grandmotherly clubwomen do form working relationships in this effort. Perception of common interests and shared desire for change, together with mutual experience of coping with resistance, appear to bring people together.

The development of this movement is revealing with respect to relationships between the community and other sectors of society. Many institutional, bureaucratic, and political networks linking local districts to outside centers can be explored by observing the course of local initiatives for change. Forms of resistance mounted by political hierarchies, centralized bureaucracies, and professional associations are varied and instructive. The observer can learn much about the whole social field as local change advocates develop tactics to match central opposition measures ranging from administrative obfuscation to armed force.

Conceptions of the movement's goals differ among its diverse constituencies. Many neighborhood participants simply look forward to bringing particular institutions up to the standards of the wider society as these are understood locally. Some leaders envision a broadly revitalized community in which democratic processes will insure that all major institutions serve local interests. The desired long-range result is that today's slums and ghettos should become comfortable and dignified communities tomorrow. Other leaders project visions of more radical change. According to one such projection, local accountability of institutions is but a step on the way to total community self-determination. This in turn would lead to the establishment of a new non-white nation in North America. Such a program may sound utopian or disingenuous to outsiders. Yet it is by no means dismissed by everyone in the community under study or in similar areas elsewhere. We have been in local audiences numbering many hundreds and in citywide gatherings several thousand strong where lengthy disquisitions on the steps from community control to nationhood are set forth. These discussions are accorded rapt attention and enthusiastic applause.

Inside and Outside Views of the Changing Scene

Through the approaches outlined earlier, the structures and processes of our chosen community seem to be unfolding before us. We are of course not yet in a position to make fully defensible statements about the theoretical significance of our findings. Nevertheless, we do have a growing impression that prominent models of life among low-income minority Americans do not fit our data very well. Thus far, what we are living in the midst of just doesn't look or feel like what books and articles offer us as the "sub-culture of poverty," "lower-class structure," and kindred formulations.

These doubts are not confined to the specific inconsistencies between data and models cited earlier. There is also a strong feeling that some major qualities are ignored or denied by well known portrayals of life among the poor. There certainly are real contrasts between social patterns in our community and those of typical middle-class areas. Yet the essence of these contrasts does not seem to reside in the alleged sub-cultural differences so often suggested.

First, there are major areas of life in which local analogues of wider institutions are dilapidated or low-quality versions of standard culture elements common to the society as a whole. This type of difference is most conspicuous in those institutional areas where direct external control has long limited the quality and quantity of resources flowing into the community. Such seems to be the case with the local units of many centralized public institutions and facilities. Examples range from sanitation services which leave the community continuously heaped with refuse, to schools with substandard teaching staffs which fail to educate community children.

Further external determinants operate through other centralized institutions which devote disproportionately *large* measures of their resources to low-income districts. Most prominent here are the welfare establishment and the police. Like other wider institutional complexes already cited, these organizations tend to play a highly manipulative role with the general effect of preserving existing conditions within the community. To this inventory must be added the commercial and financial enterprises, equally controlled from outside the community in all major cases. Without any other stake in the local situation, they appear simply to profit from whatever money is available to local people and to demand heavy police protection for their property. It is difficult to avoid the conclusion that all these agencies and enterprises together establish and maintain the larger socio-economic environment to which the poor must adapt.

It is the quality of this adaptation by poor people that seems most distorted in many writings. Contrary to most descriptions of slums, life in the community where we are working is neither drab nor dull. We see much energetic activity, great aesthetic and organizational variety, quite a number of highly patterned and well displayed behavior styles. Apathetic resignation does exist, but it is by no means the dominant tone of the community. Social disorganization can be found, but it occurs only within a highly structured context. Individual pathology is certainly present, but adaptive coping with adversity is more common. Positive strengths (often ignored in the literature) include the ability to deal with misfortune through humor, the capacity to respond to defeat with renewed effort, recourse to widely varied sacred and secular ideologies for psychological strength, and resourceful devices to manipulate existing structures for maximum individual or group benefit. Perhaps least expectable from popular models is the capacity to mobilize initiatives for large-scale change, like the movement for local control.

Both ethnic contrasts and social stratification are certainly among the most arresting dimensions of human variation continually demanding our attention. Yet the shape and dynamism of human affairs in this community seem to correspond only here and there with major delineations of these dimensions in anthropological publications. Our experience strengthens our conviction that class structures, part-societies, subcultures, and revitalization movements are conceptions of great importance for understanding our complex society. Yet we are developing an equally impelling sense that these conceptions may serve as hardly more than labels for unsolved theoretical problems.

This inadequacy of expert and specialist formulations is matched by the failure of another professional field. This is the incapacity of lay and popular media to record or communicate either the texture or the flux of life in our community. Recently there has been unprecedented attention by the mass media and other public information sources to minority communities and poverty areas. Nevertheless, the phenomena reported in this paper have generally either received no attention from the media or have been projected in a form that is difficult to recognize from within the community. Because so many community members follow the news media closely, these projections cause confusion and anger.

Leaders and followers alike increasingly believe that media policies thrust newsmen and information organs into active alliance with the resistance to community-oriented change. This experience has gradually led to exclusion of reporters from some otherwise public events. It has also produced forceful insistence that certain types of events which have been systematically ignored should be covered by the news people. The press and electronic media are thus now being added to the list of centralized institutions over whose local operations community forces demand a measure of control. The negative or exclusionist aspect of this initiative has so far been more effective than the positive demands for expanded coverage or more accurate coverage. As might be expected, it is far easier to bar journalists from a gathering than to influence the policies of their editors and publishers.

This situation has stimulated us to make a running study comparing observed events with projections from the metropolitan information media. Our preliminary conclusion is that citizens dependent on the media cannot obtain a remotely accurate perception of what is going on in this community. In this metropolitan area—like most in the United States—the general public is increasingly called upon to make political judgments with respect to minority peoples and poverty districts. Thus far our experience indicates that these public judgments must be made almost entirely without benefit of valid empirical information.

Neither the failure of the news media nor the inadequacies of the specialized published material can be ascribed to lack of interest or effort. Both seem to have in common a lack of appropriate conceptual frameworks. We suspect, however, that the common difficulty has another origin which is at once simpler and more profound. This is a problem of incomplete perception which is in turn part of a limitation on total experience. How many American newsmen, and how many social scientists, have recently lived a significant segment of their own lives as part of a low-income minority community? The numbers must be both absolutely and proportionally insignificant.

The question thus arises as to what kind of qualifications by experience are relevant to the task of portraying and interpreting the communities at issue here. How well are most writers and others who describe, analyze, and generalize about the life of the minority poor in the United States actually qualified in terms of experience? This problem takes on special significance for anthropologists. We may apply traditional ethnographic criteria to the question of qualifications for producing valid presentations of sociocultural realities. One need not necessarily challenge the legitimacy of all other perspectives. One need only ask whether the absence of an anthropological perspective may help explain the sense of unreality that arises when available portrayals are compared with direct experience in ghetto slums.

The overlapping publics who read books and articles on social science and follow the popular media are in serious need of valid information. They need the opportunity to form realistic conceptions about what is going on in disadvantaged minority communities in the United States. The need for these phenomena to be accurately perceived and meaningfully interpreted by the public at large is equally serious from the viewpoints of non-white poverty areas. White America and the darker ghettos are already engaged in a struggle which may easily have wholly destructive results if some degree of realistic knowledge and humane understanding is not established for the national public as a whole. Anthropology has risen to similar challenges in past times and different contexts. It may soon be too late for a comparable response to the present national crisis.

Who Gets the Information—and for What?

In closing we wish to raise one further issue which is also directly related to our present research experience. This is an issue which has been dealt with in recent discussions and resolutions by the anthropological association. We believe anthropologists must take care not to confuse or contaminate the provision of socially useful information with an intelligence function serving the existing concentrations of power and privilege in our society. Researchers may certainly proceed from, or be influenced by, quite a variety of ideological viewpoints. This need not cast any doubt either on the intellectual worthiness of their work or on its utility and relevance to human welfare. There is, however, one value position which *cannot* be reconciled by any humane judgment with direct experience of ghetto existence: support—active, passive, or "neutral"—for the socio-economic and political status quo as it exists in the communities of the minority poor.

We would venture to say that every adult in the community we are studying knows or feels this in one way or another—allowing for a wide range of individual and group variations on the theme. More concretely, we have never met a ghetto inhabitant who positively accepts all aspects of the ghetto as it exists. Consequently, it seems to us that nothing could be more contrary to the underlying ethical values of anthropology than to provide information of certain kinds to certain agencies. We must refuse to supply data or make reports to increase the resources of any agency that functions, for whatever reason, to prolong the existing sociopolitical position of the minority poor. Among institutions which have been shown in the past to have such functions are some which are common sources of research funds, including certain governmental agencies and a number of private foundations.

We are convinced that any anthropologist in a situation like ours must uncompromisingly refuse to contribute to the political operations of such agencies. It seems to us that any other position on this particular point would be a betrayal of the fundamental contract—explicit or implicit—between the anthropologist and the people he studies. This position may, of course, conflict with the obvious fact that public information can be used by anyone. Then the individual scholar must exercise his judgment and take full responsibility for weighing the probable effects of publication, or particular forms of publication, on community welfare. The specifics of this concluding argument are clearly open to much discussion. With this in mind we invite comment.

TELLING IT LIKE IT IS: POSTSCRIPT, 1969

Making It: Performance and Proving Oneself

Comments by others and reflections of our own, since this paper was first composed, lead us to offer a few further thoughts. Some of these expand upon matters already dealt with briefly. Others broach new problems.

Before we undertook this fieldwork we were repeatedly told, either directly or by implication, that what we hoped to do would be extremely risky and probably impossible. The burden of this prediction seemed to be a notion that the angry ghetto would make it quite unfeasible to achieve the necessary rapport and at the same time subject us to serious personal danger. No doubt those who felt this way took into account the fact that one of us is black, and the other is not. Indeed we have been given strong reason to believe that sources of financial support avoided funding our work at least partly because of doubts along these lines. We went into the field with one half academic salary, but without any supporting grant; funding began to materialize only when we had demonstrated that our field situation was viable.

There are probably many reasons why such fears about this kind of fieldwork are so wide of the mark. We expect to write about this at length later. Here it is only possible to touch on one important aspect of a complex situation. We are convinced that one factor above all others has enabled us to succeed in the early months of our work. That is, our empathy with the community under study is real, strong, and active. This means, first of all, that in our own block we are neighbors in the full sense that we actively share the discomforts and misfortunes as well as the adaptations and pleasures of living here. So for example, when large amounts of looted foodstuffs flowed into the neighborhood toward the end of a particularly lean month, the people knew that we were just as glad as they to be included in the distributional networks of the block.

As our son learns to talk, people use him to predict the number for the day, and if this little ritual should ever pay off it is quite predictable that we will be asked to share in the proceeds.

One early event went far toward establishing our rapport with the neighborhood. Our tenement apartment was broken into and the few possessions that combined some value with ready salability (including all our field equipment) were stolen. Every local household is fully familiar with this kind of event, and sharing this experience immediately established the beginnings of important bonds. In this context it may be mentioned that our 1967 model car, always parked in our block, is never locked and all the neighbors know this. (This block is one among very many in which stolen autos are stripped and left as empty but expressive hulks.) The neighbors also know that our vehicle is frequently available for errands ranging from shopping trips and outings for children to transportation to public demonstrations.

This quality of involvement has additional implications in relation to public events beyond the confines of the block-neighborhood. When local community people resort to activist behavior in service of their movements for social change, we have to be there too. We insist that our role as anthropologists makes it impossible for us to become leaders or initiators in these situations. Yet we feel just as strongly that the same role requires us to be genuine and trustworthy followers of community initiatives. So we have spent a good deal of time as observers in the middle of mass street demonstrations, sometimes under heavy constabulary aggression. And when community people have physically captured local institutions from centralized bureaucratic control, we have again been with the people. Though still eschewing leadership functions, we have worked long and hard with others to restore the operation of such captured establishments—e.g., repairing plumbing and wiring sabotaged by the external opposition or doing office work.

No one reading this should underestimate the risks entailed by these courses of behavior. Notice, however, that the principal threats we worry about do not come from the angry ghetto. They come rather from external agencies such as police forces. Most important, this is understood by the people we work with every day. Mutual respect and trust are thus based on shared experience. The legitimacy of our role as participant observers is not established by any ascribed status or external authentication. On the contrary, it develops from achieving, in the local setting, an observably consistent pattern of actual behavior. As a result of these approaches, we are not only living *in* the community but becoming a functioning part *of* it. We believe that this enables us to explore a living social entity as no other technique could.

The barriers to be overcome are not confined to generalized suspicion toward outsiders. They also include local forms of ethnic self-assertion, black nationalism and separatism, complex and powerful anti-white feelings, and hostilities specifically directed at academic researchers as such. Most of these orientations are not universal in our chosen community, but they are all present in quite significant forms. The important point here is that the approach we have described has succeeded well in spite of these barriers. This remains true even though one of us is white and we have never disguised our identity as social scientists. We do not wish to exaggerate our success in this regard. There are important local organizations to which we have only very limited access because of highly developed hostilities toward one or another of the wider social categories to which we belong. Whether these barriers will dissolve in time remains to be seen; but because of our experience thus far we are confident that at least some of them will. Six months of this experience has given us a strong feeling that the impenetrability of the angry ghetto is currently being greatly exaggerated by outsiders.

Yet like any community with boundary-maintaining mechanisms, this one too sets requirements for any would-be member who seeks full and free access. Much of the quality of these requirements can be communicated through an experience that is vividly remembered by the lighter member of our team. In a ticklish situation early in our field work, a black man who knew us only slightly could have been helpful; instead he said, "Any white man gotta *prove* himself to me." (Knowledge of both the man and the situation convinces us that he might just as well have said, "Any broad with some higher degree gotta prove herself to me—I don't care if she *is* black.") Today, however, this man is one of our many friends in the community. There have been a number of important subsequent occasions when he has vouched for us to others who did not know us as well as he came to.

Somehow we have "proved" ourselves to this man and to a great many like him—though as already noted, not to everyone. And we have done this without compromising our commitments as anthropologists, at least as we see these commitments. Perhaps the essential point is that, ultimately, the community test is one of performance, not of ascription whether by racial category, class status, or what-have-you. Possibly, it is this more than anything else which middle class and white Americans misunderstand when they overestimate the impenetrability of the darker ghettos today. At the same time, it is certainly a strong tentative conclusion of our brief experience that any serious attempt to enter into today's aroused black communities would be futile or worse for an outsider who does not take the test of performance seriously and empathetically.

Running It Down, or Writing It Up

Closely connected with all this is a phenomenon of field work which we did not anticipate. We feel that this may well be increasingly important for anthropologists working in circumstances like ours. Not long ago anthropologists became concerned about the consequences and implications of emerging literacy among their once non-literate subjects, including the possibility that the objects of study might begin to read some of the reports written about them. Our situation has taken us well beyond that stage, as indeed must by now be the case for many urban anthropologists.

Writing is the principal output of our special role in the community of which local people are aware. There is much interest in this at several different levels. A not infrequent formulation, usually delivered with a beguiling smile, is, "Hey man, how's the book coming, and is my name in it?" (Among other things, this provides many opportunities to repeat that we would not dream of writing a book about this community until we had lived here for a good two years.) We have also begun to receive direct requests to record individual first-person life stories for possible publication.

Another level of response is illustrated by the behavior of a local man who happened to be present when the version of this paper delivered at a scholarly meeting was being prepared. He showed great interest in hearing what was going to be said to the professional audience. So we did a practice delivery for him, and his reactions were instructive. The less complimentary references to the community at first angered him, he said, but he felt that everything in the paper was true, and taking it altogether he was glad we were "telling it like it is."

The most complex and demanding outgrowth of our function as writers, however, has emerged in relation to public events connected with one of the community movements for change. Musing angrily or despondently on the distortions and misrepresentations of the news media, local people began to suggest that we help set the record straight. They wanted us to do this by publishing accounts of recent developments from a community viewpoint. This suggestion made us recognize that we were uniquely qualified by circumstances to do what was asked.

So we produced several published descriptions and analyses, drawing on the systematic comparison of news reports and direct observation of events mentioned earlier. These publications are anonymous and will not be cited here, for reasons which we hope are obvious. They are known in the community, however, and local reactions to them are quite significant for our work. Community leaders and others have said spontaneously that our accounts are accurate and valuable. In one or two cases it has been specifically mentioned that we report community faults and weaknesses as well as virtues or strengths, and this is again presented as "telling it like it is."

It is perhaps unnecessary to point out that this makes us privy to a great deal that is hidden from outsiders. The principal point we wish to make is that we have found it necessary to extend the commitments of participant involvement to the work of writing as well as other aspects of our research. This is not to be taken lightly, for it is undoubtedly a delicate and difficult task. It does produce great rewards in terms of the primary object of the research, to obtain a full and deep picture of all possible aspects of community life. Yet it confronts us, as perhaps nothing else could, most sharply and directly with several interrelated issues: of scientific objectivity, scholarly integrity, and the influence of values upon research. This experience tears away from our minds' eyes any vestiges there may have been of the veil of "value-free social science." It brings home most forcefully and concretely the need for effectively combining empirical accuracy of a high order with a genuine commitment to humane valuation of community interests and welfare. Any lingering, naïve hopes of detachment have to be abandoned, while safeguards against factual inaccuracy or distortion must be redoubled.

The local response to knowledge of us as persons and to published results of our work has led to a group action which illustrates these problems. This is a formal action approving extension of our research to an area of the movement for community control which had a long-standing ban on all research. Naturally this gives us a warm sense of both personal and professional success. Yet it also makes us more aware of the dangers of becoming mouthpieces for a segment of the community, however sympathetic we may feel toward that segment. In this respect we count heavily on our already established reputation for reporting phenomena as we see them, even if in some respects they may not reflect credit on local groups or institutions. We also muster all ability to listen to and respect other points of view on these issues. Special recognition and requests of this kind tempt us to neglect many other aspects of our holistic study where comparable rewards may not be immediately forthcoming. In this connection we point out our own research needs, commitments, and values. Moreover, we attempt to remind community people of the accurate images we have projected because as anthropologists we are concerned with the *entire* community.

6

Adaptive Strategies
of Urban Nomads:
The Ethnoscience
of Tramp Culture

James P. Spradley

Urban anthropology includes a variety of approaches. Nearly every sub-field of anthropology can bring its methods, techniques, and theories to bear upon human life in the urban setting. At the same time, there are certain unique contributions which anthropologists may be able to make by virtue of their cross-cultural and and non-Western orientation. In fact, it is argued here that we may be in danger of selling our birthright for orientations developed by others who have been studying the city for decades. Research in non-Western societies has helped us lay aside our cultural blinders, a prerequisite for discovering the behavioral environment or socially constructed reality of those we study. This is not an easy task in any society, but for the urban anthropologist there are additional problems. Urban groups do not live in the "city" but in their own socially constructed definition of the city. This paper [1] begins with a discussion of five interrelated problems faced by the researcher: (1) cultural plural-

SOURCE: Thomas Weaver and Douglas White, eds., *The Anthropology of Urban Environments,* Monograph no. 11 (1972): 21–38. Reprinted by permission of the Society for Applied Anthropology.

[1] This paper is a revised and expanded version of "Ethnoscientific Study of a Tramp Subculture," a paper presented to the 67th annual meeting of the American Anthropological Association, November 21–24, 1968, Seattle, Washington. Some of the material used to illustrate the methods of research are drawn from Spradley (1970), where they receive much fuller treatment along with many other domains in the culture of urban nomads.

ism, (2) ethnocentrism, (3) subcultural interpreters, (4) similar cultural forms, and (5) relevant social units. An ethnographic approach to an urban subculture will then be presented as an effective strategy for urban research. Five major steps in the research will be discussed along with data from the subculture under consideration. Finally, I shall raise a number of issues which need further exploration by urban anthropologists.

URBAN RESEARCH PROBLEMS

Cultural Pluralism

When the ethnographer studies his own urban society, attempting to discover the meaning of objects and events according to the conceptual systems of city dwellers, he is confronted with a complex multicultural situation. In addition to the thousands of different roles in the city, resulting from specialization, there are many distinct life styles in a myriad of subcultural groups. Considerable strain is placed upon the holistic bias of the anthropologist in conceptualizing the city as a cultural phenomenon. Concepts such as "rural-urban," "primitive-civilized," and "ecological zone" have been used to understand cities as a whole, but they often obscure the cultural pluralism of the urban situation. If we are to understand the city as a functioning whole, we must begin by looking at the different units of that whole. Only then will we be in a position to fruitfully develop conceptual models of the city as a unit to be compared with other cities as well as peasant villages and nomadic tribes. After the various parts of an urban culture have been described and compared, even wider comparisons will be more valid; in fact, we may find that the minority group described here has more in common with nomadic tribes than it does with other urban subcultures. It is of utmost importance, then, for anthropologists to recognize, identify, and describe the various subcultures within the city, for, as Wallace (1962:351) has pointed out, "All of the comparative and theoretical work of cultural anthropology depends upon thorough and precise ethnographic description."

Ethnocentrism

The belief that one's traditions, values, and ways of life are better than those which exist in other societies is probably universal. Anthropologists have long championed the need to recognize the validity and dignity of diverse cultural traditions while not abandoning a commitment to one's own heritage. The contemporary urban scene throughout the world is heavily influenced by Western culture and the researcher has learned values and definitions about urban life which will profoundly influence the questions he asks and the research he undertakes. The use of hallucinogenic drugs by students in American cities is evaluated differently from their use by an isolated Indian tribe living in the Amazon basin. The drinking behavior of men in the Skid Road district of the city is similar to that of the Camba Indians, but Westerners define and evaluate them quite differently.[2] It may not be easy for one studying a remote tribe in New Guinea to overcome his feelings that their way of life is inferior to his own, but that difficulty is even greater when one studies the culture of those who live in his own society but have a very different style of life. Much of the research on the urban population considered here has been criticized for such an ethnocentric bias. Wallace (1965:159) discusses this problem:

> When the sociologist arrives on skid row with precoded, pretested survey questionnaire in hand, every one of his questions implicitly assumes the person is a failure and asks why. Even though this question remains unstated, both questioner and questioned perceive its fundamental reality.

It is naive for the researcher to believe that he can study urban subcultures without being influenced by his own culture. While "value free" research is impossible, the problems in approaching this ideal are much greater in the study of urban subcultures for which the researcher's own socialization has provided him with traditional definitions.

Subcultural Interpreters

Isolated tribesmen or villagers have little knowledge of the anthropologist's culture and informants have no basis for responding to questions based upon that culture. The field worker does not expect them to translate their way of life into the categories and terms which have significance in his way of life. Instead, he immerses himself in the field situation, learns the native language, discerns not only the answers to questions but also which questions to ask, and finally describes the culture in a way which his colleagues and students will understand. The ethnographer's job is one of translating and interpreting the culture he studies into terms which can be understood by the outsider. Urban anthropologists are faced with a different situation. Literacy, communication, and interaction among

2 Skid Road is used here in preference to "skid row," which appears in much of the literature. Skid Road is a term which originated in Seattle to describe the road down which logs were skidded to the sawmill and where bars, flophouses, and gambling houses were prevalent. There is an extensive literature on Skid Road and the men described in this paper. Those who are interested may consult Wallace (1965).

members of different subcultures have provided informants with a knowledge of the researcher's culture. This is especially true among the groups which are deprived of status and power within the city, for their very survival requires that they know the life styles of members of superordinant status groups. They are keenly aware of attitudes, values, and individual differences among the power holders. As a result the anthropologist who studies an urban population encounters many informants with the ability to translate their way of life into his language and culture. Informants act as subcultural interpreters; their translation competence may lead the anthropologist to describe another subculture in terms of his own without realizing he is doing so. Questions are formulated in the researcher's dialect of English and based on the categories of his culture. When they are put to an informant, they are quickly translated and thus "understood." Then the informant responds to questions he has imperfectly understood with answers phrased in the idiom of the researcher's culture. The ethnographer may thus guide his informants to conceptualize their culture from the perspective of the outsider. Such interpreters may provide a wealth of data which can be analyzed, but the investigator has been effectively prevented from discovering the meaning and definition of experience from the insider's point of view.

Similar Cultural Forms

Urban communities contain distinct subcultural groups which share many similar cultural forms and appear to live in the same environment. They live in the same geographic area and climatic zone, often sharing transportation systems, law enforcement agencies, educational institutions, and many other facets of city life. It would be easy to conclude that different groups actually have the same culture and that a description of these aspects of urban life for one group would be an accurate description for all groups. This appearance of sharing similar forms may even be empirically verified if culture is treated as a statistical description of behavior. But if culture involves the forms people have in mind, the fact that people share the "same" urban environment and institutions may obscure important cultural differences. "In actuality not even the most concrete, objectively apparent physical object can be identified apart from some culturally defined system of concepts (Frake 1962b:74). Men who live on Skid Road participate in many of the major institutions of the city. They visit missions, work in jail, go to the theater, walk the streets, get into bathtubs, visit cemeteries, and go to junkyards. Other city dwellers also engage in these activities but define them differently. The underlying attributes, values and meanings which each group assigns to urban life must be discovered if we are to do justice to the pluralistic nature of the city. This paper is based on Goodenough's (1957:173) premise that:

> The great problem for a science of man is how to get from the objective world of materiality, with its infinite variability, to the subjective world of form as it exists in what for lack of a better term, we must call the minds of our fellow men.

Relevant Social Units

All behavioral science is faced with the task of specifying the units and classes of behavior to be described and explained. This has always been a thorny problem for anthropologists and may be seen in such controversies as what is meant by a "tribe." The task has been easier in studying nonurban societies by the coincidence of geographical and social unit boundaries, less mobility, limited communication among social units, and greater linguistic variation. If the city is not a homogeneous sociocultural unit, how are we to identify the unit we are studying and establish its boundaries? Some scholars have studied "Skid Road" using geographical criteria to identify the subculture reported on here. Some even determine the boundaries of this area by asking professionals who attempt to help those who live on Skid Road. Are such professionals to be considered as part of this social unit? Is every individual in such a locale to be treated as part of that subculture? If the city is multicultural in nature then the identification of units which make up this pluralistic phenomenon is of utmost importance. The criteria for treating minority groups, black ghettos, urban Indans, and other units as relevant for research must be explicitly stated in order to make replication and comparison possible. All too often urban research has been carried out with an implicit mixture of biological, social, geographical, historical and cultural criteria which leads to confusing results. Even more crucial is the arbitrariness involved in the selection of criteria for identification of a subculture. Conklin (1964:29) has pointed to two aspects of this problem:

> We should like especially to avoid the pitfalls of (1) *translation-labeling analysis,* wherein the *units* are provided not by the culture studied, but by the metalanguage given before the investigation begins; (2) *translation-domain analysis,* wherein the boundaries and establishment of larger contexts are similarly provided by prior agreement instead of by ethnographic investigation.

Different approaches or models have been used in the many studies made of the urban population to be considered here. A brief consideration of these models may highlight some of the research problems discussed above for this particular group. The social units which appear to be similar have been referred to variously as "Skid Road alcoholics," "homeless men," "vagrants," "hoboes," "tramps," or "indigent public intoxicants." The *folk model* is the stereotype of this population held by the majority of urban society. They are seen as people who fail abysmally, are dependent on society, lack self-control, drink too much, are unpredictable, and often end up in jail for criminal behavior. In a word, they are bums. The *medical model* defines this social unit in terms of its primary illness—alcoholism. The concept of being an alcoholic is hardly better defined among medical professionals than the idea of being a bum among others in society. Skid Road alcoholics in particular are sometimes considered to be like "burned-out, backward schizophrenic" (Solomon 1966:165) patients who are almost without culturally organized behavior. The *legal model* defines these people as criminals guilty of many minor crimes, but especially public drunkenness. The criminal court in the city studied had a special file for keeping track of this population and they were officially designated as common drunkards. The *sociological model* defines this unit in terms of a variety of criteria including homelessness, age, sex, race, income, drinking behavior, and geographic location. Each of these four models tends to predefine the social unit in terms which are considered relevant to the outsider, using criteria determined by folk, medical, legal, or sociological standards. The folk model in particular has heavily influenced the criteria used by the others. The focus upon drinking behavior and homelessness, for instance, reflects the American cultural values of sobriety, self-control, and the home. All of these approaches are, in different ways and to different degrees, outsiders' models. The *ethnographic model* to be presented here avoids the predefinition of what is to be considered relevant and aims at discovering the insider's view of his social world. While all of these models are useful for certain purposes, it is argued here that, because of their training and experience, anthropologists can make a unique contribution by discovering the insider's model for any particular urban subculture.

AN ETHNOSCIENTIFIC APPROACH TO THE STUDY OF URBAN AREAS

The methods of ethnoscience hold promise of partially overcoming some of the problems of urban research. I consider the task of ethnography to be the discovery of the characteristic ways in which members of a society categorize, code, and define their experience. Ethnographic descriptions based on techniques of ethnoscience have been largely limited to a few selected domains in non-Western societies, such as kinship, color categories, and plant taxonomies.[3] The application of these techniques to an urban subculture is based on the premise that "the units by which the data of observation are segmented, ordered, and interrelated be delimited and defined according to conrtasts inherent in the data themselves and not according to a priori notions of pertinent descriptive categories" (Frake 1962a:54).

The various ethnic and social groups within the city have developed different strategies of adaptation. Each subculture provides such strategies in the form of cognitive maps which are learned through socialization. These cognitive maps categorize the world of experience into equivalence classes which eliminate the necessity of responding to every unique event in the environment. This is one of the most important ways that culture enables human beings to survive. Following Bruner and his associates (1956:2), it is maintained that "The learning and utilization of categories represent one of the most elementary and general forms of cognition by which man adjusts to his environment." If we are to discover different strategies of adaptation among urban groups we must discover the different category systems they use to reduce the complexity of their environment and organize their behavior. Category systems enable the individual to identify those aspects of the environment which are significant for adaptation, provide direction for instrumental activity, and permit the anticipation of future events (Bruner et al. 1956:11–14). Thus, an important avenue to understanding both the strategies of adaptation and the environment to which urban groups are adjusting is in the study of category systems through ethnoscientific techniques (Frake 1962a:54).

An ethnographic description of an urban subculture, must tap the cognitive world of one's informants. It must discover those features of objects and events which they regard as significant for defining concepts, formulating propositions, and making decisions.

How shall we approach this goal? The present study was begun by means of participant observation at an alcoholism treatment center on

[3] Since there are many studies which have not been published it is difficult to estimate the degree to which ethnoscience techniques have actually been used in the study of urban groups. There are a number of reports on American kinship terms: Ward Goodenough (1965); A. K. Romney and R. G. D'Andrade (1964); one on American law terms, Mary Black and Duane Metzger (1965); and one on German beer terms, Per Hage (1968)—all pertaining to urban problems.

Skid Road and in a municipal criminal court. The first few months were spent in observation and recording casual conversations among informants in order to discover relevant questions. This was followed by more formal ethnographic interviews using a number of different discovery and testing procedures. Although these procedures will be discussed in more detail later in this paper, we may note five major steps in the research at this point. After some familiarity had been established with this population and several informants had been selected, I began by (1) hypothesizing that certain areas were culturally significant, and then (2) recording a corpus of relevant statements in the language of informants. It was then possible to (3) examine the corpus of statements for possible domains, question frames, and substitution frames and go on to (4) elicit the categories of culturally relevant domains. This last step resulted in a folk taxonomy or native category system for identifying significant objects in the subculture. Finally, a number of eliciting techniques were used to (5) discover the semantic principles of a number of domains.

THE SUBCULTURE OF URBAN NOMADS

Tramps and Their Domains

The category of men considered in this paper could be characterized in many different ways depending upon the criteria selected. They live part of their lives on Skid Road (geographic criteria); join small groups for drinking (behavioral criteria); violate city ordinances which prohibit public drunkenness, begging, urinating in public, and drinking in public (legal criteria); and are characterized by low income and homelessness (sociological criteria). Table 1 provides a summary of several characteristics for a group of 216 men who had been arrested and committed to an alcoholism treatment center.

While most of the social characteristics given in Table 1, as well as those noted above, are useful for some purposes, few go very far toward an ethnographic identification of the urban population under consideration. The data which are gathered in any research are determined, to a large part, by the questions asked. With the ethnoscience approach questions are derived, not from previous research studies, theories, or one's own research interest, but primarily from informants. This approach involves "a search for sets of questions that the people of a society are responding to when they behave in systematic ways, and for the relations existing among these questions and responses" (Black and Metzer 1965:141). Thus, the first task was to discover how these men identified themselves and to formulate appropriate questions. Using the methods

Table 1. Social Characteristics of Tramps

	Social Characteristic	Percentage *
AGE	Under 25	3
	25–40	25
	41–50	43
	Over 50	29
MARITAL STATUS	Married	8
	Single	26
	Separated	8
	Divorced	48
	Widowed	10
LIVING SITUATION	Living alone	83
	Other	17
EDUCATION	College graduate	3
	Some college	8
	High school graduate	20
	Grades 9–12	31
	Completed eighth grade	17
	Less than eighth grade	19
INCOME	Under $500	15
	$500–1000	33
	$1001–3000	28
	Over $3000	24
TIMES IN JAIL	Less than 10	9
	10–25	23
	26–50	22
	51–100	24
	101–200	12
	Over 200	7
TIMES MOVED IN LAST FIVE YEARS	5 or less	26
	6–20	32
	Over 20	38
RACE	Caucasian	74
	Negro	7
	Indian	11
	Other	8
JOBS HELD IN LAST FIVE YEARS	1–5	21
	6–15	26
	16–50	31
	Over 50	19

* Since all the men in this sample did not answer every question, some of the percentages do not total 100. The remainder represents those who did not respond.

discussed in the section above it was found that informants identified their subcultural membership with the lexeme *tramp*. There were at least eight major categories of tramps recognized by informants: *working stiffs, mission stiffs, bindle stiffs, airedales, rubber tramps, home guard tramps, box car tramps,* and *dings*. This category system constitutes one of the major social identity domains in this subculture. The significance of these findings is that the identity of this subculture has most often been based on *external* criteria. External definitions of the primary social identity of any group profoundly influence the kinds of questions asked and data gathered by the researcher. It may be important for some purposes to identify this population as "homeless men" or "chronic alcoholics," but it does not necessarily reflect the insider's conception of his own social identity. It may even preclude discoveries of great cultural significance.

A semantic analysis of this domain revealed that the underlying criteria in statements elicited from informants were mobility-related. The different kinds of tramps were differentiated in terms of their degree of mobility, mode of travel, type of home base, and economic survival strategies. For example, *homeguard tramps* travel very little while the other kinds of tramps travel extensively. *Box car tramps* customarily travel by freight train in large continental circuits which cover most of the United States. *Rubber tramps* travel in their own cars, while *working stiffs* may ride freight trains or use commercial vehicles. The criterion of homelessness was not significant to these men in defining their social identity but rather the type of home base they had. The *airedale* and *bindle stiff* both carry their "homes" with them in the form of a pack and bedroll. *Rubber tramps* live in their cars, *mission stiffs* at the mission, and *dings* who are professional beggars have no home base. While many tramps drink and drunkenness is institutionalized in their world, drinking behavior was not a defining criterion for their social identity. Once it was established that informants conceived their primary social identity to be anchored to a mobile, nomadic life style, the importance of other facts which might have appeared trivial came to light.

Tramps are arrested often and taken to jail where they move through a series of inmate identities. Initially they are *drunks,* whether their crime has been public drunkenness, begging, shoplifting, or urinating in public. After a period of waiting in a drunk tank they are taken to a criminal court for arraignment where over 90 percent of them plead guilty and are sentenced for their crimes. Most courts follow a sentencing procedure which is graduated so that on each successive conviction, especially for public drunkenness, a man's sentence is increased. Sentences for this crime may begin with two to five days in jail and increase to as much as one year in jail where a man will work as a *trusty,* remain confined to a time tank as a *lockup,* and finally become a *kickout* just prior to his release. The judges often believe that this approach curbs the drinking behavior in the constant repeater. The validity of this belief need not concern us here, but graduated sentences act as a strong reinforcement for a nomadic way of life and the individual's identity as a tramp. After several arrests in one city he is motivated to move on to another in order to escape the longer sentences. Even a suspended sentence often induces a man to increased mobility since, if he stays in town and is arrested too soon, it will mean serving time on the earlier suspended sentence in addition to the current charge. Evidence of mobility is seen in some of the social characteristics—number of jobs, times moved, and times in jail—presented in Table 1. Even sleeping behavior is influenced by the nomadic quality of their lives, as we shall see later in this paper. While observations, interview data, and life histories all support the contention that the dominant life style of these men is nomadic, most important is the fact that these reflect their cognitive world. These men are *tramps,* members of a subculture which is present in most large American cities, the subculture of *urban nomads.*

The problems and vicissitudes of urban nomads are different from those encountered by members of other urban groups. As socialization occurs in this subculture a variety of strategies are learned for satisfying biological needs, achieving subcultural goals, and adjusting to the environment. In each of the major scenes in the world of the tramp there are specialized modes of action for solving common problems. These scenes include *buckets* (jails), *farms* (treatment centers), *jungles* (encampments), *skids* (Skid Roads), and *freights* (railroad cars). Tramps learn to solve certain problems in the bucket, for example, as they acquire the categories and rules of this subculture. In jail there are the common problems of restricted freedom, restricted communication, and lack of resources such as food, cigarettes, and clothing. The specialized modes of action for alleviating these perceived deprivations are referred to as *hustling.* Hustling is a cover term for a large number of specific actions which tramps group into the following equivalence classes: *conning, peddling, kissing ass, making a run, taking a rake-off, playing cards, bumming, running a game, making a pay-off, beating, making a phone call.*[4] These adaptive struggles used in jail are very important to this group of men who often find themselves in a new jail with no other way to meet their needs. Many have actually spent years in jail on short sentences. One tramp had been sentenced to a total of fourteen years in one city alone on convictions for public drunkenness. As one informant stated,

[4] A more detailed analysis of *hustling* may be found in two other publications on tramp culture: Spradley (1968) and (1970).

"You aren't a tramp if you don't make the bucket." While "hustling in the bucket" is important, tramps have a large number of adaptive strategies which may be employed in almost any scene. In the remainder of this paper we shall consider those related to satisfying their need for sleep in the wider urban environment.

Making a Flop

The ethnographic description which follows has resulted from a variety of research methods and techniques. Previous studies in ethnoscience and cognitive psychology have been especially valuable in this regard.[5] Some aspects of this research are difficult to make explicit, such as the values of the researcher, intuitive insights, and the complex relationship between researcher and informant. While these factors can never be eliminated, a major goal in ethnography is to increase the degree to which all operations may be explicitly stated. This will provide the possibility for replication, an important criterion for evaluating the adequacy of ethnographic descriptions (Conklin 1962). It is for this reason that the following description includes a statement of the procedures used in gathering and analyzing the data presented. While interviewing, recording, observing, and analyzing often occurred simultaneously, the data will be presented here in terms of several research steps. These data represent a partial description of the cognitive map for some members of the population studied. The extent to which other members of the population share this map is an empirical problem. It is assumed that systematic differences will occur depending on social identity, length of socialization into this subculture, geographical area of major socialization experiences, and other characteristics of each informant. Some of these have been examined and all are important areas for further research.[6] It is beyond the scope and purpose of this paper to deal with many of these theoretical and methodological problems in detail.

1. *Hypothesizing the area as culturally significant.* The researcher's cultural background precluded the prediction that sleeping and places

[5] The work of George Kelly (1955) provides one of the closest links between psychology and ethnoscience. Anthropologists whose work has been especially helpful include: Harold C. Conklin (1962, 1964); Charles O. Frake (1961; 1962a; 1962b); Ward Goodenough (1956); Paul Kay (1966); Duane Metzger and Gerald E. Williams (1963; 1966); and Black and Metzger (1965).

[6] Some differences among informants regarding different kinds of tramps have been investigated. A sample of about sixty-five men were asked to respond to a questionnaire based on the criteria used by informants to define the domain of "tramps." Relationships between a self-image adjective checklist, social identity as a kind of tramp, and knowledge of this particular taxonomy are being analyzed.

to sleep would be culturally revealing or significant. The popular image of the "bum" or "derelict" in American culture portrays these men as sleeping in cheap hotels or passing out in an alcoholic stupor. Although very little review of previous studies on this population was done prior to beginning the study, subsequent research has shown that, with a few exceptions, sleeping has not been considered very important in the published works. Participant observation, carried out among the population at the alcoholism treatment center, revealed the importance of "making a flop." Conversations among tramps at informal gatherings, meals, card playing groups, and "bull sessions" were recorded. As these men related their experiences to one another there were many references to "making a flop." Friends were identified as someone you would "make a flop with." Comments about making a flop were often linked to other important behavior such as being arrested, drinking, and traveling. Informants made such statements as "The most important thing is something to eat and a place to flop." A study (Wallace 1965:29) of Skid Road in a midwestern city emphasized the importance of this aspect of behavior:

> A place to sleep is, in some ways, more important to the men who live on skid row than food to eat or something to drink. This is so for two reasons. First, a man sleeping in the open is an easy victim for the weather, as well as for assailants be they jack rollers or police. Secondly, the law uniformly requires that "everyone must have a bedroom" if he is not to be charged with vagrancy. . . .

This author then discusses the different places where these men sleep, giving the following list: single room hotels, cubicle hotels, mission hotels, dormitories, transportation depots, buses, subways, movie houses, flop houses, box cars, hobo jungles. Thus, in discovering which questions to ask and by examining other studies, it was hypothesized that making a flop was a significant aspect of this subculture.

2. *Recording a corpus of relevant statements.* At this stage, conversations were recorded and statements gathered which all related to the general focus of sleeping. Earlier field notes on other subjects were combed for verbatim statements made by informants about this domain. The tramps' membership at some time in the dominant American society enables them to translate their concepts into those of the researcher. Because of this, very few questions were asked at this stage of the research. One approach that helped overcome their bias in interpreting similar cultural forms was to ask a group of informants to discuss their "experiences of making a flop." In such situations the individuals often talked among themselves rather than to the researcher. The following examples are drawn from these tape recorded sessions:

I took a nose dive (laughter by all) in the Bread of Life when it was real cold because they just pick out certain ones you know (laughter). If you're not sitting in the right position there, why, they're liable not to give you a ticket. And I just walked back in that little room (laughter). But it was cold! Had to take a nose dive to get it (flop).

A lot of guys make them halls over at the Puget Sound. Either they sleep in the hallway or they sleep in the bathtub over at the Puget Sound (laughter). I've gone up to sleep in the bathroom. You know where they got those trash cans, up on the fourth floor. No one ever looks up there. That Jap says, "I got 300 rooms," he says, "and twelve hundred tramps come out every morning" (laughter).

You know where they got this little private club, down at the end of the block, towards Alaska Way from the Bread of Life, that little dock back there? (Others: yea) There's garbage cans back there, but they're paper cans, not garbage. They're clean. And many a night, you know, in the summer time, I'd go in there, turn the barrels over, and put a pasteboard box there, and turn that barrel and stick my feet in it, and maybe I'd stick my head and shoulders in this damn pasteboard box, well I was out of sight. I'd lay there with half my body in a garbage can and the upper half in a pasteboard box. Until someone kicks that can or tries to load it and you'd better get out! (laughter) (Another informant: I never corked out like that!) Well, that way no one knows.

You know where I used to flop when I went out there to Interbay? I knew those Great Northern switchmen there. I'd go into those crummies, those cabooses. The guy would tell me to come down there and go ahead and build a fire in one of those stoves.

I usually hit a car lot, I'd either get in the back row, or go right up by the office. They're gonna look for you in the dark. But you pick out the best lighted place and they ain't looking for you in the light, but you get in a dark place and they come looking for you with a flashlight, right by the office, crawl in a car, cause they ain't looking for you in the light.

Statements made by one member of this subculture to another member and those which could be placed within a larger verbal context were most valuable. At the same time, written statements, statements made to the researcher, and fragmentary statements were extremely useful. The following examples indicate the variety and range of such data:

"I got my flop for the night."

"Where you gonna bed down for the night?"

"I flopped out in the weeds."

"In a stairway you got to sleep with one eye open or someone will bang you on the head or start taking your shoes off."

"I'm not bothered if I flop in a broom closet."

"I paid for my banner."

"In a flophouse you can cop a heel, double up, hit the deck."

"The Sally is one night flop."

"I robbed a whole clothesline to make a bed."

"Head for the weeds."

"You lay down there and . . ."

"Got me ten or twelve newspapers back in the Frye Hotel . . . had a bed that thick."

While most of these statements could easily be judged relevant because they were elicited in the defined context of "sleeping," this was not true for others which were provisionally accepted. The first two steps were important in reducing the degree to which categories were imposed on the data from outside. As Metzger and Williams (1963: 1077) have pointed out, the purpose of recording verbal interaction is "to arrive at a description that parallels the discriminations of the people under study."

3. *Examining the corpus of statements for possible domains, question frames, and substitution frames.* For this study, a domain was considered to be a category system which was labeled with a cover term or a set of terms which all occurred in some restricted environment. There are a number of domains or category systems within the general focus of making a flop which could be analyzed. These include, but are not limited to, the following: (1) kinds of "flops;" (2) ways to "make a flop;" (3) ways to "make your own flop;" (4) kinds of "people who bother you when you flop;" (5) ways to "make a bed;" and (6) kinds of "beds." Some of these domains are sets of terms referring to objects; others refer to modes of action. This does not exhaust the possible domains and subdomains within this area, nor does it consider "covert categories" (Berlin et al. 1968:290–299) which tramps utilize but which do not have cover terms. While several of these domains will be discussed, the focus of this study is primarily on kinds of "flops." Question frames were derived primarily from the cover terms for the various domains. Such questions as the following were developed:

"What kinds of flops are there?"

"What are the different ways to make your own flop?"

"What kinds of persons can bother you when you sleep?"

Substitution frames were discovered by inspecting the statements related to making a flop for those with terms that appeared to be replaceable by other terms. The following examples show several frames which were utilized:

"(*The sally*) is a one night flop."

"I'm not bothered if I flop in (*a broom closet*)."

"I flopped in a bathtub in (*a flophouse*)."

4. *Eliciting the categories of the domain.* The most important question frame for eliciting the categories of the domain labeled "flop" was, "What kinds of flops are there?" This resulted in a large number of terms which are ordered on the principle of inclusion and form a folk taxonomy (Table 2). Some of the terms were discovered through examination of previously recorded texts and others overheard in informal conversations. While the taxonomy appears to be clear cut, the persistent application of the above question frame with different informants did not yield unambiguous results. The final taxonomy given in Table 2 is a result of informant responses, intuitive insights, and some ordering of categories during analysis to satisfy the aesthetic values of the researcher! There are no doubt alternative ways to structure some aspects of this taxonomy as well as the componential definition to follow. I do not feel that such facts appreciably limit the possibility of replication and I would maintain that this analysis is still more rigorous than other approaches to this kind of material. In order to avoid the impression that all indeterminacy was ruled out and to identify the choices which I made, a number of factors may be examined in relation to this taxonomy.

First, there were a number of terms which were excluded from the taxonomy because they were extremely rare or very little information could be gathered on them for further analysis. One informant indicated that one kind of flop was a *mortar box*. He recalled "My wife and I were hitchhiking to Chattanooga and we slept in an old filling station that was closed, in an old mortar box. We picked up some grass they had just cut along the highway and used it for a bed." Further investigation may reveal that there is a category of flops called *boxes* which would include *mortar box* and *trash box,* but the latter was the only box included here as a kind of flop. Another informant reported that a friend has flopped in a *junky cart*. Tramps have a variety of "ways of making it," modes of action which bring some kind of economic gain. One of these is *junking*. In this case, two tramps in Chicago had acquired a junky cart and were traveling the streets of the city picking up bottles, metal, and any other object of value to sell to the junk dealer. Their *junky cart* was large enough to sleep in, so one man would crawl in and cover himself with an overcoat to keep out of sight while he slept and the other man

Table 2. Taxonomic Definition of Flops

1. Paid flop
   A. Motel
   B. Hotel
   C. Apartment
   D. Flea bag
      1. Dormitory
      2. Wire cage
      3. Flop house

2. Empty building
   A. Motel
   B. Hotel
   C. House
   D. Apartment
   E. Abandoned
   F. Under construction
   G. Being torn down

3. Weed patch
   A. Pasture
   B. Cemetery
   C. Viaduct
   D. Bridge
   E. Riverbank
   F. Field
   G. Orchard
   H. Between buildings
   I. Park
   J. Sidewalk
   K. Jungle
      1. Town
      2. Railroad
   L. Railroad track
   M. Alley
   N. Dump

4. Railroad flop
   A. Switchman's shanty
   B. Conductor's quarters
   C. Coal car
   D. Box car
   E. Flat car
   F. Reefer
   G. Piggyback
   H. Station
   I. Gondola
   J. Passenger car
   K. Sand house
   L. Crummy

5. Mission flop

6. Car flop
   A. Truck
   B. Used car lot
   C. Junk yard
   D. Transit bus
   E. Harvest bus
   F. Car on street
   G. Own car

7. Places in a paid flop
   A. Lobby
   B. Toilet floor
   C. Hallway
   D. Bathtub
   E. Closet
      1. Broom
      2. Clothes

8. Window well

9. Under building

10. All night laundromat

11. All night bar

12. All night restaurant

13. All night show

14. Paddy wagon

15. Cotton wagon

16. Hay barn

17. Furnace room

18. Newspaper building

19. Bar room

20. Night club

21. Bus depot

22. Brick yard

23. Scale house

24. Harvest shack

25. Bucket

26. Tool house

27. Stairwell

28. Park bench

29. Penny arcade

30. Church

31. Trash box

32. Doorway

33. Apple bin

34. Haystack

35. Loading dock

pushed the cart along. I was unable to discover how common such a practice was nor any other information which would enable me to define the junky cart from the tramps' point of view. There is reason to believe that further research would validate such terms and undoubtedly other categories would be discovered.

Second, there were a variety of places "in buildings" which informants identified that were not included, and the taxonomic status of those which were included is problematical. In most urban environments there are many public buildings which are accessible to tramps. Within these buildings there are public places which make good sleeping quarters because they are heated. These include depots, hotels, business buildings, police stations, etc. Many men reported that one kind of flop was a *toilet floor*. Further inquiry revealed that there were many different places where *toilet floors* could be found. For instance, informants reported: "I slept in jail in Mississippi. We went into the jail toilet and slept all night." "I've slept in a railroad station toilet and a bus depot toilet." "I have no trouble walking in a second floor, second rate hotel upstairs and curling up and going to sleep in the men's room. If it's very late at night I know there's a very poor possibility of anyone wanting to take a bath, so I just sleep in the bathtub." These places are not considered kinds of "paid flops," yet very often they are in hotels or flophouses. One arrangement that might have been used was to consider *toilet floor* a cover term for a great many location concepts such as *in jails, in hotels,* and *in buildings*. Since most informants reported that they usually found these places in *flophouses*, it was decided to consider "places in flophouses" as a category which included *toilet floors, lobbies, hallways*, etc., and exclude the other locations from the present analysis.

Third, the discovery of some middle level terms in the taxonomy presented certain difficulties. Informants responded freely with the most generic term, *flop*. They also responded freely with specific instances of places where they had flopped, such as "I slept in a crummy," or "We slept in a big truck that was loaded with cotton from seats of old cars." Initially the taxonomy appeared to be primarily made up of a generic and specific level. In order to discover the middle levels, the question frame, "What kind of a flop is that?" was used with the specific terms elicited. Through this process it was possible to discover that a *crummy* (a caboose on a train) was a railroad flop, and the big truck noted above was a *junk yard truck* which is a kind of *junk yard car flop*. When informants indicated that a certain term was to be included in a higher level term, it was possible to elicit other specific terms or place those already discovered by using substitution frames. For example, the substitution frame "A *crummy* is a railroad flop" led to expanding the list of kinds of railroad flops.

Fourth, there was a tendency to assume taxonomic relationships by confusing the form and function, as well as different functions, of an object. It will be noted by examining the taxonomy given in Table 2 that the terms categorize objects, not according to their physical form, but according to the function they serve for tramps and not other members of urban society. While this phenomenon has long been recognized by anthropologists, urban anthropologists face greater problems because they often share similar forms with those they study, but the functions are defined differently. One cannot assume similarity of taxonomic relationships but must test all such relationships empirically. For instance, at first it appeared that *paddy wagon* and *cotton wagon* might be included in the term *wagon flop*, but informants denied this relationship. There are several terms which include the phrase "all night," such as *all night laundromat*. When asked to sort these into similar categories, or asked if they were to be considered similar kinds of flops, informants refused to include them in any more generic term than flop. The discovery of taxonomic relationships for similar terms which exist in two or more urban subcultures is one way of demonstrating that such terms are or are not homonyms. Many terms in the domain of flops would be classed only as *vehicles* by this researcher. Informants classified some objects which were vehicles separately and some objects which were not vehicles, such as *sand house*, together with vehicles.

Fifth, it was necessary to check those terms constantly which might be homonyms or synonyms. The problem of intercultural homonyms has already been noted in the preceding paragraph. I shared the term *cemetery* with my informants, yet it was included in the terms *weed patch* and *flop* for them but not for me. This type of intercultural homonym contrasts with intracultural homonyms such as informants' dual use of the term *hotel*. One refers to a kind of *paid flop* and the other a kind of *empty building flop*. There were many synonyms used by informants such as *flea bag-flop house*. Some men referred to all kinds of cheap Skid Road hotels as *flea bags;* others used the term *flop houses*. There was some confusion over this since in the city studied there were no *dormitory flops* or *wire cage flops*, so informants could use the cover term *flophouse* without specifying the level of contrast, i.e., what terms it contrasted with, since there were only specific flophouses in that city.[7] Some other synonyms encountered were the following: *crummy-caboose, mission-sally*, and *jail-bucket-can*. When a choice was to be made between terms which informants reported "meant the same thing," preference was given to terms used by those who had been members of this subculture for a longer period of time and also reflected the predominant

---

[7] See Frake's discussion of the use of the same linguistic form at different levels of contrast for further discussion of this kind of problem (Frake 1961).

usage of the geographical location of the research. Dialectal variation among tramps was encountered frequently, especially among those who had been socialized into this subculture in the southern part of the United States.

It should be noted that the lower level terms in the taxonomy do not refer to specific objects, but classes of objects judged as equivalent. For some of these terms it was possible to elicit more specific named objects which were members of the class. For instance, *park* is a kind of *weed patch flop,* but there were many different parks where informants had slept. Some different kinds of parks were elicited which are not included here, such as *hobo park.* The discovery of more specific terms was carried out in some cases with the question frame, "What are the different kinds of ———?" or "Can you tell me the names for the different ——— where tramps flop?" Some category terms such as *box car* refer to a large number of different objects, but these are not named. Instead, informants would distinguish between members of a set by such statements as "I slept in a box car outside of Omaha on a rip track where I was bothered by the railroad bulls." While *empty buildings, weed patches,* and *railroad flops* are not generally named at a very specific level, other subdomains such as *flophouse* and *mission* have many specific named members reflecting the importance of these sub-domains for this population.

We may now ask what this taxonomy says about the subculture of urban nomads. How culturally revealing is it to elicit the categories which this group uses to order their environment in relationship to sleeping behavior? While this category system is not exhaustive it contains nearly one hundred *categories* of sleeping places. Furthermore this taxonomy has five levels and could have been extended to at least six by including more specific terms. Several tentative conclusions may be drawn from these facts. First, the importance of nondrinking behavior such as sleeping appears to have been underestimated by most researchers in this field. Even the study quoted earlier which stressed the importance of finding a place to sleep lists only eleven categories of places to sleep. While the initial participant observations led to the impression that "making a flop" was important and would be culturally revealing, we now have a basis for comparison with other domains, both intraculturally and interculturally. While I would not contend that a simple count of the number of terms or the levels of a taxonomy are conclusive evidence of importance, they cannot be easily dismissed. Preliminary work with other domains in this subculture have not revealed any other category system which organizes so much of the environment or in such a detailed fashion. There are many different kinds of *bars, bulls, time,* and *ways of making it,* but none of these domains are as elaborate as the different kinds of *flops.* The domain which comes closest to being as elaborate is the kind of *people in the bucket,* or social roles in jail. Further research is necessary to make a more complete intracultural comparison.

Only superficial intercultural comparisons are possible at this time, since, to my knowledge, similar domains in other cultures have not been studied by this means. Sleeping places do not appear to be culturally revealing in the rest of American culture. In fact, the eleven categories of sleeping places noted above from other research are probably more than most Americans use. It is interesting to compare the usage of the two terms *flop* and *sleep. Flopping* is used by tramps to refer to the activity which other Americans refer to as *sleeping,* although most tramps will also use *sleeping.* When we consider the use of these two terms in their noun form, an interesting difference appears. The noun *flop* refers to a place in the environment where the activity takes place, while the noun *sleep* refers to the bodily state of rest or to the occasion of sleeping. Thus the verbs may be considered translations of each other but this is not so for the nouns. Tramps, in their language, stress the place where sleeping occurs, while other Americans do not. Frake (1961:121–122) has proposed the following hypothesis related to taxonomic differences between cultures:

> The greater the number of distinct social contexts in which information about a particular phenomenon must be communicated, the greater the number of different levels of contrast into which phenomenon is categorized. . . . If the botanical taxonomy of tribe A has more levels of contrast than that of tribe B, it means the members of tribe A communicate botanical information in a wider variety of sociocultural settings.

It seems apparent that tramps communicate information regarding places to sleep in a wider variety of sociocultural settings than do members of the larger American society. One is not surprised that sleeping behavior has been largely overlooked by those who have studied this group. The social scientist in his own culture has learned that there are relatively few places to sleep, that places to sleep do not enter into a wide variety of sociocultural settings, and probably holds the implicit assumption that places to sleep are not culturally relevant. While the major basis for designating these men as urban nomads was their own definition of social identity, this taxonomy strongly supports such a designation. Although a nomadic way of life does not necessarily require a large number of categories for places to sleep, we are not surprised to find that this is so for these men. We might well be surprised to discover a group which is sedentary and also had such an elaborate category system for places to sleep.

A taxonomic definition is culturally revealing but it does not take us far enough in understanding this group of men. It tells us that tramps have many places to sleep but it does not tell us very much about what they consider significant about each place for sleeping purposes. It does not tell us much about how they choose one place to sleep instead of another. There are a very large, if not infinite, number of criteria which could be used to define such objects as *cemeteries, box cars, bridges,* and *bathtubs.* All of these items have at least one feature of meaning in common for the population under consideration: they are all *flops,* places to sleep. If we are to understand what meaning these places hold for tramps, we must discover the underlying semantic principles by means of which tramps differentiate one kind of flop from another. This leads us to the next step in the research.

5. *Discovering the semantic principles of the domain.* The procedures used to discover the underlying semantic principles of a domain have been referred to as componential analysis (Goodenough 1956). A set of objects or events which are identified as equivalent and labeled with a category term are not necessarily identical. All of the objects referred to by the terms in Table 2 are classed as equivalent. They all share at least one feature of meaning but there are many differences among them. Each term *contrasts* with the other terms and those at the same level of contrast make up a *contrast set.* The dimensions of meaning which are important in differentiating among members of a contrast set are the *dimensions of contrast.* Each dimension of contrast has two or more values. The differences in meaning among members of a contrast set are indicated in terms of the values on each dimension of meaning. By specifying how each term included in the *flop* domain contrasts with every other term, we would be stating, in part, the underlying semantic principles which organize the domain. If the dimensions of contrast reflect the cognitive world of our informants, we would also be stating, in part, the significant criteria which they use in selecting one place to sleep over another. This study was aimed at a description which approximated the psychological reality of informants. Wallace and Atkins (1960:75) have distinguished between analyses which are psychologically real and those which are structurally real:

> The psychological reality of an individual is the world as he perceives and knows it, in his own terms; it is his world of meanings. A "psychologically real" description of a culture thus is a description

which approximately reproduces in an observer the world of meanings of the native users of that culture. "Structural reality," on the other hand, is a world of meanings, as applied to a given society or individual, which is real to the ethnographer, but it is not *necessarily* the world which constitutes the mazeway of any other individual or individuals.

Table 3. Dimensions of Contrast for Flop Domain (Highest level of contrast)

1.0 Monetary resources	6.0 Civilian interference
1.1 Not required	6.1 Waitress
1.2 Required to pay for the flop	6.2 Night watchman
1.3 Required to pay for something else	6.3 Bartender
	6.4 Manager
	6.5 Owner
2.0 Atmospheric conditions (weather)	6.6 Farmer
2.1 Almost no protection	6.7 Engineer
2.2 Out of the rain/snow	6.8 Tramps
2.3 Out of the wind	6.9 Anybody
2.4 Out of the wind, possibly out of the cold	6.10 Minister or priest
2.5 Out of the wind and rain/snow	6.11 Truck driver
2.6 Out of the wind and rain/snow, possibly out of the cold	6.12 Probably no civilian
2.7 Out of the wind, rain/snow, and cold	7.0 Police interference
	7.1 Police check and may also be called
3.0 Body position	7.2 Police check
3.1 May lie down	7.3 Police must be called
3.2 Must sit up	7.4 Police do not interfere
3.3 Should sit up but may lie down	8.0 Security
	8.1 Public/Concealed/Protected
4.0 Intoxication	8.2 Public/Concealed/Unprotected
4.1 Must be sober	8.3 Public/Unconcealed/Protected
4.2 Must be drunk	8.4 Public/Unconcealed/Unprotected
4.3 Any state of intoxication	8.5 Nonpublic/Concealed/Protected
	8.6 Nonpublic/Concealed/Unprotected
5.0 Drinking restrictions	8.7 Nonpublic/Unconcealed/Unprotected
5.1 Low risk drinking	
5.2 High risk drinking	
5.3 Purchase drinks	

It is assumed here that any componential analysis of a category system will fall somewhere between an exact replica of the cognitions of informants and one which is completely divorced from how they perceive the world. As the above authors (Wallace and Atkins 1960:78) note, "A problem for research, then, must be to develop techniques for stating and identifying those definitions which are most proximate to psychological reality."

Several techniques were used to elicit the dimensions of contrast employed by tramps and to avoid imposing dimensions relevant only to the investigator. The underlying goal of all these techniques was to elicit from informants those differences in meaning which they felt existed among members of the set. Probably the most useful approach was the triadic sorting task (Kelly 1955; Romney and D'Andrade 1964). Informants were presented with three terms for different categories of *flops* and asked to indicate which two were most alike and/or which one was different. *After* a selection was made they were queried regarding the basis of their choice. Substitution frames were formulated from these responses or from other textual material. For example, an informant would be presented with the frame "If you flop in the (*main jungle*) you may be bothered by other (*tramps*)" and asked to indicate what other terms would appropriately go together in the two spaces. This approach is very similar to the "grid method" discussed by Bannister and Mair (1968) in a recent work based on Kelly's personal construct theory of personality. Another approach was to ask informants to sort the terms into two or more groups in any way they desired. Then they would be asked to indicate why they had grouped the terms in a particular way. These techniques led to the discovery of the dimensions of contrast for this domain. Those which are used for defining the terms at the highest level of contrast are listed in Table 3 and a componential definition of these terms is provided in Table 4. A more complete discussion of these dimensions of contrast as well as those used in analyzing several other subdomains has been provided by Spradley (1970).

A componential definition does not tell us everything there is to know about a domain. The definition in Table 4 does provide us with the information which some tramps use to identify objects they consider places to sleep with the appropriate label. It also enables us to see how most terms are distinguished from one another. Sleeping *under a building* is both similar to and different from sleeping in a *window well*, and this componential definition shows us how these places are alike and different from the tramp's perspective. They are similar kinds of flops because they require no money, permit lying down, allow any state of intoxication, involve low risk of arrest for drinking, are relatively free from civilian interference, and are checked occasionally by the police. They differ in that when a man sleeps *under a building* he has more protection from rain and snow as well as concealment from other people. At this level of contrast there are two sets of terms with identical values for each dimension of contrast and thus it is not possible to discriminate among them by means of elicited criteria. A *barroom, all night bar,* and *night club* have the same values, a fact which suggests that there may be a covert category which includes these three sleeping places. *Apple bin* and *cotton wagon* are not distinguished; they are both rather concealed places in the vicinity of farms or orchards. Further research would probably yield more criteria which would distinguish among these terms.

Another problem with this analysis involves the criteria of economy which has been suggested for evaluating the adequacy of ethnographic statements (Conklin 1964). Are all the dimensions of contrast necessary to define this contrast set? Except for the terms noted above which are not distinguished at the first level of contrast, only the first seven dimensions of contrast are necessary to discriminate among all the other terms. This means that the dimension of *security* (8.0) does not add anything to the goal of economy, although I would suggest that it is culturally revealing and thus should be included. In any componential analysis one may choose the criteria of economy or exhaustiveness. The analysis presented here does not measure up to either of these criteria completely. In some cases it could be more exhaustive and in other cases more economical. It seems likely that there are often more dimensions of contrast than are necessary to economically define a particular set of terms. The following hypothesis is proposed to account for this: *The semantic criteria used to identify events and objects in the environment are determined by situational variables.* These variables may be external to the organism, such as time of year, climate, and presence of other people. They may be within the organism in the form of need states. For example, a tramp with a few dollars may contemplate going to a *paid flop* or selecting some other place to sleep. An *empty building, church,* and *stairwell* are all nearby and since the weather is warm all seem to be possible flops which will not cost him anything. Then he remembers that his arrest record is such that another conviction will mean several months in jail and since these three flops are all checked by the police they are ruled out. A paid flop would protect him from the police and provide the greatest security, but he would like to use his money to purchase something to drink. He recalls that nearby there is an *all night show* which would cost less than a *paid flop,* leave him enough money

Table 4. Componential Definition of Flops (Highest level of contrast)

Flops	Dimensions of Contrast *							
	1.0	2.0	3.0	4.0	5.0	6.0	7.0	8.0
Paid Flop	1.2	2.7	3.1	4.3	X	X	7.4	X
Empty Building	1.1	2.6	3.1	4.1	5.1	6.2,6.8	7.1	8.6
Weed Patch	1.1	X	3.1	X	5.1	X	X	X
Railroad Flop	1.1	X	X	X	X	X	X	X
Mission Flop	1.1	2.7	3.1	4.1	5.2	6.8	7.4	8.4?
Car Flop	X	X	3.1	X	5.1	X	X	X
Places in Paid Flop	1.1	2.7	X	X	X	X	7.3	X
Window Well	1.1	2.4	3.1	4.3	5.1	6.8	7.2	8.7
Under Building	1.1	2.6	3.1	4.3	5.1	6.8	7.2	8.6
All Night Laundromat	1.1	2.7	3.3	4.3	5.2	6.5	7.2	8.4
All Night Bar	1.3	2.7	3.2	4.3	5.3	6.1,3,4	7.1	8.4
All Night Restaurant	1.3	2.7	3.2	4.3	5.2	6.1	7.1	8.4
All Night Show	1.3	2.7	3.3	4.3	5.1	6.8	7.4	8.2
Paddy Wagon	1.1	2.5	3.1	4.2	5.2	6.12	7.2	8.7
Cotton Wagon	1.1	2.5	3.1	4.3	5.1	6.12	7.4	8.6
Hay Barn	1.1	2.6	3.1	4.3	5.1	6.6	7.4	8.6
Furnace Room	1.1	2.7	3.1	4.3	5.1	6.2,7	7.3	8.6
Newspaper Building	1.1	2.7	3.1	4.3	5.2	6.4	7.3	8.6
Bar Room	1.3	2.7	3.2	4.3	5.3	6.1,3,4	7.1	8.4
Night Club	1.3	2.7	3.2	4.3	5.3	6.1,3,4	7.1	8.4
Bus Depot	1.1	2.7	3.2	4.3	5.2	6.9	7.1	8.4
Brick Yard	1.1	2.7	3.1	4.3	5.1	6.4	7.3	8.6
Scale House	1.1	2.6	3.1	4.3	5.1	6.8	7.3?	8.6
Harvest Shack	1.1	2.7	3.1	4.3	5.1	6.8	7.4	8.1
Bucket	1.1	2.7	3.1	4.3	5.2	6.8	7.4	8.4
Tool House	1.1	2.5	3.1	4.3	5.1	6.12	7.3	8.6
Stairwell	1.1	2.4	3.1	4.2	5.1	6.5,8	7.1	8.7
Park Bench	1.1	2.1	3.1	4.3	5.2	6.8	7.2	8.7
Penny Arcade	1.1	2.7	3.2	4.3	5.2	6.12	7.2	8.4
Church	1.1	2.6	3.1	4.3	5.2	6.2,10	7.1	8.6
Trash Box	1.1	2.5	3.1	4.3	5.1	6.12	7.2	8.6
Doorway	1.1	2.1	3.1	4.2	5.1	6.8,9	7.1	8.7
Apple Bin	1.1	2.5	3.1	4.3	5.1	6.12	7.4	8.6
Haystack	1.1	2.7?	3.1	4.3	5.1	6.12	7.4	8.6
Loading Dock	1.1	2.1	3.1	4.2	5.1	6.2,8,11	7.1	8.7

* See Table 3 for the meaning of each numerical symbol. A question mark (?) indicates lack of information while an X indicates variability among the terms at the next lowest level. In column 1.0, car flop has an X because some kinds require money and others do not.

for his drink, and allow him to escape detection by the police. As he decides on the *all night show* he notes that he is tired enough to sleep sitting up, he may even be able to lie on the floor, especially after he has finished off the bottle he can now purchase. He has taken account of the variety of situational variables and finally made a selection based on his definition of flops. The definition of situational variables and their relationships to the semantic criteria for this domain remains an important research task.

Does this analysis provide insight into broader aspects of the culture of tramps or is it merely an exercise in analyzing trivial "ethnoscientific trait lists" (Berreman 1966b:351)? Although a more complete discussion of this domain and its relationship to other important features of the culture of urban nomads is presented elsewhere (Spradley 1970), we may note several important themes which have emerged from this analysis. Tramps define sleeping places in terms of some of the most important concerns in their lives: they experience poverty (1.0); as nomads they must be aware of changing weather conditions (2.0); drinking groups and drunkenness are institutionalized (4.0, 5.0); they experience the rejection and harassment from the dominant society which is common to many minority groups (6.0); many do life sentences on the installment plan as a result of their encounters with the police (7.0); and they survive, in part, by reducing their visibility and thus increasing their security (8.0). The ethnographic approach not only led to the discovery that "making a flop" was one of the most important features of life for tramps, but through an analysis of this domain many other significant aspects of their culture were revealed.

CONCLUSION

This paper presented a study of the adaptive strategies of urban nomads by means of an ethnoscientific analysis of one domain in their culture. This approach, based on a recognition of the multicultural nature of urban life, allowed informants to identify the relevant social units and the criteria for membership in these categories. The methods used were designed to reduce the influence of that form of ethnocentrism which not only prejudges the value of tramp culture but also predefines the categories and meanings of that culture. Native terminological systems were studied in ways which avoided the tendency of informants to act as subcultural interpreters, translating their way of life into terms which are acceptable to members of the dominant culture. It was shown that while tramps share such objects as cars, missions, jails, brick yards, cemeteries, and bathtubs with other urban dwellers, the meaning of such objects varies greatly from one subculture to another. Those who live in cities may share the same locality but they are actually cultural worlds apart. One important part of *urban* anthropology must be the careful ethnographic description of these cultural worlds.

Ethnography is only a beginning and this study raises many questions for further research. How do those living by different subcultures within the city interact in predictable ways, i.e., how do urban societies manage to "organize diversity" (Wallace 1961)? Can the methods of ethno-science enable us to map the equivalence structures of the interaction between tramps and the police, bartenders, or social workers? Would it be possible to correlate certain features of tramp culture, as viewed from the inside, with the categories of behavior which are the focus of the medical and sociological approaches? How is mobility related to al-coholism, homelessness, and criminal behavior? What are the inherent limitations of the ethnographic approach outlined here in studying urban cultures? Ethnoscience and similar approaches to ethnography cannot begin to answer all the questions which must be asked to in-crease our understanding of urban man. They can, however, make us sensitive to the culture-bound nature of human existence, whether as social scientists we are investigating other cultures or as tramps we are looking for a place to flop.

7

Urban Families: Conjugal Roles and Social Networks[1]

Elizabeth Bott

In this paper I should like to report some of the results of an intensive study of twenty London families.[2] The study was exploratory, the aim being to develop hypotheses that would further the sociological and psychological understanding of families rather than to describe facts about a random or representative sample of families. Ideally, research of this sort might best be divided into two phases: a first, exploratory phase in which the aim would be to develop hypotheses by studying the interrelation of various factors within each family considered as a social system, and a second phase consisting of a more extensive inquiry designed to test the hypotheses on a larger scale. In view of the time and resources at our disposal, the present research was restricted to the first phase.

SOURCE: *Human Relations* 8 (1955): 345–84. Reprinted by permission.

[1] A first version of this paper was read at the UNESCO Seminar "Problems of the Family in the Changing Social Order" at Cologne in June 1954. Later versions were read at seminars at the London School of Economics in October 1954, and at Manchester University in November 1954. I am grateful to members of all three seminars, and most particularly to several friends and colleagues, for their painstaking and constructive criticisms. Under the title of "A Study of Ordinary Families," an earlier version of the paper will be included in a forthcoming book of research papers of the International Seminar on Family Research, to be issued by the UNESCO Institute for Social Sciences, Cologne.

[2] This research was sponsored jointly by the Family Welfare Association and the Tavistock Institute of Human Relations; it was financed for three years by the Nuffield Foundation. The core research team consisted of Dr. A. T. M. Wilson (medical psychoanalyst), Miss I. Menzies (psychoanalyst), Dr. J. H. Robb (sociologist), and the author (social anthropologist). Dr. Wilson supervised the project and conducted clinical interviews; Miss Menzies assisted Dr. Wilson in the analysis of the psychological material and supervised many of the home interviews; Dr. Robb and the author carried out the sociological field work, which consisted of home visits and interviews. Mr. H. Phillipson and Mr. J. Boreham of the Tavistock Clinic administered and interpreted Thematic Apperception Tests.

The paper will be confined to one problem: how to interpret the variations that were found to occur in the way husbands and wives performed their conjugal roles. These variations were considerable. At one extreme was a family in which the husband and wife carried out as many tasks as possible separately and independently of each other. There was a strict division of labour in the household, in which she had her tasks and he had his. He gave her a set amount of housekeeping money, and she had little idea of how much he earned or how he spent the money he kept for himself. In their leisure time, he went to football matches with his friends, whereas she visited relatives or went to a cinema with a neighbour. With the exception of festivities with relatives, this husband and wife spent very little of their leisure time together. They did not consider that they were unusual in this respect. On the contrary, they felt that their behaviour was typical of their social circle. At the other extreme was a family in which husband and wife shared as many activities and spent as much time together as possible. They stressed that husband and wife should be equals: all major decisions should be made together, and even in minor household matters they should help one another as much as possible. This norm was carried out in practice. In their division of labour, many tasks were shared or interchangeable. The husband often did the cooking and sometimes the washing and ironing. The wife did the gardening and often the household repairs as well. Much of their leisure time was spent together, and they shared similar interest in politics, music, literature, and in entertaining friends. Like the first couple, this husband and wife felt that their behaviour was typical of their social circle, except that they felt they carried the interchangeability of household tasks a little further than most people.

One may sum up the differences between these two extremes by saying that the first family showed considerable segregation between husband and wife in their role-relationship, whereas in the second family the conjugal role-relationship was as joint as possible. In between these two extremes there were many degrees of variation. These differences in degree of segregation of conjugal roles will form the central theme of this paper.

A *joint conjugal role-relationship* is one in which husband and wife carry out many activities together, with a minimum of task differentiation and separation of interests; in such cases husband and wife not only plan the affairs of the family together, but also exchange many household tasks and spend much of their leisure time together. A *segregated conjugal role-relationship* is one in which husband and wife have a clear differentiation of tasks and a considerable number of separate interests and activities; in such cases, husband and wife have a clearly defined division of labour into male tasks and female tasks; they expect to have different leisure pursuits; the husband has his friends outside the home and the wife has hers. It should be stressed, however, that these are only differences of degree. All families must have some division of labour between husband and wife; all families must have some joint activities.

Early in the research, it seemed likely that these differences in degree of segregation of conjugal roles were related somehow to forces in the social environment of the families. In first attempts to explore these forces, an effort was made to explain such segregation in terms of social class. This attempt was not very successful. The husbands who had the most segregated role-relationships with their wives had manual occupations, and the husbands who had the most joint role-relationships with their wives were professionals, but there were several working-class families that had relatively little segregation and there were several professional families in which segregation was considerable. An attempt was also made to relate degree of segregation to the type of local area in which the family lived, since the data suggested that the families with most segregation lived in homogeneous areas of low population turnover, whereas the families with predominantly joint role-relationships lived in heterogeneous areas of high population turnover. Once again, however, there were several exceptions. But there was a more important difficulty in these attempts to correlate segregation of conjugal roles with class position and type of local area. The research was not designed to produce valid statistical correlations, for which a very different method would have been necessary. Our aim was to make a study of the interrelation of various social and psychological factors within each family considered as a social system. Attempts at rudimentary statistical correlation did not make clear how one factor affected another; it seemed impossible to explain exactly how the criteria for class position or the criteria for different types of local area were actually producing an effect on the internal role structure of the family.

It therefore appeared that attempts to correlate segregation of conjugal roles with factors selected from the generalized social environment of the family would not yield a meaningful interpretation. Leaving social class and neighbourhood composition to one side for the time being, I turned to look more closely at the immediate environment of the families, that is, at their actual external relationships with friends, neighbours, relatives, clubs, shops, places of work, and so forth. This approach proved to be more fruitful.

First, it appeared that the external social relationships of all families assumed the form of a *network* rather than the form of an organized group.[3] In an organized group, the component individuals make up a larger social whole with common aims, interdependent roles, and a distinctive subculture. In network formation, on the other hand, only some but not all of the component individuals have social relationships with one another. For example, supposing that a family, X, maintains relationships with friends, neighbours, and relatives who may be designated as A, B, C, D, E, F . . . N, one will find that some but not all of these external persons know one another. They do not form an organized group in the sense defined above. B might know A and C but none of the others; D might know F without knowing A, B, C, or E. Furthermore, all of these persons will have friends, neighbours, and relatives of their own who are not known by family X. In a network, the component external units do not make up a larger social whole; they are not surrounded by a common boundary.[4]

Secondly, although all the research families belonged to networks rather than to groups, there was considerable variation in the *connectedness* of their networks. By connectedness I mean the extent to which the people known by a family know and meet one another independently of the family. I use the term *dispersed network* to describe a network in which there are few relationships amongst the component units, and the term *highly connected network* to describe a network in which there are many such relationships.[5] The difference is represented very schematically

[3] In sociological and anthropological literature, the term "group" is commonly used in at least two senses. In the first sense it is a very broad term used to describe any collectivity whose members are alike in some way; this definition would include categories, logical classes, and aggregates as well as more cohesive social units. The second usage is much more restricted; in this sense, the units must have some distinctive interdependent social relationships with one another; categories, logical classes, and aggregates are excluded. To avoid confusion I use the term "organized group" when it becomes necessary to distinguish the second usage from the first.

[4] The term "network" is usually employed in a very broad and metaphorical sense, e.g., in Radcliffe-Brown's definition (1940) of social structure as "a complex network of social relations." Although he does not define the term, Moreno (1934) uses it in roughly the sense employed in the present paper. In giving the term a precise and restricted meaning, I follow the usage of John Barnes: "Each person is, at it were, in touch with a number of people, some of whom are directly in touch with each other and some of whom are not . . . I find it convenient to talk of a social field of this kind as a *network*. The image I have is of a set of points some of which are joined by lines. The points of the image are people, or sometimes groups, and the lines indicate which people interact with each other" (1954:43).

[5] Barnes uses the term "mesh" to denote network connectedness. In a network with a small mesh, many of the individuals in X's network know and meet one another independently of X; in a network with a large mesh, few of the individuals in X's network know and meet one another independently of X (1954:44).

in *Figure 1*. Each family has a network containing five external units, but the network of Family X is more connected than that of Y. There are nine relationships amongst the people of X's network whereas there are only three amongst the people of Y's network. X's network is highly connected, Y's is dispersed.

FIGURE 1. SCHEMATIC COMPARISON OF THE NETWORKS OF TWO FAMILIES

Family X:
Highly connected network

Family Y:
Dispersed network

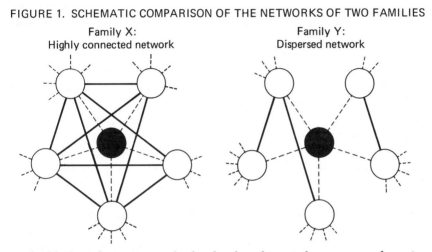

The black circles represent the family, the white circles represent the units of the family's network. The broken lines represent the relationships of the family with the external units; the solid lines represent the relationships of the members of the network with one another. The dotted lines leading off from the white circles indicate that each member of a family's network maintains relationships with other people who are not included in the family's network. This representation is of course highly schematic; a real family would have many more than five external units in its network.

A detailed examination of the research data reveals that the degree of segregation of conjugal roles is related to the degree of network connectedness. Those families that had a high degree of segregation in the role-relationship of husband and wife had a highly connected network; many of their friends, neighbours, and relatives knew one another. Families that had a relatively joint role-relationship between husband and wife had a dispersed network; few of their relatives, neighbours, and friends knew one another. There were many degrees of variation in between these two extremes. On the basis of our data, I should therefore like to put forward the following hypothesis: *The degree of segregation in the role-relationship of husband and wife varies directly with the connectedness of the family's social network.* The more connected the network, the more segregation between the roles of husband and wife. The more dispersed the network, the less segregation between the roles of husband and wife. This relationship between network connectedness and segregation of conjugal roles will be more fully illustrated and discussed below.

No claim is made here that network connectedness is the only factor affecting segregation of conjugal roles. Among the other variables affecting the way conjugal roles are performed, the personalities of husband and wife are of crucial importance. Most of this paper will be devoted to a discussion of the effect of network connectedness, however, because the importance of this variable has been insufficiently stressed in previous studies of family role structure.

It thus appears that if one is to understand segregation of conjugal roles, one should examine the effect of the family's immediate social environment of friends, neighbours, relatives, and institutions. The question remains, however, as to why some families should have highly connected networks whereas others have dispersed networks. In part, network connectedness depends on the family themselves. One family may choose to introduce their friends, neighbours, and relatives to one another, whereas another may not. One family may move around a great deal so that its network becomes dispersed, whereas another family may stay put. But these choices are limited and shaped by a number of forces over which the family does not have direct control. It is at this point that the total social environment becomes relevant. The economic and occupational system, the structure of formal institutions, the ecology of cities, and many other factors affect the connectedness of networks, and limit and shape the decisions that families make. Among others, factors associated with social class and neighbourhood composition affect segregation of conjugal roles, not solely and not primarily through direct action on the internal structure of the family, but indirectly through their effect on its network. Conceptually, the network stands between the family and the total social environment. The connectedness of a family's network depends on the one hand on certain forces in the total environment and on the other hand on the personalities of the members of the family and on the way they react to these forces.

In this paper a first attempt will be made to carry out an analysis in terms of these concepts. Part I will be devoted to a discussion of conjugal role-segregation in relation to network connectedness. In Part II the relation of networks to the total environment will be discussed.

Whether my central hypothesis, the direct relationship between network connectedness and segregation of conjugal roles, is valid for other families I do not know. At this stage I am not attempting to make generalizations about all families, and I am not concerned with whether or not the families we have studied are typical of others. What I am trying to do is to make a comparative study of the relationship between conjugal role-segregation and network connectedness for each of the twenty families considered as a social system. In so doing I have developed a hypothesis that, with further refinement of definition, preferably in quantifiable terms, might be tested on other families and might facilitate further and more systematic comparisons.

PART I. CONJUGAL ROLE-SEGREGATION AND NETWORK CONNECTEDNESS

A. Methods of Collecting Data [6]

Although this paper will be devoted primarily to discussion of the effect of external social relationships on the role-relationship of husband and wife, the research as a whole was designed to investigate families not only sociologically but also psychologically. The research techniques accordingly consisted of a combination of the field-work method of the social anthropologist, in which the group under investigation is studied as a working whole in its natural habitat in so far as this is possible, and the case-study method in which individuals are studied by clinical interviews. No attempt was made to use statistical procedures.

The families studied were "ordinary," in the sense that they did not come to us for help with personal or familial problems, and they were usually able to cope themselves with such difficulties as they had. We sought them out, they did not come to us. In order to simplify the task of comparison, only families with young children were selected; the discussion of conjugal role-segregation and network formation will accordingly be restricted to families in this phase of development. In order further to restrict the number of variables that had to be taken into account, only English families who were Protestant or of mainly Protestant background were selected. All twenty families lived in London or Greater London, but they were scattered all over the area and did not form an organized group. Although the families thus resembled one another in phase of marriage and in national and religious background, they varied considerably in occupation and in socio-economic status; the net incomes of the husbands after tax ranged from £325 to £1,500.

Much difficulty was encountered in contacting suitable families, although the effort to find them taught us a good deal about the way families are related to other social groups. The twenty families were

6 For an account of field techniques, see J. H. Robb (1953).

eventually contacted through the officials of various service institutions, such as doctors, hospitals, schools, local political parties, and the like, and through friends of the family. Introductions were most successful when the contact person was well known and trusted by both husband and wife, and the most satisfactory channel of contact was through friends of the family.

After the contact person had told a prospective family about the research and had got their agreement to an explanatory interview by one of the research staff, one of the field workers visited the family at their home to describe what the research was about and what it would involve for the family. The field worker explained the background of the research, the content of the interviews, and the time they would take. He (or she) made it clear that the family could withdraw at any time, that the material would be treated with professional discretion, and that if we wished to publish any confidential material that might reveal the couple's identity, we should consult them beforehand. The research staff also undertook to pay any expenses that the couple might incur as a result of the investigation. Although the provisional and explanatory nature of the first interview was always emphasized, we found that most of the couples who got as far as this interview had usually decided to take part in the research before they met the field worker, chiefly on the basis of what the contact person had told them. We have no systematic information about couples who were consulted but decided not to participate.

After a family had agreed to take part, the field worker paid several visits to them at home in the evening for joint interviews with the husband and wife. He also went at least once during the day at the weekend when he could meet the children and observe the whole family together. There were thirteen home interviews on the average, the range being from eight to nineteen. Each home interview began with half an hour of casual chatting followed by more focused discussions on particular topics during which notes were taken. The topics were kinship, family background, and personal history until marriage; the first phase of the family from marriage until the birth of the first child; an account of family life at the time of interviewing, including a daily, weekly, and yearly diary, a description of external social relationships with service institutions such as schools, church, clinic doctor, and so forth, with voluntary associations and recreational institutions, and more informal relationships with friends, neighbours, and relatives; an account of the division of labour between husband and wife in overall planning, in the economic support of the family, in domestic tasks, and in child care; and finally, questions were asked about values and ideology concerning family life, social class, money and financial management, and general political, social, and religious questions. These topics were used as a general guide by the field worker; the order of topics and the form of questioning were left to his discretion. Usually he raised a topic, and the couple carried on the discussion themselves with occasional additional questions by the field worker. The discussion frequently wandered away from the assigned topic, but little attempt was made to restrict such digressions, since all the behaviour of husband and wife towards one another and towards the field worker was held to be significant data.

When the home interviews had been completed, the field worker explained the second part of the research, which had been briefly mentioned in the first interview. This consisted of a clinical investigation in which the husband and wife were interviewed at the Tavistock Institute of Human Relations. Fifteen of the twenty families came for clinical interviews. The first such interview consisted of a brief joint meeting of the couple, the field worker, and the psychoanalyst, followed by the individual administration of the Thematic Apperception Tests by two psychologists from the Tavistock Clinic. The husbands and wives then returned separately on future occasions for two or three clinical interviews with the psychoanalyst. The topics covered were health; personal development, and relationships with parents, siblings, and friends; sexual development; the personal relationship between husband and wife, and the effect of the children on the individual and on the family as a whole. Here again the topics were used only as a general guide. The informants were allowed to express their ideas and feelings as freely as possible.

After the clinical interviews were over, the sociological field worker paid a final home visit to bring the investigation to a close. Frequent supplementary visits have been made, however, partly to fill in gaps in the information and partly to work material through with the families prior to publication. All the families know that a book is to be written about them and most of them intend to read it. We plan to publish detailed sociological and psychological accounts of two families; this material has been disguised so that even people who knew the families would have difficulty in recognizing them; in these very detailed, exhaustive accounts, however, it was impossible to work out a disguise so complete that the couple would not reconize themselves, because many of the things that would have had to be altered for such a disguise were essential to the analysis. We have therefore discussed the material with the two families concerned. This process is somewhat upsetting, but the families found it much more acceptable than the prospect of suddenly recognizing themselves laid bare in print without any prior consultation. We took it for granted that the process of digesting an analysis of themselves in sociological and psychological terms would be disturbing, and we accepted the responsibility of helping them with it in so far as they felt the need of assistance. We did not force therapy on them, and we chose families whom we felt could stand the stress with comparative ease. Working the material through with the families was also important for the analysis itself; the reactions of the couples to our interpretations of the facts which they had told us helped us to evaluate and revise our analysis.

In addition to the interviews with the twenty families, discussions about families in general were held with various persons, particularly doctors, who had considerable knowledge of family life. Discussions were also held with various organized groups such as Community Centres and Townswomen's Guilds. These groups had no direct connection with the families we interviewed, and in most cases they were composed of people, usually women, who were considerably older than the research husbands and wives. These discussions were therefore not directly relevant to the analysis of the research families, but they provided useful information on the norms of family life. In a public, group situation, especially one which lasts for only one session, people seem much more willing to talk about norms than to discuss their actual behaviour.

B. Description of the Data

If families are classified according to the extremes of the two dimensions of conjugal role-segregation and network connectedness, four patterns are logically possible: 1. segregated conjugal-role-relationship associated with a highly connected network; 2. segregated conjugal role-relationship associated with a dispersed network; 3. joint conjugal role-relationship associated with a highly connected network; and 4. joint conjugal role-relationship associated with a dispersed network. Empirically, two of these patterns, the second and third, did not occur. There were no families in which a highly segregated conjugal role-relationship was associated with a dispersed network; there were no families in which a joint conjugal role-relationship was associated with a highly connected network.

Six of the research families were clustered in the first and fourth patterns. There was one family that conformed to the first pattern, a high degree of conjugal role-segregation being combined with a highly connected network. There were five families that conformed to the fourth pattern, a joint conjugal role-relationship being associated with a dispersed network. These six families represent the extremes of the research set. There were nine families that were intermediate in degree of conjugal role-segregation and similarly intermediate in degree of network connectedness. Finally, there were five families that appeared to be in a state of transition both with respect to their network formation and with respect to their conjugal role-relationship.

Among the twenty families, there was thus some clustering at certain points along a possible continuum from a highly segregated to a very joint conjugal role-relationship, and along a second continuum from a highly connected to a dispersed network. The families did not fall into sharply separated types, however, so that divisions are somewhat arbitrary, but for convenience of description, I shall divide the families into four groups: 1. highly segregated conjugal role-relationship associated with highly connected network; 2. joint conjugal role-relationship associated with dispersed network; 3. intermediate degrees of conjugal role-segregation and network connectedness; and 4. transitional families. No claim is made here that these are the only patterns that can occur; further research would probably reveal others. In the following discussion I shall be chiefly concerned not with these divisions, but rather with the fact that the order according to degree of conjugal role-segregation follows the order according to degree of network connectedness, and I shall attempt to show the mechanisms by which this relationship operates.

1. *Highly Segregated Conjugal Role-Relationship Associated with Highly Connected Network*

The research set contained only one family of this type.[7] For convenience I shall call them Mr. and Mrs. N. They had been married four years when the interviewing began and had two small children. In the following discussion, I shall describe their actual behaviour, indicating the points at which they depart from their norms.[8]

[7] As stated above, I am not primarily concerned in this paper with whether the research families are typical of others, but it is perhaps of some interest that families with highly connected networks and pronounced conjugal role-segregation are by no means rare, and that they appear to occur primarily in long-established working-class areas. Supplementary data about such families was collected in group discussions. See also Michael Young (1954a, b) and J. H. Robb (1955). In Part II of the present paper I shall discuss some of the factors involved in living in long-established working-class areas, and how these factors affect network connectedness.

[8] Problems concerning norms will be taken up in a subsequent paper. I use the term "norm" to mean those items of behaviour which are felt by the members of a family to be prescribed and/or typical in their social circle. Ideal norms are those prescribed roles of behaviour which it is felt that people ought to follow; norms of expectation are those behaviours which are felt to be typical or usual. In my view, norms are partly internalized through experiences with other people and through reading, listening to the radio, and so forth; in part norms are a construction of the members of the family, who re-interpret and re-order the received norms, within limits, in accordance with their own needs. It follows that families vary considerably in their norms, although families with similar social experiences will tend to have broadly similar norms.

EXTERNAL SOCIAL RELATIONSHIPS. Mr. N. had a semi-skilled manual job at a factory in an East End area adjacent to the one in which he and Mrs. N lived. He said that many other men in the local area had jobs at the same place, or were doing the same sort of work at similar factories and workshops nearby. Mrs. N did not work, but she felt that she was unusual in this respect. Most of the neighbouring women and many of her female relatives had jobs; she did not think there was anything morally wrong with such work, but she said that she had never liked working and preferred to stay at home with the children. Mr. N said that he thought it was best for her and the children if she stayed at home, and added that he felt it was a bit of a reflection on a man if his wife had to go out to work.

The Ns used the services of a local hospital and a maternity and child welfare clinic. They expected to send their children to the local elementary school. They were also in touch with the local housing authority because they were trying to find a new flat. These various service institutions were not felt to have any particular relationship to one another, except in the sense that they were all felt to be foreign bodies, not really part of the local life. Mrs. N was a little bit afraid of them, particularly of the hospital and of doctors. On one occasion, while waiting with her baby and the field worker in an otherwise empty hospital room for a doctor to attend to the baby, she said in a whisper, "My husband says that we pay for it [the hospital services, through National Health subscriptions] and we should use it, but I don't like coming here. I don't like hospitals and doctors, do you?"

To the Ns, the local area was definitely a community in the social sense, a place with an identity of its own and a distinctive way of life. They spoke of it with great pride and contrasted it favourably with other areas. "It has a bad name, they say we are rough, but I think it's the best place there is. Everyone is friendly . . . there is no life in the West End compared with the East End. They drink champagne and we drink beer. When things are la-di-da you feel out of place." They took it for granted that the other inhabitants had similar feelings of local pride and loyalty. Both the Ns had grown up in the same area, as had most of their relatives and friends. Trips outside the area were like adventures into a foreign land, especially for Mrs. N, and very few informal social relationships were kept up with people outside the area. Physical distance was felt to be an almost insuperable barrier to social contact.

Physically, the area was far from ideal as a place to live, for the houses were old-fashioned, inconvenient, and crowded. The Ns were faced with a difficult choice of whether to move out of London to a modern flat on a new housing estate, or to stay put in cramped quarters, in the old familiar local area with their friends and relatives. They knew of several other young couples who were faced with a similar dilemma. Group discussions at a local community centre and the research of the Institute of Community Studies indicated that many local residents feel this to be an important social and personal problem (Young, 1954b).

The Ns felt that their neighbours were socially similar to themselves, meaning that they had the same sort of jobs, the same sort of background, the same sort of outlook on life.[9] Because the Ns had grown up in the area, as had many of their relatives and neighbours, they knew a very considerable number of local people, and many of the people they knew were acquainted with one another. In other words, their social network was highly connected. In fact there was considerable overlap of social roles; instead of there being people in three or four separate categories —friend, neighbour, relative, and colleague—the same person frequently filled two or three or even four of these roles simultaneously.

The Ns took it for granted that Mr. N, like other husbands in their social circle, would have some form of recreation that he carried on with men away from home. In his case it was football, although the most common form of recreation was felt to be drinking and visiting in the local pub, where many husbands spent an evening or two a week with their friends; quite frequently some of these men were friends of old standing, men who had belonged to the same childhood gang, and others were colleagues at work. Mr. N had kept in touch with one or two friends of his childhood; he also played football and went to matches with some of his colleagues at work; he mentioned that several of his friends knew one another. Mrs. N knew a bit about these men, but she did not expect to join in their activities with her husband. She had a nodding acquaintance with the wives of two or three of these men, and occasionally talked to them when she was out shopping.

Mrs. N also had her own separate relationships in which her husband did not expect to join. She knew many of her female neighbours, just as they knew one another; she took it for granted that a friendly relationship with a neighbour would be dropped if the woman moved away. Neighbours saw one another on the landings, in the street, in shops, occasionally over a cup of tea inside the flat or house. They talked over their own affairs and those of other neighbours. Neighbours frequently accused one another of something—of betraying a confidence, of taking the wrong side in a children's quarrel, of failing to return borrowed articles, of gossip. One has little privacy in such a situation. But if one

[9] Unless otherwise noted, the phrase "socially similar" will be used throughout this paper to describe people who are felt by a husband and wife to belong to the same social class as themselves.

wants to reap the rewards of companionship and small acts of mutual aid, one has to conform to local standards, and one has to put up with being included in the gossip. Indeed, being gossiped about is as much a sign that one belongs to the neighbourly network as being gossiped with. If one refuses to have anything to do with one's neighbours one is thought odd, but eventually one will be left alone; no gossip, no companionship.

With the exception of visiting relatives and an occasional Sunday outing with the children, the Ns spent very little of their leisure time in joint recreation with each other; even though they could have got their relatives to mind the children for them, they rarely went out together. In particular, there was no joint entertaining of friends at home. From time to time Mr. N brought a friend home and Mrs. N made tea and talked a bit to the friend; female neighbours often dropped in during the evening to borrow something, but they did not stay long if Mr. N was there. There was no planned joint entertaining in which Mr. and Mrs. N asked another husband and wife to spend an evening with them. Such joint entertaining as existed was carried on with relatives, not with friends. Poverty does not explain the absence of joint entertaining, for the Ns considered themselves to be relatively well off. It did not seem to occur to them that they might spend their surplus money on entertainment of friends; they felt that such money should be spent on furniture, new things for the children, or on large gatherings of relatives at weddings, funerals, and christenings.[10]

There was much visiting and mutual aid between relatives, particularly by the women. The Ns had far more active social relationships with relatives than any other research family, and there was also a great deal of independent contact by their relatives with one another in addition to their contacts with the Ns themselves. In brief, the network of kin was highly connected, more highly connected than those of neighbours or

[10] The absence of the pattern of joint entertainment of friends made our technique of joint interviews with husband and wife somewhat inappropriate for the Ns. Mrs. N was more relaxed and talked much more freely when she and I were alone or when we were together with other women. This was not because of bad relations with her husband; in fact she felt that they had a very successful conjugal relationship and that she was fortunate in having an unusually generous and thoughtful husband. But in spite of this, she could not talk as freely when he was there, and in all probability he had similar feelings. Because of the difficulty in conducting joint interviews, we considered the possibility of interviewing them separately, Mrs. N by the female field worker and Mr. N by the male field worker. But there were two difficulties: first, we wanted to use the same technique with all families so as to simplify the task of comparison, and secondly we felt that separate home as well as clinical interviews would make each partner too suspicious and anxious about what the other was saying.

friends. The women were more active than the men in keeping up contacts with relatives, with the result that the networks of wives were more highly connected than the networks of their husbands. Although husbands were recognized to be less active in kinship affairs than their wives, Mr. N paid occasional visits to his mother, both by himself and with Mrs. N. Furthermore, there were some activities for which joint participation by husband and wife was felt to be desirable. At weddings, funerals, and christenings, there were large assemblages of relatives, and on such occasions it was felt to be important that both husband and wife should attend. Recent and prospective weddings, twenty-first birthday parties, and christenings formed an important topic of discussion throughout the interviews with the Ns.

In a group discussion, a man living in the same local area as the Ns and having a similar sort of family life and kinship network summed up the situation by saying, "Men have friends. Women have relatives." Very succinctly he had described the overlapping of roles mentioned above. For Mrs. N, there was no independent category of "friend"; friends were either neighbours or relatives. She had had a succession of girl friends in her adolescence, but she said that she did not see so much of them since they had all got married and had had children. She always described them as "girl friends," not as "friends." Both Mr. and Mrs. N used the term "friend" as if it applied only to men; the term "neighbour," on the other hand, seemed to refer only to women. Mr. N looked rather shocked when I asked him if he saw much of the neighbours.

Later on in the group discussion, the same man observed, "Women don't have friends. They have Mum." In Mrs. N's case the relationship between herself and her mother was indeed very close. Her mother lived nearby in the same local area, and Mrs. N went to visit her nearly every day, taking her children along with her. She and her mother and her mother's sisters also went to visit Mrs. N's maternal grandmother. Together these women and their children formed an important group, helping one another in household tasks and child care, and providing aid for one another in crises.[11] Within the network of relatives, in other words, there was a nucleus composed of the grandmother, her daughters, and her daughters' daughters; the relationships of these women with one another were sufficiently intense and distinctive to warrant the term "organized group" in the sense defined above. Mrs. N's female relatives provided some of the domestic help and emotional support that, in other research families, a wife expected to get from her husband. Mrs. N felt tremendously attached to her mother emotionally. She felt that a bad relationship between mother and daughter was unnatural, a complete catastro-

[11] See also Michael Young (1954a).

phe. She would, I feel sure, have been deeply shocked by the seemingly cold and objective terms in which many of the women in the other research families analysed their mothers' characters. The close tie with the mother is not only a source of help, however, but may also be a potential source of friction, for if her husband and her mother do not get along well together, a young wife is likely to feel torn by conflicting loyalties. Mrs. N felt that she was particularly fortunate in that her husband and her mother liked each other.

In brief, there was considerable segregation between Mr. and Mrs. N in their external relationships. In effect, Mrs. N had her network and Mr. N had his. The number of joint external relationships was comparatively small. At the same time, there were many links between their networks: the husbands of some of Mrs. N's neighbours were men who were colleagues of Mr. N, some of Mrs. N's relatives also worked at the same place as Mr. N, and in a general way, his family was known to hers even before Mr. and Mrs. N got married. In other words, the connectedness of the combined networks of Mr. and Mrs. N was high compared to that of the families to be discussed below. But the Ns' total network was sharply divided into the husband's network and the wife's network. Furthermore, her network was more highly connected than his: many of the relatives and neighbours with whom she was in contact saw one another independently of her, whereas there were fewer independent links between Mr. N's colleagues, his football associates, and his friends from childhood.

CONJUGAL ROLE-SEGREGATION. The previous description reveals considerable segregation between Mr. and Mrs. N in their external relationships. There was a similar segregation in the way they carried out their internal domestic tasks. They took it for granted that there should be a clear-cut division of labour between them, and that all husbands and wives in their social circle would organize their households in a similar way. One man said in a group discussion: "A lot of men wouldn't mind helping their wives if the curtains were drawn so people couldn't see." Although the Ns felt that major decisions should be made jointly, in the day-to-day running of the household he had his jobs and she had hers. He had control of the money and gave her a housekeeping allowance of £5 a week. Mrs. N did not know how much money he earned, and it did not seem to occur to her that a wife would want or need to know this. Although the Ns said that £5 was the amount most wives were given for housekeeping, Mrs. N had great difficulty in making it cover all the expenses of food, rent, utilities, and five shillings' saving for Christmas. She told

Mr. N whenever she ran short, and he left a pound or two under the clock when he went out the next morning. She said that he was very generous with his money and she felt that she was unusually fortunate in being spared financial quarrels.

Mrs. N was responsible for most of the housework and child care, although Mr. N did household repairs and helped to entertain the children at week-ends. Mrs. N expected that he would do some of the housework if she became ill, but this was usually unnecessary because her mother or her sister or one of her cousins would come to her aid. Indeed, these female relatives helped her a great deal even with the everyday tasks of housework and child care.

ATTITUDES TOWARDS THE ROLE-RELATIONSHIP OF HUSBAND AND WIFE. Mr. and Mrs. N took it for granted that men had male interests and women had female interests and that there were few leisure activities that they would naturally share. In their view, a good husband was one who was generous with the housekeeping allowance, did not waste money on extravagant personal recreation, helped his wife with the housework if she got ill, and took an interest in the children. A good wife was a good manager and an affectionate mother, a woman who kept out of serious rows with neighbours and got along well with her own and her husband's relatives. A good marital relationship was one with a harmonious division of labour, but the Ns placed little stress on the importance of joint activities and shared interests. It is difficult to make any definite statement on the Ns' attitudes towards sexual relations, for they did not come to the Institute for clinical interviews. Judging from Mrs. N's references to such matters when Mr. N was absent, it seems likely that she felt that physical sexuality was an intrusion on a peaceful domestic relationship rather than an expression of such a relationship; it was as if sexuality were felt to be basically violent and disruptive. The findings of clinical workers and of other research workers suggest that among families like the Ns, there is little stress on the importance of physical sexuality for a happy marriage (Slater and Woodside 1951).

2. Families Having a Joint Conjugal Role-Relationship Associated with a Dispersed Network

Among the research set there were five families of this type. All the husbands had professional or semi-professional occupations. Two of the husbands had been upwardly mobile in occupation relative to the occupations of their fathers. All five families, however, had a well-established pattern of external relationships; they might make new relationships, but the basic pattern was likely to remain the same. Similarly, all had worked out a fairly stable division of labour in domestic tasks.

EXTERNAL SOCIAL RELATIONSHIPS. The husbands' occupations had little intrinsic connection with the local areas in which they lived. All five husbands carried on their work at some distance from the area in which their homes were located, although two husbands did some additional work at home. But in no case was there any feeling that the occupation was locally rooted.

Whether or not wives should work was considered to be a very controversial question by these families. Unless they were very well off financially—and none of these five families considered themselves to be so—both husband and wife welcomed the idea of a double income, even though much of the additional money had to be spent on caring for the children. But money was not the only consideration; women also wanted to work for the sake of the work itself. It was felt that if she desired, a woman should have a career or some sort of special interest and skill comparable in seriousness to her husband's occupation; on the other hand, it was felt that young children needed their mother's care and that ideally she should drop her career at least until the youngest child was old enough to go to school. But most careers cannot easily be dropped and picked up again several years later. Two of the wives had solved the problem by continuing to work; they had made careful (and expensive) provision for the care of their children. One wife worked at home. One planned to take up her special interest again as soon as her youngest child went to nursery school, and the fifth wife was already doing so.

These husbands and wives maintained contact with schools, general practitioners, hospitals, and in some cases local maternity and child welfare clinics. Most of them also used the services of a solicitor, an insurance agent, and other similar professional people as required. Unlike the first type of family, they did not feel that service institutions were strange and alien, it did not bother them when they had to go out of their local areas to find such services, and they were usually well informed about service institutions and could exploit them efficiently. They were not afraid of doctors. There was no strict division of labour between husband and wife in dealing with service institutions. The wife usually dealt with those institutions that catered for children, and the husband dealt with the legal and financial ones, but either could take over the other's duties if necessary.

These husbands and wives did not regard the neighbourhood as a source of friends. In most cases husbands and wives had moved around a good deal both before and after marriage, and in no case were they living in the neighbourhood in which they grew up. Four were living in areas of such a kind that only a few of the neighbours were felt to be socially similar to the family themselves. The fifth family was living in a suburb that the husband and wife felt to be composed of people socially similar to one another, but quite different from themselves. In all cases these husbands and wives were polite but somewhat distant to neighbours. In order to have become proper friends, the neighbours would have had to be not only socially similar to the family themselves, but would also have had to share a large number of tastes and interests. Establishing such a relationship takes a long exploratory testing, and the feeling seems to have been that it was dangerous to make the test with neighbours since one ran the risk of being pestered by friendly attentions that one might not want to return. Since many of the neighbours probably had similar feelings, particularly when the neighbourhood was socially heterogeneous, it is not surprising that intimate social relationships were not rapidly established. Since these families had so little social intercourse with their neighbours, they were very much less worried than the first type of family about gossip and conformity to local norms. Indeed, in the circumstances one can hardly say that there were any specifically local norms; certainly there was not the body of shared attitudes and values built up through personal interaction since childhood that was characteristic of the local area inhabited by the Ns.

The children were less discriminating than their parents. Unless restricted by their parents, they played with anyone in the street. This caused some of the parents a certain amount of anxiety, particularly when they felt that the area was very heterogeneous. Other parents adopted the view that mixing with children of other social classes was a good thing. In any case, all parents relied on their own influence and on the education of the children to erase any possibly bad effects of such contact.

It seemed very difficult for these families to find the sort of house and local area in which they wanted to live. They wanted to own a reasonably cheap house with a garden in central London, a house within easy reach of their friends, of plays, concerts, galleries, and so forth. Ideally they wanted a cheap, reliable cleaning-woman-cum-baby-sitter to live nearby, possibly even with the family if they could afford it. Only one family had achieved something approaching this aim. The others were making do with various compromises, impeded by lack of money as well as by the scarcity of suitable houses.

For these families, friends were felt to provide the most important type of external relationship. Not all of each family's friends knew one another; it was not usual for a large number of a family's friends to be in intimate contact with one another independently of their contact with the family. In brief, the network of friends was typically dispersed (unconnected). Husband and wife had usually established friendships over a period of years in many different social contexts—at school, during the course of their professional training, in the Services, at various jobs, very occasionally even because of living in the same neighbourhood. Their friends were scattered all over London, sometimes even all over Britain. Because the network of friends was so dispersed, their social control over the family was dispersed and fragmented. The husband and wife were very sensitive to what their friends thought of them, but since the friends had so little contact with one another, they were not likely to present a unified body of public opinion. Amongst all the different bits of advice they might receive, husband and wife had to make up their own minds about what they should do. They were less persecuted by gossip than the first type of family, but they were also less sustained by it. Their friends did not form a solid body of helpers.

In marked contrast to the Ns, nearly all of the husband's and wife's friends were joint friends; it was felt to be important that both husband and wife should like a family friend, and if a friend was married, then it was hoped that all four partners to the relationship would like one another. Exceptions were tolerated, especially in the case of very old friends, but both husband and wife were uncomfortable if there was real disagreement between them over a friend. Friendship, like marriage, required shared interests and similar tastes, although there was some specialization of interests among different friends. For example, one couple might be golfing friends whereas others might be pub and drinking friends; still others were all-round friends, and it was these who were felt to be the most intimate.

Joint entertainment of friends was a major form of recreation. Even when poverty made invitations to dinner or parties impracticable, friends were still asked over jointly even if only for coffee or tea in the evening. It was considered provincial for husbands to cluster at one end of the room and wives at the other; everyone should be able to talk to everyone else. These husbands and wives usually had enough shared interests to make this possible. Many of them were highly educated, so that they had a common background of general topics, but even those who lacked such education usually make an attempt to talk about matters of general interest.

After these couples had had children, it had become increasingly difficult for them to visit their friends. Since their friends often lived at a considerable distance, and since most of them were also tied down by young children, mutual visiting had become more and more difficult to arrange. Considerable expense and trouble were taken to make such visiting possible. It was obvious that friends were of primary importance to these families.

There were usually other forms of joint recreation besides visiting friends, such as eating in foreign restaurants, going to plays, the cinema, concerts, and so forth. After children were born, there had been a marked drop in external joint recreation in preference for things that could be done at home. Going out had become a special occasion with all the paraphernalia of a baby-sitter and arrangements made in advance.

These five families had far less contact with their relatives than the Ns. Their relatives were not concentrated in the same local area as themselves, and in most cases they were scattered all over the country, and did not keep in close touch with one another. They formed a dispersed network. It was felt that friendly relations should be kept up with parents, and in several cases the birth of the children had led to a sort of reunion with parents. It seems likely that becoming a parent facilitates a resolution of some of the emotional tensions between adult children and their own parents, particularly between women and their mothers. It is possible that in some cases the arrival of children may exacerbate such tensions, but none of these five families had had such an experience. There are of course some obvious practical advantages in increased contact with parents; they are usually very fond of their grandchildren, so that they make affectionate and reliable baby-sitters; if they live close enough to take on this task their services are greatly appreciated.

Among the families with dispersed networks, there was not the tremendous stress on the mother-daughter relationship that was described for Mrs. N, although women were usually rather more active than men in keeping up kinship ties. There were also fewer conflicts of loyalty; it was felt that if conflicts arose between one's parents and one's spouse, one owed one's first loyalty to one's spouse. Unless special interests, particularly financial interests, were operating among relatives, there was no very strong obligation towards relatives outside the parental families of husband and wife. Even towards siblings there was often very little feeling of social obligation. These families were very much less subject to social control by their relatives than the Ns, partly because they saw less of them, but also because the network of kin was dispersed so that its various members were less likely to share the same opinions and values.

In brief, the networks of these families were less highly connected than that of the Ns: many of their friends did not know one another, it was unusual for friends to know relatives, only a few relatives kept in touch with one another, and husband and wife had very little contact with neighbours. Furthermore, there was no sharp segregation between the wife's network and the husband's network. With the exception of a few old friends and some colleagues, husband and wife maintained joint external relationships.

CONJUGAL ROLE-SEGREGATION. As described above, these families had as little segregation as possible in their external relationships. There was a similar tendency towards joint organization in their carrying out of domestic tasks and child care. It was felt that efficient management demanded some division of labour, particularly after the children had been born; there had to be a basic differentiation between the husband's role as primary breadwinner and the wife's role as mother of young children. But in other respects such division of labour as existed was felt to be more a matter of convenience than of inherent differences between the sexes. The division of labour was flexible, and there was considerable helping and interchanging of tasks. Husbands were expected to take a very active part in child care. Financial affairs were managed jointly, and joint consultation was expected on all major decisions.

Husbands were expected to provide much of the help that Mrs. N was able to get from her female relatives. The wives of these families with dispersed networks were carrying a tremendous load of housework and child care, but they expected to carry it for a shorter time than Mrs. N. Relatives sometimes helped these wives, but only occasionally; they usually lived at some distance so that it was difficult for them to provide continuous assistance. Cleaning women were employed by four families and a children's nurse by one; all families would have hired more domestic help if they could have afforded it. In spite of their affection for their children, all five couples were looking forward to the time when their children were older and the burden of work would decrease. In so far as they could look so far ahead into the future, they did not expect to provide continuous assistance to their own married children.

It seems likely that in the cases of Mrs. N and other wives with highly connected networks, the burden of housework and child care is more evenly distributed throughout the lifetime of the wife; when she is a girl she helps her mother with the younger children; when she herself has children, her mother and other female relatives help her; when she is a grandmother she helps her daughters.

ATTITUDES TOWARDS THE ROLE-RELATIONSHIP OF HUSBAND AND WIFE. Among the families with dispersed networks, there were frequent discussions of whether there really were any psychological or temperamental differences between the sexes. These differences were not simply taken for granted as they were by the Ns. In some cases, so much stress was placed on shared interests and sexual equality (which was sometimes confused with identity, the notion of equality of complementary opposites being apparently a difficult idea to maintain consistently) that one sometimes felt that the possibility of the existence of social and temperamental differences between the sexes was being denied. In other cases, temperamental differences between the sexes were exaggerated to a point that belied the couple's actual joint activities and the whole pattern of shared interests that they felt to be so fundamental to their way of life. Quite frequently the same couple would minimize differences between the sexes on one occasion and exaggerate them on another. Sometimes these discussions about sexual differences were very serious; sometimes they were witty and facetious; but they were never neutral— they were felt to be an important problem. Such discussions may be interpreted as an attempt to air and to resolve the contradiction between the necessity for joint organization with its ethic of equality on the one hand, and the necessity for differentiation and recognition of sexual differences on the other. "After all," as one husband said, to conclude the discussion, *"vive la différence,* or where would we all be?"

It was felt that, in a good marriage, husband and wife should achieve a high degree of compatibility, based on their own particular combination of shared interests and complementary differences. Their relationship with each other should be more important than any separate relationship with outsiders. The conjugal relationship should be kept private, and revelations to outsiders, or letting down one's spouse in public, were felt to be serious offences. A successful sexual relationship was felt by these couples to be very important for a happy marriage; it was as if successful sexual relations were felt to prove that all was well with the joint relationship, whereas unsatisfactory relations were indicative of a failure in the total relationship. In some cases one almost got the feeling that these husbands and wives felt a moral obligation to enjoy sexual relations, a feeling not expressed or suggested by the Ns.

The wives of these families seemed to feel that their position was rather difficult. They had certainly wanted children, and in all five cases they were getting a great deal of satisfaction from their maternal role. But at the same time, they felt tied down by their children and they did not like the inevitable drudgery associated with child care. Some were more affected than others, but most of them complained of isolation, boredom, and fatigue. "You must excuse me if I sound half-witted. I've been talking to the children all day," was a not uncommon remark. These women wanted a career or some special interest that would make them feel that they were something more than children's nurses and house-maids. They wanted more joint entertainment with their husbands, and more contact with friends. These complaints were not levelled spe-cifically at their husbands—indeed in most cases they felt that their husbands were doing their best to make the situation easier—but against the social situation in which they found themselves and at the difficulty of satisfying contradictory desires at the same time. One wife summed it up by saying, "Society seems to be against married women. I don't know, it's all very difficult."

It may be felt that the problem could be solved if such a family moved to an area that was felt to be homogeneous and composed of people similar to themselves, for then the wife might be able to find friends among her neighbours and would feel less isolated and bored. It is diffi-cult to imagine, however, that these families could feel that any local area, however homogeneous by objective criteria, could be full of poten-tial friends, for their experience of moving about in the past and their varied social contacts make them very discriminating in their choice of friends. Further, their dislike of having their privacy broken into by neighbours is very deeply rooted; it diminishes after the children start playing with children in the neighbourhood, but it never disappears entirely.

3. Intermediate Degrees of Conjugal Role-Segregation and Network Connectedness

There were nine families of this type in the research set. There was con-siderable variety of occupation amongst them. Four husbands had pro-fessional or semi-professional occupations very similar to the occupations of the second type of family described above. It was in recognition of the fact that these four families were similar in occupation but different in conjugal role-segregation from the second set of families that I con-cluded that conjugal role-segregation could not be attributed to occupa-tional level alone. Of the five remaining husbands, one was a clerical worker, three had manual occupations similar in general level to that of Mr. N, and one changed from a highly skilled manual job to an office job after the interviewing was completed.

There was considerable variation among these nine families in con-jugal role-segregation. Some tended to have a fairly marked degree of segregation, approaching that of the Ns described above, whereas others were closer to the second set of families in having a relatively joint role-relationship. These variations in degree of segrega-tion of conjugal roles within the nine intermediate families did not follow exactly the order according to occupational level. If the occupations of the husbands are arranged in order from the most joint to the most segregated conjugal role-relationship, the order is as follows: manual worker, professional, professional, clerical worker, professional, manual worker, professional, manual worker, manual worker. The variations in degree of segregation follow more closely the variations in degree of network connectedness. The families with the most dispersed networks had the most joint role-relationships, and the families with the most connected networks had the most conjugal role-segregation. The families with the most dispersed networks were those who had moved around a great deal so that they had established relationships with many people who did not know one another.

For brevity of description, I shall treat these nine intermediate families collectively, but it should be remembered that there were variations in degree amongst them, and that both network connectedness and conjugal role-segregation form continua so that it is somewhat arbitrary to divide families into separate types.

EXTERNAL SOCIAL RELATIONSHIPS.   The data suggest two possible reasons for the intermediate degree in the connectedness of the networks of these families. First, most of them had been brought up in families whose networks had been less connected than that of the Ns but more connected than that of the second set of families. Furthermore, with one exception these couples had moved around less than the second type of family both before and after marriage, so that more of their friends knew one another; several of these families had had considerable continuity of relationships since childhood, and they had not developed the pattern of ignoring neighbours and relying chiefly on friends and colleagues that was described as typical of families with very dispersed networks.

Secondly, these families were living in areas where they felt that many of the neighbours were socially similar to themselves. In four cases these were "suburban" areas; in five cases they were mixed working-class areas in which the inhabitants were felt to be similar to one another in general occupational level although they worked at different jobs. Five families were living in or near the area where one or both of the partners had lived since childhood. In two of the remaining four cases, the area was similar to the one in which husband and wife had been brought up. In two cases, the present area differed considerably from the childhood area of one or other partner, but the couple had acclimatzed themselves to the new situation.

If the husband and wife were living in the area in which they had been brought up, each was able to keep up some of the relationships that had been formed before their marriage. This was also true of the Ns. The intermediate families differed from the Ns chiefly in that their jobs, and in some cases their education, had led them to make relationships with people who were not neighbours. Many neighbours were friends, but not all friends were neighbours. Even in the case of families in which one or both partners had moved to the area after marriage, each partner was able to form friendly relationships with at least some of the neighbours, who were in most cases felt to be socially similar to the couple themselves. Husband and wife were able to form independent, segregated relationships with neighbours. In particular, many of the wives spent a good deal of their leisure time during the day with neighbouring women. Husband and wife also joined local clubs, most of these clubs being unisexual. (Voluntary associations appear to thrive best in areas where people are similar in social status but do not know one another well; the common activity gives people an opportunity to get to know one another better.)

In local areas inhabited by the intermediate families, many of the neighbours knew one another. There was not the very great familiarity built up over a long period of continuous residence such as was described for the area inhabited by the Ns, but there was not the standoffishness described as typical of the families with very dispersed networks. The intermediate families had networks of neighbours that were midway in degree of connectedness, and the husbands and wives were midway in sensitivity to the opinions of neighbours—more susceptible than the second set of families, but better able to maintain their privacy than the Ns.

Husbands and wives had some segregated relationships with neighbours, but they could also make joint relationships with them if all four partners to the relationship liked one another. Some relationships were usually kept up with friends who had been made outside the area. Couples usually tried to arrange joint visits with these friends. These friends usually did not become intimate with the neighbours, however, so that the network remained fairly dispersed.

Relations with relatives were much like those described above for the second set of families. But if the relatives were living in the same local area as the family, there was considerable visiting and exchange of services, and if the relatives lived close to one another, the kinship network was fairly well connected.

The networks of these families were thus less highly connected than that of the Ns, but more highly connected than that of the second set of families. There was some overlapping of roles. Neighbours were sometimes friends; some relatives were both neighbours and friends. The overlapping was not as complete as it was with the Ns, but there was not the complete division into separate categories—friend, neighbour, relative—that was characteristic of the second set of famlies. The networks of husband and wife were less segregated than those of the Ns, but more segregated than those of the second set of families.

CONJUGAL ROLE-SEGREGATION. In external relationships, husband and wife thus had some joint relationships, particularly with relatives and with friends, and some segregated relationships, particularly with neighbours and local clubs.

In carrying out household tasks and child care, there was a fairly well-defined division of labour, a little more clearly marked than in the second type of family, more flexible than in the case of the Ns. Husbands helped, but there was a greater expectation of help from neighbours and relatives (if they lived close enough) than among the second set of families.

ATTITUDES TOWARDS THE ROLE-RELATIONSHIP OF HUSBAND AND WIFE. Although there were variations of degree, considerable stress was placed on the importance of shared interests and joint activities for a happy marriage. In general, the greater the stress that was placed on joint organization and shared interests, the greater was the importance attached to sexual relations. Like the families with dispersed networks, the intermediate families stressed the necessity for conjugal privacy and the precedence of the conjugal relationship over all external relationships, but there was a greater tolerance of social and temperamental differences between the sexes, and there was an easier acceptance of segregation in the activities of husband and wife. Wives often wanted some special interest of their own other than housework and children, but they were able to find activities such as attending evening classes or local clubs that could be carried on without interfering with their housework and child care. And because, in most cases, they felt that at least some of the neighbouring women were similar to themselves, they found it relatively easy to make friends among them, and they had people to talk to during the day. They complained less frequently of isolation and boredom than did the wives in families with very dispersed networks.

4. Transitional Families

There were five families in varying stages of transition from one type of network to another. Two phases of transition can be distinguished among these five families. (a) Families who were in the process of deciding to move from one local area to another, a decision that was requiring considerable restructuring of their networks, and (b) somewhat "de-socialized" families (Curle and Trist 1947), that is, families who had radically changed their pattern of external relationships and had not yet got used to their new situation. There were other families who had gone through the process of transition and had more or less settled down to the pattern typical of families with dispersed or intermediate networks.

(a) FAMILIES IN THE PROCESS OF DECIDING TO MOVE. There were two such families. Both had relatively highly connected networks, and both had been socially mobile and were contemplating moving to suburban areas, which would be more compatible with their new social status. In both cases this meant cutting off old social ties with relatives and neighbours and building up new ones. One couple seemed to feel too bound to the old network to make the break; they also said they did not want to lower their current standard of living by spending a lot of money on a house. The second family moved after the interviewing was completed, and a brief visit suggested that they would in time build up the intermediate type of network and conjugal role-segregation.

(b) SOMEWHAT DE-SOCIALIZED FAMILIES. There were three families of this type. All three had been brought up in highly connected networks similar to that described for the Ns, and all had moved away from their old areas and the people of their networks. For such a family, any move outside the area is a drastic step. This contrasts with the intermediate families who are not too upset by moving, provided that they move to an area of people who are felt to be socially similar to themselves.

One family had been very mobile occupationally, although they had moved primarily because of the requirements of the husband's occupation rather than to find a neighbourhood compatible with their achieved status. They were living in relative isolation, with very few friends, almost no contacts with neighbours, and very little contact with relatives, most of whom were living at a considerable distance. They seemed to be a bit stunned by the change in their immediate environment. They had some segregated interests, but they felt that joint organization and shared interests were the best basis of a conjugal relationship.

The other two families were working-class and had not been occupationally mobile. These two families were particularly important to the conceptual analysis of conjugal role-segregation, for although they were similar to the Ns in occupational level and in general cultural background, their conjugal role-relationship was more joint. It was their relatively dispersed networks that distinguished them from the Ns.

These two families had moved to a different local area because they could not find suitable accommodation in their old neighbourhoods. They also wanted the amenities of a modern flat, and since their parents had died and many of their relatives had moved away, they felt that their main ties to the old local area were gone. Both these couples seemed to feel that they were strangers in a land full of people who were all strangers to one another, and at first they did not know how to cope with the situation. They did not react to their new situation in exactly the same way. In both cases, husband and wife had turned to one another for help, especially at first, but for various personal reasons, one husband and wife were making a concerted effort to develop joint activities and shared interests, whereas the other couple did not take to the idea of a joint role-relationship with any enthusiasm.

In the first case, husband and wife tried to develop more joint relationships with friends, but this was difficult for them because they had had so little practice; they did not know the culture of a joint role-relationship, and their new acquaintances were in a similar predicament so that they got little external support for their efforts. The husband tried to get his wife to join in his club activities, but the structure of the club was such that her activities remained somewhat segregated from his. The husband helped his wife extensively with household tasks and child care, although he continued to plan the family finances. In the second case, the husband busied himself with his work and friends and spent a great deal of time on various committees with other men; his wife was becoming isolated and withdrawn into the home. They had more joint organization of domestic tasks than they had had before; she urged him to help her because her female relatives lived too far away to be of much assistance.

In both cases, however, nothing could really take the place of the old networks built up from childhood, and both couples felt a good deal of personal dissatisfaction. The husbands were perhaps less drastically affected, since they continued to work at their old jobs and their relationships with colleagues gave them considerable continuity. Both husband and wife often blamed their physical surroundings for their malaise, and they idealized their old local areas. They remembered only the friendliness and forgot the physical inconvenience and the unpleasant part of the gossip. On the whole, although one family had carried the process further than the other, both seemed to be developing a more joint division of labour than that which they had had before, and it seemed likely that they would eventually settle down in some intermediate form of network connectedness and conjugal role-segregation.

The research set did not contain any families who had moved in the other direction, that is, from a dispersed to a more connected network. But personal knowledge of families who had been accustomed to a dispersed network and were having to come to grips with a fairly highly connected one suggests that this type of change is also felt to be somewhat unpleasant. The privacy of husband and wife is encroached upon, and each is expected to take part in segregated activities, a state of affairs that they regard as provincial. These families could have refused to enter into the local network of social relationships, but in most cases they felt that the husband's career required it.

C. The Nature of the Relationship Between Conjugal Role-Segregation and Network Connectedness

The data having been described, the nature of the relationship between conjugal role-segregation and network connectedness may now be examined in more detail.

Connected networks are most likely to develop when husband and wife, together with their friends, neighbours, and relatives, have all grown up in the same local area and have continued to live there after marriage. Husband and wife come to the marriage each with his own highly connected network. It is very likely that there will be some overlap of their networks; judging by the Ns' account of their genealogy, one of the common ways for husband and wife to meet each other is to be introduced by a person who is simultaneously a friend of one and a relative of the other .

Each partner makes a considerable emotional investment in relationships with the people in his network; each is engaged in reciprocal exchanges of material and emotional support with them; each is very sensitive to their opinions and values, not only because the relationships are intimate, but also because the people in his network know one another and share the same values so that they are able to apply consistent informal sanctions to one another.

The marriage is superimposed on these pre-existing relationships. As long as the couple continue to live in the same area, and as long as their friends, neighbours, and relatives also continue to live within easy reach of the family and of one another, the segregated networks of husband and wife can be carried on after marriage. Some rearrangement is necessary; the husband is likely to stop seeing some of the friends of his youth, particularly those who work at a different place and go to different pubs and clubs; after children are born, the wife is likely to see less of her former girl friends and more of her mother and other female relatives. But apart from these readjustments, husband and wife can carry on their old external relationships, and they continue to be very sensitive to external social controls. In spite of the conjugal segregation in external relationships, the overlapping of the networks of husband and wife tends to ensure that each partner finds out about the other's activities. Although a wife may not know directly what a husband does with his friends away from home, one of the other men is likely to tell his wife or some other female relative who eventually passes the information on, either directly or through other women, to the wife of the man in question. Similarly any defection on the part of the wife is likely to be made known to her husband.

Because old relationships can be continued after marriage, both husband and wife can satisfy some of their personal needs outside the marriage, so that their emotional investment in the conjugal relationship need not be as intense as in other types of family. Both husband and wife, but particularly the wife, can get outside help with domestic tasks and with child care. A rigid division of labour between husband and wife is therefore possible, since each can get outside help. In other words, the segregation in external relationships can be carried over to activities within the family.

Networks become dispersed when people move around from one place to another, or when they make new relationships that have no connection with their old ones. If both husband and wife have moved around a good deal before marriage, each will bring an already dispersed network to the marriage; many of the husband's friends will not know one another; many of the wife's friends will not know one another. After the marriage they will meet new people as well as some of the old ones, and these people will not necessarily know one another. In other words, their external relationships are relatively discontinuous both in space and in time. Such continuity as they possess lies in their relationship with each other rather than in their external relationships. In facing the external world, they draw on each other, for their strongest emotional investment is made where there is continuity. Hence their high standards of conjugal compatibility, their stress on shared interests, on joint organization, on equality between husband and wife. They must get along well together, they must help one another as much as possible in carrying out familial tasks, for there is no sure external source of material and emotional help. Since their friends and relatives are physically scattered and few of them know one another, the husband and wife are not stringently controlled by a solid body of public opinion, but they are also unable to rely on consistent external support. Through their joint external relationships they present a united front to the world and they reaffirm their joint relationship with each other. No external person must seriously menace the conjugal relationship; joint relationships with friends give both husband and wife a source of emotional satisfaction outside the family without threatening their own relationship with each other.

In between these two extremes are the intermediate and transitional families. In the intermediate type, husband and wife have moved around a certain amount so that they seek continuity with each other and make their strongest emotional investment in the conjugal relationship. At the same time, they are able to make some segregated relationships outside the family and they are able to rely on considerable casual help from people outside the family, so that a fairly clearly defined division of labour into male tasks and female tasks can be made.

The transitional families illustrate some of the factors involved in changing from one type of network to another. Husbands and wives who change from a connected to a dispersed network find themselves suddenly thrust into a more joint relationship without the experience or the attitudes appropriate to it. The eventual outcome depends partly on the family and partly on the extent to which their new neighbours build up relationships with one another. An intermediate form of network connectedness seems to be the most likely outcome. Similarly, in the case of families who change from a dispersed to a more highly connected network, their first reaction is one of mild indignation at losing their privacy, but in time it seems likely that they will tend to develop an intermediate degree of network connectedness and conjugal role-segregation.

PART II. NETWORKS IN RELATION TO THE TOTAL ENVIRONMENT

Having discussed the relation of the family to its network, I should like now to consider the factors affecting the form of the network itself. First the general features characteristic of all familial networks in an urban industrialized society will be examined, then I shall turn to consider some of the factors affecting variations from one urban familial network to another.

A. Factors Affecting the General Features of Urban Familial Networks

As described above, all the research families maintained relationships with external people and institutions—with a place of work, with service institutions such as schools, church, doctor, clinic, shops and so forth, with voluntary associations such as clubs, evening classes, and recreational institutions; they also maintained more informal relationships with colleagues, friends, neighbours, and relatives. It is therefore incorrect to describe urban families as "isolated"; indeed, no urban family could survive without its network of external relationships.

It is correct, however, to say that urban families are not contained within organized groups, for although they have many external relationships, the institutions and persons with which they are related are not linked up with one another to form an organized group. Furthermore, although individual members of a family frequently belong to groups, the family as a whole does not. There are marginal cases, such as the situation arising when all the members of the family belong to the same church or go to the same general practitioner, but in these cases the external institution or person controls only one aspect of the family's life, and can hardly be said to "contain" the family in all its aspects.

In the literature on family sociology, there are frequent references to "the family in the community," with the implication that the community is an organized group within which the family is contained. Our data suggest that the usage is misleading. Of course every family must live in some sort of local area, but very few urban local areas can be called communities in the sense that they form cohesive social groups. The immediate social environment of urban families is best considered not as the local area in which they live, but rather as the network of actual social relationships they maintain, regardless of whether these are confined to the local area or run beyond its boundaries.

Small-scale, more isolated, relatively "closed" local groups provide a marked contrast. This type of community is frequently encountered in primitive societies, as well as in certain rural areas of industrialized societies. A family in such a local group knows no privacy; everyone knows everyone else. The situation of the urban family with a highly connected network is carried one step further in the relatively closed local group. The networks of the component families are so highly connected and the relationships within the local group are so clearly marked off from external relationships that the local population can properly be called an organized group. Families are encapsulated within this group; their activities are known to all, they cannot escape from the informal sanctions of gossip and public opinion, their external affairs are governed by the group to which they belong.

In many small-scale primitive societies, the elementary family is encapsulated not only within a local group, but also within a corporate kin group. In such cases, the conjugal role-segregation between husband and wife becomes even more marked than that described above for urban families with highly connected networks. Marriage becomes a linking of kin groups rather than preponderantly a union between individuals acting on their own initiative.

These differences between the immediate social environment of families in urban industrialized societies and that of families in some small-scale primitive and rural communities exist, ultimately, because of differences in the total economic and social structure. The division of labour in a small-scale society is relatively simple; the division of labour in an industrial society is exceedingly complex. In a small-scale, relatively closed society, most of the services required by a family can be provided by the other families in the local group and in the kin group. In an urban industrialized society, such tasks and services are divided up and assigned to specialized institutions. Whereas a family in a small-scale, relatively closed society belongs to a small number of groups each with many functions, an urban family exists in a network of many separate, unconnected institutions, each with a specialized function. In a small-scale, relatively closed society the local group and the kin group mediate between the family and the total society; in an urban industrialized society there is no single encapsulating group or institution that mediates between the family and the total society.

One of the results of this difference in the form of external relationships is that urban families have more freedom to govern their own affairs. In a small-scale, relatively closed society, the encapsulating groups have a great deal of control over the family. In an urban industrialized society, the doctor looks after the health of individual members of the family, the clinic looks after the health of the mother and child, the school educates children, the boss cares about the individual as an employee rather than as a husband, and even friends, neighbours, and relatives may disagree amongst themselves as to how the affairs of the family should be conducted. In brief, social control of the family is split up amongst so many agencies that no one of them has continuous, complete governing power, and within broad limits, a family can make its own decisions and regulate its own affairs.

The situation may be summed up by saying that urban families are *more highly individuated* than families in relatively closed communities. I feel that this term describes the situation of urban families more accurately than the more commonly used term "isolated." By "individuation" I mean that the elementary family is separated off, differentiated out as a distinct, and to some extent autonomous, social group. Of course, in most societies the elementary family is individuated to some extent; one could not say that it existed as a distinct group if it were not. The difference in individuation between an urban family and a family in a relatively closed community is one of degree. It should be remembered, however, that urban families differ among themselves in degree of individuation; families with highly connected networks are less individuated than those with dispersed networks.

The individuation of urban families provides one source of variation in role performance. Because families are not encapsulated within governing and controlling groups, other than the nation as a whole, husband and wife are able, within broad limits, to perform their roles in accordance with their own personal needs. These broad limits are laid down by the ideal norms of the nation as a whole, many of which exist as laws and are enforced by the courts. But informal social control by relatives and neighbours is much less stringent and less consistent than in many small-scale societies, and much variation is possible.

B. Factors Affecting Variation in Urban Families' Networks

Although the immediate social environments of all urban families resemble one another in assuming network form, there are important differences from one urban family's network to another. As has been demonstrated in Part I above, these differences lie in the degree of connectedness of families' networks. Such differences are most clearly marked in the area of informal relationships, that is, in relationships with friends, neighbours, and relatives. These relationships are felt to be of much greater personal and emotional importance than the more specialized and formal relationships that are maintained with doctors, clinics, schools, and so forth, and they are usually maintained with people who are felt to be socially similar to the family themselves.

In the introduction to this paper it was suggested that network connectedness is a function on the one hand of certain forces in the total environment and on the other hand of the family themselves. It now becomes appropriate to discuss this statement in greater detail.

The highly developed division of labour in an industrial society produces not only complexity but also variability. Sometimes conditions are created that favour the development of relatively highly connected networks, sometimes conditions are created that favour relatively dispersed networks. To examine these conditions in detail would take the discussion far away from families and their networks into a study of the ecology of cities and the economic structure of industries and occupations, a task obviously beyond the scope of this paper. I should like, however, to suggest tentatively several factors that appear likely to affect network connectedness.

(1) *Economic Ties among the Members of the Network*

Economic ties operate more forcibly between relatives than between friends and neighbours, but there is a wide range of variation in the operation of such cohesive forces even among relatives. The connectedness of the kinship network is enhanced if relatives hold property rights in common enterprises, or if they expect to inherit property from one another.

The connectedness of kinship networks is also enhanced if relatives can help one another to get jobs. Only certain types of occupation allow such help; in occupations requiring examinations or other objective selection procedures—and most professional and semi-professional occupations fall into this category—relatives cannot give one another much help in this respect, whereas in some less skilled occupations and in certain businesses, particularly family businesses, relatives are able to help one another more directly.

The important point here is that neither the occupational system nor the distribution of property is uniform. Different families are affected in different ways. This means that although families' networks in general and their kinship networks in particular do not play a very large part in the economic and occupational structure, there is a great deal of variation in the way in which economic forces affect families' networks.

(2) *Type of Neighbourhood*

Type of neighbourhood is important not so much in and of itself, but because it is one of the factors affecting the "localization" of networks. If a family's network is localized, that is, if most of the members live in the same local area so that they are accessible to one another, they are more likely to know one another than if they are scattered all over the country.

Since the members of the informal network are usually felt by the family to have the same social status as themselves, localized networks are most likely to develop in areas where the local inhabitants feel that they are socially similar to one another, that they belong to the same social class, whatever their definition of class may be. Such feelings of social similiarity appear to be strongest in the long-established working-class areas in which there is a dominant local industry or a small number of traditional occupations. As described above, the Ns, the family with the most highly connected network, were living in such an area. It was also an area of low population turnover, at least until the recent war. Formerly people were born, brought up, and died there. Highly connected networks could develop not only because the local area was homogeneous but also because people stayed put. Now, as some of the inhabitants move away, the networks of even those people who remain in the area are becoming more dispersed.

There were no comparable homogeneous neighbourhoods of people belonging to one of the full professions.[12] Neighbourhoods were found, however, in which the inhabitants were relatively homogeneous with regard to income, although they had different occupations. The type and cost of the dwelling was probably an important factor contributing to this type of homogeneity. Such neighbourhoods were found in suburbs; they were also found in certain mixed working-class areas in which there was no dominant local industry. Most of the families with intermediate and transitional networks were living in such areas; one family with a dispersed network was living in such an area, but they ignored their neighbours, whom they felt were socially similar to one another but not to themselves. Finally, there were some areas that were extremely heterogeneous with regard to occupational level, income, educational background of the inhabitants, and so forth; most of the families with very dispersed networks were living in such areas.

In a very complex way, neighbourhood composition is related to occupation and social class. It is possible to have fairly homogeneous areas of, say, dockworkers or furniture workers, although not all manual occupations are heavily localized, but the structure of professions is such that it would be most unusual to find a homogeneous area of, say, doctors or lawyers or chartered accountants. On the basis of our data on families, no attempt can be made to analyse the many factors contributing to the formulation of local neighbourhoods. The most one can say is that the industrial and occupational system is so complex that it gives rise to many different types of urban neighbourhood. Some are more homogeneous and stable than others. If one were making a detailed study of network connectedness in relation to neighbourhood composition, it would be necessary to work out detailed criteria of homogeneity so that neighbourhoods could be systematically compared; one could then study

12 University towns are perhaps the closest approximation to a homogeneous area of a single profession. Study of networks and conjugal role-segregation in such areas should be of considerable interest, for certain factors in the situation would be likely to foster a high degree of network connectedness whereas others would discourage it. A homogeneous local area, if perceived as such by the local inhabitants, encourages a high degree of network connectedness. The sexual segregation in the social structure of the colleges may also tend to increase connectedness among men and to reinforce segregation between husband and wife. But most professional men move around during their education and early occupational training, and have professional contacts with people outside their local area, which would discourage network connectedness. As described below, continuity of residence by all members of the network is also an important factor; it seems likely that the population turnover of university towns is relatively high, and that there are few families in which husband and wife are born, brought up, and die in the same university town. Such lack of continuity would tend to prevent a high degree of connectedness.

the relation of different degrees and types of objective homogeneity to the attitudes of local inhabitants towards one another; one could also compare the formation of the networks of families in different types of area. My guess would be that one would not find families with highly connected networks in heterogeneous areas of high population turnover, but that one might find both families with highly connected networks and families with dispersed networks in relatively homogeneous, stable areas.

It is most unlikely that one would be able to predict degree of network connectedness from knowledge of the local area alone. Too many other factors are involved—type of occupation, where the husband works, how long the family has lived in the area, perception of the area, and so forth. The family's perception of the people in the area is particularly important. Objective measures of social homogeneity give only a rough indication of how families will feel about their neighbours. Furthermore, it is always necessary to remember that a neighbourhood does not simply impose itself on a family. Within certain limits families can choose where they will live, and even if they feel that their neighbours are similar to themselves they are not compelled to be friendly with them; other criteria besides felt social similarity enter into the selection of friends.

(3) *Opportunities to Make Relationships outside the Local Area*

Networks are more likely to be highly connected if members do not have many opportunities to form new relationships with persons unknown to the other members of the network. Thus, in the case of the family with a highly connected network described above, the husband's work, the relatives of husband and wife, and their friends were all concentrated in the local area. There are no strong sanctions preventing such families from making relationships with outsiders, but there is no unavoidable circumstance that forces them to do so. In the case of the professional families in the research set, their education and professional training had led them to make many relationships with colleagues and friends who did not know one another. Even if such families keep on living in the same area throughout their lives, which is unusual though possible, the husband's pursuit of an occupational career leads him to make relationships with people who do not belong to the family's neighbourhood network, so that the network tends to become dispersed.

In brief, network connectedness does depend, in part, on the husband's occupation. If he practises an occupation in which his colleagues are also his neighbours, his network will tend to be localized and his connectedness will tend to be high. If he practises an occupation in which his colleagues are not his neighbours, his network will tend to become dispersed. One cannot predict this solely from knowledge of occupational level. Most professional occupations require a man to get his training and do work in different areas from the one he lives in. Some manual occupations require or permit this too; others do not.

(4) *Physical and Social Mobility*

Network connectedness depends on the stability and continuity of the relationships; a family's network will become more dispersed if either the family or the other members of the network move away physically or socially so that contact is decreased and new relationships are established.

Among the research set, there were clear indications that networks became more dispersed when physical mobility had been great. When the number of local areas lived in by both husband and wife before and after marriage is added up, the averages according to network formation are as follows: Families with dispersed networks, 19; families with intermediate networks, 8.2; families with transitional networks, 9.6, and the Ns, the family with the most highly connected network, 2. (In all cases, Service career was counted as one "area.")

Many factors affect physical mobility. Here again the occupational system is a relevant factor. Some occupations permit or encourage social and physical mobility so that networks become dispersed; other occupations encourage stability of residence and social relationships. Social mobility is often accompanied by physical mobility. In the research set, seven families had been occupationally mobile and three had moved or were contemplating moving to an area appropriate to their achieved status. The other four had moved too, but not primarily for status reasons. In general, the networks of socially mobile families tend to become less connected not only because they move physically but also because they are likely to drop old social ties and form new ones. Among the mobile families of the research set, most of the rearranging had been done in adolescence and in the early years of the marriage, and it involved chiefly friends and distant relatives. However mobile the family, husband and wife felt an obligation to maintain contact with their parents; occupational and social achievements were usually felt to be a positive accomplishment for parents as well as for the husband and wife themselves.

Occupation may affect physical mobility even when there is no social mobility. Among the research families many of the professional couples had moved frequently from one local area to another and even from one city to another, and they tended to treat the requirements of the husband's career as the most important factor in deciding whether to move or not; this applied as much to families who were not socially mobile as to those who were. The manual and clerical workers were less likely to give the demands of the husband's career as a chief reason for moving, and only one such family had moved very frequently. The relations between occupation and physical and social mobility are obviously very complex. The important fact is that the occupational system is not uniform; it permits much variation in physical and social mobility and hence much variation in network connectedness.

But decisions to move depend not only on occupational considerations but also on the housing shortage, the type and cost of the house or flat, the family's views on the welfare of their children, relations with relatives, neighbours, and friends in the old area, and on potential relations in the new area, and doubtless many other factors as well. All these considerations must be weighed together when the decision to move is made, although one or other factor may be dominant. Sometimes all considerations point in the same direction; more frequently they have to be balanced against one another. But whatever the reasons, once the move has been made the family's network becomes more dispersed. Even if the family itself does not move, its network will become dispersed if friends and relatives move away.

Network connectedness thus depends on a very complex combination of economic and social forces. Instead of the relatively homogeneous environment of a small-scale, relatively closed society, the total environment of an urban family is exceedingly complex and variable. Many forces affect a family's network, so that there is considerable latitude for the family to choose among several courses of action, and a wide range of variation is possible.

(5) *Individual Decision and Choice*

The connectedness of a family's network depends not only on external social forces, but also on the family itself. Although the members of a family cannot control the forces of the total environment, they can select from among the various courses of action to which these forces give rise. It is the variability of the total environment that makes choice possible, but it is the family that makes the actual decisions. Decisions are shaped by situational factors but they also depend on the personalities of the members of the family, on the way they react to the situational factors.

Through acts of personal decision and choice, husband and wife may affect the connectedness of their network, often without any deliberate intention of doing so; by changing the connectedness of their network they affect in turn their conjugal role-segregation. Thus, if a family with a highly connected network moves out of their old area to a new housing estate, their network will rapidly become more dispersed, and for a time at least they will develop a more joint relationship with each other. If a professional family with a dispersed network moves to a university town because of the husband's career, their network is likely to become slightly more connected even though they may not plan to make it so. If a family with a dispersed network decides to move to a distant suburb because that is the only place where they can find a house that they can afford to buy, they may find themselves extremely isolated—cut off from their friends, unable to make relationships easily with their neighbours, and even more dependent on each other than usual.

Among the research set there were several couples who, for various personal reasons, had almost no informal network at all. Thus two families were living in a state of voluntary isolation or near isolation; they kept up necessary contacts with service institutions and paid a few duty visits to relatives, but that was all. Or again, a husband and wife of the second set of families, for various personal reasons, had almost no friends, although they saw a good deal of their relatives and rather more of their neighbours than the other families of this set. In so far as they had an informal network it was dispersed, but there were far fewer members in it than usual. One of the intermediate families could, if they had wished, have had a network almost as highly connected as that of the Ns, but for various personal reasons they had cut themselves off and had adopted a more home-centred outlook and a more joint role-relationship. Slightly deviant families of this type are aware that their behaviour does not coincide exactly with their own norms, although they usually do not like to discuss their deviance unless they feel that they are above their norm rather than below it.

Personality characteristics may thus affect conjugal role-segregation indirectly because they are a factor in shaping choices that affect the form of the family's network. But personal needs and attitudes, both conscious and unconscious, also affect performance of conjugal roles directly. Two families may have similar networks but slightly different degrees of conjugal role-segregation. Thus the two transitional families discussed above were living in approximately the same social situation, but in one case the husband and wife were trying to develop as joint a conjugal relationship as possible whereas in the second case they were not. Personality factors are of necessity involved in performance of familial roles —and of any role for that matter—but it is only where there is a lack of fit between the personal needs of husband and wife, the social situation in which they find themselves, and the expectations of the members of their networks, that such needs stand out as a separate factor.

Social Class, Network Connectedness, and Segregation of Conjugal Roles

Because of the complexity of the situation it is not surprising that we could not find a simple correlation between class position and segregation of conjugal roles. In my view such segregation is more directly related to network connectedness than to class status as such, although there are probably some aspects of class position that affect conjugal role-segregation directly. For example, if both husband and wife are highly educated, they are likely to have a common background of shared interests and tastes, which makes a joint relationship easy to conduct. Although it is unlikely that teachers deliberately plan to teach children about joint conjugal relationships, higher education is probably a chief means of passing on the ethic appropriate to a joint relationship from one generation to another, and of teaching it to socially mobile individuals whose parents have had a more segregated relationship. It is doubtful, however, whether such education alone could produce joint conjugal relationships; it works in conjunction with other factors.

But for the most part factors associated with class—however one defines that complex construct—affect segregation of conjugal roles indirectly through having an effect on the connectedness of the family's network. To sum up the empirical resultant: Families with highly connected networks are likely to be working-class. But not all working-class families will have highly connected networks.

It is only in the working-class that one is likely to find a combination of factors all working together to produce a high degree of network connectedness: concentration of people of the same or similar occupations in the same local area; jobs and homes in the same local area; low population turnover and continuity of relationships; at least occasional opportunities for relatives and friends to help one another to get jobs; little demand for physical mobility; little opportunity for social mobility.

In contrast, the structure of professions is such that this pattern of forces almost never occurs. Homogeneous local areas of a single profession are very rare; a man's place of work and his home are usually in different local areas; professional training leads him to make relationships with people who do not know his family, school friends, and neighbours; in most cases getting a job depends on skill and training rather than on the influence of friends and relatives; many professional careers require physical mobility. Almost the only factor associated with high-class status that tends to foster network connectedness is owner-ship of shares in common enterprises by relatives—and this is less likely to occur among professional people than among wealthy indus-trialists and commercial families.

But because a man has a manual occupation he will not automatically have a highly connected network. He may be living in a relatively heterogeneous area, for not all manual occupations are localized. He may live in one place and work in another. He may move from one area to another. Similarly his friends and relatives may move or make new relationships with people he does not know. A high degree of network connectedness *may* be found in association with manual occupations, but the association is not necessary and inevitable.

In brief, one cannot explain network connectedness as the result of the husband's occupational or class status considered as single deter-minants. Network connectedness depends on a whole complex of forces —economic ties among members of the network, type of local area, op-portunities to make new social contacts, physical and social mobility, etc.—generated by the occupational and economic systems, but these forces do not always work in the same direction and they may affect different families in different ways.

Finally, network connectedness cannot be predicted from a knowledge of situational factors alone. It also depends on the family's personal response to the situations of choice with which they are confronted.

In a situation of such complexity, little is to be gained by trying to explain conjugal role-segregation in terms of single factors. In the ap-proach to this problem, the most useful conceptual model has proved to be that of field theory: "behaviour is a function of a person (in this case a family) in a situation." Performance of conjugal roles is a function of the family in its social network. The form of the social network de-pends, in turn, partly on the members of the family and partly on a very complex combination of forces in the total social environment.

SUMMARY

1. The conjugal role-relationships of all twenty urban families studied in this research contained both segregated and joint components. There were differences of degree, however. Some couples had considerable *segregation* in their conjugal role-relationship; in such families, husband and wife expected to have a clear differentiation of tasks and a consider-able number of separate interests and activities. At the other extreme there were couples who had as much *joint organization* as possible in

the role-relationship of husband and wife; in such families husband and wife expected to carry out many activities together with a minimum of task differentiation and separation of interests. There were many degrees of variation between these two extremes.

2. The immediate social environment of an urban family consists of a network rather than an organized group. A *network* is a social configuration in which some, but not all, of the component external units maintain relationships with one another. The external units do not make up a larger social whole. They are not surrounded by a common boundary.

The network formation of the immediate environment of an urban family is brought about by the complexity of the division of labour in the total society. Whereas a family in a relatively closed community belongs to a small number of groups each with many functions, an urban family exists in a network of many separate institutions each with a specialized function. Urban families are not isolated, but they are *more highly individuated* than families in relatively closed communities; urban families are not encapsulated within external governing groups other than the nation as a whole, and they have a relatively large measure of privacy, of autonomy, and of opportunity to regulate their own affairs.

3. The networks of urban families vary in degree of *connectedness*, namely in the extent to which the people with whom the family maintains relationships carry on relationships with one another. These variations in network connectedness are particularly evident in informal relationships between friends, neighbours, and relatives.

These differences in network connectedness are associated with differences in degree of conjugal role-segregation. *The degree of segregation in the role-relationship of husband and wife varies directly with the connectedness of the family's social network.* Four sets of families have been described, and the relationship between the connectedness of their networks and the degree of their conjugal role-segregation has been discussed.

4. Conceptually, the network stands between the family and the total social environment. Variations in network connectedness cannot be explained in terms of any single factor. Such variations are made possible by the complexity and variability of the economic, occupational, and other institutional systems that create a complex of forces affecting families in different ways and permitting selection and choice by the family. It is suggested that the connectedness of a family's network is a function on the one hand of a complex set of forces in the total environment, and on the other hand of the family themselves and their reaction to these forces. Several situational factors possibly relevant to the connectedness

of families' networks have been suggested, including the extent to which members of the network are bound to one another by economic ties; the type of neighbourhood; opportunities to make new relationships even while continuing to live in the same area; opportunities for physical and social mobility.

SELECTED READINGS

ARONSON, DAN R., ED.

1970 Special Issue: Social Networks. Canadian Journal of Sociology and Anthropology Vol. 7, No. 4.

This collection of articles, arising out of a symposium at the Central States Anthropological Society meetings in 1969, demonstrates some of the lines in network analysis along which American anthropologists are working.

BARNES, J. A.

1954 Class and Committees in a Norwegian Island Parish. Human Relations 7:1:39–58.

The original statement on the use of network analysis, in which Barnes found that the traditional holistic approach could not be used fruitfully in understanding social interaction in a Norwegian fishing community.

BOTT, ELIZABETH

1971 Family and Social Network: Roles, Norms, and External Relationships in Ordinary Urban Families. Second Edition. New York: The Free Press.

This book is a more complete presentation of Bott's research reported in Selection 7. From it, the reader will gain a good understanding of the operation of social networks in the lives of selected London families.

HANNERZ, ULF

1969 Soulside: Inquiries into Ghetto Culture. New York: Columbia University Press.

Appendix: In The Field, pp. 201–210.
Like Whyte's account, this personal description by a Swedish anthropologist of the work he did in Washington, D.C., is essential reading for the student of urban anthropology.

MITCHELL, J. CLYDE, ED.

1969 Social Networks in Urban Situations: Analyses of Personal Relationships in Central African Towns. Manchester: University of Manchester Press, for the Institute of Social Research, University of Zambia.

This collection of reprinted and original articles using network analysis in African urban studies is the best source of such information now available on the use of that method.

SPRADLEY, JAMES P., and DAVID W. MCCURDY

1972 The Cultural Experience. Chicago: Science Research Associates.

Explicitly laying out the problems and techniques of urban research, the authors also include examples of the research that may be done by undergraduates in urban situations.

VIDICH, ARTHUR, JOSEPH BENSMAN, and MAURICE STEIN

1964 Reflections on Community Studies. New York: John Wiley and Sons.

This wide-ranging collection of researchers' feelings and perspectives is a valuable resource for an urban scholar in any behavioral science discipline. To some extent, these may replace the stories heard at the knee of one's major professor.

WHYTE, WILLIAM FOOTE

1955 Street Corner Society: The Social Structure of an Italian Slum. Second Edition. Chicago: University of Chicago Press.

A classic study of an Italian slum. The second edition contains a new appendix, "On the Evolution of Street Corner Society." This statement by Whyte of his research experiences remains one of the best introductions to the techniques of urban field research. His discussion of the ethics of such research is particularly relevant today.

Part Three
CATEGORIES OF URBAN DWELLERS

The heterogeneity of its population is a significant feature of Wirth's assessment of the city. The great variety of types of people and positions they occupy results in the formation of numerous distinct populations, across whose boundaries communication and association are limited. Wirth contrasts this situation with that of traditional societies in which major categorical distinctions are made largely on the basis of age, sex, and kinship. The selections in this part are concerned with the increase of social categories in urban settings, exploring the factors which underlie this heterogeneity.

Specifically referring to Wirth's earlier work, Gans suggests that "economic condition, cultural characteristics, life-cycle stage, and residential instability explain ways of life more satisfactorily than number, density, and heterogeneity." Thus the five categories of inner city residents Gans identifies react to the same ecological settlement area in different ways, which he ascribes to differences in the above-quoted traits among the categories. Gans's comments on the importance of residential instability may be profitably read in conjunction with Selection 6 by Spradley and Selection 16 by Jacobson. The variations in approach are characteristic of those who study the city and valuable for understanding different aspects of the same problem.

Another approach is found in Berreman's essay, a significant contribution to the literature in urban anthropology and ethnic studies, in which he not only describes the large number of categories utilized in a North Indian city but also discusses the subtle processes of interaction among and within categories. Because of its importance in demonstrating the use of ethnomethodology, this article could also have been placed in Part 2. Berreman points out that "identity is to a significant extent a matter of choice in the relatively anonymous and momentary arena of much urban interaction." Yet, at the same time, traditional identifiers such as sex, caste status, and region of origin continue to be major reference points for interaction.

According to Bascom, the worlds of urban dwellers in the old "Yoruba cities were heterogeneous only in terms of craft specialization, social stratification, and socio-political segmentation." In Selection 10, one of the major anthropological responses to Wirth, Bascom shows that the more traditional and pre-European cities contrast sharply with Western cities and with African cities that developed after European contact. Instead of heterogeneity and social disorganization, Bascom found that individuals are enmeshed within lineages and other cultural groups and that traditional forms of social control continue to be effective. Even though impersonal and segmental social relationships exist in Yoruba cities, these are characteristic of the marketplace, leading Bascom to suggest that economic interdependence might be more important than heterogeneity in an urban definition. Such interdependence makes possible settlements of larger size, greater density, and more permanence —the defining characteristics of cities for Bascom.

In its stress upon permanence and social stability, Bascom's essay is similar to Gans's in that both recognize that urban inhabitants need not live insecure and chaotic lives in the city. Bascom found anomie only among recent migrants; the remainder of the population was well integrated into stable residential lineages. We need not assume that kin groupings are the only social units reducing anomie, however; research reports included in Parts Four and Five suggest other urban social groups in which stable personal participation is possible.

8

Urbanism and Suburbanism as Ways of Life: A Re-evaluation of Definitions

Herbert J. Gans

The contemporary sociological conception of cities and of urban life is based largely on the work of the Chicago School, and its summary statement in Louis Wirth's essay, "Urbanism as a Way of Life" (1957).* In that paper, Wirth developed a "minimum sociological definition of the city" as "a relatively large, dense and permanent settlement of socially heterogeneous individuals" (1957:50). From these prerequisites, he then deduced the major outlines of the urban way of life. As he saw it, number, density, and heterogeneity created a social structure in which primary-group relationships were inevitably replaced by secondary contacts that were impersonal, segmental, superficial, transitory, and often predatory in nature. As a result, the city dweller became anonymous, isolated, secular, relativistic, rational, and sophisticated. In order to function in the urban society, he was forced to combine with others to organize corporations, voluntary associations, representative forms of government, and the impersonal mass media of communications (Wirth 1957:54–60). These replaced the primary groups and the integrated way of life found in rural and other pre-industrial settlements.

Wirth's paper has become a classic in urban sociology, and most texts have followed his definition and description faithfully (Dewey 1960). In recent years, however, a considerable number of studies and essays have questioned his formulations (Axelrod 1956; Dewey 1960; Form *et al.*

SOURCE: Arnold M. Rose, ed., *Human Behavior and Social Processes* (Boston: Houghton Mifflin Company, 1962), pp. 625–48. Reprinted by permission of the publisher.

* I am indebted to Richard Dewey, John Dyckman, David Riesman, Melvin Webber, and Harold Wilensky for helpful comments on earlier drafts of this essay.

1954; Gans 1959; Greer 1956; Greer and Kube 1959; Janowitz 1952; Reiss 1955, 1959; Seeley 1959; Smith *et al.* 1954; Stone 1954; Whyte 1955; Wilensky and Lebeaux 1958; Young and Willmott 1957).[1] In addition, a number of changes have taken place in cities since the article was published in 1938, notably the exodus of white residents to low- and medium-priced houses in the suburbs, and the decentralization of industry. The evidence from these studies and the changes in American cities suggest that Wirth's statement must be revised.

There is yet another, and more important reason for such a revision. Despite its title and intent, Wirth's paper deals with urban-industrial society rather than with the city. This is evident from his approach. Like other urban sociologists, Wirth based his analysis on a comparison of settlement types, but unlike his colleagues, who pursued urban-rural comparisons, Wirth contrasted the city to the folk society. Thus, he compared settlement types of pre-industrial and industrial society. This allowed him to include in his theory of urbanism the entire range of modern institutions which are not found in the folk society, even though many such groups (e.g., voluntary associations) are by no means exclusively urban. Moreover, Wirth's conception of the city dweller as depersonalized, atomized, and susceptible to mass movements suggests that his paper is based on, and contributes to, the theory of the mass society.

Many of Wirth's conclusions may be relevant to the understanding of ways of life in modern society. However, since the theory argues that all of society is now urban, *his analysis does not distinguish ways of life in the city from those in other settlements within modern society.* In Wirth's time, the comparison of urban and pre-urban settlement types was still fruitful, but today, the primary task for urban (or community) sociology seems to me to be the analysis of the similarities and differences between contemporary settlement types.

This paper is an attempt at such an analysis; it limits itself to distinguishing ways of life in the modern city and the modern suburb. A reanalysis of Wirth's conclusions from this perspective suggests that his characterization of the urban way of life applies only—and not too accurately—to the residents of the inner city. The remaining city dwellers, as well as most suburbanites, pursue a different way of life, which I shall call "quasi-primary." This proposition raises some doubt about the mutual exclusiveness of the concepts of city and suburb and leads to a yet broader question: whether settlement concepts and other ecological concepts are useful for explaining ways of life.

[1] I shall not attempt to summarize these studies, for this task has already been performed by Dewey (1960), Reiss (1955), Wilensky (1958), and others.

THE INNER CITY

Wirth argued that number, density, and heterogeneity had two social consequences which explain the major features of urban life. On the one hand, the crowding of diverse types of people into a small area led to the segregation of homogeneous types of people into separate neighborhoods (Wirth 1957:56). On the other hand, the lack of physical distance between city dwellers resulted in social contact between them, which broke down existing social and cultural patterns and encouraged assimilation as well as acculturation—the melting pot effect (1957:52). Wirth implied that the melting pot effect was far more powerful than the tendency toward segregation and concluded that, sooner or later, the pressures engendered by the dominant social, economic, and political institutions of the city would destroy the remaining pockets of primary-group relationships (1957:60–62). Eventually, the social system of the city would resemble Tönnies' Gesellschaft—a way of life which Wirth considered undesirable.

Because Wirth had come to see the city as the prototype of mass society, and because he examined the city from the distant vantage point of the folk society—from the wrong end of the telescope, so to speak—his view of urban life is not surprising. In addition, Wirth found support for his theory in the empirical work of his Chicago colleagues. As Greer and Kube (1959:112) and Wilensky (1958:121) have pointed out, the Chicago sociologists conducted their most intensive studies in the inner city.[2] At that time, these were slums recently invaded by new waves of European immigrants and rooming house and skid row districts, as well as the habitat of Bohemians and well-to-do Gold Coast apartment dwellers. Wirth himself studied the Maxwell Street Ghetto, an inner-city Jewish neighborhood then being dispersed by the acculturation and mobility of its inhabitants (1928). Some of the characteristics of urbanism which Wirth stressed in his essay abounded in these areas.

Wirth's diagnosis of the city as Gesellschaft must be questioned on three counts. First, the conclusions derived from a study of the inner city cannot be generalized to the entire urban area. Second, there is as yet not enough evidence to prove—nor, admittedly, to deny—that number, density, and heterogeneity result in the social consequences which

[2] By the inner city, I mean the transient residential areas, the Gold Coasts, and the slums that generally surround the central business district, although in some communities they may continue for miles beyond that district. The outer city includes the stable residential areas that house the working- and middle-class tenant and owner. The suburbs I conceive as the latest and most modern ring of the outer city, distinguished from it only by yet lower densities, and by the often irrelevant fact of the ring's location outside the city limits.

Wirth proposed. Finally, even if the causal relationship could be verified, it can be shown that a significant proportion of the city's inhabitants were, and are, isolated from these consequences by social structures and cultural patterns which they either brought to the city, or developed by living in it. Wirth conceived the urban population as consisting of heterogeneous individuals, torn from past social systems, unable to develop new ones, and therefore prey to social anarchy in the city. While it is true that a not insignificant proportion of the inner city population was, and still is, made up of unattached individuals (Rose 1947), Wirth's formulation ignores the fact that this population consists mainly of relatively homogeneous groups, with social and cultural moorings that shield it fairly effectively from the suggested consequences of number, density, and heterogeneity. This applies even more to the residents of the outer city, who constitute a majority of the total city population.

The social and cultural moorings of the inner city population are best described by a brief analysis of the five types of inner city residents. These are:

1. the "cosmopolites";
2. the unmarried or childless;
3. the "ethnic villagers";
4. the "deprived"; and
5. the "trapped" and downward mobile.

The "cosmopolites" include students, artists, writers, musicians, and entertainers, as well as other intellectuals and professionals. They live in the city in order to be near the special "cultural" facilities that can only be located near the center of the city. Many cosmopolites are unmarried or childless. Others rear children in the city, especially if they have the income to afford the aid of servants and governesses. The less affluent ones may move to the suburbs to raise their children, continuing to live as cosmopolites under considerable handicaps, especially in the lower-middle-class suburbs. Many of the very rich and powerful are also cosmopolites, although they are likely to have at least two residences, one of which is suburban or exurban.

The unmarried or childless must be divided into two subtypes, depending on the permanence or transience of their status. The temporarily unmarried or childless live in the inner city for only a limited time. Young adults may team up to rent an apartment away from their parents and close to job or entertainment opportunities. When they marry, they may move first to an apartment in a transient neighborhood, but if they can afford to do so, they leave for the outer city or the suburbs with the arrival of the first or second child. The permanently unmarried may stay in the inner city for the remainder of their lives, their housing depending on their income.

The "ethnic villagers" are ethnic groups which are found in such inner city neighborhoods as New York's Lower East Side, living in some ways as they did when they were peasants in European or Puerto Rican villages (Gans 1959). Although they reside in the city, they isolate themselves from significant contact with most city facilities, aside from workplaces. Their way of life differs sharply from Wirth's urbanism in its emphasis on kinship and the primary group, the lack of anonymity and secondary-group contacts, the weakness of formal organizations, and the suspicion of anything and anyone outside their neighborhood.

The first two types live in the inner city by choice; the third is there partly because of necessity, partly because of tradition. The final two types are in the inner city because they have no other choice. One is the "deprived" population: the very poor; the emotionally disturbed or otherwise handicapped; broken families; and, most important, the non-white population. These urban dwellers must take the dilapidated housing and blighted neighborhoods to which the housing market relegates them, although among them are some for whom the slum is a hiding place, or a temporary stopover to save money for a house in the outer city or the suburbs (Seeley 1959).

The "trapped" are the people who stay behind when a neighborhood is invaded by non-residential land uses or lower-status immigrants, because they cannot afford to move, or are otherwise bound to their present location.[3] The "downward mobiles" are a related type; they may have started life in a higher class position, but have been forced down in the socio-economic hierarchy and in the quality of their accommodations. Many of them are old people, living out their existence on small pensions.

These five types all live in dense and heterogeneous surroundings, yet they have such diverse ways of life that it is hard to see how density and heterogeneity could exert a common influence. Moreover, all but the last two types are isolated or detached from their neighborhood and thus from the social consequences which Wirth described.

When people who live together have social ties based on criteria other than mere common occupancy, they can set up social barriers regardless of the physical closeness or the heterogeneity of their neighbors. The ethnic villagers are the best illustration. While a number of ethnic groups are usually found living together in the same neighborhood, they are able to *isolate* themselves from each other through a variety of social devices.

[3] The trapped are not very visible, but I suspect that they are a significant element in what Raymond Vernon has described as the "gray areas" of the city (1959).

Wirth himself recognized this when he wrote that "two groups can occupy a given area without losing their separate identity because each side is permitted to live its own inner life and each somehow fears or idealizes the other." (1928:283). Although it is true that the children in these areas were often oblivious to the social barriers set up by their parents, at least until adolescence, it is doubtful whether their acculturation can be traced to the melting pot effect as much as to the pervasive influence of the American culture that flowed into these areas from the outside.[4]

The cosmopolites, the unmarried, and the childless are *detached* from neighborhood life. The cosmopolites possess a distinct subculture which causes them to be disinterested in all but the most superficial contacts with their neighbors, somewhat like the ethnic villagers. The unmarried and childless are detached from neighborhood because of their life-cycle stage, which frees them from the routine family responsibilities that entail some relationship to the local area. In their choice of residence, the two types are therefore not concerned about their neighbors, or the availability and quality of local community facilities. Even the well-to-do can choose expensive apartments in or near poor neighborhoods, because if they have children, these are sent to special schools and summer camps which effectively isolate them from neighbors. In addition, both types, but especially the childless and unmarried, are transient. Therefore, they tend to live in areas marked by high population turnover, where their own mobility and that of their neighbors creates a universal detachment from the neighborhood.[5]

The deprived and the trapped do seem to be affected by some of the consequences of number, density, and heterogeneity. The deprived population suffers considerably from overcrowding, but this is a consequence of low income, racial discrimination, and other handicaps, and cannot be considered an inevitable result of the ecological make-up of the city.[6] Because the deprived have no residential choice, they are also forced to

[4] If the melting pot has resulted from propinquity and high density, one would have expected second-generation Italians, Irish, Jews, Greeks, Slavs, etc. to have developed a single "pan-ethnic culture," consisting of a synthesis of the cultural patterns of the propinquitous national groups.

[5] The corporation transients (Whyte 1956; Wilensky and Lebeaux 1958), who provide a new source of residential instability to the suburb, differ from city transients. Since they are raising families, they want to integrate themselves into neighborhood life, and are usually able to do so, mainly because they tend to move into similar types of communities wherever they go.

[6] The negative social consequences of overcrowding are a result of high room and floor density, not of the land coverage of population density which Wirth discussed. Park Avenue residents live under conditions of high land density, but do not seem to suffer visibly from overcrowding.

live amid neighbors not of their own choosing, with ways of life different and even contradictory to their own. If familial defenses against the neighborhood climate are weak, as is the case among broken families and downward mobile people, parents may lose their children to the culture of "the street." The trapped are the unhappy people who remain behind when their more advantaged neighbors move on; they must endure the heterogeneity which results from neighborhood change.

Wirth's description of the urban way of life fits best the transient areas of the inner city. Such areas are typically heterogeneous in population, partly because they are inhabited by transient types who do not require homogeneous neighbors or by deprived people who have no choice, or may themselves be quite mobile. Under conditions of transience and heterogeneity, people interact only in terms of the segmental roles necessary for obtaining local services. Their social relationships thus display anonymity, impersonality, and superficiality.[7]

The social features of Wirth's concept of urbanism seem therefore to be a result of residential instability, rather than of number, density, or heterogeneity. In fact, heterogeneity is itself an effect of residential instability, resulting when the influx of transients causes landlords and realtors to stop acting as gatekeepers—that is, wardens of neighborhood homogeneity.[8] Residential instability is found in all types of settlements, and, presumably, its social consequences are everywhere similar. These consequences cannot therefore be identified with the ways of life of the city.

THE OUTER CITY AND THE SUBURBS

The second effect which Wirth ascribed to number, density, and heterogeneity was the segregation of homogeneous people into distinct neighborhoods,[9] on the basis of "place and nature of work, income, racial and

[7] Whether or not these social phenomena have the psychological consequences Wirth suggested depends on the people who live in the area. Those who are detached from the neighborhood by choice are probably immune, but those who depend on the neighborhood for their social relationships—the unattached individuals, for example—may suffer greatly from loneliness.

[8] Needless to say, residential instability must ultimately be traced back to the fact that, as Wirth pointed out, the city and its economy attract transient—and, depending on the sources of outmigration, heterogeneous—people. However, this is a characteristic of urban-industrial society, not of the city specifically.

[9] By neighborhoods or residential districts I mean areas demarcated from others by distinctive physical boundaries or by social characteristics, some of which may be perceived only by the residents. However, these areas are not necessarily socially self-sufficient or culturally distinctive.

ethnic characteristics, social status, custom, habit, taste, preference and prejudice." (1957:56) This description fits the residential districts of the *outer city*.[10] Although these districts contain the majority of the city's inhabitants, Wirth went into little detail about them. He made it clear, however, that the socio-psychological aspects of urbanism were prevalent there as well (Wirth 1957:56).

Because existing neighborhood studies deal primarily with the exotic sections of the inner city, very little is known about the more typical residential neighborhoods of the outer city. However, it is evident that the way of life in these areas bears little resemblance to Wirth's urbanism. Both the studies which question Wirth's formulation and my own observations suggest that the common element in the ways of life of these neighborhoods is best described as *quasi-primary*. I use this term to characterize relationships between neighbors. Whatever the intensity or frequency of these relationships, the interaction is more intimate than a secondary contact, but more guarded that a primary one.[11]

There are actually few secondary relationships, because of the isolation of residential neighborhoods from economic institutions and workplaces. Even shopkeepers, store managers, and other local functionaries who live in the area are treated as acquaintances or friends, unless they are of a vastly different social status or are forced by their corporate employers to treat their customers as economic units (Stone 1954). Voluntary associations attract only a minority of the population. Moreover, much of the organizational activity is of a sociable nature, and it is often difficult to accomplish the association's "business" because of the members' preference for sociability. Thus, it would appear that interactions in organizations, or between neighbors generally, do not fit the secondary-relationship model of urban life. As anyone who has lived in these neighborhoods knows, there is little anonymity, impersonality, or privacy.[12] In fact, American cities have sometimes been described as collections of small towns.[13] There is some truth to this description, especially if the city

[10] For the definition of *outer city*, see Footnote 2.

[11] Because neighborly relations are not quite primary, and not quite secondary, they can also become *pseudo-primary*; that is, secondary ones disguised with false affect to make them appear primary. Critics have often described suburban life in this fashion, although the actual prevalence of pseudo-primary relationships has not been studied systematically in cities or suburbs.

[12] These neighborhoods cannot, however, be considered as urban folk societies. People go out of the area for many of their friendships, and their allegiance to the neighborhood is neither intense nor all-encompassing. Janowitz has aptly described the relationship between resident and neighborhood as one of "limited liability." (1952)

[13] Were I not arguing that ecological concepts cannot double as sociological ones, this way of life might best be described as small-townish.

is compared to the actual small town, rather than to the romantic construct of anti-urban critics (Vidich and Bensman 1958).

Postwar suburbia represents the most contemporary version of the quasi-primary way of life. Owing to increases in real income and the encouragement of home ownership provided by the FHA, families in the lower-middle class and upper working class can now live in modern single-family homes in low-density subdivisions, an opportunity previously available only to the upper and upper-middle classes (Wattell 1958).

The popular literature describes the new suburbs as communities in which conformity, homogeneity, and other-direction are unusually rampant (Berger 1960; Vernon 1959). The implication is that the move from city to suburb initiates a new way of life which causes considerable behavior and personality change in previous urbanites. A preliminary analysis of data which I [collected] in Levittown, New Jersey, suggests, however, that the move from the city to this predominantly lower-middle-class suburb does not result in any major behavioral changes for most people. Moreover, the changes which do occur reflect the move from the social isolation of a transient city or suburban apartment building to the quasi-primary life of a neighborhood of single-family homes. Also, many of the people whose life has changed reported that the changes were intended. They existed as aspirations before the move, or as reasons for it. In other words, the suburb itself creates few changes in ways of life. Similar conclusions have been reported by Berger in his excellent study of a working-class population newly moved to a suburban subdivision (Berger 1960).

A COMPARISON OF CITY AND SUBURB

If urban and suburban areas are similar in that the way of life in both is quasi-primary, and if urban residents who move out to the suburbs do not undergo any significant changes in behavior, it would be fair to argue that the differences in ways of life between the two types of settlements have been overestimated. Yet the fact remains that a variety of physical and demographic differences exist between the city and the suburb. However, upon closer examination, many of these differences turn out to be either spurious or of little significance for the way of life of the inhabitants (Wattell 1958).[14]

The differences between the residential areas of cities and suburbs which have been cited most frequently are:

[14] They may, of course, be significant for the welfare of the total metropolitan area.

1. Suburbs are more likely to be dormitories.

2. They are further away from the work and play facilities of the central business districts.

3. They are newer and more modern than city residential areas and are designed for the automobile rather than for pedestrian and mass-transit forms of movement.

4. They are built up with single-family rather than multi-family structures and are therefore less dense.

5. Their populations are more homogeneous.

6. Their populations differ demographically: they are younger; more of them are married; they have higher incomes; and they hold proportionately more white collar jobs. (Duncan and Reiss 1956:131)

Most urban neighborhoods are as much dormitories as the suburbs. Only in a few older inner city areas are factories and offices still located in the middle of residential blocks, and even here many of the employees do not live in the neighborhood.

The fact that the suburbs are farther from the central business district is often true only in terms of distance, not travel time. Moreover, most people make relatively little use of downtown facilities, other than work-places (Foley 1957; Jonassen 1955). The downtown stores seem to hold their greatest attraction for the upper-middle class (Jonassen 1955:91–92); the same is probably true of typically urban entertainment facilities. Teenagers and young adults may take their dates to first-run movie theaters, but the museums, concerts halls, and lecture rooms attract mainly upper-middle-class ticket-buyers, many of them suburban.[15]

The suburban reliance on the train and the automobile has given rise to an imaginative folklore about the consequences of commuting on alcohol consumption, sex life, and parental duties. Many of these conclusions are, however, drawn from selected high-income suburbs and exurbs, and reflect job tensions in such hectic occupations as advertising and show business more than the effects of residence (Spectorsky 1955). It is true that the upper-middle-class housewife must become a chauffeur in order to expose her children to the proper educational facilities, but such differences as walking to the corner drug store and driving to its suburban equivalent seem to me of little emotional, social, or cultural import.[16]

[15] A 1958 study of New York theater goers showed a median income of close to $10,000 and 35 per cent were reported as living in the suburbs (Enders n.d.)

[16] I am thinking here of adults; teenagers do suffer from the lack of informal meeting places within walking or bicycling distance.

In addition, the continuing shrinkage in the number of mass-transit users suggests that even in the city many younger people are now living a wholly auto-based way of life.

The fact that suburbs are smaller is primarily a function of political boundaries drawn long before the communities were suburban. This affects the kinds of political issues which develop and provides somewhat greater opportunity for citizen participation. Even so, in the suburbs as in the city, the minority who participate are the professional politicians, the economically concerned businessmen, lawyers and salesmen, and the ideologically motivated middle- and upper-middle-class people with better than average education.

The social consequences of differences in density and house type also seem overrated. Single-family houses on quiet streets facilitate the supervision of children; this is one reason why middle-class women who want to keep an eye on their children move to the suburbs. House type also has some effects on relationships between neighbors, insofar as there are more opportunities for visual contact between adjacent homeowners than between people on different floors of an apartment house. However, if occupants' characteristics are also held constant, the differences in actual social contact are less marked. Homogeneity of residents turns out to be more important as a determinant of sociability than proximity. If the population is heterogeneous, there is little social contact between neighbors, either on apartment-house floors or in single-family-house blocks; if people are homogeneous, there is likely to be considerable social contact in both house types. One need only contrast the apartment house located in a transient, heterogeneous neighborhood and exactly the same structure in a neighborhood occupied by a single ethnic group. The former is a lonely, anonymous building; the latter, a bustling microsociety. I have observed similar patterns in suburban areas: on blocks where people are homogeneous, they socialize; where they are heterogeneous, they do little more than exchange polite greetings (Gans 1961).

Suburbs are usually described as being more homogeneous in house type than the city, but if they are compared to the outer city, the differences are small. Most inhabitants of the outer city, other than well-to-do homeowners, live on blocks of uniform structures as well—for example, the endless streets of rowhouses in Philadelphia and Baltimore or of two-story duplexes and six-flat apartment houses in Chicago. They differ from the new suburbs only in that they were erected through more primitive methods of mass production. Suburbs are of course more predominantly areas of owner-occupied single homes, though in the outer districts of most American cities homeownership is also extremely high.

Demographically, suburbs as a whole are clearly more homogeneous than cities as a whole, though probably not more so than outer cities. However, people do not live in cities or suburbs as a whole, but in specific neighborhoods. An analysis of ways of life would require a determination of the degree of population homogeneity within the boundaries of areas defined as neighborhoods by residents' social contacts. Such an analysis would no doubt indicate that many neighborhoods in the city as well as the suburbs are homogeneous. Neighborhood homogeneity is actually a result of factors having little or nothing to do with the house type, density, or location of the area relative to the city limits. Brand new neighborhoods are more homogeneous than older ones, because they have not yet experienced resident turnover, which frequently results in population heterogeneity. Neighborhoods of low- and medium-priced housing are usually less homogeneous than those with expensive dwellings because they attract families who have reached the peak of occupational and residential mobility, as well as young families who are just starting their climb and will eventually move to neighborhoods of higher status. The latter, being accessible only to high-income people, are therefore more homogeneous with respect to other resident characteristics as well. Moreover, such areas have the economic and political power to slow down or prevent invasion. Finally, neighborhoods located in the path of ethnic or religious group movement are likely to be extremely homogeneous.

The demographic differences between cities and suburbs cannot be questioned, especially since the suburbs have attracted a large number of middle-class child-rearing families. The differences are, however, much reduced if suburbs are compared only to the outer city. In addition, a detailed comparison of suburban and outer city residential areas would show that neighborhoods with the same kinds of people can be found in the city as well as the suburbs. Once again, the age of the area and the cost of housing are more important determinants of demographic characteristics than the location of the area with respect to the city limits.

CHARACTERISTICS, SOCIAL ORGANIZATION, AND ECOLOGY

The preceding sections of the paper may be summarized in three propositions:

1. As concerns ways of life, the inner city must be distinguished from the outer city and the suburbs; and the latter two exhibit a way of life bearing little resemblance to Wirth's urbanism.

2. Even in the inner city, ways of life resemble Wirth's description only to a limited extent. Moreover, economic condition, cultural

characteristics, life-cycle stage, and residential instability explain ways of life more satisfactorily than number, density, or heterogeneity.

3. Physical and other differences between city and suburb are often spurious or without much meaning for ways of life.

These propositions suggest that the concepts urban and suburban are neither mutually exclusive, nor especially relevant for understanding ways of life. They—and number, density, and heterogeneity as well—are ecological concepts which describe human adaptation to the environment. However, they are not sufficient to explain social phenomena, because these phenomena cannot be understood solely as the consequences of ecological processes. Therefore, other explanations must be considered.

Ecological explanations of social life are most applicable if the subjects under study lack the ability to *make choices*, be they plants, animals, or human beings. Thus, if there is a housing shortage, people will live almost anywhere, and under extreme conditions of no choice, as in a disaster, married and single, old and young, middle and working class, stable and transient will be found side by side in whatever accommodations are available. At that time, their ways of life represent an almost direct adaptation to the environment. If the supply of housing and of neighborhoods is such that alternatives are available, however, people will make choices, and if the housing market is responsive, they can even make and satisfy explicit *demands*.

Choices and demands do not develop independently or at random; they are functions of the roles people play in the social system. These can best be understood in terms of the *characteristics* of the people involved; that is, characteristics can be used as indices to choices and demands made in the roles that constitute ways of life. Although many characteristics affect the choices and demands people make with respect to housing and neighborhoods, the most important ones seem to be *class*—in all its economic, social and cultural ramifications—and *life-cycle stage*.[17] If people have an opportunity to choose, these two characteristics will go far in explaining the kinds of housing and neighborhoods they will occupy and the ways of life they will try to establish within them.

Many of the previous assertions about ways of life in cities and suburbs can be analyzed in terms of class and life-cycle characteristics. Thus, in the inner city, the unmarried and childless live as they do, detached from neighborhood, because of their life-cycle stage; the cosmop-

---

[17] These must be defined in dynamic terms. Thus, class includes also the process of social mobility, stage in the life-cycle, and the processes of socialization and aging.

olites, because of a combination of life-cycle stage and a distinctive but class-based subculture. The way of life of the deprived and trapped can be explained by low socio-economic level and related handicaps. The quasi-primary way of life is associated with the family stage of the life-cycle, and the norms of child-rearing and parental role found in the upper working class, the lower-middle class, and the non-cosmopolite portions of the upper-middle and upper classes.

The attributes of the so-called suburban way of life can also be understood largely in terms of these characteristics. The new suburbia is nothing more than a highly visible showcase for the ways of life of young, upper-working-class and lower-middle-class people. Ktsanes and Reissman have aptly described it as "new homes for old values." (1959) Much of the descriptive and critical writing about suburbia assumes that as long as the new suburbanites lived in the city, they behaved like upper-middle-class cosmopolites and that suburban living has mysteriously transformed them (Duhl 1956; Fromm 1955:154–162; Reisman 1958; Whyte 1956). The critics fail to see that the behavior and personality patterns ascribed to suburbia are in reality those of class and age (Dobriner 1958). These patterns could have been found among the new suburbanites when they still lived in the city and could now be observed among their peers who still reside there—if the latter were as visible to critics and researchers as are the suburbanites.

Needless to say, the concept of "characteristics" cannot explain all aspects of ways of life, either among urban or suburban residents. Some aspects must be explained by concepts of social organization that are independent of characteristics. For example, some features of the quasi-primary way of life are independent of class and age, because they evolve from the roles and situations created by joint and adjacent occupancy of land and dwellings. Likewise, residential instability is a universal process which has a number of invariate consequences. In each case, however, the way in which people react varies with their characteristics. So it is with ecological processes. Thus, there are undoubtedly differences between ways of life in urban and suburban settlements which remain after behavior patterns based on residents' characteristics have been analyzed, and which must therefore be attributed to features of the settlement (Fava 1958).

Characteristics do not explain the causes of behavior; rather, they are clues to socially created and culturally defined roles, choices, and demands. A causal analysis must trace them back to the larger social, economic, and political systems which determine the situations in which roles are played and the cultural content of choices and demands, as well as the opportunities for their achievement.[18] These systems determine income distributions, educational and occupational opportunities, and in turn, fertility patterns, child-rearing methods, as well as the entire range of consumer behavior. Thus, a complete analysis of the way of life of the deprived residents of the inner city cannot stop by indicating the influence of low income, lack of education, or family instability. These must be related to such conditions as the urban economy's "need" for low-wage workers, and the housing market practices which restrict residential choice. The urban economy is in turn shaped by national economic and social systems, as well as by local and regional ecological processes. Some phenomena can be explained exclusively by reference to these ecological processes. However, it must also be recognized that as man gains greater control over the natural environment, he has been able to free himself from many of the determining and limiting effects of that environment. Thus, changes in local transportation technology, the ability of industries to be footloose, and the relative affluence of American society have given ever larger numbers of people increasing amounts of residential choice. The greater the amount of choice available, the more important does the concept of characteristics become in understanding behavior.

Consequently, the study of ways of life in communities must begin with an analysis of characteristics. If characteristics are dealt with first and held constant, we may be able to discover which behavior patterns can be attributed to features of the settlement and its natural environment.[19] Only then will it be possible to discover to what extent city and suburb are independent—rather than dependent or intervening—variables in the explanation of ways of life.

This kind of analysis might help to reconcile the ecological point of view with the behavioral and cultural one, and possibly put an end to the conflict between conceptual positions which insist on one explanation or the other (Duncan and Schnore 1959). Both explanations have some

18 This formulation may answer some of Duncan and Schnore's objections to socio-psychological and cultural explanations of community ways of life (Duncan and Schnore 1959).

19 The ecologically oriented researchers who developed the Shevsky-Bell social area analysis scale have worked on the assumption that "social differences between the populations of urban neighborhoods can conveniently be summarized into differences of economic level, family characteristics and ethnicity." (Bell and Force 1956:26) However, they have equated "urbanization" with a concept of life-cycle stage by using family characteristics to define the index of urbanization (Bell and Force 1956; Greer 1960; Greer and Kube 1959). In fact, Bell has identified suburbanism with familism (Bell 1958).

relevance, and future research and theory must clarify the role of each in the analysis of ways of life in various types of settlement (Dobriner 1958:xxii). Another important rationale for this approach is its usefulness for applied sociology—for example, city planning. The planner can recommend changes in the spatial and physical arrangements of the city. Frequently, he seeks to achieve social goals or to change social conditions through physical solutions. He has been attracted to ecological explanations because these relate behavior to phenomena which he can affect. For example, most planners tend to agree with Wirth's formulations, because they stress number and density, over which the planner has some control. If the undesirable social conditions of the inner city could be traced to these two factors, the planner could propose large-scale clearance projects which would reduce the size of the urban population, and lower residential densities. Experience with public housing projects has, however, made it apparent that low densities, new buildings, or modern site plans do not eliminate anti-social or self-destructive behavior. The analysis of characteristics will call attention to the fact that this behavior is lodged in the deprivations of low socio-economic status and racial discrimination, and that it can be changed only through the removal of these deprivations. Conversely, if such an analysis suggests residues of behavior that can be attributed to ecological processes or physical aspects of housing and neighborhoods, the planner can recommend physical changes that can really affect behavior.

A RE-EVALUATION OF DEFINITIONS

The argument presented here has implications for the sociological definition of the city. Such a definition relates ways of life to environmental features of the city qua settlement type. But if ways of life do not coincide with settlement types, and if these ways are functions of class and life-cycle stage rather than of the ecological attributes of the settlement, a sociological definition of the city cannot be formulated.[20] Concepts such as city and suburb allow us to distinguish settlement types from each other physically and demographically, but the ecological processes and conditions which they synthesize have no direct or invariate consequences

[20] Because of the distinctiveness of the ways of life found in the inner city, some writers propose definitions that refer only to these ways, ignoring those found in the outer city. For example, popular writers sometimes identify "urban" with "urbanity," i.e., "cosmopolitanism." However, such a definition ignores the other ways of life found in the inner city. Moreover, I have tried to show that these ways have few common elements, and that the ecological features of the inner city have little or no influence in shaping them.

for ways of life. The sociologist cannot, therefore, speak of an urban or suburban way of life.

CONCLUSION

Many of the descriptive statements made here are as time-bound as Wirth's.[21] Twenty years ago, Wirth concluded that some form of urbanism would eventually predominate in all settlement types. He was, however, writing during a time of immigrant acculturation and at the end of a serious depression, an era of minimal choice. Today, it is apparent that high-density, heterogeneous surroundings are for most people a temporary place of residence; other than for the Park Avenue or Greenwich Village cosmopolites, they are a result of necessity rather than choice. As soon as they can afford to do so, most Americans head for the single-family house and the quasi-primary way of life of the low-density neighborhood, in the outer city or the suburbs.[22]

Changes in the national economy and in government housing policy can affect many of the variables that make up housing supply and demand. For example, urban sprawl may eventually outdistance the ability of present and proposed transportation systems to move workers into the city; further industrial decentralization can forestall it and alter the entire relationship between work and residence. The expansion of present urban renewal activities can perhaps lure a significant number of cosmopolites back from the suburbs, while a drastic change in renewal policy might begin to ameliorate the housing conditions of the deprived population. A serious depression could once again make America a nation of doubled-up tenants.

These events will affect housing supply and residential choice; they will frustrate but not suppress demands for the quasi-primary way of life. However, changes in the national economy, society, and culture can affect people's characteristics—family size, educational level, and various other concomitants of life-cycle stage and class. These in turn will stimulate changes in demands and choices. The rising number of college graduates, for example, is likely to increase the cosmopolite ranks. This might in turn create a new set of city dwellers, although it will probably

---

21 Even more than Wirth's they are based on data and impressions gathered in the large Eastern and Midwestern cities of the United States.

22 Personal discussions with European planners and sociologists suggest that many European apartment dwellers have similar preferences, although economic conditions, high building costs, and the scarcity of land make it impossible for them to achieve their desires.

do no more than encourage the development of cosmopolite facilities in some suburban areas.

The current revival of interest in urban sociology and in community studies, as well as the sociologist's increasing curiosity about city planning, suggest that data may soon be available to formulate a more adequate theory of the relationship between settlements and the ways of life within them. The speculations presented in this paper are intended to raise questions; they can only be answered by more systematic data collection and theorizing.

9

Social Categories and
Social Interaction
in Urban India[1]

Gerald D. Berreman

> *Say "Hindu" if you have in mind a human type
> common to the whole continent; otherwise,
> according as you want to refer to this or that
> group, say "Bengali, Hindustani, Marathi, Tamil,
> Sikh, Muslim," and so on. As to the word "Indian,"
> it is only a geographical definition, and a very
> loose one at that.*
>
> CHAUDHURI 1967:34

The research to be reported here was an inquiry into social identity and how it is defined and acted upon in the highly differentiated, hierarchical, competitive, and economically depressed plural society of urban India. Its aim was to throw light on the methodology of such a study as well as on substantive issues relating to the nature and functioning of caste organization, pluralism, ethnic relations, conflict, and accommodation in a heterogeneous, rigidly stratified, urban population. It was carried out in 1968–69 in Dehra Dun, a quite modern, rapidly growing, ethnically diverse North Indian city of 165,000.

The research was undertaken from a "symbolic interactionist" perspec-

SOURCE: *American Anthropologist* 74, no. 3 (1972): 567–87. Reprinted by permission of the American Anthropological Association.

[1] This paper was presented in preliminary and abbreviated form at the 68th Annual Meeting of the American Anthropological Association, in New Orleans, November 21, 1969, and in expanded form at the Burg Wartenstein Symposium No. 51, on "Ethnic Identity: Cultural Continuity and Change," September 5–13, 1970, sponsored by the Wenner-Gren Foundation for Anthropological Research. The research upon which it is based was carried out under a Fulbright-Hayes Fellowship for Advanced Research and a supplementary grant from the National Institute of Mental Health, Behavioral Science Research Branch.

tive, using detailed observation and inquiry regarding what people do in face-to-face interaction, to discover how they choose among alternative behaviors in terms of the meanings specific attributes, actions, and social situations have for them and for those with whom they interact (cf. Blumer 1969; Cicourel 1964, 1968; Garfinkel 1967; Goffman 1959a, 1963, 1967; Schutz 1962). The approach was also cognitive in that I was interested in the people's own views of their social world and in the principles upon which they organize its constituent elements, define systems of relevance, and make choices. My inquiries were directed primarily at discovering the subjective experience of social identity in the society, its variations and manipulations, and the relationship of that experience to interpersonal (reciprocal) behavior and the decisions which underlie that behavior.

The research was based upon four fundamental kinds of questions which I asked of myself and my data:

1. What are the social categories—the social identities—of people composing the society as defined by themselves?

2. What characteristics are attributed to members of these social categories, i.e., what stereotypes or empirical generalizations are expressed about them?

3. How—by what cues and in what circumstances—do people identify individuals as belonging to a particular social category?

4. How are the above three questions related to interpersonal behavior—to interaction? That is, given that certain categories of people are defined and recognized and that they are regarded as having significant and shared characteristics, how do these facts affect how people behave in one another's presence (or behind their backs)?

I treated the last of these as the crucial question to which the others were necessarily preliminary. To answer it is to get directly at social behavior, its context and meaning.

In order to answer the four questions through research, I observed and talked to people in many circumstances and in many walks of life. I worked primarily in "public places" (cf. Goffman 1963), where most distinctively urban interaction takes place. I began in the bazaar, where urbanites of many groups and statuses interact and where people from an extensive rural hinterland extending into three major linguistic and culture areas and representing several religions and numerous castes come to buy, sell, and pass the time. I sat in teashops, retail stores, barber shops, and the like, observing and talking with the proprietors and their customers. Later I moved to other settings: to wholesale markets, residential areas, craftsmen's places of work, small factories, government offices, hospitals, recreation areas, political rallies, public transportation depots, religious centers and events, the stalls of sidewalk vendors—wherever I could interact with people naturally or in interview situations. I talked with people of all sorts—businessmen, laborers, students, Gypsies—including those such as letter-writers and itinerant dentists who deal with a wide range of people. My favorite setting was a little teashop run by a Punjabi Sikh. Over the entrance was a conspicuous sign proclaiming it the "Data Hotel and Restaurant." One could hardly ask for more clearly documented evidence of the legitimacy of his data source.

SOCIAL CATEGORIES AND ETHNIC IDENTITY

My initial question was, "What kinds of people come here?" (or do business here, pass by here, work here, live here, etc., as the situation dictated). I soon learned that social categories could be elicited to the exclusion of individual social types by the wording of the inquiry: by asking "Who all comes here?" (*kaun kaun . . .*) rather than literally "What kinds of people come here?" (*kis kisim kē . . .*). In the early stages, especially, I was interested in terms employed which defined the general categories—the domains—which respondents had in mind when giving specific answers, as well as the specific answers themselves; that is, I was interested in words such as the Urdu *quōm* (nation, race, tribe —almost literally "ethnic group"), the Hindi *jātī* ("descent group," which carries much the same connotation), and *nāshtā* (belief or creed) as well as terms for specific named categories of varying degrees of inclusiveness. To elicit the latter, I asked not only in the abstract, but in the concrete instance: "Who is he?" "What kind of person was that?" I also listened for unsolicited terms of address and reference. I pursued these matters in such a way as to be able to make use of the method of contrastive analysis of terms and behaviors as prescribed by componential analysts.

As I collected the data, I kept detailed notes on the context of use of the various terms: who used them, with reference to whom, and in what situations. Where possible, I recorded further contextual material on the background of the individual who used the term: his own ethnic identity, where he came from, his native language, where he had been, his education, his occupation, etc. I also attended to any explanation or elaboration on the term's use that he or others might provide, including the reaction of the one to whom it was applied, if possible. These data proved invaluable because, as I shall elaborate below, the terms used varied greatly according to just these kinds of factors.

In this manner, I accumulated a considerable number of terms for specific social identities of varying degrees of specificity and depending upon a wide range of criteria. I cannot list them all, but the pattern is clear. A single interview or observation sequence might provide a small sample such as the following, covering most of the major social dimensions but few of the specific categories: Punjabi, Muslim, Kūmhār (potter caste), Untouchable, Khatri (caste), Vaisya (caste category), Baniya (Vaisya merchant), Agarwāl (a Vaisya caste), Garg (an Agarwal sib), Shīā (a Muslim sect), Pathān (a Muslim "tribe"), "villager," Vaishnavite (a Hindu sect), Pahari (mountain people), *refūjī* (refugee—from West Pakistan), Sikh, *bābū lōg* (white-collar workers), "eating-drinking people" (well-to-do), "man from Delhi," Anglo-Indian, Chamār (leatherworker caste), Shūdra (artisan caste-category), "small castes" (low castes), Nepali, etc. In other words, there was a variety of terms used to describe people and the terms referred to various aspects of their identities. These terms can be analyzed according to the criteria or components which are common and distinctive to each category and those which distinguish constituent sub-categories although, as I shall show, this cannot be done fully or consistently without detailed reference to behavioral and situational context. Thus, the terms listed above fall into such broad categories as these:

1. *Religious groups:* Muslim and Sikh, for example, as contrasted with Hindu, Christian, Jain, Parsi, etc.;

2. *Regional-linguistic-national-racial groups:* Punjabi and Pahari, for example, as contrasted with Hindīwālā (person of Hindi-speaking area), Madrasi (South Indian, sometimes including people from western India: Marathi and Gujerati), Bengali, Anglo-Indian Englishman, Tibetan, Nepali, etc.;

3. *Caste-categories* (the *varnas*): Brahman, Kshatriya, Vaisya, Shudra; "high castes" (comprising the highest three of the *varnas*—the "twiceborn"—usually); "small castes" (comprising roughly the Shudra *varna* of low status artisans); "low castes" (comprising, roughly, untouchables);

4. *Social class, life-style, and occupational categories:* villager, laborer, well-to-do, white-collar, etc.

Each of these major categories comprises sub-sets of differentiated and often contrasting categories, not all of which can be accurately presented in a two-dimensional paradigmatic outline. But a vastly abbreviated indication can be made that is consistent with the data without claiming that this particular system of presenting the material is the only, or even the best, one.

(1) Religious Groups

Religious groups (*dharam*) are subdivided as follows:

(A) *Muslims* into: (a) sects (*firkā*): Shīā, Sūnnī, Wāhābī, Kādiyānī; (b) tribes and castes (see 3, below);

(B) *Hindus* into: (a) sects by primary deity or mode of worship (e.g., Shaivite, Vaishnavite), and sects by philosophical and textual tradition (e.g., Sanatham Dharam [traditional], Arya Samaj [reform]); (b) caste-categories and castes (see 3, below);

(C) *Sikhs, Jains, Christians, Parsis* and others can be similarly divided into: (a) sects, e.g., Sikh: Akali, Namdhari, Ram Raiya, etc. Christians: Catholic, Protestant (Baptist, Presbyterian, etc.); (b) caste (see 3, below).

(2) Regional-Linguistic Groups

Regional-linguistic groups, of which there are a great many, are subdivided by locality and dialect so that, for example, Hindīwālā includes Purbīā (people from eastern Uttar Pradesh) and, as remoteness decreases, "man from Delhi," "man of Agra," "man of Meerut," etc. *Refūjī* (refugee) seems also to be a term of this order.

(3) Caste-Categories

Caste-categories, which are ideally limited to Hindus, but are in fact terminologically (and behaviorally) distinguished in all religious groups, with or without a religious designation appended (e.g., "high caste Muslim"). Caste-categories comprise various specific castes (*jātī*: named, birth-ascribed, ranked groups). Hindu terms for these groups are often applied outside the Hindu fold, either on the basis of pre-conversion ancestral caste status (e.g., "Muslim Rajput") or, in the case of the lower-ranked groups, on the basis of occupation (see F, below).

In order to illustrate the system and the bases for subdividing caste-categories, I will select one Hindu category, (A), and one subdivision thereof at each of three levels, (B), (C), (D), and then comment briefly on other categories among low caste Hindus, (E), and on non-Hindu caste homologues, (F).

(A) "High castes," or "big castes," are a category comprising the highest three ("twiceborn") *varna:* Brahman, Kshatriya, Vaisya.

(B) *Kshatriya varna* includes, among others, Rajput and Khatri castes (*jati*). (But note that some non-Khatri informants would assign Khatri to the lower Vaisya category.)

(C) Within each of these castes are numerous phratries (groups with putatively common patrilineal ancestry, in which endogamy is usually preferred). Thus, Khatri include Arora, Khukran, Banjahi, etc.

(D) The phratries are subdivided again into sibs (closer relatives patrilineally defined, among whom exogamy is enforced). Arora, for example, are subdivided into many sibs including Kumar, Gulhati, Madan, Dhingra, Matta, Sachdeva, etc.

In addition, any of the terms in (A), (B), (C), and (D), may be regionally or subregionally designated, e.g., "Madrasi Brahman," "Rajasthani Rajput," "Amballa Khatri," "Lahore Arora," etc.

(E) Among the lower castes, subdivisions of castes may be made on different principles, e.g., on traditional occupational subspecialty, on region of origin, or on patron deity, rather than on phratry. Also, the caste categories at these levels may be far broader in scope, less specific in content, and less agreed upon in inclusiveness and rank than among the high castes. "Untouchables" include Chamar (leather-workers), Sweepers and, depending upon the informant and circumstances, anywhere from a dozen other castes to no other castes. Chamar, for example, are divided into two distinct groups in Dehra Dun (although the division is unknown to higher castes): the Jatiya who originated in Gwalior, and the Raidasi from Bijnore (cf. Bhatt, 1960).

(F) Non-Hindu groups generally claim to have no castes, for these minority religions of India are equalitarian or at least caste-free in ideology. Nevertheless, all religious groups do in fact contain ranked subgroups displaying some degree of occupational specialization and social separation. The influence of the dominant Hindu society has been powerful. Even the anti-caste Sikhs have, for example, in addition to sects, several caste-like categories including the very low status Bhātrā (an almost Gypsy-like group) and Mazbhī (essentially the untouchable category).

In order to illustrate non-Hindu caste, we will choose Islam, India's largest minority religion and an aggressively equalitarian one. Many sophisticated Muslims, loyal to their religion's precepts, deny that there are ranked groups among Muslims. Yet it is clear, and most will admit, that ranked categories of tribes and castes do exist in Muslim India as follows: (a) Tribes (generally designated by the broad term *quōm*) including Pathān, Mōgul, Sheikh, Sayid, and in some regions, Rājpūt, Gūjar, etc. These are similar in status and some features of structure to the higher Hindu castes. For the most part, they are distinguished by their claimed relationship to the prophet or other religious figures, or by ethnic origin, rather than by occupational status. (b) Occupational groups (generally called *zāt* by Muslims), including weavers, washermen, barbers, butchers, etc., and corresponding in status, structure, and frequently name, to the lower Hindu castes (cf. Karim, 1956:111–160). (c) Phratry, sib, and other subdivisions are similar to those described for Hindus in (C), (D) and (E) above, although there are differences in marriage rules, inheritance rules and other features (even as there are among some Hindu castes).

(4) Parallel Terms Not Implyng Ethnicity

In addition to the obviously ethnic categories and sub-categories listed in (1), (2) and (3) above—obvious in that they suggest common ancestry, common status, common culture, and their concomitants—are terms which appear in parallel linguistic and social context without implying ethnicity as social scientists understand the concept. These designate social class, life-style or occupational status, e.g., *bābū lōg*, student, soldier, "eating-drinking people," laboring people, beggar, villager, official. Subdivisions within these categories are often made on the basis of specifics: particular occupation or office, roles within the category, degree of wealth or poverty, ethnic identity, etc.

These are significant social categories and hence refer to social identities. Their character is objectively different from ethnic groups, however, for cultural homogeneity is likely to be less within them; ancestry irrelevant. Membership in ethnic groups is ascribed; in these categories it is acquired or imposed. People are assigned their class status because they display its attributes and behaviors; conversely, people display the attributes and behaviors of their caste or ethnic group because they are members of it (cf. Berreman 1972b). In the cognitive and behavioral world of the urban Indians with whom I worked, however, this analytical distinction is not made in practice (it *is* recognized when pointed out). I therefore deal with these terms together with the ethnic terms, as social categories. They are so regarded by my informants.

Similarly, since my informants *did not* consistently separate corporate groups (castes, religions) from non-corporate categories (regions, languages, classes), I did not do so in this study. I tried to follow their taxonomies, not my own (cf. Silverberg 1968:127f.).

Terms for social types and personality types—heroes, villains, and fools (Klapp 1962), liars, men of God, charlatans, etc.—were also easily elicited and frequently occurred spontaneously in conversation. These, however, were *not* used in contexts parallel to those I am discussing here—social categories. Urban Indians thus distinguished clearly in usage between social categories and individual social types. I have followed their distinction and have chosen to confine my analysis to the former except where a social type is relevant as a putative characteristic of a social category (see Stereotypes and Indicators, below).

The terminological categories I discuss are real to those who use them. They come continually into play in conversation and behavior. The terms themselves were collected from many people in many situations. They can be organized and charted into an inclusive or maximal terminology (cf. Sebring 1968:196ff.), and I am in the process of doing so. But the total terminology would be known to no one; its contrasts and categories would fail to find agreement among many, and there would be numerous points at which no clearcut paradigmatic relationship between terms could be drawn—only the contexts of use could show this relationship. Thus, "Muslim" is often contrasted with "Punjabi" or "Purbia," although it is a religious designation whereas they are regional-linguistic designations. "Sikh" is contrasted by some informants with Hindu *varnas* such as Brahman and Kshatriya, and is ranked relative to them. An Anglo-Indian woman contrasted Hindu, Sikh, and Punjabi, but was unable to specify the religion of her "Punjabi" category when asked. What is more important for the research is that this was irrelevant to her. Recently an Indian sociologist has written a book on caste in which he cites Arora as a caste contrasting with Khatri, whereas all of my informants cite Arora as a phratry within Khatri (cf. Chhibbar 1968:6). The Khatri caste itself was not consistently identified as to its *varna* (caste-category) status. The analytical utility of an inclusive chart of terminology is thus perhaps limited to the fact that, to the extent that it is complete, it identifies the widest range of categories available to people in this city from which they can select, and which they can apply to themselves and their fellows and translate into behavior.

In working out the terminological system, a very complex picture emerges. First, there is a wide variety of terms which may apply to the same individual. Thus, to take a simple case, a man might well be identifiable as (1) a Punjabi, (2) Muslim of (3) Teli (oil-presser) caste, who is (4) an urbanite working in (5) a white-collar job—five designations which are usually non-contrastive. Another individual might be (1) a Purbia (that is, from eastern Uttar Pradesh), (2) Hindu of (3) Kumhar (potter) caste who is (4) a villager working as (5) a laborer. The latter five terms are also non-contrastive with one another and each is usually constrastive with the correspondingly numbered term in the preceding five. All five contrast pairs can vary more or less independently, although there are correlations among some of them and a few combinations are unlikely. Other terms can be added within each of these contrast sets (other regions, other religions, other castes, other life-styles, and other occupations); sub-categories could be designated within many of these terms (sects within Islam, phratries and sibs within castes, localities within regions) and super-categories could be designated for some (caste categories, more inclusive cultural-linguistic regions, etc.). This gives some idea of the terminological complexity of social categories. Clearly, social identity cannot be understood without understanding the variation in peoples' knowledge and use of the categorical terms and the individual and circumstantial sources of that variation. These matters, of necessity, became a major focus of the research.

The number and specificity of terms which could be applied to an individual, and which ones would be applied in a particular instance, varied from one informant to another and from one situation to another. The total range of terms available and appropriate for an individual was never socially and situationally applicable at any given time. Individual variation in the use of terminology proved to be largely a function of one's own social identity relative to those of whom he spoke or with whom he interacted. This is partly a matter of knowledge which, in turn, is a matter of subculture, social distance, and social relevance. For example, most Muslims could tell me in considerable detail and with consistency about several sub-categories of Muslims: the sects, tribes, and caste-like occupational categories and their characteristics. Few Hindus could give even a minimally coherent picture. Muslims, on the other hand, had a fairly clear picture of Hindu social categories (though not as clear as Hindus). Similarly, all Chamars (untouchable leather-workers) distinguished two endogamous and culturally distinct castes among themselves. No one of any other group made this distinction or even knew of it when it was suggested to them. "Leather-workers are all alike," they said. For them, Chamar was a caste; for leather-workers it was a caste category. The Chamars, on the other hand, knew a good deal about the culture and social organization of their caste superiors.

Generally, upwardly mobile individuals and groups defined those they regarded as competitors for status differently than those same people were defined by people with whom they were non-competitive. The audience to statements about social identity seemed to influence heavily the nature of those statements: behind-the-back statements were different from face-to-face ones; statements before peers were different from statements before social superiors; statements before strangers were different from statements before acquaintances; statements in haste or anger were different from considered statements; statements to un-identified individuals were often cautious, those to misidentified individuals were often regretted.

In a chart of all of the terms collected and their relationships, one could demonstrate with a series of overlays how people in different social positions differentially view the categories which compose their social environment (cf. Sebring 1968:186f.). In a preliminary attempt, I find, not surprisingly, that people are most detailed and consistent in the use of terms for their own groups and less so for those socially adjacent. They become more vague as social distance increases, but especially as that distance increases downward in the social hierarchy or toward greater social stigma or outward toward more alien identity; that is, people are most knowledgeable about those in their own and nearby groups. They are more knowledgeable about those superior to themselves in status and power than about those inferior. People know well those who dominate them, but know little about those they dominate. As I have suggested above, untouchables know a great deal about Brahmins; Brahmins know little about untouchables. Muslims know a great deal about Hindus; Hindus know little about Muslims. And this applies not only to terminology and social structure, but to general ethnographic knowledge. There are good functional reasons for this—those of lower or stigmatized status have both the opportunity (as people who perform services for others) and the need to know their powerful superiors, and these are not reciprocal. There is cross-cultural confirmation, especially in studies of American society. Waller noted thirty years ago that "it is usually the subordinated member of any pair who tends to develop insight into the other" (Waller 1938:356).[2] This is true of groups as well as individuals.

In the case of regional designations, the specificity of terminology is a function of physical, social, and cultural proximity. For example, all South Indians are called "Madrasi" by most local informants although they come from widely divergent cultures and areas within the Dravidian region. In fact, some informants identified people of Maharashtra and Gujerat, who come from western India and share the Indo-Aryan culture of the North, as "Madrasi" and refused to alter the identification even when these facts were pointed out. Within a radius of 200 miles of Dehra Dun, on the adjacent and culturally similar plains, the distinctions are refined—people are designated by sub-region or city. The culturally and linguistically distinct mountain people, even from only a few miles

[2] I wish to thank my father, Joel V. Berreman, for suggesting this citation together with the reference to Faris and the concepts "primary" and "secondary" relationships, below. I never cease to be impressed at how much of what we discover has been discovered before.

away, are relatively undifferentiated by Dehra Dun informants, even though among themselves the distinctions are many and minute (cf. Berreman 1960, 1972a). Within the sixty mile long Dehra Dun valley, with the city in the center, distinctions are made between the eastern and western ends, and within the city people are (or can be) designated by neighborhoods.

Situational differences in the use of terminology are more complex. An outsider can learn quite quickly to make conventionally accurate assessments of a wide range of social identities. Learning which ones are relevant in a given situation is more difficult, for a number of alternatives are always open. Familiar situations elicit varying terminologies. A man of merchant caste who is fastidious about matters of ritual purity and pollution will discuss an impending wedding with detailed reference to the caste, subcaste, sib, and family affiliations of the participants, the caste and religion of those who will be hired to provide services, the region and social class of guests. A wide range of statuses will be important to him. In his drygoods shop, however, he will categorize customers only in ways relevant to the customer role, relying on stereotypes about the honesty, tight-fistedness, propensity to bargain, and buying preferences of various social categories he encounters. Evidently "everyone's money is green" (in the Indian case, more often blue)—he simply notes who is likely to spend it, how readily, and for what. If, however, someone crosses him or taxes his patience, he may hurl an ethnic slur at the low status customer ("dirty Chamar," "lying Muslim," "hill-billy") or mutter one under his breath after the departure of a high status one ("stupid Sikh," "greedy Baniya," "arrogant Bengali"). A teashop proprietor, on the other hand, will look at potential customers in terms of religion and major caste categories because he has to attend to his customers' notions of ritual purity and the jeopardy in which inter-dining puts them. A barber will attend to certain categories of class, religion, and region in order to assure that he can please his customers in the hair styles they prefer and expect. Customers behave in complementary fashion. It is clear that these relations are not defined by the "whole persons" involved—by the sum of the statuses of those interacting—but by those segments of the social selves which are relevant in the situation. The relations outside one's own ethnic group are impersonal and fractionated; they are what sociologists have often termed "secondary relationships." They contrast with the personal, holistic, "primary" relationships in the family, the village, and other traditional settings where all of one's statuses are known, relevant, and likely to be responded to (cf. Faris 1932)—relationships found in the city only within the ethnic group or neighborhood, if at all.

What I find terminologically, then, are several sets of social categories which are employed simultaneously, alternatively, or in various mixtures depending upon who is speaking and the situation in which he is speaking, as he defines it. There is no "correct" or "complete" taxonomy of social categories. One man's contrasting terms often prove to be another man's interchangeable terminological variations. For some people and in some circumstances, untouchables contrast with Hindus; for others they are a subcategory of Hindus. For some, "untouchable" includes all Shudra castes; for others it includes only leather-workers and sweepers, while for still others it includes three or four or more castes in addition to these. It may or may not be congruent with "low caste." For no one does it include his own caste. For some, "little castes" means Shudra castes; for others it means Shudras and untouchables; for still others it means "castes lower than us." For some, Purbia (people of eastern Uttar Pradesh), is a subcategory of laborer or a synonym for laborer; for others it is a purely regional term. Some apply it across religious and caste lines; others reserve it for low caste (or lower class) Hindus of the region. For some, Jain and even Sikh are subcategories of Hindu; for others, including themselves, they contrast with Hindu (and some regard Jains as a subgroup of the Vaisya caste category). Innumerable additional examples could be given. Differential experience, differential aspirations, various audiences, differential definition of the situation, differential relevance, all lead to differential designations and interpretations of social identity.

There is order in the use of terminology, but it is order explicable only by reference to social, cultural, personal, and situational context, and is not derivable from the terminological system itself or from the relationship of terms to their referents out of context.

STEREOTYPES AND INDICATORS

The second and third questions addressed in my research, inquiry into stereotypes and the indicators by which people are identified as members of social categories, are relatively straightforward matters which seem not to require extensive discussion here. Suffice it to say that stereotypes were many and relatively consistent with terminology. There is no term of social identity which is not richly characterized in stereotypic metaphor and simile. These were discovered through inquiry, spontaneous comments, folklore, epithets, and a wide variety of similar sources. They cover character traits, mental and physical prowess, physical appearance, habits and proclivities. Anant has recently presented the results of social-psychological research on caste, religious, and regional stereotypes in North India, which give tabulated results of extensive surveys utilizing

88 stereotypic traits (Anant 1970 n.d.(a), n.d.(b); cf. Rath and Sircar 1960; G. and R. Sinha 1967). These are consistent with my qualitative materials.

Indicators were also many and relatively closely correlated with terminology. They were discovered through inquiry, observation, and interaction, "natural experiments," photograph identification, characterizations in mass media, and the like. Readily apparent but often subtle indicators of identity that were most used and most diagnostic in casual interaction were speech, dress and adornment, manners, life style, and physiognomy, in roughly that order (cf. Sebring 1969). They ranged from conspicuous indicators (the traditional Muslim woman's all-concealing *burkā* contrasted to the stylishly worn middle class Hindu woman's *sari*), to subtle ones (the regional and sub-regional differences in mode of wearing the *sari*), and to unverifiable stereotypes (including many of the alleged physical differences among groups such as the "loose skin" of Paharis). Distinctive cultural and social structural attributes also symbolize identity (ceremonies, myths, systems of kinship, social organization, traditional occupations, dietary preferences, etc.). Some of these are not readily apparent but are nonetheless important as symbols of identity and foci of self-esteem. Muslims are proud of their cross-cousin marriage, polygyny, kosher standards of meat preparation, prohibition on pork, prohibition on graven images, and prohibition on portraits and music in mosques—Hindus are repelled or amused by them. Muslims are repelled or amused by Hindu deities, ceremonies, cow worship, eating habits, and marriage customs. Mountain people are proud of their brideprice marriage; plains people are proud of their dowry marriage. And so it goes.

Interaction is also a key indicator of ethnic identity. People of common status tend to interact more freely and intimately with one another than with those who do not share their status. The caste, for example, is the maximum unit of status-equal interaction in many contexts and especially in those which are intimate or ritual in nature. Those of common ethnic status are likely to live, eat, work, converse, worship, and marry together. Even those sharing only common language interact in casual conversation more freely than with others, while common regional origin may bring people together in ethnic restaurants, regional associations, or at regional celebrations. The identity of a person is often discovered by the company he keeps.

People put as much effort into conveying the desired symbols of identity to others—in trying to get the desired response—as they do in discerning them in others. Conventional cues obvious to the initiate are often subtle to the stranger. In Dehra Dun, proprietors of teashops, for example, conventionally indicate their religion (and hence that of their expected clientele) by the cooking utensils they display prominently to passersby: stainless steel or aluminum for Muslims, brass for Hindus. I have never seen an exception to this rule, and the only instances in which both types were displayed together were in shops owned by people of neither of these groups. That this is symbolic behavior is suggested by the fact that both groups use both kinds of utensils in their homes. Shopkeepers from each group rationalized the superiority of their utensils in terms of beauty and cleanliness. Thus the utensils displayed in Hindu and in Muslim teashops were used not only for purposes of identification, but to verify favorable self-images and unfavorable images of the competing group (in this case, in terms of cleanliness-slovenliness). Similarly, the differing Hindu and Muslim methods of slaughtering animals were used by each group to verify the cruelty, immorality, and crudity of the other. In general, competing groups engaged in what might appropriately be called mutual status degradation, implicit in which was status affirmation of one's own group.

A stark reminder that the question of indicators is not academic appeared in a news item from Ahmedabad, reported in the *San Francisco Chronicle,* on October 1, 1969. Describing the Hindu-Muslim riots there in which 1000 were reported to have died, the article noted: "Since would-be killers identify their victims through dissimilar Hindu and Moslem ways of dressing, many Ahmedabadis have started wearing Western clothes as a measure of safety." But appearances do not always provide safety. Ved Mehta, reporting the tragic communal strife attending the birth of Bangla Desh, noted: "Hindus and Muslims in East Pakistan were often indistinguishable, and in those cases the only way the [Pakistani] Army could tell them apart was by making them strip, for Muslims are circumcised and Hindus are not" (Mehta 1971:174). Fortunately, ethnic identification and interaction are not often immediately matters of life and death; unfortunately, as we know in America, they *are* often crucial to the well-being of those involved.

INTERACTION

The fourth and, in my estimation, the most important question addressed in the research was that of the relation of behavior to the categories expressed in terminology, to associated stereotypes and to other aspects of the social situation. I focused on people's responses to others, but was also alert to management of the self in conveying a desired impression and eliciting a desired response (cf. Goffman 1959a, 1967, Berreman 1962). My aim was to find out how people act in terms of the identities available to them and confronted by them.

In this phase of the research, I wanted to rely primarily on observation—to see and hear behavior that was conditioned by cognitive assessments of social identity. I listened, for example, to the drivers of horse-drawn vehicles as they shouted to clear the path of pedestrians.[3] I was rewarded not only with an enriched vocabulary of threats and epithets, but with modes of address corresponding to the drivers' judgments of the social identity of the people they were addressing—ranging from the deferential request that the well-to-do Brahmin save himself, to the insulting threat directed at the country bumpkin. I saw teashop keepers send Muslim and untouchable potential customers on their way, or, more often, require them to wash their own utensils after use. I saw passengers move away from undesirable seat partners on public buses. I saw and heard people deferred to, abused, flattered, patronized, welcomed, avoided—in contexts where it was apparent (and often explicitly verified) that this was a consequence of their ethnic identity. This was ethnic identity, social hierarchy and social separation in action. I also saw votes courted on ethnic appeals, and abrupt repudiation of that appeal if misidentification of ethnic identity occurred or if the appeal was regarded as spurious.

A wide range of data on behavior was obtained indirectly—by talking extensively with people about inter-ethnic experiences. One could observe for days before seeing behavior identifiable as ethnically conditioned, but cooperative individuals could recall instances from a lifetime of experience and observation.

Symbols of identity and in fact identity itself can be and are manipulated in order to maximize the rewards or minimize the sanctions which adhere to them in the rigid social inequality of India's plural and stratified society (cf. Isaacs 1964; Srinivas 1966). Sanskritization (the adoption of traditional symbols of high caste status) is a well-documented method of identity manipulation, as are Islamicization and analogous processes of status emulation among members of ethnic groups attempting mobility, revitalization, or solidarity. Westernization is an individual means to status enhancement and material advantages. Retreat into special religious roles, and recourse to deviant status are other forms of individual mobility (cf. Berreman 1972a, ch. 10).

Most indicators of social identity are under some degree of individual and group control.[4] Skin color, physiognomy, and other unalterable features are of relatively minor importance. Hence, identity is to a signif-

---

[3] I am grateful to J. Michael Mahar for suggesting this particular technique to me in the field.

[4] This section has benefited significantly from discussions with Lucile F. Newman, based on her own fieldwork in India.

icant extent a matter of choice in the relatively anonymous and momentary arena of much urban interaction. Most of the indicators are *assumed* to be intrinsic to groups or categories; in *fact* they are often manipulated. The effectiveness of their manipulation is largely a function of the credibility of the assumption that they cannot or will not be—that indicators in fact indicate the ethnic identity of those who display them (cf. Berreman 1972b).

In the manipulation of identity, people make use of the currency that is available to them in the marketplace of public esteem, advantage, and other rewards. Thus, in the city, students, white-collar workers, and other employed non-menials can often maximize their status through obscuring ethnic ties and adopting Western clothes and manners, and they proceed to attempt to do so. These are the people hardest to distinguish ethnically, and whose ethnic identity is least relevant in most of their social relations. Among people in menial or traditional occupations and those who have retained strong rural ties, status enhancement may be most attainable and relevant through Sanskritization—conformity to a high status traditional ideal of behavior. To some who regard themselves as discriminated against but who are numerous and/or well organized and cognizant of common interest, organization into caste associations (Rudolph and Rudolph 1960), into ethnic nationalist movements (Orans 1965; cf. Geertz 1963), into political action groups, into unions and the like, is most advantageous.

Every conceivable urban occupation and small business category from coolies to drygoods merchants is organized into an association in Dehra Dun, as is every regional group represented in town. The effectiveness of the organizations varies widely. For those of high status, fraternal groups, professional associations, and chambers of commerce may be avenues to status enhancement or status protection. To the most marginal, the tradition of marginality itself may pay off, as in the case of itinerant blacksmiths, resident puppeteers, basket-makers, utensil sellers, certain groups of beggars, animal trainers, etc.—all of whom live on the physical and social periphery of the city and who are tolerated and rewarded (however grudgingly) partly because of their traditionally esoteric cultural characteristics which often derive from a distant homeland or a glorious or mysterious past. For them, no other avenue to social survival and enhancement is realistically available, so they emphasize their group identity and uniqueness through dress, manner, and style of life, as do Gypsy fortune-tellers in American society. In all of these cases, corporate groups are formed and utilized to promote self interest. That tradition—fundamental to rural caste organization—runs deep, and as circumstances change, it surfaces in many guises.

Identity manipulation, although possible, is not easy because most indicators are not easily dissimulated, especially in intense or extended interaction. As a mountain villager lamented, "We don't know how to dress or act in town. There even a poor untouchable puts on a shirt and pajama and looks respectable, but we can't look like that. Even if we spend Rs.200 on the finest cloth and have the best clothes made, we still look like fools in town" (Berreman 1972a:307). Moreover, in the most crucial circumstances, ethnic credentials are sure to be closely checked through acquaintances, kinsmen, and one's natal village. This is a deterrent to ambitious plans for "passing."

There is a traditional kind of entertainer (*bahūrūpiyā,* lit. one of many [disguises]), who travels among Indian towns and cities making his living from the amusement he affords others by skillfully simulating various identities (policemen, meter-reader, fakir, sadhu, transvestite, Anglo-Indian, rich man, blind woman, etc.) and fooling shopkeepers and others in repeated interaction in many guises and on successive days. Few could get away with it; it is an art at least as difficult as that of the juggler, who does easily what others find impossible. His remuneration is a gauge of his skill, revealed only when, after a series of successful encounters over a period of several days, he reveals himself to those whom he has fooled and requests payment. This is identity manipulation made into entertainment and into a profession.

Identity manipulation is often expressed as casual, situational, or instrumental impression management (Goffman 1959a, 1963; cf. Berreman 1962). I saw many examples: young village men affected Western dress in town; high caste Bengali men changed from regional to Western dress depending upon the social situation; politicians adopted the dress identified with Congress Party leaders or the dress of the ethnic community whose votes they sought; applicants for waiters' jobs in high class or high caste restaurants concealed low caste status by their manner and the temporary adoption of high caste names, while Muslims did the same. It is proverbial that mountain men who emigrate to work as cooks and servants in homes and hotels in the cities are largely of low caste, while mountain men who work in such places invariably report themselves to be of high caste. Speech patterns are manipulated much as are manners and patterns of dress, and for the same purposes—but perhaps with more difficulty or less success (cf. Gumperz 1962, 1964).

RELATIONSHIPS AMONG ASPECTS OF IDENTITY

In general, I found that stereotypes and indicators of ethnic identity were closely tied to one another and to terminology. Once the ethnographic information had been collected on these three kinds of data, one could predict with fair accuracy in a new situation from any one of the three to the other two.

Interpersonal and intergroup behavior, however, was *not* closely related to terminology and its correlates. As sociologists of race relations in America have repeatedly demonstrated, people often do not act as their attitudes suggest or even as they say they would when confronted by an individual of a despised or honored or feared group (cf. La Piere 1934; Kutner et al. 1952). They behave as the situation demands or makes most comfortable rather than as consistency with belief would seem to dictate. Ethnic identity is relevant to, but far from determinative of, behavior; people act in context, not in the abstract. The structure of interpersonal and intergroup behavior, then, lies in the interplay of situational and motivational factors underlying choices among alternative behaviors, wherein cognitively distinguishable and terminologically specifiable identities are relevant but not determinative.

Behavior proved to be less specific than terminology: people knew many more social distinctions than they acted upon in any given situation. They tended to assimilate terminological categories into broader behavioral categories and to apply them as the purpose and context of the interaction dictated. Rough analysis suggests that the most common behavioral categories in impersonal, short-term, face-to-face interaction were: superiors (those honored, feared, or obeyed), equals (often far broader, as a category, than the caste system would suggest, and often with far more suppressed reservations and anxieties on the part of participants than their behavior would reveal), inferiors (those disparaged, dominated, or shunned), aliens (those regarded warily and avoided), and non-entities (those irrelevant, unimportant, or inexplicable, hence ignored). To which of these broad categories a representative of a particular group would be behaviorally assigned often varied with the situation. A poor Brahmin, treated as superior in a ritual context, might be treated as an equal in a Western setting, and as an inferior in a business transaction. An untouchable sweeper or low caste tailor might be treated as a non-entity when performing his job in a high caste home, an inferior in a tea shop, an equal in a dry-goods store.

Certain social categories or identities tended to obscure or take precedence over others in their influence on behavior. With notable consistency, those identities which were most stigmatized or alien in an individual were the ones to which others responded. To Hindus, the fact that someone was Christian or Muslim was more relevant than that he was Punjabi or Purbia, usually; if he were untouchable, that took precedence over his being Hindu and over his being Punjabi or Purbia; his being a villager, a hill-billy or a laborer took precedence over his being Brahman or Rajput. The most consistent exception seemed to be that middle-class status—particularly at the upper end of the scale—often took precedence over virtually all else: over religion, region, and even caste. Middle-class status was not so transcendent, however, in narrowly ritual, patently traditional, or intimately familial contexts, of which the epitome in all respects is marriage. These contexts tended to draw out traditional identities, with their attendant obligations and behaviors. Such behaviors are conspicuous when they appear in what Western ideology defines as situations beyond the sphere of traditional corporate-group responsibility: employment, credit transactions, legal testimony, bureaucratic functions, etc., where they are often described as "nepotism" (cf. Sharma 1969). Most of my informants regarded these as, to a significant degree, extensions of familial, caste, and ethnic functions, where "primordial sentiments" of group identity, loyalty, and commitment are held to be morally primary.

The facts and processes described here seem to be generally true of contemporary life in urban India as secularization, political participation, and Westernization increase, as new criteria of social identity assume importance, and as avenues to power and privilege become available.

CONCLUSIONS

As highly structured as Indian society is in terms of traditional corporate groups—notably castes—and as often as they appear or reappear in urban situations, these are only part of the basis for urban social interaction. Their traditional functions seem to be diminishing in importance (cf. Béteille 1969:30–56; Silverberg 1968:127f.). In urban society, other named and readily distinguishable social categories are becoming at least equally important. But even knowing all of these categories does not afford an adequate understanding of urban social interaction and urban social structure for such interaction and structure depend upon—in fact compromise—complex behavioral choices within the ideal structural framework and its associated values. These choices are based largely on implicit rules which take into account a variety of situations, goal-orientations, matters of personal and temporal circumstance, the immediate and ultimate audience to behavior, the actors' own definitions of the social situation, their respective roles in it, and its probable outcome.

The terminological system of social categories reveals some important parameters within which the choices are made, but it by no means reflects them all. To understand urban society one must also know the context of the use of terms, the behavioral alternatives available and the criteria for choice among them.

These are the most general conclusions of this research. In order to elaborate upon them and to point out some of their implications, I will divide the final discussion between methodological-analytical conclusions and empirical-theoretical conclusions, suggesting the practical significance of the latter.

METHODOLOGICAL-ANALYTICAL CONCLUSIONS

To discover the significant social categories in urban India, it is necessary to find out what people say and how they act with reference to one another. Terminology, its meaning and use, is important in this regard. The discovery and description of social categories requires attention to the subtle as well as the conspicuous aspects of social behavior, to verbal and non-verbal communcation, to social situations including their participants and the participants' identities—in short, to the total context of interpersonal behavior and how it is perceived by its participants. This can only be derived by intensive participant-observation, extensive interviewing, and the willingness to secure information and insights wherever and however they appear. This is as true in seeking to learn the terminological system of social categories as it is in the investigation of their stereotypes, identifying characteristics, and their behavioral manifestations in interaction.

The methods used in the research reported here have been briefly described in earlier sections. Most of the data were derived by observation of, and listening to, natural interaction and natural conversations, by discussing my observations with participants and observers, and by inquiry about interactional experiences. Formal elicitation procedures (cf. Frake 1964) were used from time to time to check terminology, meanings, and relationships among terms. These procedures were found to be useful after I had acquired relatively complete ethnographic knowledge about social categories and their significance in interaction. They proved inadequate to the initial acquisition of that knowledge and especially to the discovery of the existence, situational relevance, and meaning of the full range of social categories (beyond the most obvious ones). Formal procedures, in short, tended to produce formal answers, depicting ideal, conventional, and stereotyped, rather than actually employed social categorization. Their utility was thus severely limited.

As a result of this research experience, I find myself in agreement with Perchonock and Werner (1969:238) when, after pursuing their componential analysis of Navajo classifications, they concluded that "every statement uttered by informants [and, I would add, every bit of social behavior] is worthy of consideration and analysis." This conclusion is not surprising in ethnography—it is axiomatic in participant observation, the traditional method of ethnography. It becomes significant in the context of "the new ethnography" (as componential analysis has been called by some of its practitioners) where it has been largely ignored, only to be recently rediscovered (cf. Berreman 1966b). Analysis of terminological systems is a useful—even necessary—tool, as the formal analysts have emphasized, but without behavioral, interactional, and contextual analysis it remains, as Perchonock and Werner suggest, "simply a process of description and enumeration." [5] It is especially sterile, and likely to be both fragmentary and misleading when it deals with terminology which is complex, acutely relevant to behavior, and when that behavior is heavily laden with vested interest and affect, as is the case with social categories in urban India. In short, it is inadequate precisely where understanding is most crucial. Similar sterility results from a purely social structural approach or a purely cultural description, as too many accounts of caste in India demonstrate. Inquiry into the subjective meaning of behavior in social context seems to stand the best chance of providing an understanding of how inter-ethnic relations work—in this instance, of comprehending what is going on among the ethnic groups and social categories which compose India's pluralistic, urban society—and of illuminating similar processes in the societies of most contemporary nations (cf. Barth 1969; Bruner 1961, n.d.).

EMPIRICAL-THEORETICAL CONCLUSIONS

This research suggests some inferences about the nature of urban society and ethnic relations in India and about the way in which they contrast with the better-known and more thoroughly researched rural situation. I will discuss the latter first as a basis for discussing the former.

[5] This view is shared by increasing numbers of componential analysts, just as some symbolic interactionists have come to recognize the importance of terminology—a convergence which may contribute to a productive synthesis. Thus, Kay (1969:19), in summarizing formal analysis, says, perhaps a bit optimistically: "Cognitive models alone do not predict overt behavior. But when the cognitive model is supplied with the information it specifies as necessary for reaching a decision, it can predict overt behavior accurately." In the case of social categories, that necessary information is largely situational and interactional information.

Rural-Urban Contrast

The village comprises people whose statuses are largely a function of their membership in corporate groups (families, sibs, castes). They tend to remain in their "home territory"—the familiar setting of the village and its local region. Religious diversity is often absent, and where this is not the case, it is handled in traditional fashion, very often on the model of caste differences. Villagers interact in terms of their total identities on a personal basis with others who know them well. Status summation is the rule: well-to-do people are powerful people of high ritual and social status; poor people are relatively powerless and of low status (with the exception of some religious roles where poverty is defined as consistent with or even necessary to high ritual status). As a consequence of these facts, there is relatively rarely a novel interactional situation to be figured out, rarely status incongruity to be coped with, rarely important interaction with strangers. In the city, on the other hand, ethnic diversity is great. A large proportion of one's interaction is outside the "home territory" of one's neighborhood, and is with strangers or casual acquaintances. Even those who are not strangers often know little about one another and see one another in limited, stereotyped situations. Therefore, a large proportion of interaction occurs in contexts where only specific statuses—parts of the social identity—are relevant or even known, and the elements of individual status (ethnic, ritual, economic, occupational, political statuses) are not as highly correlated as in the village. People therefore have to figure out how to interact on the basis of minimal information in highly specific, impersonal situations, rather than responding on the basis of thorough knowledge, consistent statuses, and generalized relevance.

City people usually know very little about the corporate groups to which their fellow city-dwellers belong and the internal structure of those groups. This does not mean that the city is socially unstructured or even less structured than the village, but rather that its structure is less conspicuous. The structure lies largely in the regularity of behavioral responses to subtle cues about social identity and its situational relevance which come out of face-to-face interaction which is impersonal and often fleeting. This is reflected in the stereotypic differences between the social knowledge and skills of the country bumpkin and the city slicker, each of whom is a laughing stock in the other's milieu where his hard-won social knowledge and skills are as inappropriate and irrelevant as they are effective and appropriate on his home ground. Both survive socially by reacting to the social identities of others, but the expression, definition, and recognition of those identities and the appropriate responses are quite different. The villager is well-versed on corporate groups, the individuals who compose them, the history and characteristics of the groups and their members, and the traditional social, economic, political, and ritual interrelations among them. He depends on ramified knowledge rather than superficial impressions. The urbanite is well-versed in the identification of a wide variety of strangers as representatives of both corporate and non-corporate social categories. He knows the superficial signs of their identity, their stereotypically defined attributes, the varieties of situations and the social information necessary for interaction with them, and methods of defining and delimiting interaction in the impersonal, instrumental world of urban interaction. He knows also when situations are not impersonal and instrumental, and how to act accordingly and appropriately. Urban residential neighborhoods are often relatively homogeneous ethnically, and stable over time, so that interaction approximates that in the village. Indian cities have for these reasons often been described as agglomerations of villages. What I have noted above about urban interaction applies, therefore, to the work-a-day world of the city—the bazaar and other public places. It is less applicable to interaction within residential neighborhoods and relatively "private" settings.

In the urban situation, where status summation is less and is less relevant than in the village, and where livelihood is not dependent on high caste landowners, power and privilege are not tied so closely or necessarily to traditional ritual status. People of low ritual status who have essential services to offer may be able to organize themselves, for they are in a position to exercise political and economic influence and to acquire or demand social amenities. Thus, the sweepers of Dehra Dun, one of the most despised groups in the society, have been able to organize and surpass other low status groups in security of employment, standard of living, and morale, because they are the exclusive practitioners of an essential service: providing the city's sewage and street cleaning systems. They are also a significant political bloc and a self-confident people. This is a distinct contrast to the situation of their caste-fellows in surrounding villages where their untouchability and dependence upon farming castes of high status insure deprivation, discrimination and all of their consequences. The position of urban sweepers also contrasts sharply to that of the equally low-status Chamars (leather-workers) in Dehra Dun. The latter are unorganized, impoverished, almost powerless, and despondent. Their despised status is compounded by technological displacement (commercial shoes are replacing their hand-crafted ones). Only those individuals who have escaped to non-traditional, non-menial occupations (and they are few) have escaped the full consequences of their untouchability.

Ethnic Identity, Social Relations, and Change

Despite ethnic heterogeneity, impersonal interaction, the situational specificity of ethnic relevance, and the prevalence of impression management, urban residents of Dehra Dun cannot and do not, for the most part, change their ethnic identity. In this respect they are unlike the Kachin described by Leach (1954). Instead, they manipulate aspects of it, bringing to the fore that which the situation or their goals require. Caste is a matter of birth and religion; region and language are matters of birth or early socialization in most cases. Class status and even occupation are not easily altered because of the relatively closed nature of the society and the limited opportunity structure. Thus, in a world where status manipulation and impression management are frequent, status change is infrequent.

This structural rigidity is reflected in terminology: *jāti* (descent group) or *quōm* (tribe, ethnic group) may refer to religion, region, or language as well as to caste. Béteille has discussed this matter explicitly, concluding that "the word *jāti* may thus be applied to units based on race, language and religion as well as to castes in the narrower sense of the term. How easily these different kinds of identity are confused can best be illustrated by a common remark I used to hear in Bengal where I grew up. It would be said of a person: 'He is not a Bengali, he is a Muslim (or Christian)'" (Béteille 1969:48). The system is based on an assumption of status stability for which caste is the model.

It is possible to change religious identity: by conversion to Christianity or Sikhism or to the reformist Arya Samaj sect; a woman may marry and become a Jain or Sikh; a Hindu family may vow that if a son be granted them by the deity, he will be raised as a Sikh—but these are unusual and virtually irrevocable shifts.

Within a broad status category, shifts may be made in response to changes in prosperity, education or other circumstances, not unlike the shifts Leach describes for the Kachin. This is the message implicit in an ironic proverb about Muslims: "The first year we were butchers, the next Sheikhs. This year, if prices fall, we shall become Sayids" (cf. Blunt 1931:184).[6] Such shifts are claimed far more often than they are accorded

[6] This can be interpreted roughly as follows: First we were poor and of low status; then we became prosperous and claimed higher status. Now, if prices fall, we will save our pride by using our poverty as the rationalization for an audacious claim to

by other groups in the society. Across major boundaries (Hindu-Christian, touchable-untouchable, tribal-non-tribal), the likelihood of successful shifts decreases drastically.

The comment by Béteille quoted above points up the fact that although changes in identity are difficult and unsual, it is usual and expectable that people will be called upon to make choices among alternative and complementary statuses in various circumstances, especially where status summation is far from perfect, as it characteristically is in the city. People expend considerable effort trying to assure that the statuses they regard as advantageous and appropriate for themselves are conveyed in particular contexts, and they expend considerable energy in trying to discern and respond to the relevant (if possible the most stigmatized) and appropriate identities of others. This is where knowledge of the meanings attached to attributes and behaviors in various social and situational contexts is crucial to successful interaction, and where the manipulation of these meanings is crucial to identity maintenance. This is the crux of urban social organization.

The distinctiveness of social groups in Dehra Dun, as in India generally, tends to be translated into social ranking—into differential social valuation and differential access to goods, services, and other rewards in society. Hierarchy is deeply pervasive and contagious (cf. Opler 1968). Social identity thus makes a very tangible difference in one's life chances. This is epitomized in caste (cf. Berreman 1966a), but carries over into most sets of social categories.

The insight and understanding upon which successful social behavior depends, therefore, includes not only knowing the characteristics of groups and their members, but also understanding the relationship of group membership to privileges, to the power which confers those privileges, and to the sanctions which enforce them. On the individual level this means knowing the social capabilities as well as the social identities of those one meets: what they expect and what they can be expected to do, what resources they have at their command, how they can be expected to act and react in particular circumstances and with what effect. To the extent that inter-group relations are characterized by stability, it is primarily a consequence of balance of power, not consensus on the desirability of, or the rationale for, the system. No stigmatized, oppressed, or even relatively deprived ethnic group or social category that I encoun-

---

high status based on religious merit rather than wealth. In a personal communication explaining the humor in this proverb, Joanna Kirkpatrick points out that the Sayid, as a *pir*, lives off the worshipful charity of others. Hence, in the proverb, "the structural opposition is between sacred and secular beggary." The speaker claims the first when reduced to the latter.

tered in Dehra Dun or in its rural hinterland accepted its status as legitimate. But many—perhaps most—individuals in such statuses accepted that status as fact and accommodated to it while cherishing a hope or nursing a plan or pursuing action to alter it.

The fact of cultural differences within the society is an expression of social relations, as Leach has noted for the Kachin (Leach 1954:17), as well as a factor influencing the nature of those relations. That a man is a Sikh ensures that Hindus, Muslims, and Sikhs as well, will assume certain things about his character, his abilities, his motives, and his habits, and will in various situations act differently toward him than toward non-Sikhs. The same is true of all socially defined groups. At the same time, these identities are sources of self-esteem, and mutual esteem, and trust among those who hold them, even if they are denigrated by others. They serve to define social entities whose members can count upon one another to have common values, goals, and interests, whose behavior can be predicted, who can be trusted, and who can therefore be called upon and mobilized for purposes of individual and group welfare and enhancement. These assumptions cannot be made about those of alien ethnic identity. It is in these facts that much of the dynamics of India's plural society can be understood. It is in insightful comprehension and skillful manipulation of the social identity of oneself and others that individuals are successful in negotiating their society, and in acting to change it.

Increased availability of education, mass media, and political participation, together with conspicuous consumption of luxury goods by the well-to-do, and callous disregard for the needs and desires of the poor by many of the well-to-do, contribute to and accelerate the likelihood of change through enhancing awareness of alternatives, providing an understanding of the means to change, and increasing the accessibility of those means. Urban India is the arena in which this is happening most rapidly. There the social structure is loose enough to allow experimentation with various alliances and social structures which have been elsewhere inhibited by the rigidity of traditional, rural social organization and the unitary relationship between that social organization and the distribution of power. Effective mechanisms for change may result, actuated by newly mobilized interest groups growing out of significant urban social categories.

As people thread their ways through the intricate networks of urban social structure, they choose or forge paths which accommodate their needs, reward their aspirations, and justify their humanity. People travel these paths in groups more often than alone. Many of the paths are closed to those of particular groups, but new ones are opening, and old ones are being circumvented. Future trends in Indian social, economic, and political organization will be largely determined by which paths are open, which are followed and which reward their followers. In this respect, the analysis of urban Indian social organization takes on an acutely practical significance, and the role of ethnic identity, its maintenance and manipulation, assumes critical importance. Similar processes can be seen at work in complex ethnically plural, rigidly separated, and sharply stratified societies in many parts of the world, including the United States.

10

The Urban African and His World

William Bascom

By millions, Africans have been moving from rural areas into cities. The rate of urbanization has been increasing, and there is no sign of a decline. Leaving their homes and traditional way of life, they face a new setting in an urban environment.

In South Africa, cities founded by white settlers are being swelled by Bantu from the reserves, despite the policy of apartheid and to the increasing discomfiture of its proponents. Johannesburg, the largest city south of the Sahara, is over a million, Cape Town over 700,000, Durban over 600,000, Pretoria over 400,000, and Port Elizabeth over 200,000. Benoni, Bloemfontein, East London, Germiston, Springs, and Vereeniging-Vanderbiljpark in the Union of South Africa, Lourenço-Marques in Mozambique, and Bulawayo in Southern Rhodesia have passed 100,000, and Salisbury is over 200,000. Before the Europeans arrived, the Africans of this region lived in scattered homesteads. There were regimental camps and tribal capitals whose populations numbered in the thousands, or perhaps tens of thousands, but which lacked the permanency of cities. Capitals were moved to new sites each time a new ruler was installed, and men left the regimental camps to marry and establish their own homes when their military service was completed.

Three centuries ago the population of San Salvador, Angola, the capital of the Bakongo empire, was estimated at 70,000 but soon afterwards it declined in size and importance. Luanda, which was founded by the Portuguese in 1573, now exceeds 200,000.

Leopoldville, now approaching 500,000, had passed 300,000 by 1954, in-

SOURCE: *Cahiers D'Etudes Africaines* 14 (1964): 163–85. © by Ecole Pratique des Hautes Etudes, Paris and Mouton & Co., Paris–The Hague. Reprinted by permission.

creasing six fold in less than twenty years; only 50,0000 of the 300,000 inhabitants were born in the city, most of whom were children. Nairobi in Kenya and Khartoum-Omdurman in the Sudan are over 200,000 and the 100,000 mark has been passed by Elizabethville, Luluaburg, Stanleyville, and Brazzaville in the two Congos, Dar-es-Salaam in Tanganyika, Mombasa in Kenya, and Douala in the Cameroun. Throughout most of this part of Africa also there had been no cities before the arrival of white settlers, miners, traders, missionaries, and colonial officials, due in large part to the practise of shifting agriculture. African villages were moved as the soil became exhausted or for other reasons, precluding large, stable settlements.

In West Africa, Dakar expanded from 54,000 in 1931 to 300,000 in 1960, only a century after it was founded by the French in 1857. The 100,000 mark has been passed by Bamako in Mali, Conakry in Guinée, Freetown in Sierra Leone, Abidjan in the Ivory Coast, Sekondi-Takoradi and Kumasi in Ghana, while Accra is approaching 500,000. In Nigeria, Ibadan probably exceeds 500,000 today and Lagos 300,000, while four other Yoruba cities and Kano had passed 100,000 by 1952.

Some of these cities are also new, but West Africa had cities before the advent of Europeans, some dating back at least a thousand years. In the Western Sudan, inland from the Guinea Coast, there were Kumbi and Kangaba, capitals of the ancient empires of Ghana and Mali. The latter is a small village today, and the former extinct; but other ancient cities still exist: Kano, Sokoto, Wagadugu, Gao, Segu, Jenne, and Timbuctoo. And along the Guinea Coast there were Kumasi in the Ghana of today, and Benin and the Yoruba cities in Nigeria.

Africa had its cities before the outside forces from Europe impinged upon it, south of the Sahara as well as in Egypt and North Africa. These outside forces caused the decline of some ancient cities, the expansion of others, and the development of what I call here the new or modern cities. Some of the new cities are several centuries old, but they were founded by Europeans since the period of exploration.

These new cities, and many smaller ones that have not been mentioned, have developed as important ports, as in the case of Cape Town and Dakar, as governmental headquarters like Leopoldville, Pretoria, Salisbury, and Nairobi, and as mining centers like Johannesburg and Elizabethville. Railroads have contributed to the development of smaller cities, and to the growth of the larger ones, but none of the largest new cities has developed solely as the result of either railroads or trade. Similarly industrialization, in the sense of manufacturing as distinguished from mining and shipping, does not in itself explain the development of any city over 100,000 in Africa south of the Sahara. It has been important in South

Africa and the Congo, and it will become increasingly important in other parts of Africa, but it is both a recent and a localized cause of urban growth.

There are, then, two kinds of African cities, the old and the new, both of which are rapidly expanding. And there are two kinds of urban Africans, those who have moved to the cities from rural areas, and those who were born and raised in the city, who have married and raised their families in the city, who will live their lives, and will die and be buried there with their ancestors. The "urban worlds" of these two kinds of urban Africans are quite different. We will discuss first the recent migrants to the urban environment.

All over the continent and in increasing numbers, Africans have been moving into the cities from farms and villages. Some come voluntarily, in hopes of a better standard of living and in search of novel goods and new experiences which are not provided in the rural "tribal" setting in which they were born and raised. Some come out of desperation, when their land becomes too poor or too crowded to support them, and they see nowhere else to turn. Many come only temporarily to earn money to pay taxes, or to buy imported goods for their own satisfaction. Some spend a considerable part of their life in the city, but return to their rural homes to spend their old age and be buried.

What they find in the city, and what happens to them, depends in part on the city they go to and the country in which they live. The tragic picture of urban life in Johannesburg, South Africa, under apartheid, has been tellingly portrayed by Ellen Hellman, a sociologist, in her study of *Rooiyard: A Sociological Survey of an Urban Native Slum Yard* (1948), Wulf Sachs, a psychoanalyst, in *Black Hamlet* (1937), Alan Paton, a novelist, in *Cry the Beloved Country* (1951), and Trevor Huddleston, a priest, in *Naught for Your Comfort* (1956). The frustrations of Africans to whom the attractions of European life were denied, particularly in Nairobi, made themselves known through the Mau-Mau uprisings in Kenya, and may well have added fuel to the recent conflict in the Congo. The gayety, bustle, and the temptations of Lagos, as well as the disillusionment and cynicism of those who move there are being described by Nigerian writers themselves.

The cities also attract the educated Africans, students from universities and schools who do not wish to return to their fathers' farms. And children are sent to the cities of West Africa to attend school or to learn a trade. They were focal points for nationalist movements for independence, and, after independence, have remained more concerned with national problems than the rural areas, where traditional rivalries between ethnic groups and subgroups persist. The cities are a hope for a national unity that transcends the traditional boundaries of language and culture.

The process of urbanization has created new problems, and urban life for Africans has its seamy side. Many men who go to the cities leave their wives and children on the farms, some hoping to bring them to the cities eventually. But high rents and the scarcity of housing for Africans, aggravated in some areas by segregated patterns of residence, may make it difficult for their families to join them. The more rapid the process of urbanization and the more restrictive the policies of segregation, the more difficult this problem is. In the rural areas, the wives, the children, and the aged who are left behind must take care of the farms and do the work that is normally performed by young men. This creates hardship on individuals and often leads to shortages of food.

Unmarried men also go to the cities in search of work, so that many cities have a preponderance of young men, but few women, children, or elderly people. On the mining camps, there may be no quarters for wives and children, to say nothing of polygynous wives and their children, and there may be regulations which prohibit wives and children from accompanying their husbands. On the gold fields of Witwatersrand, in the Union of South Africa, Phillips (1938) found that less than one percent of all Africans had their wives with them.

In cities and in mining camps a common result is prostitution, or at least extra-marital relations which are condemned by the codes of both African and European society. The disproportion of males and females, in both urban and in rural areas, has undermined and weakened the family and, particularly in urban areas, extra-marital relations result in children born out of wedlock by mothers who cannot or do not give them proper attention.

Juvenile delinquency, which was practically unknown on the farms and villages and even in the traditional African cities with little immigration, is becoming a problem in the new and rapidly growing African cities. Statistics from Salisbury in Southern Rhodesia for a five year period (1939–43) showed no general upward trend in the number of juveniles charged, but an increasing number of these charged with more serious offenses. Juvenile delinquency, as distinct from petty crimes by first offenders, was increasing. Charges of theft and housebreaking were responsible for more than half of the prosecutions, and a number of African juveniles were developing into habitual thieves. This study cited unsatisfactory home control as the main factor contributing to juvenile delinquency, due to the breakdown of family life, and lack of parental control, loose living by one or both parents, unsatisfactory care of orphans, or crowded and unsatisfactory living conditions. In this study poverty was considered as a cause of many cases of theft, but not the sole factor, and the lack of adequate leisure activities and of schooling and educational discipline were considered only as contributing factors.

A study of juvenile delinquency in West Africa, in what is now Ghana, showed a ten percent increase in juvenile offenders over a period of ten years (1936–45). This increase, and in fact eighty percent of the total offenses for this period, were accounted for by offenses against property by boys in five large cities. The same proportion was found in the sample of delinquents selected for intensive study, with most of the offenses being petty thefts by individuals, or less frequently by gangs. Again, there was no evidence that poverty alone was a cause of delinquency, although it played a secondary role, while boys from better-class homes were more prone to become recidivists. More than half the boys in the sample had attended school at some time, though very few had risen above junior schools. More important, children whose parents were dead or separated were significantly more frequent among delinquents; delinquents came from families which were significantly smaller than the control group; and the majority of offenses in the large towns were committed by boys who had come from rural areas, that is whose families had recently moved to the city. Rates of juvenile delinquency and other social disorders are useful measures of change; although increasing in Africa, they are still far below the rates in European and American cities.

The new cities of Africa usually bring Africans into contact, not only with European culture, but with other African cultures as well. In Poto-Poto, the main African town of Brazzaville with 55,000 inhabitants, less than ten percent of whom were born in that city, Balandier (1952) found over 60 ethnic groups from other parts of French Africa, plus immigrants from other African territories. And Busia (1950) found representatives of more than 60 different ethnic groups in Takoradi-Sekondi in 1950 in what is now Ghana. The new city provides an opportunity for acculturation to other African traditions, as well as to Western forms.

Western observers, living in or visiting Africa's new cities, have often spoken of the detribalization that accompanies urbanization, and at one time detribalization was considered as a natural consequence of urbanization. Seeing Africans going to work as bookkeepers, stenographers, and clerks in European shops and offices, seeing them dressed in European clothes and engaged in European leisure-time activities, may give the impression that urban Africans have cut their ties with the past, that they have left both the society and the culture of their parents, and that they are without either in the new context of the city.

In her early and important work on urban Africans in "Rooiyard," which was evacuated for a furniture factory before the study was pub-

lished, Ellen Hellman (1948) concluded that "the rapidity and complete-
ness of the process of detribalisation has been exaggerated." She writes:

> Much is heard nowadays of the detribalised Native and the great
> increase in detribalisation. In every discussion dealing with the Na-
> tive, the cry is raised: "But what of the detribalised Native?" So
> much so that there is a widespread impression that the majority of
> urban and many rural Natives are detribalised. The growth of this
> concept, dangerous because the term "detribalisation" is not defined
> and is not used to convey any definite meaning, but rather a host
> of vague impressions, is gradually tending to merge the meanings
> of the terms "detribalisation" and "Europeanisation." That the pro-
> cess of detribalisation and of assimilation to Western civilisation
> are not one and the same is shown by a more careful analysis of a
> sample of urban population such as the Natives of Rooiyard.
>
> The average European would unhesitatingly classify these Na-
> tives as detribalised. And in doing so he would advance as proof
> the numerous manifestations of the adoption of European material
> culture which he would perceive in Rooiyard. But what is detribal-
> isation? I have taken as my standard the following three criteria:
> permanent residence in an area other than that of the chief to
> whom a man would normally pay allegiance; complete severance
> of the relationship to the chief; and independence of rural relatives
> both for support during periods of unemployment and ill-health or
> for performance of ceremonies connected with the major crises of
> life.

According to her definition, Hellman found few detribalized Africans
in this slum yard of Johannesburg. Most were only temporary urban
residents who had come to the city to earn money to pay taxes or to
buy goods, and hoped to spend their old age in their rural homes. Of
100 families, 13 had lived in Rooiyard for more than four years, 27 for
periods of one to four years, and 60 for less than one year with an
average residence of only five months. Of these 100 families, 74 maintained direct connections with rural families, either through having
their children reared by relatives at home or by sending a part or the
whole of their families to their rural homes. The doctor-diviner of the
city also served as a link with the rural areas by stressing the ties of
kinship with both the living relatives and the dead ancestors.

Yet the effects of acculturation can hardly be exaggerated. European
material culture was being rapidly and sometimes indiscriminately absorbed. The disintegrating effects of urban conditions were nowhere
more apparent than in the change in family relationship, with an un-

dermining of the permanence of marriage, the exclusiveness of the sexual bond, kinship obligations, and parental control. Illegitimacy was accepted, but not condoned. In religion, the inhabitants of Rooiyard hesitated between two worlds, their own and that of the European, secure in neither. Magic, which gave them a sense of security and power, retained its force. All Rooiyard families were technically criminals, because the brewing of beer, which was a traditional duty of a wife for her husband and an economic necessity in the city, was illegal.

Traditional African culture had not disappeared in Rooiyard. Native custom still flourished despite the unfavorable circumstances in which its inhabitants lived, yet a new feeling of unity with other Bantu speaking peoples was developing. Tribal loyalties and rivalries had not been forgotten, which is not surprising considering the short residence in the city, but a broader sense of loyalty was beginning as the result of intermarriage and common disillusionment, suffering, and persecution.

When Africans first move to the city, they are isolated from their relatives, even if they maintain contact with them. They are separated from the lineage, which is the most important kinship group in African societies. Yet when others follow them to the city, they try to settle near a lineage member, and it is in terms of lineages that relatives are invited to the city and that they try to find housing. In the course of time it is possible for the lineage to be reestablished in the new urban setting, if only on a skeletal basis, and as this happens it is possible to reestablish control over marriage and childcare, and to find a decline in extramarital relations and in juvenile delinquency. From what is known of the traditional African cities, it is not unreasonable to expect that this may happen in the newer cities in time.

When Africans move to the city, and have no relatives there, they at least try to settle near someone who speaks their own language, and if possible the same dialect, or someone who comes from their own village. In many new cities, ethnic groupings develop which bring together people of similar linguistic and cultural backgrounds, although scarcity of housing may make this impossible or cause established groupings of this kind to break down. Even where ethnic or linguistic groupings cannot live together, they usually maintain contact. In the unfamiliar and often unfriendly settings of the city, traditional rivalries and antagonisms between peoples who are basically similar in language and culture are diminished, at least temporarily, and a feeling of solidarity may develop which is far stronger than in the rural situations.

As ethnic groups grow larger, new types of voluntary associations may be established, based on ties of ethnic origin, occupation, or common interests, and devoted to mutual benefit, entertainment and recreation, or other interests. Some of these, particularly the "tribal unions" or "improvement societies" undertake to advise and guide local politics back home, democratizing traditional councils, urging better roads and other amenities, and giving the chief the benefit of the wisdom and broader experience of the select few who are more familiar with city life and European ways. If relations with the chief have been severed, they are reestablished, but in a new, advisory role.

The literature on these tribal unions or improvement societies implies that they have developed as a means of aiding recent immigrants to adjust to life in the new urban setting, and they clearly fulfill this function as Little (1957) has pointed out. However, they are not restricted to the new cities of Africa nor to Africans who have recently moved into them. In the ancient Yoruba city of Ife in Nigeria, an improvement society of this type was established prior to 1920, not to improve conditions in the areas from which its members had come, but to influence politics in Ife itself, where its members had been born and raised. This type of voluntary association is new, and has probably resulted from education in schools of the European type, but at least one type of mutual aid society, the credit institution of the Yoruba, Ibo, Ibibio, Efik and other West African peoples, often known as the savings or contribution club, dates back to the period before European penetration in the villages. Nevertheless, recent urbanization has produced a wider range of friendly societies and other voluntary associations, church groups, associations of students from the same school, athletic, musical, and social clubs than was ever known in the traditional cities. These voluntary associations have an adaptive function for new urban immigrants, even when some have as their main raison d'être the "fostering and keeping alive an interest in tribal song, history, language, and moral beliefs, and thus maintaining a person's attachment to his native town or village and to his lineage there."

In an important article on Africa, Mitchell (1956a) has pointed out the danger of confusing the demographic sense of urbanization with its sociological sense. The demographic sense has to do with residence in a large city, and the sociological sense has to do with its effect on the individual's behavior, as for example, the *anomie*, or sense of loneliness and isolation associated with life in the large cities of Europe and America, which urban sociologists, following Durkheim, have stressed. Mitchell emphasizes the danger of assuming that if a man is urbanized in a demographic sense, he is also urbanized in the sociological sense. It is all too easy to assume that the longer a man has been in town, the more severe is his state of *anomie*.

In fact, as Mitchell has pointed out, there is some evidence that *anomie* is most severe among those who have only recently come to the city, and that those who have lived there for longer periods accept certain standards of behavior and conform to them. *Anomie* seems to be not the product of urban conditions of life in Africa, per se, but rather a form of "cultural shock" such as even anthropologists experience when first moving into a different culture, with a new set of rules and standards.

Mitchell's conclusion is borne out by research among the traditional cities of the Yoruba in the Western Region of Nigeria, but before turning to them let us look more closely at a demographic and a sociological definition of the city. For this we will take a study which, though recent, is already a classic, because of the influence it has had on urban studies in Africa and elsewhere. This is *Urbanism as a Way of Life* by Louis Wirth (1938), a sociologist who was a contemporary of Robert Redfield at the University of Chicago, and whose definition of the city relates to Redfield's folk-urban continuum. Wirth's description of the sociological aspects of the urban way of life was based mainly on his studies of American cities, but it provides a useful background against which to compare life in both the newer cities of Africa and the traditional Yoruba cities.

Wirth defines a city for sociological purposes as "a relatively large, dense, and permanent settlement of socially heterogeneous individuals." The first three criteria are clearly demographic; and are qualified by the word "relative." Different countries take populations of over 2,000, 2,500, or 5,000 as a basis for classifying communities as cities for census purposes, and densities of 1,000 and 10,000 per mile have been proposed by Wilcox and by Jefferson as a criterion of urban settlement. But as Wirth points out, whatever figure is taken for size or density it must be an arbitrary one, and the same is true for the number of years which constitute permanence.

Wirth's definition has been widely accepted, but it has proved difficult to apply cross-culturally because of the factor of "social heterogeneity." Because this factor was not clearly defined it has proved difficult, in Africa, for example, to distinguish between social heterogeneity and homogeneity. Probably the difficulty also lies in the fact that however it is defined, social heterogeneity is a sociological result of urbanization under certain circumstances, rather than a feature essential or even pertinent to a demographic definition of the city.

The shortcomings of the criterion of social heterogeneity are suggested by the equivocal positions taken by those who have attempted to apply it to traditional African communities. In his study of a Yoruba city in Nigeria, William Schwab (n.d.) concludes that "if Oshogbo was viewed on the level of form, it was an urban community; if viewed in terms of social organization and process, it was folk." In an earlier study, Horace Miner (1953) described Timbuctoo as "a primitive city" and its inhabitants as a "city-folk." Yet he concluded that "Timbuctoo is a city. It has a stable population of over six thousand persons, living in a community roughly a square mile in area, and patterning their lives after three distinct cultural heritages. The size, density and heterogeneity of the city are all evident." Timbuctoo, of course, was known as an important center of trade and learning long before European contact.

Miner, who studied at the University of Chicago at the time of Wirth and Redfield, commented on "the lack of any concise benchmark from which to appraise the degree of homogeneity." He admittedly rests his case for heterogeneity on the cultural diversity of the three distinct ethnic groups which inhabit Timbuctoo, the Songhai people, the Tuareg, and the Arabs. Yet neither he nor Wirth suggests that ethnic diversity is essential to a definition of the city. American and European cities, and many of the new cities of Africa, include peoples of different racial, linguistic, and cultural backgrounds, but this can be regarded as a secondary feature of urbanization, and a basis for distinguishing two types of cities, which I have called cosmopolitan and non-cosmopolitan.

Compared to Timbuctoo's 6,000 inhabitants, over half of the 5,000,000 Yoruba in Nigeria live in cities over 5,000. Over thirty percent live in cities of over 40,000, of which six are larger than 100,000, including Ibadan, the largest Negro city in Africa, with a population today of over half a million.

In 1952 the Yoruba had an index of urbanization (as developed by Davis and Casis 1951) of 39.3. This falls below Great Britain with 65.9, Germany with 46.1, and only slightly below the United States with 42.3; but it exceeds that of Canada with 34.3, France with 31.2, Sweden with 28.7, Greece with 25.2, and Poland with 17.4. The Yoruba are the most urban of all African people of any considerable size, and their urban way of life is traditional.

Official figures on population density of Yoruba cities are lacking except for Lagos, where they are given as 25,000 per square mile in 1901, 50,000 in 1921, 58,000 in 1931, and 87,000 in 1950. In 1950 the three wards of Lagos Island had densities of 67,000, 111,000, and 141,000 per square mile. Grant (1960) gives an area of nine square miles for Ibadan with an estimated 500,000 inhabitants in 1960, or 55,555 per square mile. It has been possible to calculate approximate densities for three other cities as of 1931, giving 5,720 for Abeokuta, 13,914 for Oyo, and 43,372 for Ogbomosho. These figures compare with 24,697 per square mile for New York City, 15,850 and 15,743 for Chicago and Philadelphia,

Table 1. Yoruba Cities with Populations over 40,000 in 1952

	1952 Census	1931 Census	1921 Census	1911 Census	1890 Moloney	1860 Delany and Campbell	1856 Bowen
Ibadan	459,196	387,133	238,094	175,000	150,000	150,000	70,000
Lagos	276,407	126,108	99,690	73,766	86,559	30,000	20,000
Ogbomosho	139,535	86,744	84,860	80,000	60,000	50,000	25,000
Oshogbo	122,728	49,599	51,418	59,821	60,000	—	—
Ife	110,790	24,170	22,184	36,231	—	—	—
Iwo	100,006	57,191	53,588	60,000	60,000	75,000	20,000
Abeokuta	84,451	45,763	28,941	51,255	100,000	110,000	60,000
Oyo	72,133	48,733	40,356	45,438	80,000	75,000	25,000
Ilesha	72,029	21,892	—	—	40,000	—	—
Iseyin	49,680	36,805	28,601	33,262	20,000	20,000	20,000
Ede	44,808	52,392	48,360	26,577	50,000	—	20,000
Ilorin	40,994	47,590	38,668	36,342	100,000	100,000	70,000

and 5,451 for Los Angeles in 1960, the four largest cities in the United States.

Because of the high ratio of inhabitants per room and per square foot and the compactness of the traditional housing, the size of older Yoruba cities is easily underestimated by visitors. Abeokuta, for example, appears much larger than Ogbomosho, which is actually eight times as dense and half again as large.

Yoruba cities are large, and even the traditional ones are dense. Their permanence over the past 100 years is documented by the estimates of Bowen of about 1856, of Delany and Campbell in 1960, of Moloney in 1890, and in the census reports of 1911, 1921, 1931, and 1952 (Table 1). Bowen gave no estimates of the population of Ife, Ilesha, or Oshogbo, but he mentions that the countries of Ife, Ilesha, Igbomina, and Efon-Alaiye had not yet been visited by missionaries, adding "we are assured that there are many large towns in that region." [1]

Yoruba territory was first penetrated in 1825 by the expedition of

[1] For historical references on Yoruba cities see Bascom, "Urbanization among the Yoruba" (1955) and "Les premiers fondements historiques de l'urbanisme yoruba" (1959b). For full references, and for other sources, see Bascom (1952, 1958, 1959a, 1960). This paper was originally prepared for a series on "The African Character" given at the University of Minnesota in March 1961.

Clapperton and Lander, who travelled inland west of the large cities of today. They estimated the size of some of the cities they visited, including eight to ten thousand for Ijana, five to six thousand for Assula, upwards of 10,000 for Assoudo, ten to fifteen thousand for Duffo, and upwards of 7,000 for Chiado. No estimate is given for the "large and populous town" of Shaki, although they were told that its chief had two thousand wives. Beyond Shaki lay Kooso which "at least contains twenty thousand people." At this point Lander wrote, "the further we penetrated into the country, the more dense we found the population to be, and civilization became at every step more apparent. Large towns at the distance of only a few miles from each other, we were informed lay on all sides of us." Yet of the remaining Yoruba towns visited, estimates are given only for Adja with four thousand, Ateepa with six thousand, Leobadda with six or seven thousand, and Tshow with four thousand.

Of all these towns, only Ijana and Shaki can be identified today. Presumably all the rest were destroyed or abandoned during the wars of the last century. Bowen, the first American missionary in Nigeria, who travelled through much of Yoruba country in 1849–56, wrote:

> I have counted the sites of eighteen desolated towns within a distance of sixty miles between Badagry and Abbeokuta—the legitimate result of the slave trade. The whole of Yoruba country is full of depopulated towns, some of which were even larger than Abbeokuta is at present. Of all the places visited by the Landers, only Ishakki (Shaki), Igboho, Ikishi (Kishi) and a few villages remain. Ijenna (Ijana) was destroyed only a few weeks after my arrival in the country. Other and still larger towns in the same region have lately fallen. At one of these Oke-Oddan, the Dahomy army killed and captured 20,000 people, on which occasion the king presented Domingo, the Brazilian slaver, with 600 slaves. The whole number of people destroyed in this section of the country, within the last fifty years, can be not less than five hundred thousand.

Clapperton and Lander went on to visit Old Oyo, and by comparing their statements about it and other Nigerian cities like Kano, we can judge that it was at least 20,000 and perhaps 40,000. One can also judge that they felt that Ilorin, Igboho and perhaps Kishi, which still exist today, exceeded 20,000. Clapperton described Old Oyo as surrounded by a dry moat and a mud wall about twenty feet high. The wall was oval in shape, "about four miles in diameter one way and six miles the other," fifteen miles in circumference, and entered by ten gates. Following another visit by Richard Lander and his brother John in 1830, Old Oyo was evacuated about 1839, after a defeat by Ilorin, and was reestablished farther south at the present site of Oyo, today a city of 72,000 and traditional in character. Recent archaeological investigations at the site of Old Oyo suggest that it was inhabited by a large, dense population.

From reports from Dahomey to the west, which was explored earlier, we know that Old Oyo intervened in the affairs of this powerful state at least since 1724. For a century, from about 1729 Old Oyo received gifts and tribute from Dahomey until about 1827, when Oyo was deeply involved with the wars from Ilorin, and King Gezo of Dahomey sized his opportunity to end the payment of annual tribute.

Ijebu-Ode near the coast, which had a population of 28,000 in 1952, appears on a Portuguese map of about 1500 and is described as "a very large city called Geebu, surrounded by a moat" by Pacheco Pereira, writing in 1507–1508. From 1500 onwards, Ijebu-Ode or 'Jebu is mentioned repeatedly in the literature or shown on maps, at least six times in the seventeenth century, four times in the eighteenth century, and four times in the nineteenth century before it was visited by Hinderer and Irving in 1854. Recent investigations at Ijebu-Ode have discovered an enormous earth rampart, 80 miles long, enclosing an area of 400 square miles, which surrounds the city at distances from about 5 to 15 miles. It is formed by a bank which is still 15 to 20 feet high and 50 feet wide at the base, and a ditch 20 to 25 feet deep and 40 feet wide, which together create a wall 40 feet high.

Even earlier, before discovery of America, when Portuguese explorers of Nigeria first reached Benin in 1485, they brought back in 1486 to the King of Portugal an ambassador from the King of Benin, which was itself an important city of considerable size. From him they learned of Ogané, "the most powerful monarch in these parts." Spurred on to their exploration of the African coast by the belief that Ogané was Prester John, they passed the cape of Good Hope in 1487 and reached India by sea in 1498. Recent studies in Benin make it almost certain that Ogané was the Oni or King of the Yoruba city of Ife, whose successor became the first Governor of the Western Region of independent Nigeria. Yoruba and Benin traditions agree that the ruling dynasty of Benin originally came from Ife, and archaeological discoveries at Ife, today a city of over 110,000, indicate that it was far more important as a center of elaborate ritual and art in earlier times.

The evidence is incomplete, because Yoruba territory remained *terra incognita* for centuries after Benin to the east and Dahomey to the west had been explored. Nevertheless it is clear that the Yoruba have cities which are relatively large, dense, and permanent, and that urbanism as a traditional feature of the Yoruba way of life cannot be explained in terms of industrialization, acculturation, or the development of colonial administrative headquarters, ports, and mining centers.

Acculturative factors have affected the traditional Yoruba cities in the past century, but urbanism as a way of life clearly antedated the earliest European contact, and is clearly not an outgrowth of European acculturation. Urbanization is related to acculturation, as Ralph Beals (1951) has said. Urbanization is a process which involves an adjustment to the new urban setting, and the adoption of new standards and forms of life; but urbanism as a way of life is distinct from acculturation, and it existed among the Yoruba before the first penetration of their area of Europeans.

Ibadan and Abeokuta are not old cities, having been founded in the first half of the last century by refugees from the wars with Ilorin, and Ilorin was only a small village before these wars began. Ibadan and Abeokuta differ from the ancient Yoruba cities in house types and other features but, clearly, neither they nor Ilorin are in the category of the new cities of Africa. Oyo is far more traditional, even though it moved to a new site in the same period. Of all the large Yoruba cities, only Lagos, which is the capital of Nigeria and its principal port and railhead, is a new African city. The site of Lagos had long been known as the entrance to the lagoon from which it is named, and as a small village which numbered only 5,000 at the end of the eighteenth century.

Of all major Yoruba cities, only Lagos is ethnically heterogeneous and in this sense cosmopolitan, yet in 1950 its population was still seventy three percent Yoruba. Ilorin, which is neither ancient nor one of Africa's modern cities, is eighty four percent Yoruba although it has been ruled by Fulani from the north for more than a century and is now included in the Northern Region of Nigeria. All other major cities range from over ninety four to over ninety nine percent Yoruba according to the census, though in many cases the only published official figures included outlying rural areas.

With the end of the slave wars of the last century, Hausa from the North, Ibo and Jekri from the East, and other peoples have settled in Yoruba cities, but in relatively small numbers except for Lagos. Even in the present century the European population of the twelve largest Yoruba cities was negligible compared with South, East, and North Africa. In 1931 the non-native population, which includes Europeans, numbered only 1,443 for Lagos, the capital, 226 for Ibadan, and 159 for the remaining ten major cities combined. The wars of the last century flooded some cities with refugees from others which were evacuated or destroyed, including those from different Yoruba kingdoms and subcultures; but even on this level of subcultural variation we may assume that in earlier times Yoruba cities were ethnically homogeneous, and that non-Yoruba probably consisted mainly of slaves and transient traders.

How did these traditional cities exist without industrialization, which caused the development of urban life in Europe and America? The real base of the Yoruba economy was, and still is, farming, but farming is not an exclusively rural occupation. Many farmers are city dwellers who would regard American suburbia as a curious inversion of their way of life. They are commuters, not from the suburbs to their places of work in the city, but from their city homes to the belt of farms which surround each city.

Nearly all Yoruba engage in farming, but the production of many other goods is specialized. Weaving, dyeing, ironworking, brass-casting, woodcarving, ivory-carving, calabash-carving, beadworking, leatherworking, and pottery, as well as drumming, divining, the compounding of charms and medicines, and certain other activities are crafts whose techniques are known only to a small group of specialists, and often protected as trade secrets through supernatural sanctions. These specialists, who are organized into guilds, may engage in farming, but they supply all other members of the community with their goods and services.

Farming, specialization and trade were the three cornerstones on which the Yoruba economy rested. Intercommunity and intertribal trade was in the hands of specialists in earlier times, either the King's wives or male traders, though this was ended when British control was established and they were replaced by European trading firms. Local retail trade has remained primarily in the hands of women, who tend to specialize in yams, corn, chickens, cloth or other commodities, and who, like the craftsmen, are organized into guilds.

The size and importance of Yoruba markets, visited by many tens of thousands in the large cities, impress the visitor today as they did the early explorers. Trade does not involve a simple exchange of goods between the producer and consumer, as in the Pacific for example, but was carried on by middlemen whose role and motivations are similar to those in our own society. In the simplest case a trader buys from a producer and sells at a higher price for a monetary profit; but in some cases the goods are sold and resold through a chain of middlemen with so many links that it becomes difficult to distinguish wholesaler from retailer. Before European contact the Yoruba had money in the form of cowrie shells, a pecuniary society, large markets, and true middlemen.

Yoruba cities were of course nonindustrial, and lacked the degree of specialization based upon the machine. Yet Wirth himself specifically excludes industrialism as an essential feature of urbanism although it accounted for the development of cities in Europe and America.

> It is particularly important to call attention to the danger of confusing urbanism with industrialism and modern capitalism. The rise of cities in the modern world is undoubtedly not independent

of the emergence of modern power-driven machine technology, mass production, and capitalistic enterprise. But different as the cities of earlier epochs may have been by virtue of their development in a preindustrial and precapitalistic order from the great cities of today, they were, nevertheless, cities.

Yet among the Yoruba the craft form of specialization made each individual economically dependent upon the society as a whole. The weaver depended upon the blacksmith for tools and upon the farmer, the hunter, and the trader for food. The blacksmith depended upon others for food and upon the weaver for clothes. The farmer depended upon the hunter for his meat, the smith for his hoe and cutlass, and the weaver for his clothing. Each of these, moreover, had to rely upon the herbalist, the priest, the chief, the drummer, the potter, the woodcarver, and other specialists for goods and services which they could not provide for themselves. Specialization, even on this level, resulted in an economic interdependence of all members of the city, a factor which I consider as extremely significant.

In Yoruba cities today one can buy a can of food, a machette, or a piece of cloth from Europe, Japan, or India, but food from the local farms is still for sale and the craftsmen are still producing at their looms and smithies, and competing effectively with imported goods from the factories of the world.

Wirth (1938) emphasizes economic interdependence as a result of the size of cities.

> The specialization of individuals, particularly in their occupations, can proceed only, as Adam Smith pointed out, upon the basis of enlarged market, which in turn accentuates the division of labor. This enlarged market is only in part supplied by the city's hinterland; in large measure it is found among the large numbers that the city itself contains. The dominance of the city over the surrounding hinterland becomes explicable in terms of the division of labor which urban life occasions and promotes. The extreme degree of interdependence and instability is increased by the tendency of each city to specialize in those functions in which it has the greatest advantage.

This statement fits Yoruba cities which produce primarily for their own inhabitants, while Oyo and Iseyin, for example, export weaving and iron goods to other Yoruba cities. Yet local or regional specialization is the basis of inter-tribal trade in many parts of the world where cities are lacking. To cite only one example, it is found in the islands of the Pacific where the people of the interior specialize in the production of agricultural foods which they export to the coast in exchange for fish and other products of the sea, but where cities, money, and true middlemen are lacking. The important feature here is that a city, even though nonindustrial as among the Yoruba, finds its market mainly within its own boundaries. The degree of specialization, even though limited to the craft level, makes individuals economically interdependent and provides a basis for the development of larger, denser, and more stable communities. One might also postulate that these results may give rise to the need for some broader forms of political control, which formally unite neighboring kinship groupings into larger communities, but this remains an unsupported hypothesis.

Yoruba cities were heterogeneous only in terms of craft specialization, social stratification, and socio-political segmentation. The city is divided into clearly defined "quarters" or wards, sub-quarters or political precincts, and lineages. In Ife the heads of each patrilineage constituted the precinct council, with one of their number serving as precinct chief. Precinct chiefs formed the ward council, which again was headed by one of its members. The five ward chiefs and three other city chiefs whose titles were "owned" by certain lineages represented the interests of the townspeople, and with eight palace chiefs from the King's retinue, served as the King's council and chief tribunal of the capital of the kingdom. The King, or Oba, whose position was hereditary within the related lineages of the royal clan, was responsible for the affairs of the capital city and of the outlying towns and villages within his kingdom.

Wirth cites the delegation of individual interests to representatives as another feature of urban life which derives from its size:

> In a community composed of a larger number of individuals than can know one another intimately and can be assembled in one spot, it becomes necessary to communicate through indirect mediums and to articulate individual interests by a process of delegation. Typically, in the city, interests are made effective through representation. The individual counts for little, but the voice of the representative is heard with a deference roughly proportional to the numbers for whom he speaks.

This clearly is the case in Yoruba cities, where an individual makes his interests known to the head of his family, and through him to the head of his lineage, the head of his precinct, the head of his ward, the town chiefs, the King's council, and ultimately to the King. However deference is based on the social status of his lineage, as well as its size. Within the lineage, individual relationships were dependent on such factors as seniority, sex, wealth, personal qualities and status as slave, pawn, or free, but between lineages individual relationships were defined by the relative status of the lineages. The individual counted for little, except as a member of the lineage. In Ife social stratification involves nine social strata of which five, comprising perhaps ninety five percent of the population, were ascribed or attributed on the basis of lineage affiliation. The four highest strata were primarily achieved, but often within specific lineages or clans.

Wirth says "the contacts of the city may indeed be face to face, but they are nevertheless impersonal, superficial, transitory, and segmental." All these characteristics are exemplified in Yoruba market transactions, where the principle of *caveat emptor* is as well established as in Timbuctoo. As in our own urban centers, one may have regular customers with whom relations are not transitory or superficial, but one must also deal with casual customers of whom one must always beware in either buying or selling.

Wirth emphasizes that urbanism refers to a distinctive mode of life, and this is evident among the Yoruba in clothing, food, habits, manners and attitudes. City dwellers ridicule the unsophisticated "bush" people, and their attitudes toward the non-urban Yoruba, as expressed in conversation and proverbs, closely parallel our concepts of the "rube" or the "hick." The attitudes of the rural Yoruba toward the city dweller also seem to resemble those in our society.

Yoruba cities are secondary in the sociological sense, as Wirth says, while the lineages are primary. Wirth dismisses the factor of political organization as an unsatisfactory criterion of urbanism. Yet it is the presence of a formalized government which exercises authority over neighboring primary groups, such as lineages, and incorporates them into larger secondary grouping like the city, town, or village. And it is this factor which distinguishes the Yoruba, who are urban, from the Ibo of Nigeria's Eastern Region, who had no cities until recently, despite their larger numbers and higher population densities.

Some Yoruba cities, such as Oyo, Ife, Ilesha, Ijebu-Ode, Ondo and Ketu served as capitals and centers of whole kingdoms and in this sense can be considered as metropolitan. They maintained regular communications with the outlying cities, towns, and villages through representatives stationed in them, collected taxes through them, and tried serious crimes which were reserved to the court of the King. Other large cities such as Iseyin, Ogbomosho, and more recently Ibadan, had formalized city governments but were ruled by a town Chief (*Bale*) under the authority of the King (*Oba*). These cities were not capitals, but they served as centers of trade and warfare. From them the goods and services of specialists reached the smaller towns and villages. This was also true of the capitals, which served not only as centers of warfare and trade, but also of political authority, religion, and arts and crafts.

Here, however, the parallels end. *Anomie* is not apparent, except among those who have recently come to the cities from rural areas. Since the residential unit is the lineage, which involves reciprocal social and economic obligations, the city dweller need not feel lonely and insecure. Yoruba society is pecuniary and highly competitive, and economic failure can lead to frustration, aggression, or suicide, but not to starvation because one can count on the support of his lineage. And one can count on it for social as well as economic support. Lineages were differentiated in status, but these statuses were stable.

Wirth says:

> The bonds of kinship, of neighborliness, and sentiments arising out of living together for generations under a common folk tradition are likely to be absent or, at best, relatively weak in an aggregate the members of which have such diverse origins and backgrounds. Under such circumstances competition and formal control mechanisms furnish the substitutes for the bonds of solidarity that are relied upon to hold a folk society together.

In Yoruba cities, formal mechanisms were not developed as substitutes for those of kinship, but rather as mechanisms of political control on a secondary, supra-kinship level, transcending the primary groups such as lineages. Yoruba cities clearly lack the diversity of origins and backgrounds of other cities, and kinship bonds were not weakened either by urban life or political control on a higher level by city governments. The lineage, rather, was the basis of Yoruba political structure, both urban and rural. A small village might contain only one or a few lineages, but the social and political structure of Yoruba cities were founded on the lineage. The many lineages of the cities were united as a community by the superior authority of city government. To the extent that lineage and other kinship bonds have been weakened among the Yoruba, this has been the result of acculturation, rather than of urbanism as a way of life. And more recent studies of American cities have revealed a greater strength of ties of kinship and neighborhood than were realized by sociologists at the time when Wirth wrote.

In earlier publications on this subject, I suggested that either economic interdependence or centralized political organization, or both, might be substituted for the criterion of social heterogeneity, as a basis for a definition of cities which might be more meaningful cross-culturally. I still regard these factors as important and as less subjective and no more arbitrary than the factor of social heterogeneity and as less likely to be the results of urbanization in certain cases, than prerequisites for the development of cities.

Now, however, I am inclined to go even farther than Mitchell suggested and to recommend that cities should be defined strictly in terms of demographic factors: relative size, density, and permanence. There will still be room for argument about how large, how dense, and how permanent communities must be to be accepted as cities, but the range of disagreement does not seem large, and should eventually be narrowed. There can be little question that the Yoruba had cities as defined in demographic terms, and once this definition is accepted we can proceed to examine the social, economic, political and other cultural features of urban life in the hope of being able to distinguish its consequences from causes of its development.

Defined demographically, urbanism as a way of life and urbanization as the process of urban growth may have a cause-or-effect relationship with cultural and social factors, such as acculturation, Europeanization, detribalization, cosmopolitanism, and other types of social heterogeneity, with the economic or technological factors of specialization and industrialization, and with political factors such as city government. All of these factors should be considered separately to determine whether they are necessary to city growth or are the results of urban life, and whether they pertain to all cities.

Wirth explicitly distinguished urbanism from industrialism; Hellman's study shows that both urbanization and Europeanization are distinct from detribalization; and while Beals maintains that acculturation is related to urbanization as a process, I have tried to show that it differs from urbanism as a way of life. The Yoruba, who were urban before their country was even explored by Europeans, show that urbanism as a way of life differs from urbanization, Europeanization, acculturation, detribalization, industrialization, and ethnic heterogeneity, though there was social heterogeneity in terms of craft specialization, social stratification, and socio-political segmentation.

A comparison of the ancient cities of Africa, as illustrated by the traditional Yoruba cities, with the more modern cities which have developed as a result of direct European contact, reveals some significant differences which may shed some light on the future of the urban Africans.

In the traditional cities most of the inhabitants are born and raised, marry and raise their children, live with their families throughout most of their lives, and die and are buried within the city and their own lineage. Statistical data are lacking, but my guess would be that this held for over ninety percent of the population of the major traditional Yoruba cities until only twenty years ago, and that it is probably not much different even today. This is in very marked contrast to the newer cities of South and East Africa where a high proportion of the African inhabitants have come to the city only very recently, where they are only temporary urban residents, and where they hope to return to their homes before they die.

In Africa's traditional cities, husbands lived together with their wives, their children, and their lineages most of their lives in an urban environment. Ties with the family and lineage were not broken by urban life, nor even temporarily suspended. The authority of the family, lineage, and the chiefdom were maintained according to traditional standards. Traditional forms of discipline were maintained in the cities through the family and lineage, and through the town chiefs and the Kings of the independent Yoruba states. As a result illegitimacy, juvenile delinquency, and crime were surprisingly low, in comparison with the new African cities and with cities of America and Western Europe.

In newer Africa cities urbanization involves separation from the lineage and family and has resulted in the weakening of the family as an institution, with the increase of extra-marital relations, and of illegitimate children raised in poor home surroundings with inadequate care and discipline, and the development of juvenile delinquency. As families and lineages are reestablished in the new cities and populations stabilize, one may expect illegitimacy, juvenile delinquency and crime to decline, if one can judge from the pattern of urbanism in the traditional African cities.

Yet even the traditional Yoruba cities are being affected by the outside influences which have changed Africa so rapidly during the present century. Newcomers from the farms and villages face problems similar in many ways to those of the new cities, and both the new and old urban residents must adapt to the changes resulting from European acculturation.

The strength of Yoruba religion, and its sanctions of behavior have also been undermined by missions, both Christian and Moslem, and by schools and government. Old beliefs have been destroyed for some, without having been replaced by new sanctions or internalized controls, though the number of such individuals is probably smaller than is to be found in Europe and America. The authority of Yoruba chiefs and Kings was weakened during the period of colonial administration, but they have retained the respect of the large majority of the people. The major question here is where they will fit in the political structure of Nigeria as an independent nation.

Western concepts of individual salvation and individual responsibility, which have been taught by the missions and by the schools, have been undermining the traditional respect for the elders, lineage responsibilities, and the strength of lineage controls. The Yoruba are eager for schooling, and grateful to the missions for their role in providing it. Schooling has been a major source of social change, and has added to mobility, as those who leave school often seek suitable employment in other towns and cities where they are separated from their lineages. Industrialization, which has been taking place at a surprising rate in Nigeria since 1956, will further contribute to mobility from the farms and villages to the towns and cities, and to urban growth.

It is easy to predict that urbanization will continue at a rapid rate in Africa for some time, but it is difficult to go much farther. I would suggest that although African cultural features will be retained, probably to a greater degree than many are willing to admit, the new and old cities of Africa will tend to approximate each other and the cities of Europe and America in their sociological characteristics. The evidence from New York, Detroit, Chicago, Havana, and other cities in the Americas indicates the adaptability of descendants of Africans to Westernized urban life, and their preference for it.

SELECTED READINGS

DORE, RONALD P.

1958 City Life in Japan. Berkeley: University of California Press.

A neighborhood study in Tokyo, focusing upon a heterogeneous population of one ward. Valuable as a contrasting approach to the macroanalysis discussed in the preceding parts.

GANS, HERBERT J.

1962 The Urban Villagers: A Study of the Second Generation Italians in the West End of Boston. New York: The Free Press.

The study of an Italian slum in Boston, offering an example of the type of study conducted within a city by setting off a subgroup and following the traditional holistic approach.

HANNERZ, ULF

1969 Life Styles. Chapter 2 in Soulside: Inquiries into Ghetto Culture. New York: Columbia University Press.

Exploding the common notion that there are only a few ghetto social roles, Hannerz discusses four life styles in a Washington, D.C., neighborhood. Significantly, these are related to each other and to cultural and economic conditions.

LEWIS, OSCAR

1959 Five Families: Mexican Case Studies in the Culture of Poverty. New York: John Wiley and Sons.

Lewis describes the life styles of five families ranging from poor rural peasants to wealthy urbanites. An interesting study of contrasts, this book is flavored by Lewis' vivid style of portrayal of the daily lives of various family members.

MILLER, WALTER B.

1971 Subculture, Social Reform, and the "Culture of Poverty." Human Organization 30:277–288.

In this excellent discussion of conceptual problems in the culture-of-poverty idea, Miller provides a detailed discussion of the numerous social identities available to American urban dwellers.

PLOTNICOV, LEONARD

1967 Strangers to the City: Urban Man in Jos, Nigeria. Pittsburgh: University of Pittsburgh Press.

Plotnicov characterizes both ethnic variation and the impact of economic circumstance upon the individual in this study of a few migrants to a Nigerian town. Through the eyes of these men, the reader gains an intimate view of the problems besetting African migrants.

PRESS, IRWIN

1971 The Urban Curandero. American Anthropologist 73:741–757.

Noting that traditional roles are represented in the city with a greater degree of complexity, Press describes differences in the roles of native curers in Bogotá, Colombia.

SUTTLES, GERALD

1968 The Social Order of the Slum: Ethnicity and Territory in the Inner City. Chicago: University of Chicago Press.

Concentrating upon the "Addams" area of Chicago, Suttles discusses the internal and external relationships of four ethnic groups in this inner city neighborhood. Noting, but not relying upon, native ethnic stereotypes, he explains the nature of intergroup relations on the basis of tradition, territory, and life style.

Part Four
SPECIALIZED
COMMUNITIES

Wirth and other Chicago sociologists noted the variety of communities within the early twentieth-century American cities they studied. In addition to the well-known Gold Coast and the Slum (cf. Zorbaugh 1929), such cities were also characterized by large numbers of European immigrants grouped together into neighborhoods and districts. Possessing aspects of their homeland cultures, these districts were set apart in this conceptualization of the heterogeneous city with its variety of subcultures.

The discovery and description of colorful urban subcultures have formed a predominant part of the literature of urban anthropology. Anthropologists, whose approach and background led them to the exotic in an attempt to find "the folk in the urban," gravitated toward such restricted communities, hoping to maintain continuity in the anthropological tradition. The selections in this part discuss distinct groups of urban dwellers much in the above-mentioned tradition. However, they also demonstrate another significant trend emerging as anthropologists move to the city: that of making theoretical contributions to specific anthropological problems which do not seem to fit either end of the folk-urban continuum. They occur in those places where humanity gathers.

One such gathering place, particularly in the Third World, is the squatter settlement. Epstein describes Brasilia's squatter settlements as important residential units for that city's poorer migrants. Far from seeing these localities as "marginal" or "pathological" with respect to the city, Epstein is interested in showing the "historic and continuing interconnections between two groups which give rise to and sustain the disparity between them." Explicating the relation of squatter settlements to urban and national institutions, Epstein aids us in understanding how these social units persist in the face of official policies contrary to their existence. This article pictures the external relationships of squatter settlements just as Mangin (1967) and others have shown the importance of their internal organization into voluntary associations.

In his article on overseas Chinese communities, Crissman provides data on this wide-ranging but culturally similar group in a series of urban settings. Significantly, he refers to the earlier literature on such societies in reporting upon a phenomenon frequently found among immigrants, namely, the nesting or segmentary nature of their associations. Noting that the particular "pattern of segmentation in each city or locality is unique," he alerts the reader to the adaptability of this form of organization for city life. In an approach to ethnic identity that complements Berreman's (Selection 9), Crissman also discusses the notion of the ethnic community as it contrasts with more traditional territorial communities.

In his analysis of Freemasonry in Freetown, Sierra Leone, Cohen contributes to an understanding of political change as well as voluntary associations. Noting the importance of "fraternising" in creating strong organizational bonds which have been useful in national politics, Cohen makes the dual nature of voluntary associations clearly apparent. The wider importance of this article is evident in its focus upon Freemasonry, an internationally organized voluntary association of relatively high importance in the United States, and in its discussion of an economically powerful minority group similar to the Hausa of Ibadan, Nigeria (cf. Cohen 1969).

In addition to offering a documentary view of urban life in Lagos, Marris also emphasizes spatial relationships and their social and economic significance for slum dwellers. His argument demonstrates how the crowded slum locale contributes to the maintenance of family ties, and of craft and entrepreneurial enterprises. Contrasting the integration and ease of slum life with the difficulties of residing in the rehousing area, Marris echoes some of the findings of Young and Willmott in Britain (1957). Like Gans (1962), Marris reminds urban planners that slum-dweller relocation frequently implies unpleasant consequences for the inhabitants.

11

The Genesis and Function of Squatter Settlements in Brasília

David G. Epstein

Urban squatting is the fastest-growing, and one of the most widespread forms of settlement in Brazil and in many other countries in the under-developed sector of the capitalist world. Social scientists and public officials have often failed to take into account factors on the international and national levels which account for the existence of squatting in cities such as Brasília, the new "planned" capital of Brazil. The sources of this neglect also underlie many of the widespread misconceptions and mistakes in writing about urban poverty and worldwide underdevelopment in general.

In the case of Brasília, an understanding of the development of the squatter settlement component of the urban settlement pattern requires attention to the class, urban-rural and regional disparities in the economy, and to the requirements for a low-wage labor in the face of low governmental priority for the housing and other needs of workers. Although planners and officials in Brasília inveigh against squatting, it is in fact a product of the same process of development which produced Brasília and in practice is tolerated and regulated by the same institutions that officially condemn it.

A squatter settlement in a city is an area where people build houses in violation of the formal legal rules about property rights, zoning, and type and quality of construction. Squatter settlements (or squatments) may be distinguished from slums in that most squatters (at least initially,

SOURCE: Thomas Weaver and Douglas White, eds., *The Anthropology of Urban Environments* Monograph No. 11 (1972), pp. 51–58. Reprinted by permission of the Society for Applied Anthropology.

and by their own, if not by official definition) own the houses they live in.[1] Large numbers of squatters, though by no means all of them, are members of the urban working class or the urban un- and underemployed, and large numbers of them, though again by no means all, live in housing of low prestige and durability. Slums, on the other hand, are inhabited mostly by renters, and the most common house types are the decayed town house and various types of tenements especially built for rental to the urban poor.

THE DUALIST FALLACY

One approach to squatter settlements is to regard them as fundamentally divorced from the city around them. When squatters are conceived of as in-migrants from rural areas regarded as the "traditional" sector of a dual society, the assumption of urban dualism follows naturally from the dualist image of the national society as a whole. Thus, just as Jacques Lambert (1959) argues that there are "two Brazils," a conclave of social workers in Brasília suggested that there are two Brasílias:

> The phenomenon of marginality which appears in the Latin American countries indicates the existence of a *dual urban social structure* and has in the economic factor one of the variables of its appearance.

> In addition to this economic variable, which assumes undeniable importance in the configuration of the situation of urban marginality, the concentration of marginalized groups in certain characteristic zones of urban space is observed [emphasis added] (Lambert 1967:2).

While an effort is made to give this term a technical definition, or at least usage, it should be noted that the Brazilian term *marginal* is most often used in crime reporting to refer to individuals from the lower-class, criminal milieu, such as pickpockets, illegal lottery salesmen (*bicheiros*), pimps, and muggers. Use of the term, even in a professional context, must evoke in most middle-class Brazilians associations of the squatting phe-

---

[1] In Brazil squatter settlements are known as *favelas, invasões, mocambos,* and (when over water, on stilts) *alagados*. Among other terms for them are *callampas* (Chile), *bidonvilles* (French), *barriadas* (Peru), and *gecekondu* (Turkey). In English, they are often referred to as *shantytowns*, but not all squatment structures are shanties and not all urban, shanty agglomerations are squatter settlements.

nomenon with crime, violence, and social pathology in general, in correspondence with their standard prejudices.[2]

Others argue that squatter settlements are in some sense rural, either because of the alleged similarity of architectural forms to those in rural areas or because of the supposed provenience and associated social and cultural characteristics of their inhabitants (Bonilla 1962).[3] Bastide suggests that the cultural assimilation of foreigners in Brazilian cities is easier than that of rural migrants who are ". . . bearers of a folk culture, because (a) internal migrations are family migrations . . . (and) (b) the rural family in the city continues to 'socialize' its children according to rural models." (Bastide 1964:76)

Building on the concept of subculture, Bastide goes on to suggest that shantytowns are the locales of "microcultures" which are sharply distinct from the urban milieu as a whole.

Other analysts are concerned with the effect on individual personality of the allegedly rapid cultural change taking place in rural-urban migration. Pye, for instance, suggests (and laments) that the maladjustment and insecurity he believes associated with such migration offer a threat to the national and international status quo. This argument relies very heavily on a concept of social duality similiar to the arguments of the commentators already cited. States Pye:

> Urbanization is . . . a profoundly disruptive process. In nearly all transitional societies the early emergence of urban centers has produced a *fundamental cleavage* between the worlds of the more modernized cities and the more traditional and village-based people. This *bifurcation of the social structure* is usually matched in the economic realm by the development of *dual economies.* In the psychological sphere the rapid transition from the compact and intimate world of the village to the highly impersonal and anonymous world of the city can leave people with deep personal insecurities.

[2] Norman Whitten and James Szwed (1968) use the concept of economic marginality in reference to intermittent or irregular income, a different usage from that dealt with here. Indeed, squatting not involving rent is adapted to marginality in this sense of the term. Use of the term *marginality* for this situation is confusing, however, to the extent that irregular income among sugar workers or urban squatters may be an aspect of their integration into the very heart of the functioning political economy, not of their isolation from it.

[3] Anthony and Elizabeth Leeds have effectively demolished this notion in their paper "Brazil and the Myth of Urban Rurality: Urban Experience, Work and Values in 'Squatments' of Rio de Janeiro and Lima," presented in November 1967 at the Conference on Work and Urbanization in Modernizing Societies, St. Thomas, Virgin Islands.

Thus in a multitude of ways rapid urbanization can cause social, economic, and psychological tensions which, translated into the political realm, become sources of instability and obstacles to rapid nation building [emphasis added] (Pye 1963:84).

Lewis' concept of the *culture of poverty* is more carefully hedged than any of the foregoing discussions, but it also emphasizes the distinctiveness of its bearers from the larger society, rather than the role they play in it. While on the one hand Lewis defines the culture of poverty as a subculture and hence presumably a product of Western capitalism, on the other hand he states:

It is a culture in the traditional anthropological sense in that it provides human beings with a design for living, with a ready-made set of solutions for human problems, and so serves a significant adaptive function (Lewis 1966:19).

The concept of the culture of poverty focuses attention on the relative lack of organization and the isolation of its bearers. Yet Lewis recognizes that many urban squatters may display a sense of community untypical of the culture of poverty, especially when the settlements are low rent areas of stable residence, physically and ethnically, racially or linguistically distinct from their surroundings (1966:23).

A synthesis of these outlooks would suggest that squatter settlements, contrasting so sharply with the loci of oligarchic traditionalism and the new Latin American consumerism (e.g., the modern superblocks and monumental architecture of Brasília's Pilot Plan), house people who, while they may or may not be bearers of the culture of poverty, are isolated from modern Brazilian national life and are rural, marginal, and maladjusted.[4] Fundamentally, these views suggest the squatters' living conditions and their physical separation from the city derive from their failure to pass from "traditional" rural ways to "modern" urban society, a view evocative of the new unilinealism of the bourgeois liberal development theorists such as W. W. Rostow and Cyril E. Black (Rostow 1960; Black 1966).

The empirical basis for the pathologist-dualist viewpoint lies in the blatant economic and social inequality which pervades every phase of urban life in those cities where squatting exists. The presence of this inequality is made painfully apparent by the frequently close juxtaposition of shabby and foul-smelling squatments with luxury apartments, as in

---

[4] William Mangin (1967) suggests without elaboration that urban squatters are less alienated than central-city slum dwellers.

Rio de Janeiro, or with monumental symbolic architecture, as in Brasília.

The policy implications of this view are equally clear—either eliminate these nests of social pathology and potential subversion by means of massive clearance and public housing projects or missionize their residents with community development and other professionally-mediated forms of middle-class morality in order to integrate them into the modern sphere of the society. In fact, the writings of much of this school resemble the older religious missionary forms of colonialist humanitarianism, which translated the poverty and strange customs of the natives into a mandate to provide them as soon as possible with the blessings of clothing and Methodism. Today the Peace Corps tells its applicants that "the most basic contribution a Volunteer can make is to inject some sense of community, some inkling of latent power into a village or slum." This in spite of the fact that squatters have often successfully resisted repeated legal and forcible attempts to remove them and have developed complex networks of voluntary associations of various types!

In fact, both clearance (Safa 1964; Salmen 1969) and community development have been unsuccessful by almost any objective or subjective index. In part this failure is a consequence of the errors of individual programs and their executors, but only in part. It is also a product of the empirical and theoretical inadequacy of the pathologist-dualist position. There is little evidence that squatters are "folk" unable or unwilling to become "urban," or that they have failed to become integrated into the society, and much more evidence that it is the *form* of their integration which has resulted in the spectacular contrast between their lifeways and living conditions and those of their more affluent neighbors. It is not any lack of ties with the dominant sectors of the society that is the problem, but the kinds of ties which exist.

We may apply to dualist analyses of squatting the same criticism which may be made of dualist treatments of the relationship between the Northeast and the Paraiba Valley industrial region in Brazil, Indians and the larger societies of Mexico and Peru, and blacks and whites in the United States. Emphasis on the synchronic, internal characteristics which distinguish a subordinate (satellite, colonized) social group from the group which dominates it (the metropolis) may lead to neglect or even denial of the historic and continuing interconnections between the two groups which gave rise to and sustain the disparity between them. From this first fallacy it is easy to move on to the assumption that the cure for the situation lies in the diffusion of certain characteristics from the dominant sector to the other, or in the full integration of the dependent sector into the dominant. In fact, it is often at least arguable that the solution lies in transforming the nature of the already existing interconnection, or in eliminating the tie completely. To deemphasize the importance of the metropolis-satellite relationship, as the dualists do, is of course to obscure the possibility of such a revolutionary transformation.[5]

In contrast to the cruder imputations of the dualists, many writers emphasize the adaptive or even conservative characteristics of urban squatting. These writers describe a squatting cycle leading from the first tentative efforts to invade private or, more often, public land, to resistance to official challenges to their land tenure and, sometimes, to a high degree of stability as urban neighborhoods (Mangin 1963, 1964, 1965, 1967; Turner 1963). Some writers emphasize that except on the issue of land tenure, squatters tend to be politically centrist or even conservative (Bourricard 1964; Halperin 1963; Peattie, n.d.). Many anthropologists identify with squatters as with other informants and, in particular, look askance at uncritical schemes to "eradicate" squatting, establish public housing, and "reform" squatters (Safa 1964) and emphasize the relative satisfaction of the migrants with the squatment as opposed to their places of origin, especially when these are rural (Herrick 1966; Pastore 1968).

As a policy prescription, this view seemingly would imply a cautious attitude to mass clearance programs and would tend to suggest that public housing schemes (especially high rise schemes and pay-as-you-go plans) fail to fulfill the needs of many squatters. Rather, where conditions permit, the indicated policy would seem to be one of granting land tenure free or at low cost and promoting improvements in such areas as water supply, electricity, and sewage. Some planners, as in Ciudad Guyana, a new industrial city in Venezuela (Rodwin, n.d.), have even favored regarding squatting as inevitable and setting aside areas where it can be permitted with relatively little disruption of the city plan.

Whatever the virtues of squatting as a strategy of survival or upward mobility, however, squatters continue at or near the bottom of a highly polarized urban social structure—if they are upwardly mobile, their ascent is a fairly shallow one. Even more accurate and less alarmist ethnographic data, if it is focused upon the characteristics of squatters and their settlements to the neglect of their position in the society as a whole and its development, takes the squatters' social position as a given and fails to come to grips with the roots of the problem.

ISOLATE AND SYSTEM

As anthropologists have moved from the study of the most primitive and small-scale of the social units comprising the underdeveloped sector of

[5] This discussion incorporates many of the views of A. G. Frank (1967a, 1967b).

the global society to rural units in more developed parts of the society to the study of urban society, they have striven manfully to retain two related attitudes. The first is to regard the unit under investigation, whether a tribe, a village, a neighborhood, a family, an individual, or a squatter settlement, as an isolate, a social organism, a largely self-sufficient entity. The second attitude has been characterized by Martin Nicolaus as keeping their "eyes . . . turned downwards, and their palms upwards" (Nicolaus 1968:9–10). In other words, they study the powerless under the auspices of the powerful, and the information they produce is much more readily available to the latter than to the former. This has been true in spite of the fact that many anthropologists have been sympathetic intermediaries between the rulers and the ruled (Gough 1968).

Without reducing anthropological works in general to the level of crude ideology, these two attitudes have tended to minimize the conflict of their holders with the dominant sectors of society. With a few exceptions (e.g., Leeds 1968b), anthropologists have failed to provide much that is helpful to our understanding of elites or of national and international societies, except insofar as the isolates they study may be assumed to be representative.[6] In this sense anthropology has shared what Mills criticized in his *The Sociological Imagination* as the "abstracted empiricist" retreat from the classical tradition of the social sciences.

The increased interest in cities on the part of anthropologists is to a degree a sign that some anthropologists are abandoning the traditional idealization of the exotic and the primitive.[7] Yet they have clung to emphasis upon the study of lower-class and lumpen elements studies as isolates by methods which resemble as closely as possible the methods used in primitive and peasant villages.

The facts of life in cities and the clear lack of demographic, social, and political equilibrium that are apparent on inspection, however, make the simple application of traditional research orientations untenable. Indeed, given a larger-than-local perspective it becomes apparent that the bulk of the ethnographic data we possess consists of "snapshots" (synchronic views) of primitives in the process of being peasantized, peasants in the process of being proletarized, and ruralities in the process of becoming

[6] See, for instance, one set of proposed criteria of representativity in Conrad Arensberg (1961).

[7] This is occurring only to a degree. In part, increased interest in the "urban" reflects the immediate social control and counterrevolutionary concerns of the rulers of American society, efficiently mediated through the academic marketplace, as in the case of the earlier success of "area studies" interests in the social sciences: Russia, China, Africa, Latin America, Southeast Asia. Suddenly we are confronted with poverty and urban studies.

urbanized,[8] whether through migration to cities or through the extension of formerly "urban" technology and institutions to the countryside. Most of the units traditionally studied by anthropologists as if they were microcosms are, in fact, subsegments of subsegments of a global system of social, economic, and cultural relations established in the wake of the worldwide expansion of Western power. Even the nation-states themselves, in many cases, are specialized parts of this global underdevelopment system. The investigator who seeks to explain the forms taken by component units of this system ignores its existence and its specific forms at his peril; the applied social scientist who seeks to effect piecemeal change without considering how his efforts are conditioned by the requirements of the system and its component parts may be bitterly disappointed. The NATO intellectuals and their successors, who seek to explain the global disparities of wealth, power, and prestige as a consequence of the failure of "traditional" societies or "traditional" segments of dual societies to become "modernized," are at best neglectful of the structure and history of the underdevelopment system.

None of the foregoing should be interpreted as a suggestion that specific empirical studies are a waste of time and that all research should be directed toward the characteristics of the global society as a whole. It is rather to assert that such studies must be informed by some notion of what the underdevelopment system is all about and what it implies for the specific nation, region or city, and smaller social unit under examination.

THE CASE OF BRASÍLIA

These rather broad assertions can only be exemplified within the limited scope of the present article or, indeed, even by far more extended discussion about a single city. In the late fifties, Brazil's federal government began to put into practice a century-old plan to build a new national capital in the savanna country (*cerrados*) of Southern Goiás state in the country's Central Plateau. The construction was guided by a plan written by Lúcio Costa, an eminent Brazilian architect-planner (1957:41–44). Approximately ten years after construction began in earnest, two-thirds of the population of the capital live in areas whose urban ecology and architecture are in direct contradiction to the apartment house superblocks proposed in the original plan. More than 15 percent of the population is housed in technically illegal squatter settlements and over 50 percent in satellite towns whose legality, while unquestioned, was granted in consequence of a last-ditch official effort to limit squatting to

[8] A paraphrase of a passage from Scott Cook (1968:259).

some degree. Many of the dwellings in the satellite towns are constructed of the same materials and have the same physical characteristics as those in squatter settlements.

The decision to construct Brasília in the face of the nation's scarce capital resources and the characteristics of the original plan reflected the character of the political and social stratification system of Brazil, in at least the following respects: (1) the monumentalist emphasis on dramatic architecture and broad vistas; (2) the favoring of automotive circulation in spite of the fact that cars remain a luxury for the vast majority of the Brazilian population; (3) the cursory attention paid to the needs and desires of the first residents (the construction workers) and to the lower-class residents in general; (4) the nondevelopmental, static, or skeletal character of the plan, expressed as a final output rather than a process of growth which at all stages would involve human lives; (5) the necessity, given prevailing political practice in Brazil, of finishing the city according to plan within a three-year period (Kubitschek's presidential mandate) if it was not to be later abandoned; (6) the centralized character of the planning and execution processes themselves, with no provision for consultation or participation by any but upper-level technical and political personnel; and finally, (7) the division of the city into hierarchical sectors. The plan is thus false to the nature of social interaction in cities.[9] The general neglect of the social, in any serious sense, as opposed to the esthetic and the symbolic, is one of the hallmarks of the plan and of Brazilian elite culture in general.

SQUATTING AND LABOR SUPPLY

Building Brasília required large numbers of workers, who came from the poorest sections of Brazil, the Northeast (including Bahia), and the Center-West. According to various surveys conducted, from half to two-thirds of the residents of the largest squatter settlement in Brasília, the Social Security Invasion,[10] came from the Northeast of Bahia, and from one- to two-fifths from the Center-West States of Goiás and Minas Gerais.[11] Invariably the migrants themselves cite economic motivations as primary in their decision to move, although some comments in more

[9] For a conception of this interaction patterning from a planner's viewpoint, see Christopher Alexander (1966).

[10] *Invasão do I. A. P. I.* I.A.P.I. is the acronym for the former Industrial Workers' Social Security Institute, which sponsored the hospital behind which the "invasion," or squatting, began.

[11] Discussion of this data is to be found in "Planned and Spontaneous Urban Settlement in Brasília" (D. G. Epstein 1969).

extensive discussions indicate that many migrants were not unaffected by the more glamorous aspects of the Brasília experiment.

Just as the main strategic resource supplied by Africa in the slavery period was labor, today many underdeveloped regions of economies such as Brazil's have as a principal function the exportation of cheap labor. In Brazil this function is fulfilled by the Northeast and to a lesser extent by some other rural areas, such as in Minas Gerais. The Northeast regularly disgorges migratory streams in accordance with the exigencies of the economy—to the Amazon if the revival of the rubber trade becomes necessary, to the industries of São Paulo, or to Brasília when a new capital is abuilding. Minas Gerais, a secondary source of such migrants, is also a case of the pattern of regional underdevelopment Frank calls "passive involution" (1967). To the extent that the conditions which underlie this exportation of human beings thereby serve the needs of the extant economic and political elites, serious doubts must arise as to the prospects for success of programs administered by these same elites with the declared intention of combating regional underdevelopment.

These considerations also apply to the urban squatter settlements, which serve as reception areas and places of residence for the migrants and some of their descendants and thus owe their existence to the distribution of wealth and power which underlies the migratory process. Rather than viewing such settlements (with alarm or otherwise) as the products of an alleged failure to diffuse urban-industrial values to the rural-oriented lower class or as the pathological consequences of mismanagement or bad planning, we may consider the contribution they make to the provision of an economical solution to the supply of abundant, cheap labor for the urban economy, including not only the industrial sector, but also the largely labor-intensive service sector which is such an important prop to the lifestyle of the upper and middle classes.

The squatments and to a considerable extent the satellite towns serve as reserves, at little cost to the employers, where large numbers of workers may be maintained; proximity to lines of transportation permits easy access to the work sites; high unemployment rates depress wages; domestic, service, and commercial work is available to diminish the effects of (and potential reactions against) this unemployment and ease the burdens of the middle and upper classes; official pressure permits the squatting to be confined to areas of low visibility to the outsider and at a distance from the middle-class zones sufficient to reduce casual contact between the classes; and the location, terrain, and settlement pattern are such as to facilitate military and police measures to repress or contain riot and rebellion should they arise. At the same time, the formal official condemnation of squatting as an evil to be eradicated permits the capital to maintain its symbolic "developmentist" associations in the eyes of the middle class.

On the other hand, from the viewpoint of inmigrants, the relatively high economic rewards available in Brasília as opposed to the Northeast —especially its rural sector—as well as the generally higher level of public services (education, health, social security) provide the appearance of upward mobility. Squatting, by eliminating the need for payment of rent and property taxes, enhances the squatters' economic position and, in particular, provides a form of security in an unstable labor market characterized by frequent firings, late paychecks (due in part to the dependence of the construction industry on political decisions), and other insecurities. The physical form of the shack permits it to be expanded in accord with the changes in family size and unanticipated receipts of funds. In a society characterized by occupational multiplicity at all levels, the shack may also be used as a business asset: a store, a sewing business, rental of space for a store, or as a source of capital through its sale should the owner decide to move elsewhere.

It is impossible to estimate the numbers of migrants to Brasília who have left, but the rapid growth of the population confirms that a large number, and by all accounts of officials and squatters alike, the vast majority, remain in the new capital. As long as construction continues and the transfer of civil servants from Rio de Janeiro provides a basis for the service sector of the economy, the lower class retains an economic basis. In addition, the availability of public education of better-than-average quality and of medical clinics, such as those of the District Hospital, provides an incentive to remain, even in harder times—and those who have shacks need not concern themselves with paying rent. Women also find in domestic service and in small businesses, especially dressmaking, that they can increase their income and improve their position vis-a-vis their husbands, and in several cases have successfully resisted the migratory urges of their spouses. Most squatters in Brasília, barring disaster or depression, want to stay, and a significant majority want to stay in the squatter settlement. Informants often supposed that the research was connected with the government and wanted to know if they would have any chance of obtaining legal title to their house lots.

Brasília's settlement pattern developed in response to conflicting pressures emanating from the official "planned" construction and from the housing needs of squatters. A tacit bargain was struck at Brasília between the work-hungry migrants and entrepreneurs and politicians. The workers were permitted access to undeveloped public land, readily available in the scantily-populated, relatively flat areas of the new capital and to the waste materials from the construction process, such as the wooden forms used to mold the reinforced concrete employed in most of the monumental and residential apartment buildings. Another advantage provided by employers is truck transportation from the squatter settlements to the place of work. The marginal cost to the entrepreneurs of providing these advantages was nearly nil, and the advantage to them considerable in terms of permitting the large in-migration to continue and to improve their labor-supply situation. The squatters, on the other hand, possessed a limited bargaining power by virtue of the need for their presence in menial and service roles and of their potential for organized protest and disruption. For active protest to occur required (1) settlements containing large numbers, notably the Social Security Invasion, which in 1967 had over 4,000 shacks, and (2) conditions of threat to the permanence of the settlement or some part of it.

Official and police action has had a regulatory function with respect to squatting rather than (except in occasional declarations of intent) constituting an effort to eliminate or to provide a viable alternative to it for the majority of squatters. Small squatments offering relatively slight prospects of resistance were removed from the centrally planned area housing the urban middle class to the larger and less centrally-located Social Security Invasion. This squatment was the site of two efforts, backed by police force, aimed at removing squatters from privately owned land and from a highly visible position on one of the principal interurban motor routes into the city where their presence would detract from the symbolic and prestige functions of the new capital. While long-term financing for the purchase of publicly sponsored core housing and small agricultural resettlement schemes have been discussed, there is no realistic possibility that official policy toward squatting can do more than to specify its location to some degree and declare the intention to eradicate it.

Brasília's existence up to the present and the economic survival of its poor have in fact been largely dependent upon government expenditures, notably those connected with (1) the construction of the capital, which is continuing under the military dictatorship at a reduced rate, and (2) the salaries of the civil and military employees of the government. Industrial development has been quite restricted, and even agriculture has been limited by natural conditions, the lack of a regional plan, and the commercial manipulations of São Paulo interests concerned with maintaining control of the local markets. The growth of an urban population nearing the half-million mark, more orderly governmental administration by the military, and the completion of the railroad spur to Brasília (officially inaugurated in March 1967, but not in operation until a year later) may change this somewhat pessimistic picture and lead to some industrial employment to substitute for construction work as the city ages and to supplement jobs in the tertiary sector. Yet given the increasingly capital-intensive character of recent Latin American industrialization and the off-center location of Brasília in the Brazilian distribution network, the role of industrial employment is not likely to be great. The probable future decline in expenditures for new building may seriously injure the prospects of the majority of squatters and limit, if not actually reverse, the aggregate effects of migration on population growth in the lower class.

The official policy of the government in regard to squatting, furthermore, tends to discourage—although it does not prevent—the development of small enterprises, other than strictly commercial ones, and of more permanent types of buildings in general. By insistently proclaiming the illegality and eventual demise of the squatter settlements and denying public services such as street lighting, electricity, sewage, and a permanent water system, the government does not prevent the squatter settlement from growing (especially when it moves people into the place in its own trucks!), but it does suppress or deflect some internal entrepreneurial interest and prevent the gradual improvement of many homes beyond the wood-and-tarpaper stage, for which some squatters on occasion have the money and the skills. In the light of the difficult middle-run prospects for employment for squatters in Brasília and the lack of really viable alternate forms of settlement, the governmental policy seems to be somewhat short-sighted.

Thus, what recent in-migrants today see as at least a minimal improvement in their lives may not survive the eventual diminution of the rhythm of construction in the new capital. And in fact, throughout Latin America, current industrialization is largely capital-intensive. It may be that the urban under- and unemployed, when the marginal sense of improvement gained through in-migration and squatting in its initial stages is lost (for instance in the next, urban-born generation) will become a source of political unrest and challenge to the system as a whole (Petras 1969). The development of and prospects for such a challenge, like the genesis of urban poverty and its reflexes in urban ecology, can only be understood on the basis of systemic as well as local variables. Revolutionaries (and counterrevolutionaries) understand this point. Perhaps we can ask at least as much from academic social scientists.

12
The Segmentary Structure
of Urban Overseas
Chinese Communities

Lawrence W. Crissman

Chinese communities exist in most of the major cities of the world and constitute a sizeable proportion of the total urban population in much of south-east Asia. Despite the fact that the Chinese living outside China have been subjected to widely varying pressures for and against assimilation to the dissimilar peoples they live among, it is possible to discern a similar segmentary organisation underlying the superficially different characteristics of various communities. The existence of this common structure makes it possible to describe urban Chinese society throughout south-east Asia and in North America in terms of the same generalised model. It is also a strong indication that the social organisation of the urban overseas Chinese did not originate abroad, but rather that it is derived from patterns indigenous to China itself and for this reason the overseas Chinese provide a basis for inference about the social structure of traditional Chinese cities.

What follows is an ideal-type analysis made from written sources in English.[1] The specific ethnographical facts to which reference is made

SOURCE: *Man*, 2, no. 2 (1967): 185–205. Reprinted by permission of the Royal Anthropological Institute.

I would like to thank Maurice Freedman, Stephen Morris, Barbara Ward, Howard Nelson, Hugh Baker, Philip Staniford and Nancy Chodorow for criticism of earlier drafts of this paper. I would also like to acknowledge the financial support of the Cornell Committee of the London-Cornell Project for East and South East Asian Societies, which is financed by the Carnegie Corporation of New York and the Nuffield Foundation.

[1] The data from which the analysis was made come primarily from New York City (Heyer 1953), Kuching in Sarawak (T'ien 1953), Semarang (D. Willmott 1960)

have been selected as illustrative examples and do not represent even a small fraction of the total basis of induction, which of course comprised a far greater amount of data than there is space to include. The segmentary model that the analysis has produced is a-temporai: it has no time dimension. It may, however, fit certain historical periods better than present situations and it is certainly more immediately apparent in the organisation of some communities than it is in others. In any event, it is a new way of conceptualising overseas Chinese society and contains a number of testable propositions.

CHARACTERISTICS OF THE OVERSEAS CHINESE

Permanent Chinese trading communities are known to have existed in the Philippines and in Sumatra at least as early as the twelfth and thirteenth centuries; but the migration that accounts for the 14 million or so Chinese now living abroad did not begin until the latter part of the seventeenth century, and did not become a large-scale movement until the middle of the nineteenth century (Wang 1959; Purcell 1965). Nearly all of the Chinese who emigrated came from rural areas in the two coastal provinces of south-east China, Kuangtung and Fukien. The population of these provinces is far from homogeneous, and the Chinese who went abroad must be divided into at least five ethnic categories: Cantonese from the neighbourhood of Canton; Hainanese from Hainan island; Hakka from scattered inland areas of northern Kuangtung and southern Fukien; Hokkien from near Amoy; and Teochiu from the Swatow area. These so-called dialects or speech groups are actually different, mutually incomprehensible languages.[2] Various important cultural traits distinguish the speakers of each, but they are all equally good Chinese, especially in their own estimations. Each of the respective languages contains a number of dialects, and persons from particular places within the area mentioned are further divided by superficial cultural differences.

Chinese from the various areas are not evenly distributed abroad. Nearly all those outside south-east Asia are Cantonese. There are only Hokkien and Cantonese in the Philippines, the Hokkiens with a 75 per

---

and Sukabumi (G. Tan 1963) on Java, Phnom Penh (W. Willmott 1964), Manila (Amyot 1960; Sycip 1957; Weightman 1954; 1960), Bangkok (Coughlin 1955; 1960; Laudon 1941; Skinner 1957; 1958) and Singapore (Cheng 1950; Freedman 1950; 1956; 1957; 1961a & b; Kwok 1954; Lim 1958; Song 1923; K. Tan 1962).

[2] Teochiu and Hokkien are far closer to each other than are any two of the others. They are mutually intelligible to some extent, being related in about the same degree as are Spanish and Portuguese.

cent. majority (Amyot 1960:70). In Bangkok 60 per cent. of the Chinese are Teochiu, 16 per cent. are Hakka, while Hainanese, Cantonese, Hokkien and miscellaneous northerners constitute the remaining 24 per cent. in respectively decreasing proportions (Skinner 1958:20). 72 per cent. of the Chinese in Semarang are Hokkien, Cantonese and Hakka being the only other appreciable groups (D. Willmott 1960:100–3). There are also similar disproportions in the local origins of individuals within the major speech groups; for example, 60 per cent. of the Cantonese, Hakka and Hainanese in Bangkok are each from a single county (Skinner 1958:21). Unevenness of this sort in regard to the origins of Chinese living in any one place abroad is one of the most significant features of overseas Chinese populations. It is accounted for in part by the existence of ancient trade routes linking the various ports of China with particular places in south-east Asia (Skinner 1957) and by the fact that emigrants tended to go to places where others from their own villages or small localities were already established.

New immigrants usually followed the same occupations as friends and relatives who had preceded them, with the result that in any one place abroad those with the same occupation tend to have come from the same place in China. As an example of this, in Phnom Penh carpenters and mechanics are Cantonese, hardware sellers are Hokkien, cobblers and traditional drug dealers are Hakka, shirt sellers, pepper merchants and restaurant and hotel proprietors are Hainanese. Teochiu are found in many occupations and monopolise rural peddling (W. Willmott, personal communication). Similar situations exist throughout south-east Asia, but the occupations monopolised by a given speech community in one place belong to others in different places and have nothing to do with regional specialisations back in China. Although the origins of men in all lines of endeavour are becoming more and more heterogeneous, many occupations are still monopolised by men from the same place in China or at least contain a large concentration of such men.

Until the First World War the number of Chinese women who went abroad was very small and many of those who did go went unwillingly as domestic slaves or prostitutes. Only 20 per cent. of the Singapore Chinese population was female in 1900 (Freedman 1961a:26) and there were six Chinese men for every Chinese woman in Manila before the Second War (Amyot 1960:58). There were large differences in the proportion of women in the various speech communities. In Singapore in the 1880's there were practically no Hainanese women but from 7 per cent. to 10 per cent. of the Hokkien, Teochiu and Hakka were women, as were 35 per cent of the Cantonese (Freedman 1961a:26).

The very low percentage of Hainanese women existed everywhere and was due to self-imposed but very stringent rules against women leaving Hainan. Cantonese women went to Singapore, Thailand and other places earlier and in greater numbers than women of other speech groups, probably owing to the minor tradition of economic independence for women in Cantonese areas, the predilection of Cantonese women to enter pacts and sisterhoods directed against marriage, which sometimes meant they had to leave home (Topley 1961:301–2), and the fact that Hong Kong was the great entrepôt for prostitutes among other commodities.

The imbalanced sex ratio among the Chinese abroad is explicable in light of the way the Chinese looked upon emigration. They did not set out adventurously to begin a new life abroad, but were pushed out of their homes by economic necessity, the unwilling victims of pressure on the land and lack of local opportunities for earning a living. Leaving home was not thought to be permanent but, on the contrary, was seen as a temporary expedient that would allow them to earn enough to live, support their families, and eventually return home as wealthy men. Except for a few fugitives from justice and those too poor and rootless to have homes and families, emigrants left China expecting to return home in due time, and leaving in no way cut them off from their families and natal villages. No matter how long they were away they were still considered by themselves and by those who stayed at home to be members in good standing of their home communities. This membership was passed on to sons born abroad, who in turn passed it on to their sons. This patrilineal inheritance of village membership is shown in striking fashion by the fact that the remains of foreign-born who had never seen China were sometimes sent to their fathers' or grandfathers' villages for burial. Before the First War, married emigrants usually left their wives and children at home under the watchful eyes of their mothers. Many single emigrants returned home briefly to marry local women chosen by their parents. These they soon left, pregnant if possible, in order to return to their jobs overseas. Those who could afford the passage visited their homes in China every few years and managed to raise normal sized families.

The early immigrants to south-east Asia tended to be assimilated into their host populations over the generations. In the beginning the only women available to them were non-Chinese locals and the children of these unions often grew up speaking their mother's language better than their father's brand of Chinese. Daughters, at least in the Straits, never married non-Chinese but only other half-Chinese or newcomers from China (Song 1923:3). This, together with the practice of repatriating foreign-born sons to be raised and educated by grandparents or co-mothers, helped the early Chinese communities resist assimilation. As the nineteenth century wore on, China-born newcomers became ever more numerous and it became easier for the foreign-born to retain their Chinese heritage.

Assimilation went furthest in Thailand, where there were no barriers against it, and the acculturated Chinese eventually became indistinguishable from other Thai. In Java, Dutch policy, among other things, kept the Peranakan Chinese, as those who were partially assimilated there are called, from blending completely with the indigenous population; but almost the only vestiges of 'Chineseness' left to some of them were the use of Chinese names, some patrilineal emphasis, and Chinese business methods.

The Peranakans constituted the majority of Chinese in many parts of Indonesia until the first decades of this century. They were influenced by their non-Chinese mothers and wives, and also borrowed heavily from their Dutch masters, in the same way as the Straits Chinese, or Babas, modelled themselves on the British. The Babas never constituted a large percentage of the Chinese in Singapore, but they were powerful beyond their numbers because of their early economic opportunities, their possession of daughters who could be married to successful latecomers, and their command of English words and ways which allowed them to mix socially and do business with their British overlords. The acculturated Chinese in Cambodia and the Philippines were not so numerous as those in Indonesia nor so important as those in Singapore.

ETHNIC COMMUNITIES

To complete the background to the social structure of the urban Chinese overseas it is necessary to introduce the somewhat obvious concept of 'ethnic community'.[3] References are often made to the Polish community in London, the Jewish community in the United States, or the Chinese community in Java, and it should be possible to refine this usage into a valid sociological concept of wide relevance in this heterogeneous world. As normally used by sociologists, 'community' denotes a place or a localised group; a village, town, city, or even a nation. A wider use of the term can be found in the work of MacIver, who defines a community as an area of common life based on common interests which can determine activity (1917:22). As an illustration, he says, 'The English residents in a foreign capital often live in an intimate community of their own as well as in the wider community of the capital' (1917: 23). Such a community has ethnicity as well as locality as its basis and in order to distinguish

[3] Max Weber has used the term briefly in reference to caste (Gerth & Mills 1947: 189–90).

it from territorially-based communities, it may be called an ethnic community and defined as consisting of people who share, and are conscious of, a common ethnicity different from that of their host population.

Whether a given ethnic community is a corporate group, a group, or a quasi-group is a matter for empirical verification. The fact that all ethnic communities are, in addition, categories based on ethnic criteria is important because it provides the basis for stereotyped treatment of members by outsiders. In so far as identification with the community is consciously held by the members, it is a quasi-group. When this identification is acknowledged and acted upon, the community is a group. The community is corporate if it endures over time despite changing membership, has internal organisation and leadership and its members exercise rights and have duties as members. In respect to different members the same ethnic community can be a quasi-group, a group, or a corporate group, and in respect to any particular member it can change its character with time. The ethnic communities to be considered in this article are all corporate, at least for some of their members. They form the major components in the structure of urban overseas Chinese society.

The existence of an ethnic community depends primarily on a recognised difference in ethnicity or origin. Most ethnic communities are based on gross differences, such as are found between hosts and first (and sometimes second) generation immigrants from a foreign country who do not speak the local language well and continue to act as they did at home. Even slight differences will suffice, such as those between the Irish and the English, but there is no community of New Yorkers in California or Londoners in Birmingham because differences in culture between the two states and cities are insignificant, and the fact of a common origin does not produce or modify relationships among those living in the distant place. Ethnic communities are not necessarily based on permanent immigration; they can consist of transients and expatriates, as in the case of the overseas Chinese who, ideologically at least, are not committed to staying abroad. Nor are they necessarily based on immigration at all, as in the case of the Burakumin (Eta) of Japan, or of communities consisting of converts to esoteric and marginal religious cults. Not all people with ethnic differences form communities and some never enter or soon leave existing communities by consciously identifying with and trying to assimilate to their hosts. On the other hand, some ethnic communities, such as the Amish in the American mid-west or some Peranakan Chinese in Java, can endure for a century or more even though they have forgotten their origins except in general terms and can speak only the language of their hosts.

By contrast to territorial communities, which form a single nested hierarchy (i.e., neighbourhood, village market area, county, etc.), ethnic communities are based on two criteria, each of which is capable of producing a nested hierarchy which cross-cuts the other. To give a simplified example, a Hokkien Chinese from Chiangchiu living in Manila is a member of (at least) nine possible ethnic communities produced by the intersection of two sets of three identifications. The possibilities are: the Chinese in south-east Asia, the Hokkiens in south-east Asia, the Chiangchius in south-east Asia, the Chinese in the Philippines, the Hokkiens in the Philippines, the Chiangchius in the Philippines, the Chinese in Manila, the Hokkiens in Manila, and the Chiangchius in Manila. Of the nine, three do not exist empirically: the Hokkiens in south-east Asia, the Chiangchius in south-east Asia, and the Chiangchius in the Philippines. From this it can be seen that the two dimensions are not entirely independent; the larger the host locality, the more likely are fine ethnic distinctions to be ignored. All the Chinese in south-east Asia form a community which is of real concern to the governments of the two Chinas, but at that level Hokkiens, to say nothing of Chiangchiu Hokkiens, tend not to be distinguished from Chinese in general. It is important to point out that just as the community of Manila Chinese is contained within the Philippine Chinese community, so the Manila Chiangchiu community is contained within the Manila Hokkien community and the Manila Chinese community.

The concept of ethnic community becomes more useful and real, in a sense, as it is narrowed in its two dimensions. There is a Jewish community in the United States, but more concretely, there is a Russian Jewish community in New York City. Again, something quite specific can be said about the members of a certain Zambian sub-tribe who work at a single copper mine, or about the Fukien Hakkas living in Modjokuto. The criterion of ethnicity is primarily empirical, and depends on the categories actually recognised and used as bases for forming communities. The overseas Chinese make many distinctions among themselves, and relevant ethnicity is relative and situational. It is this fact, among others, that allows a segmentary model to be applied to their society. The criterion of host locality is in a sense definitional. It determines the field under consideration, and can be varied for heuristic purposes. Although the urban Chinese throughout south-east Asia (and in New York) form the subject of this article, this is not a useful analytical level. For convenience, the community of Chinese living in a single city has been taken as the unit of analysis, and it is that to which the model applies.

CHINESE COMMUNITY SEGMENTS

All the Chinese living in a city compose a Chinese community in that they stand apart from the rest of the population and the government and because the affairs of any group of Chinese are likely to be of concern to all the Chinese living there. A Chinese community is not homogeneous, however, and is in turn divided into a number of sub-communities, or segments. The primary division is usually between the five major speech groups, and in so far as they are represented in the area, communities will be formed on the basis of language. Except for Hakka, the speakers of which come from discontinuous areas, the languages are associated with discrete localities in China, and it is common for the ethnic distinction of language to be expressed in geographical terms, such as northern Kuangtung for Teochiu.

Distinctions of provenance are by no means limited to the large areas associated with the languages, but are made with equal significance in respect to counties (which commonly align with dialect differences), market town areas, and villages, or combinations of them. These distinctions in terms of geographical origin provide the basis for division within communities which result in smaller included communities. Speech communities can segment into sub-communities based on counties or groups of counties, which in turn can be segmented on the basis of smaller territories down to the level of communities drawn from single villages.

Every Chinese has a native place, the area of China where his lineage is localised and where his ancestors are buried and worshipped. He may never have seen it, having been born elsewhere in China or abroad, but he knows it is the place where his father or forefathers originated. It is important to emphasize that a person's native place is permanent and cannot be changed. It is ascribed or inherited like a name or lineage membership, and in the foreign context one of the most important things about a Chinese is his native place back in China. In respect to someone from a nearby village, the exact place is significant, but in regard to someone from the same county it can be expressed in terms of the local market town. Within speech communities, county of origin is the significant locality, as is language area within the total Chinese community. People with the same native place (the extent of which is determined by context) have a community of interest. They recognize a bond between themselves and treat one another differently from outsiders. The content of the relationship between members of locality communities varies with the level of community in question, but even at the level of speech communities where the bond is somewhat attenuated, custom and jobs are given to co-members in preference to outsiders.

Provenance is not the only criterion of like origin which the Chinese use as a basis for forming communities. Of equal importance is the possession of the same surname. There are only a few hundred surnames in common use in the whole of China. They are inherited patrilineally and ideally form exogamous units, the idea being that all those who have the same name are ultimately descended from the same patrilineal ancestor, even though the actual lines of descent are unknown. Men who have the same name, even when no known genealogical relationship exists between them, do not consider one another to be complete strangers and treat one another as if they were in fact related, albeit remotely. This sometimes holds for people with different names, in which case there is a history of close relationship between the names based on a pact of blood brotherhood between remote ancestors, or a tradition that asserts that one of the names was changed long ago to avoid persecution (Amyot 1960:34). There is some evidence that these links between surnames can be manufactured when expedient, and the recognition of a linkage in one place by no means indicates that it will be found elsewhere.

Surname communities are analogous to ethnic communities based on provenance in that the basis of membership in both is ascribed to and consists of elements of common origin, in the one case geographical, and in the other of stipulated descent. Surname communities are different, however, in that they are discreet and cannot form a nested hierarchy. Apart from the case of linked names, no two names are any closer than any two others; there is no way in which they can be ranked, and a community based on one name cannot in any way contain communities based on others. Therefore surname communities alone cannot constitute a segmentary system. In conjunction with native place, however, they can form some of the units in such a system. Surname communities are, in fact, always formed on the basis of both a name and some criterion of locality. Although they are perhaps functionally as significant, they are structurally subordinate to locality communities. Because of their dependence on an element of locality to establish part of their boundaries they must be contained within some territorial community, even if such is taken to be the total Chinese community. They are, as a rule, limited to speech groups or smaller geographical areas.

THE SEGMENTARY SYSTEM

Every Chinese has both a surname and a native place, and some other Chinese share either one or the other, or both, giving rise to locality and surname communities which are equally units in the same segmentary system. Because each of the two criteria is capable of dividing communities based on the other, if they were applied in all possible circumstances they would cross-cut the total Chinese community, producing a vast number of interlocking, overlapping segments. Although there is some overlap, the two principles are in fact used intermittently. Only some of the total sub-communities are recognised within any one Chinese community, and the pattern of segmentation in each city or locality is unique. The actual points of segmentation and the exact criteria used vary greatly from one city to another, and even in the same place over time, and depend on the immigration history, the relative numbers from various localities with different names, and the existence of special interests held by potential communities.

It is common for most of the people in a speech community to come from a few specific counties, and for many within these areas to have the same names. In addition to influencing strongly the points and basis of segmentation in particular places, these disproportions allow for, and in some cases demand, asymmetrical segmentation analogous to that which is found in Chinese patrilineages (Freedman 1958). The existence of asymmetric segmentation means that the occurrence at any level of a group set apart by one of the principles does not necessarily call forth other units at the same level, whether based on the same principle or not. There is nothing that demands nicely paired or balanced segments at any or all points. A group within a community can be set apart on either of two criteria, leaving the remainder undivided; or other groups can be set off by the other criterion or by different uses of the same one.

It is usual, however, for one or other of the principles to be the major basis of division at any level in one sub-community. The principle has no effect on which principle is used in other sub-communities of the same inclusive community because each segment is itself an autonomous community with regard to internal segmentation. The principle on which a community is based does, however, affect the principle which can be used for internal segmentation. Communities formed on the basis of territory can segment further on the basis of either surnames or smaller localities; but surname communities can only divide on the basis of locality. This is so because people with the same name belong to many different lineages, and although they stipulate descent from the same culture hero or semi-historical figure, they do not have a common genealogy. Therefore, people with the same name must be distinguished from one another on the basis of where they come from. The members of a localised lineage are identified and set apart in terms of the small territory, usually taken to be a village or market town area, which contains the lineage in China. Speech groups are very often used as the boundaries for surname communities, partly because the pronunciation of the names changes from one language to another, but more importantly because language communities are such significant units in overseas Chinese society. Surname communities which are limited to parts of language areas can be either a reflection of important divisions within speech groups, or the result of disproportionate representation of the particular area among people with that name.

The speech groups which are found in a Chinese community constitute its major segments. These language communities can be divided on the basis of either one of the two structural principles. For example, the Hainanese community in Singapore is segmented on the basis of surnames (Lim 1958) whereas the Teochiu community in Bangkok is primarily divided by localities (Skinner 1958). Divisions within the Singapore Hainanese surname communities are necessarily on the basis of locality, but further divisions of the segments of Bangkok's Teochiu community can be based on either surnames or smaller localities, or both. When surname and locality are both independently operative at the same levels, a number of partially overlapping sub-communities are created, and it is possible for individuals and very narrow communities to belong to more than one segment of the same larger community. The division of loyalties and interests this entails is of course a powerful agent of social cohesion which serves to check the divisive tendencies of the system. Surname communities which cut across the territorial divisions of a language community, or those which include the speakers of more than one of the languages, are good examples of overlapping communities which tie segments together.

Partially assimilated Chinese participate in their various surname and locality communities inversely with the degree of their acculturation and identification with the host population, their involvement growing weaker as the generations pass. In Indonesia in the twentieth century when the distinction between the Peranakans and the China-born newcomers was sharpened by the flood of immigration and the rise of Chinese nationalism, there was in some places a primary division in the Chinese community on this basis, each half being divided separately into numerous and different segments (D. Willmott 1960:15; G. Tan 1963:250–6).

Communities composed of people from the same village are the basic units in the segmentary system. Although the possession of different names or special interests can detract from the community of interest shared by members, these do not actually segment because divisions between them do not constitute independent groups. Small communities based on either surnames or locality are composed of village communities along with stray individuals and miscellaneous groups which have the appropriate ethnicity or name. These in turn form ever larger communities until the level of speech communities and the total Chinese community is reached. The whole membership of a surname community can be contained in a large community based either on locality or the name, or both if they exist. Because it contains more than one surname, a locality community can belong in its entirety only to a larger locality community. Its members can belong to different surname communities, but this must be done individually or by small surname sub-communities. This impairs the unity of the locality community, but at the same time adds to the cohesiveness of the larger community.

Special interests such as a common occupation can provide independently the basis for communities whose members are heterogeneous in terms of provenance and surnames. These occupational communities are not frequently found outside China because of the congruence between occupation and origin engendered by the nature of Chinese immigration; but when they exist they enter into the segmentary system and are contained within the communities that embrace the bulk of their membership, usually speech groups or the total Chinese community.[4]

Various segments, or sub-communities, combine and divide in different circumstances. In some contexts the whole Chinese community is united and acts together, while in different situations small segments act independently against each other. Opponents in one situation are allies in another. Disputes between two individuals or low-level communities can escalate, bringing in other communities with the same names or localities up to the level below the community which contains both of the disputants, at which point the inclusive community, its unity threatened, will attempt to arrange a settlement. The way in which difficulties are handled, and by whom, will be touched upon in the following discussion of the activities and functions which characterise communities at different levels.

VILLAGE COMMUNITIES

The members of a village community all know one another and each other's affairs. They form a face-to-face social unit which is usually corporate. They try to live close together (but may be widely dis-

---

[4] The following is of some interest:
'Hong Kong society is accustomed to organise itself into groups not upon identity of community interest in a given area but upon traditionally accepted charitable objectives, language, place of origin, occupation, business, profession, etc. It is largely within groupings based upon such common ideals and interests that individual citizens give community service. Members of these groups generally choose for their leaders persons whom they know personally and believe to be shrewd, able, resourceful and effective organisers for action' (Dickinson et al. 1966:84).

persed), visit each other frequently, and periodically meet for meals, card games, and religious observances. There is usually a headquarters of some sort, either a place of business, a certain apartment, or a dormitory which is maintained for single male members. Each community has recognised leaders whose position may depend on genealogy or politics back home, but is more likely to be derived from wealth and status in the Chinese community abroad. The village community is (or was) in frequent communication with the village in China, both by mail and through visits to China by members who carry messages back and forth, convey money to various families, and return with gossip and instructions. Those who return from a visit home look after new immigrants who accompany them and can be charged with disciplining errant members who have been remiss in sending remittances to their families. The members are responsible for each other, give aid and support, and in fact exert considerable social control over one another. Family quarrels and disputes between members are mediated and settled at this level. If there is a conflict with another village community, the leaders take the case to a larger community which contains both disputants.

If the village in question is a lineage village, which is not uncommon in the areas of south-east China that the immigrants come from, all the members of the village community abroad will be related genealogically. They will not, however, constitute an overseas branch of their lineage, not only because they come from various branches and sub-lineages and are genealogically mixed, but also because lineages cannot be transplanted; they belong at home and cannot be separated from land and ancestors in China. Abroad, the members of a lineage village community are simply people from the same village who happen to be related. All the members of a mixed village community usually refer to one another by generalised kin terms anyway, whether or not they are actually related, just as most villagers do in China. A lineage village community may be designated by the surname rather than by the name of the village, but it is still a village community.

Typical village communities contain thirty to sixty people (extremes range from about five to well over one hundred) including stray individuals brought in through cognatic and affinal ties, a common occupation, or some other particular tie. If there are not enough people from a single village to constitute even a small community, those from neighbouring villages can join together. If, on the other hand, a village community becomes cumbersomely large, it can split into separate communities on the basis of surnames, village hamlets, or lineage sections, but part-village communities are uncommon.

COMMUNITY ORGANISATIONS

Communities above the village level are too large and heterogeneous to be cohesive face-to-face groups. Their functions are exercised by organisations, which are referred to in the literature by the term voluntary associations, a category that includes benevolent societies, funeral associations, surname temples, provincial clubs, merchant and craft guilds, chambers of commerce, and secret societies as well as a number of miscellaneous groups. It is rather a misnomer to call most of these bodies voluntary associations because all members generally do not formally associate *en masse*, and in so far as they serve as community organisations they are not strictly voluntary. Many so-called voluntary associations are in fact the administrative organs of the communities from which their membership is drawn. Their names and stated purposes, which are sometimes chosen more with an eye toward official governmental regulations than anything else, are often indexed to their primary role of community organisations and camouflage their true structural and functional importance.

Membership in a community must be clearly distinguished analytically from participation in that community's organisation. Community membership is based on the recognition of ascribed attributes of common origin; the same surname or the same native place. (In the case of occupational communities eligibility is of course achieved.) Membership in a community organisation, on the other hand, is optional, and involves registration, paying dues, and participation in formal activities. By no means everyone who belongs to a community is registered as a member of its organisation, and only a few, the wealthy or ambitious, are active in its political affairs. Only one-third to one-half of those eligible bother to become formal members even of those organisations which offer certain benefits exclusively to registered members. Despite this, a community organisation is responsible for all the members of the community it represents and they are all under its jurisdiction. Anyone with the requisite origin, including transients as well as old residents who have never registered or paid dues, can appeal to the appropriate organisation for help.

A person in trouble is referred to the proper organisation once his name or native place is known. When an organisation is involved in a large undertaking such as a building programme or competition with another community, or when it is ordered or appealed to by a higher-ranking organisation, it can mobilise the entire community it serves, irrespective of its official membership list.

Organisations representing segments, or sub-communities, commonly have corporate membership in the organisations that serve the larger communities in which they are included. This provides for an organisational hierarchy which parallels the segmentary community structure. Members of smaller included communities are represented in larger community organisations by the leaders of their own small-scale organisations, some of whom are usually officers in the large organisations. Participation in a small organisation is no bar to participation in larger ones if the bodies in question cater to mass membership, and some ordinary Chinese, as well as leaders, are active in half a dozen or more community organisations.

Any large or wealthy community will be administered by some organisation. However, a numerically preponderant segment of a larger community may not have an organisation of its own, but can use that of the larger group. For example the Hokkien community of Manila, which comprises 75 per cent. of all the Chinese living there, has no organisation serving it alone. It is administered by the Manila Chinese Chamber of Commerce which also includes Cantonese. Both the Cantonese community and the various segments of the Hokkien community have their own organisations (Amyot 1960:103).

Community organisations can be formal or informal. In many places there are, and for some time have been, government regulations designed to control or eradicate undesirable Chinese associations, principally the secret societies, and these laws require all organisations to register and obtain official approval. As a result, community organisations which own property or are at all active have been endowed with a formal constitution based on a standard format, and have high-sounding purposes which never account for their entire range of activities. They have large numbers of honorary officers, powerful executive committees, numerous sub-committees, and full-time paid secretaries who manage most of the day-to-day affairs and are often qualified in the language used by the government.

Elections are held annually or biannually, and there are periodic meetings which few but the officers attend, the quorum commonly being set as low as 1 per cent. of the membership.

MIDDLE RANGE COMMUNITY ORGANISATIONS

Village communities seldom have formally recognized organisations because their property is such that it can easily be held by private individuals and their activities are unlikely to come to official notice, although they do occasionally register purely for reasons of prestige. At levels intermediate between village communities and language communities, community organisations are almost always formally constituted, and are easily recognisable by their activities if not by their names. They usually take the form of surname associations, *huikuan* or so-called provincial clubs, funeral societies, charitable groups, and occupational organisations. Surname associations provide for ancestral tablets, occasionally organise worship and often provide mourners at funerals. *Huikuan* have a hall where feasts are held, rooms that can be rented to transients and single members, and possibly a special burial area. Funeral societies manage funerals, providing coffins, mourners, and cash for expenses; charities give aid; and guilds manage occupations. When these various groups are also community organisations, as many of them are, they also administer and represent their communities, and this, rather than their formal activities, is their primary significance in the social structure of the urban overseas Chinese. The names of the organisations usually provide a clue to the communities they serve, but are sometimes quite ambiguous. Surname associations all represent surname communities, but the other kinds of organisations can also serve them. Communities based on locality can be served by all but surname associations, but there is a preference for *huikuan* and funeral societies.

Whatever its name or stated purpose, a community organisation will be involved in regulating the businesses of its members, and if the community dominates a particular occupation or type of business, it will take the place of a guild. This is fairly common overseas, and explains why guilds are not frequently found outside China. If those who monopolise a trade or type of business have discrete common origin, either of descent or provenance, they may have a merchant trade guild which is used to administer and represent their community, including members who have various other occupations. When those following an occupation have diverse origins, guilds or business associations concerned almost exclusively with the occupation are sometimes found. These enter into the organisational structure of the Chinese community at the level that includes their diverse members, usually a speech group or the total Chinese community.

The administrative functions of organisations serving the communities that lie between village communities and the upper levels of the total community include providing charity for needy members and tickets home for the aged or stranded transients, giving aid and advice to those with problems that cannot be handled by village communities, and maintaining the peace by shipping out or otherwise discouraging troublemakers. Their leaders settle differences between individual members or community segments and represent their communities at higher levels, sometimes acting on behalf of individual members in case of a justified dispute with members of another community. Offences, especially against members of the same community, may be published and redress given. When something needs to be done for the benefit of the community or on orders from the authorities, the labour or cash to accomplish it are obtained by calling on member organisations or appropriate individuals. Funds are also collected for higher level organisations. The prestige of a community is largely dependent upon the energy and status of its leaders and on how well they manage the affairs of the community.

HIGH LEVEL COMMUNITY ORGANISATIONS

Organisations which serve major communities such as speech groups or the total Chinese community are likely to be covert due to the necessity of hiding their activities from their political rivals, the governments of the areas where the Chinese live. Their most common guises are hospital committees, school boards, and nowadays Chambers of Commerce. At one time the secret societies provided the organisation for speech groups and Chinese communities in most of south-east Asia and in north America, but they were eclipsed in the latter part of the nineteenth and the early twentieth centuries, often owing to official suppression. At present, the Chinese Benevolent Society provides overall leadership for the Chinese community in New York City (Heyer 1953:106). In Phnom Penh this leadership is in the hands of a hospital board (W. Willmott 1964: 362–4), as it was in Bangkok before the Chinese Chamber of Commerce took over (Skinner 1957:170–1). Schools, which are usually limited to speech groups, are often used as cover for the governing bodies of the language communities.

Except for Chambers of Commerce and secret societies, high level community organisations are small and highly select; and the Chambers and secret societies, while soliciting wide membership, are headed by a small group which holds all the power, making them equally exclusive in regard to leadership. The governing committees are rather like the board of directors of a large stock company where the directors control and represent large blocks of shareholders. In the Chinese case, the various members of the governing committees represent major segments of the community, representation being roughly proportional to numbers and importance. Nominally the leaders are elected or appointed for definite terms, but they are often returned, and nothing so crude as open campaigning occurs.

The leaders of the whole Chinese community and its major segments settle disputes that affect the majority of the Chinese and those that involve structurally distant communities. In addition to supervising the operation and finances of their schools and hospitals or the general conduct of business, the governing bodies provide services for the large communities, such as commissioning public works in the absence of official governmental action and donating large sums for disaster relief, both locally and in China. They also make policy decisions affecting the affairs of the communities, and even have what amounts to foreign relations with the government of China.

Perhaps the most important function of the overall community leadership is its role as mediator between the Chinese community and the government, indigenous or colonial, which claims sovereignty over it. The arrangement was formalised under the Kapitan China system (Wong 1963) used by the Dutch in Indonesia and by the British for brief periods. Under this system, a type of indirect rule, a particular Chinese was appointed Kapitan and made responsible to the authorities for all the Chinese living in an area. He was in effect given *carte blanche* for the internal management of the Chinese community so long as he kept the peace and satisfied his masters. Obviously, for such a system to work, the man invested with official recognition had to be a power within the community in his own right, and a balance had to be kept between the benefits derived from his relationship with the outside government and those obtained as a natural leader of the community. The Kapitans were, in short, brokers between the Chinese and the colonial administration. Their power over the Chinese is known to have been derived from being leaders of the secret societies, positions occupied before their selection as Kapitans, the Dutch being wise enough to accept the leaders the Chinese themselves put forward.

In the absence of an official system of brokerage such as the Kapitan China arrangement, the leaders of a Chinese community act as informal brokers between the sovereign authority and the Chinese. They have informal dealings with the powers that be, both in business and socially, and by letting it be known what their influence amounts to, they gain the recognition of those in authority. Through their offices the government is kept informed despite the absence of official channels for sounding Chinese opinion, and the Chinese find out what is expected of them and what their alternatives are. Matters are arranged backstage in a most convenient Chinese fashion.

Secret societies (see Comber 1957; 1959) have another role in the social structure besides being capable of providing community leadership. The societies abroad all derive from those that existed in China, and in fact a few lodges came *en bloc* after the Taiping rebellion. Their rituals are faintly Buddhist and/or Taoist in origin, they emphasize a bond of brotherhood that is supposed to transcend all others, and they all had a distinct anti-dynastic tradition which led the imperial government of China to persecute them. They had much more freedom overseas, where they did not actively oppose the governments. As mentioned, they are known to have been the basis of the success of the Dutch system of indirect rule, and operated quite openly in Singapore in the mid-19th century, when about one half of all the Chinese males living there were members (Freedman 1961a:30). They still exist everywhere overseas but are much less in the open than before, and fights between rival societies which in the past were large and bloody affairs are now rare and on a small scale. They have always been involved in organised vice and crime, but this has now become their major concern, and they are in many places merely gangs of petty criminals and extortionists which include many non-Chinese.

There is known to have been a nearly one-to-one correspondence between the speech communities and the lodges of the secret societies. In every place but Singapore a lodge was limited to a single speech group, and only four of Singapore's nine societies appear to have crossed language boundaries (Freedman 1961a:35–6). Certain occupations were dominated by a society to the extent that belonging was like having a union card, and perhaps the fact that some of these occupations, such as dock worker, included men in different speech groups accounts for lodges that crossed the boundaries of major segments. The typical lodge had almost no formal differentiation between members, and consisted of a few leaders and hundreds or thousands of rank and file. Internal politics and the selection of leaders took place in the context of lower level community segments and their organisations, which existed then as now (Vaughan 1879). Before they were suppressed, the secret societies provided the organisations for the language communities and the leadership of the whole Singapore Chinese community. It was only after their demise that the present organisations evolved to provide leadership for the upper levels of the Chinese community.

Apart from their criminal activities, which provided a certain amount of the income necessary for their support, it was the function of the secret societies to provide an element of force in the political system. Their leaders were also community leaders and the power of the societies was used for the benefit of the communities they drew on for their membership. Many of the fights between lodges grew out of competition over territory or control of rackets; but others, not related to the operations of the societies as such, arose out of disputes between different communities which were able to use the societies in attempts to enforce their policies. As well as being used to obtain the objectives of their communities in external dealings with other communities, the societies also exerted their power internally. They acted as police, keeping down un-authorised or independent crime, and could be used for the physical re-moval of intransigents.

The force they represented was used to implement policy decisions of leaders within their communities. Their power supported the authority of the high level community leaders and kept the system from segmenting into anarchy. One principal reason why they lost this function, and, in-cidentally, why the communities adopted other efficient organisations in their place, was that in order to suppress them efficient police forces were created which have gained a monopoly on force at their expense.

Leadership of the various communities, from the level of the village groups to that of the total Chinese community, is based on wealth and its concomitant prestige. The officers of organisations are nominally elected, but only the wealthy are considered and the surest route to office, honorary or active, is a sizeable donation to an organisation's treasury. Almost the only people who come to meetings, including elec-tions, are the rich and ambitious or those who are indebted in some way to the officers or other powerful men who direct their votes. Over-seas Chinese communities are, in short, plutocracies in which wealth breeds prestige and power. The elite of overseas Chinese society is al-most exclusively based on wealth or its derivatives, the only other basis being education in the language of the official government, which is an added asset for some highly placed leaders. A small community which cannot produce a leader rich enough to gain access to the positions of power in large communities will be poorly represented, if at all, whereas a rich community that knows how to use its wealth can have a man at the very top, no matter how small it is.

The leadership of the various organisations is heavily interlocked, so that most leaders have positions in numerous organisations at different levels. This is especially evident near the top of the hierarchy, where a solid power base in lower level communities, plus great wealth, is needed to obtain a position. Honorary offices are desired because they provide prestige and a constituency without demanding much time and most of the men who represent their communities at high levels are honorary officials of the lower level organisations. The apex of the sys-tem is the Chinese community organisation, with other major nodes representing the speech groups. There is an excellent description of the system of interlocked leadership as it exists in Bangkok's Chinese com-munity (Skinner 1958).

Until recently, no Chinese community abroad has had any say in the government of the city or country of settlement. In addition, few if any provisions were made for governing the Chinese or providing for their needs. As an extreme example, from 1825 to 1870 the British in Singapore made no formal arrangements whatever for administering the Chinese, who made up over half of the population of the city. The Dutch Kapitan China system was only a step removed from the British practice. Similar conditions existed everywhere, north America included; yet had the Chinese tried to establish explicitly governmental or political organisations even those limited to activities internal to the Chinese communities, they would have brought repression down upon themselves. This is still the situation faced by many if not most overseas Chinese communities.

The urban Chinese abroad are really in the same situation as was the urban population of traditional China. They must govern themselves without having noticeable governmental institutions, and their solution of the dilemma is the same. They use the organisational superstructure of their segmentary social structure as both a representative political system and a hierarchical administrative system, maintaining a rarely disturbed balance between the two aspects of government. The urban Chinese abroad are nearly autonomous and self-governing and their system of government is peculiarly Chinese.

CHINA AND THE SEGMENTARY MODEL

The nature of the relationship between overseas Chinese urban social structure and the social organisation of cities in China under the Ch'ing dynasty is difficult to determine with any certainty, due to the fact that the latter is so poorly documented. At first glance, the model presented above would seem to have little relevance to cities in China because of the superficially anomalous situation of the overseas Chinese. After all, they were primarily males from rural areas, immigrants to foreign lands where they lived among distinctly different peoples. As Chinese they were barred from entering the indigenous or colonial elites and had little participation in the formal governments that had sovereignty over them. They also comprised only parts of the total societies abroad, being in most places restricted to the urban class supported by commerce, trades and crafts, or wage labour. The dim picture of what is known about traditional Chinese cities shows, however, that these conditions also existed in whole or in part in China itself.

The immigration that peopled the cities overseas was in fact only a continuation in a new direction of longstanding patterns of movement within China. In all the cities of China there were large numbers of ethnically different Chinese from diverse parts of the empire (Chang 1958). Men from Fukien living in Peking or Hunanese in Canton are nearly as foreign as Cantonese in Saigon or Hakkas in Thailand. The Chinese who migrated to the cities of China were ideological transients just like those who went overseas, and men from the same area tended to monopolise lines of business or particular crafts in Chinese cities as well. Most of China's internal immigrants also went unaccompanied by their families, and owing to the difficulties of inland travel by comparison with steamship passage to south-east Asia, were often more cut off from home than those who went abroad. Wives, and especially concubines, were commonly taken from natives of the host cities and their hinter-lands, sons born to them were often sent home to be raised in their fathers' villages, and the old native place continued to be claimed after many generations, just as was done abroad. However, there were some differences owing to shared items of Chinese culture in the ease with which total assimilation took place and in the absence of intermediate categories such as the Peranakans.

By contrast to the situation abroad where all Chinese are equally foreign except those who have been partially assimilated, individuals and groups in the population of a Chinese city were more or less foreign depending on the distance and differences between their home areas and the host locality. The majority of a city's population was undoubtedly either born in the city or derived from its immediate hinterland. The proportion that came from distances so great that they were obviously different sorts of Chinese varied from city to city, but was never very large. Many others were different enough from the locals to be easily distinguished. Those who came from nearby and blended easily with the majority of the city's population identified themselves with their homes, thereby setting themselves apart. All these 'foreigners' were divided into many different ethnic communities, usually on the basis of geo-graphical origin and occupation, and Provincial 'clubs' and merchant and craft guilds were the most common forms used for community organisations. In China, surnames were likely to have been of greater functional significance as a means of joining foreign Chinese to the local majority than as a basis for differentiation within each of the ethnically foreign communities.

The criterion of common occupation, which is very commonly aligned with and expressed by locality or surname overseas, was a major organi-sational principle for the local born and the migrants (often seasonal) from nearby areas. Chinese cities had a wide variety of guilds with highly specialised occupational differentiations covering the entire spec-trum from rice merchants and restaurant waiters to mat makers and even beggars. These associations represented and administered their members, who did not necessarily constitute ethnic communities, and were functionally equivalent to community organisations. Because occupational communities are discrete, there was not such neat organisational nesting in China as there is in overseas Chinese communities, but there was usually some sort of unofficial linking of all the groups and communities present in a city. During the twentieth century this was almost universally formalised in Chambers of Commerce. Secret societies existed throughout China, but they could not operate in the open as they did at certain times in south-east Asia. They were, however, certainly more powerful in China than they now are overseas because the imperial Chinese authorities were not nearly as efficient in suppressing them as are modern or colonial governments.

China's Confucian élite, based on classical education and proximity to imperial power, was equally resident in cities and the countryside, but was closed to the mass of the urban population, including merchants as merchants, however wealthy. Those who could afford to do so patterned themselves after the literati and occasionally associated with them as near equals, just as the wealthy Babas in Singapore, for instance, acted as much as possible like Englishmen.

The official government of the cities in which they lived, as well as that of all China, was also closed to non-élite urban classes. Government was imposed from above as a part of the imperial bureaucracy, and cities were not in fact distinguished administratively from the surrounding countryside in the governmental organisation. One imperial magistrate was responsible for governing 200,000 people on the rough average, and if a territory included a large city, or part of one, it contained far more. Considering the size of these populations and the small staffs magistrates had to aid them, there is no doubt that Chinese cities were just as autonomous and self-governing as the rural population or the Chinese living in cities abroad. The leaders of urban communities in China, including those of associations based purely on occupation as well as ethnicity, acted as informal brokers between the magistrates and the masses in a manner very similar to the way in which the rural gentry mediated between the bureaucracy and the peasants or the Kapitans China represented both the Dutch and the Chinese to each other.

The urban Chinese in China were a distinct part of their total society in the same way as were the Chinese living abroad. They were different from both the peasants in the countryside and the educated élite associated with the bureaucracy and landed wealth, just as the overseas Chinese can be differentiated from the local farmers and the indigenous or colonial élites. Redfield's distinction between folk society and the city has been a fruitful concept, but there is some cause for questioning his further identification of Great Traditions with cities.[5] Although it will perhaps usually be centred in them, the élite is by no means necessarily limited to the cities and towns, nor does it usually constitute a large percentage of the total urban population. In the case of China, in particular, there is need to distinguish three 'cultures' or sections instead of only two. There are the peasant farmers with their folk cultures, there is the dispersed élite with its unitary high culture, and there are the city dwellers with their urban culture. Although the three cultures and their areas of society are relatively distinct, the differences between them are secondary in importance to their overriding similarities. Special emphasis and developments in the different 'traditions' are balanced by diffusion, with the result that shared items predominate.

The rural Chinese were peasants, but they had a thoroughgoing money economy linked to that of the cities, and sharp financial dealings were as much a part of rural life as city life (Freedman 1959). There were a great many of these cultural similarities, including the expectation of particularism, the power of in-group feeling, and the prestige and power of wealth. In addition, the actual conditions of urban life were not unknown in rural areas. Peasants habitually traded in rural market towns and had a long history of migration to and from cities all over China. In slack agricultural periods many farmers went to nearby towns and cities where they could earn a little money as craftsmen or coolies.

The inter-relationship of urban and rural Chinese culture and society provides an explanation of both the similarity between urban social structure in China and overseas, and the surprising structural uniformity of the latter. Although most of the Chinese who went overseas were from rural areas, they were able to re-create traditional urban forms wherever they went, out of the common stock of Chinese culture they took with them. The unity underlying the diversities in urban and rural life demanded a parallel, and in a sense inevitably similar, development of Chinese urban society abroad. The basic sociological principles that organise rural life—descent, locality, and occupation—are also used to order urban society. Indeed it is not just the same principles, but the same *facts* of stipulated agnation and origin which are used, a use made possible by the putatively temporary nature of migration to cities, whether in China or abroad.

[5] See 'Folkways and city ways', 'The folk society', 'The natural history of the folk society', and 'The cultural role of cities' in Redfield (1962).

13

The Politics
of Ritual Secrecy

Abner Cohen

There are about six million men in the world today who are the members
of what has been described as the largest secret society on earth—Freemasonry. The overwhelming majority of these men live in the highly
industrialised societies of western Europe and America and almost all
are members of the wealthy and professional classes.

In Britain alone there are about three-quarters of a million Freemasons (see Dewar 1966:46–7). They are organised within local lodges
which are ritually, ideologically and bureaucratically supervised by the
grand lodges of England, Scotland and Ireland. They meet periodically
in their local centres and, behind the locked and well-guarded doors
of their temples, they wear their colourful and elaborately embroidered
regalia, carry the jewels, swords and other emblems of office, and perform their 'ancient' secret rituals.

The bulk of these rituals is concerned with the initiation of new members or the promotion of existing members to higher degrees. These rites
of passage involve the enactment of lengthy dramas, in the course of
which candidates go through phases of death and rebirth, are entrusted
with new secret signs, passwords and hand clasps, and are made to take
oaths, under the threat of horrifying sanctions, not to betray these

SOURCE: *Man*, 6, no. 3 (1971): 427–49. Reprinted by permission of the Royal Anthropological Institute.

The field study on which this article is based was carried out in Freetown, Sierra
Leone, between September 1969 and September 1970. It was financed by the School
of Oriental and African Studies, University of London. During that period I was
given the status of Visiting Research Fellow by Fourah Bay College, University of
Sierra Leone. I would like to record my thanks to both institutions for their generous
help.

I am grateful to Dr. Humphrey Fisher for his detailed and critical comment on
an earlier draft of the article.

secrets to outsiders. Recurring within these rites of passage are episodes from the life and career of a mythological hero, Hiram Abiff, who is said to have designed the Temple of Solomon. In the face of continual criticism and opposition from the Church, Freemasons go out of their way to emphasize their faith in the Supreme Being, to whom they refer as 'The Great Architect of the Universe' or, at times, 'The Grand Geometrician', and prominently display the Holy Book [1] in all their meetings.

There is a vast literature on Freemasonry. A large part of it is concerned with controversies about the origins of the cult or the sources of its mythology and rituals. The long essay in the *Encyclopedia Britannica* is purely historical. Another section of this literature consists of attacks, particularly by Roman Catholic clergymen, against the movement, or of apologetic reactions by Masons against these attacks. A third section consists of speculations or disclosures about the secret rituals of the craft.

Although a great deal is now known about its history and rituals, very little is known about its social significance, or its involvement in the system of the distribution and exercise of power in our society. Our ignorance is only partly due to the secrecy in which the movement is enveloped. Freemasons repeatedly point out that they are not a secret society but a society with secret rituals. By this they mean that it is only their rituals that are secret, but that membership is not secret. But the anomalous situation today is that while these rituals are no longer secret, hardly anything is known about membership. Legally, every lodge is obliged by law to submit a list of its members to the local Clerk of the Peace. But neither clerks of the peace, nor the Masonic authorities are obliged to make public the full list of members (see Dewar 1966: 103–4). Some scanty bits of information appear in the newspapers every now and then about individual Masons and some Masons may also in one way or another reveal to friends their membership, but on the whole the majority do not go out of their way to make their membership known.

A great deal of this reluctance to disclose membership is probably the result, not of the teachings of Freemasonry as such, but of the general tendency of members of the middle and upper classes, from which Masons are recruited, to be highly individualistic and to value privacy in their lives. This is indeed one of the main reasons why so little sociological research in general has been carried out in Britain among these classes.

[1] According to Freemasonic principles, the Holy Book can be either the Bible or the sacred book of any other universal religion. To my knowledge, all Freetown lodges display the Bible only.

Added to this difficulty is the immensity of the scale of our social groups and settlements, with the result that amidst our massive and highly impersonal urban milieux, it is too difficult to identify and locate members or to be acquainted with their circles or to know much about their economic, political or other social roles.

Finally, it must be remembered that sociologists are often so immersed in the very culture of which Freemasonry is a part, that some of them are hardly aware even of its existence or of the significance of its informal symbolism.

Some of these epistemological and methodological difficulties can be overcome if Freemasonry is studied as it is practised in a totally different social and cultural context from that of our own, within relatively small-scale societies. I believe that we can learn a great deal about our own culture generally when we study its forms in foreign lands. Most anthropologists working in preindustrial societies have so far, for a variety of reasons, shied away from investigating the functions of Western cultural forms in these societies.

Even a casual look through the pages of the year books of the Masonic grand lodges will be sufficient to show that relatively large numbers of Masonic lodges exist in nearly all the new states of Africa and Asia. (There are 44 in Nigeria, 43 in Ghana, and well over 100 in India, to take only random examples.) There is practically nothing whatever known about the social significance of these Masonic lodges.

I shall discuss here the organisation and functioning of Freemasonry in Sierra Leone, west Africa. The interplay between individual motives and structural constraints in the local development and functioning of this cult will be analysed. In conclusion some observations about the social significance and political potentialities of Freemasonry within industrial societies will be made.

THE CREOLES

There are today seventeen Masonic lodges in Sierra Leone, all in Freetown, the capital. Seven of these follow the English Constitution of Freemasonry. They are organised under a District Grand Lodge and are ultimately supervised by the Grand Lodge of England. The remaining ten lodges follow the Scottish Constitution of Freemasonry, are organised under a separate District Grand Lodge, and are ultimately supervised by the Grand Lodge of Scotland (see table page 313). There are no Masonic Lodges in Sierra Leone which follow the third 'sister' Constitution of Ireland.

I estimate that there are about 2,000 members in these lodges. Only a handful of these are Europeans, mainly British, although it was originally British officials in the colonial administration who established Freemasonry in Sierra Leone.[2] Most of these Europeans are today concentrated in one particular lodge, along with other Africans. Some of the British members have been in the movement in Britain before going to Sierra Leone and want to continue their membership through affiliation within a Freetown lodge. A few have joined in Sierra Leone mainly in order to become part of the movement in Britain when they return home. These find joining much easier in Sierra Leone than in Britain. My impression is that on the whole these European Masons play no significant role in the activities of the local lodges at present and at least some of them seem to be lukewarm in their attendance at the regular meetings of the movement.

The bulk of the Masons in Freetown are thus Africans, and the Grand Masters and the other important office-bearers in both district grand lodges are African.

With very few individual exceptions, all the Africans in the Masonic lodges are Creoles, the descendants of the slaves who were emancipated by the British between the 1780's and the 1850's, and were duly settled in the 'Province of Freedom', the Freetown Peninsula, which was bought for the purpose from the local Temne chiefs (see Fyfe 1962; Porter 1963; Peterson 1969). The Creoles are predominantly literate, highly educated, and occupationally differentiated. They number today 41,783 in the whole of Sierra Leone, with 37,560 of them concentrated in the Freetown Peninsula, and 27,730 in the city of Freetown itself. The remaining 4,223 are scattered among the provincial towns and are mostly civil servants and teachers whose homes are in Freetown. (For census details, see Central Statistics Office, 1965.) The Creoles are thus essentially metropolitan. Although they comprise only 1.9 per cent. of the total population, they dominate the civil service, the judiciary and the other major professions of medicine, law, engineering, university and high school teaching. A relatively substantial number of them have completed university training in Britain or in the U.S.A.

From the very beginning of their settlement in Sierra Leone, the Creoles made a bid to have a new start in their cultural life. They adopted English names, English styles of dress, education, religion, etiquette, art, music, and a general English style of life. Even today they can truly be said to be in many ways more English than the English. I have indeed

[2] According to Fyfe (1962:146) the first lodge was opened in Freetown in 1821, but was abolished, together with other dormant lodges, in 1864 by order of the Grand Lodge of England. Freemasonry was revived in 1882 (1962:437) with Creoles and Europeans joining the same lodge.

heard Creole men who have visited 'swinging Britain' recently express personal shock and disillusionment at the departure of the English from their 'proper' tradition which, in the Creole ideology, is synonymous with civilisation and enlightenment. It is certainly no exaggeration that has led them so often to be called 'The Black Englishmen'.

After a period of interaction with the Creoles on the basis of equality and comradeship, the British administrators turned their backs on them and began to resent their attempts to be equal partners in British civilisation and in the sharing of political power with them. The British administrators gradually segregated themselves from Creole company and British writers and travellers poured scorn and ridiculed their 'rubbishy' White culture and their 'aping' of English customs and ways of life. But, as Banton (1957:96–120) points out, their culture is very far from being merely the blind result of any superficial aping of English ways. On the contrary, it represents a unique and highly sophisticated culture combining different traits, both English and non-English, in a new way. Anyone who has had close personal contacts with the Creoles would know that their style of life is genuine and natural and is deeply rooted in their personality structure and entrenched in their thinking and in their way of life. It is a culture well worth investigating in its own right.

Although they originally hailed from different parts of west Africa (principally from Nigeria) and carried different cultural traditions, the Creoles managed in the course of only a few decades to develop a homogeneous culture of their own and to set themselves sharply apart, both culturally and socially, from the rest of the population of Sierra Leone, to whom they referred derisively as the 'Aboriginies'. (For a detailed account, see Peterson 1969). During the second half of the nineteenth century and the early decades of the present century they attempted to control the Natives,[3] but the British colonial administration, for a variety of considerations, thwarted that attempt (see Fyfe 1962. 614–20). If it had not been for this British policy, the Creoles would have probably succeeded in achieving the same degree of overall domination that has been accomplished by the Americo-Liberians, a similar minority with a similar origin, in neighbouring Liberia (see Libenow 1969).

Until about the end of the first world war, the Creoles were prominent in business. But since then a number of factors have led to the rapid decline of their businesses and to the transfer of their resources and of their energies into the training and recruitment of civil servants and professionals (see Porter 1963). Extensive biographical evidence shows how one successful businessman after another spent his fortune, not on the

---

[3] I am using the term Native for non-Creole Sierra Leoneans in the same way as it is used when one writes of the natives of France, for example.

development of his business, but on giving his children higher education in Britain or America. Almost invariably the succeeding generation preferred the highly lucrative, stable, and socially esteemed positions of the professions and government service, so Creole business virtually died out, to be taken over by Lebanese, British, and Indian business firms who are still dominant today.

Creole power today stems from two major resources. The first is the extensive property in land and in housing in Freetown and in the rest of the Freetown Peninsula which they control. This property has greatly appreciated in value since the end of the second world war, more particularly so since independence, because of an increasing demand by foreign diplomatic missions, by wealthy Sierra Leoneans from the interior of the country, and by the rapidly expanding government administration. This property is freehold, while all the land in the other provinces of the country, in what was formerly referred to as the Protectorate, is still 'tribal' land which cannot be sold. Their second source of power is their predominance in the civil service and in the professions.

Both these strongholds are now being seriously challenged by the tribesmen of the provinces, particularly by the Mende (30.9 per cent. of the population) and the Temne (29.8 per cent. of the population; see Central Statistical Office 1965). By their sheer voting power, these non-Creole Sierra Leoneans completely dominate the executive and the legislature and their politicians have been frequently harassing the Creoles and denouncing them as foreigners. The Temne maintain that the very land on which the Creoles have developed their society and culture, the Freetown Peninsula, is theirs and that their forefathers were tricked into selling it to the British for a trivial price for the purpose of settling the Creoles (see Fyfe 1964: 112–13). It is significant that even now, the Creoles are still legally referred to as 'Non-Native'. And, as rapidly increasing numbers of 'Natives' are becoming educated and trained, Creole predominance in the civil service and in the professions is becoming increasingly more precarious.

The cleavage between the Creoles and the Natives has dominated Sierra Leone politics throughout this century. This cleavage is symbolically represented in the very flag of the state. The committee which designed the flag chose blue to represent 'those who came from across the seas', namely the Creoles, green for the native inhabitants, and white, signifying peace—or rather, the wish for peace—separating them. But the cleavage is becoming deeper, though its processes are operating behind new slogans and new identities. Many Creoles today claim that they are facing not just the threat of losing their property and their positions, but virtual physical annihilation and they quote in support of this claim various pronouncements by politicians and others, particularly in the provinces.

From the figures quoted earlier, it should be evident that nearly one in every three Creole men in Freetown is a Mason. Creole Masons do not hide the fact that Masonry in Sierra Leone is overwhelmingly Creole. But they argue at length that this is not the result of any kind of policy of exclusion. They invariably mention some names of non-Creole Sierra Leoneans who are Masons. The name of one man in particular was mentioned to me over and over again by different Creole Masons. A Creole Mason will eagerly tell you that there are many non-Creole Sierra Leoneans in the movement. But when you ask specifically whether there are such members in his own lodge, the answer will often be that: 'It so happens that there is no one in our own lodge, but there are many in the other lodges'. There is no doubt that there are a few Natives in the lodges but their number is insignificant and for a variety of reasons which will become clear later their membership is only nominal. It is a fact that all the important figures in the Masonic movement, including the two Grand District Masters, are Creole. No native name is ever mentioned in the newspapers in connexion with Freemasonry and all the announcements of funerals and obituaries of deceased Masons which I have been able to see or hear include no Natives.

I do not myself think that there is any consciously formulated policy of excluding non-Creole Sierra Leoneans from membership. Many Masons think that non-Creoles are rare in the movement either because they are not interested, or because they are Muslims, or because they cannot afford the expense, or simply that they are not sufficiently educated. Many Creoles would also add that the Natives have their own secret society, the 'Poro', to which they are always affiliated. The Natives do not in fact need to become members in the Masonic movement. More than that, while there is a good deal of pressure on Creole men to join the movement, there is a good deal of pressure on Natives *not* to join it.[4]

THE INCIDENCE OF MEMBERSHIP

As with every other cult, individual Masons mention a wide variety of motives for joining the movement and remaining within it. Some join because they personally want to, but others join because of pressure. Often a man may join initially for one motive, but develop others after

[4] In its agitation against the APC government in 1970, an opposition paper claimed that the Prime Minister of Sierra Leone had made history by being the first Prime Minister of the country to join Freemasonry. This was to imply that the Prime Minister had been under the influence of the Creoles.

joining. The same man may emphasise different motives for being a Mason at different times. A man who joined as a result of pressure may develop motives or sentiments that are individual and personal. If we consider the sentiments, motives, and circumstances of each individual membership, we will find that each is a unique case and, when questioned, Masons often offer conscious and rational considerations for their membership.

This, of course, is only one side of the story and it will fail by itself to tell us anything about Freemasonry as an institution in its own right or about the structural circumstances which keep it alive as a going concern. The structural consequences of Freemasonic activity are certainly largely unintended by individual Masons, as each individual's first concern is his own interests. There is thus a dialectical relation between the individual and the group. In other words, although individual members seem to be acting freely and rationally, their action is nevertheless conditioned largely unconsciously by structural factors which to some extent constrain a man to behave in certain ways. Thus, the collective and the individual are closely related, though for analytical purposes they should be kept apart if we are to understand the social significance of the movement. I want to avoid at this stage discussing this problem in the abstract and will thus proceed to consider briefly the multiplicity and complexity of factors underlying membership.

Like many other ritual systems, Freemasonry offers a body of beliefs and practices which have intrinsic value. It provides a world view which includes the place of man in the universe. The literature of speculative Freemasonry contains a large number of treatises on metaphysics and theology written by men who are passionate in their search for what they believe to be the truth. In Freetown I met young Masons who spent a good deal of their spare time reading Masonic literature for sheer intellectual satisfaction.

Some men join the movement in the belief that the secrets which they will acquire contain vital intellectual and mystical formulae. This belief is sustained for long after joining as more and more secrets and rituals are unfolded to the Mason when he passes to higher degrees within the order.

Many of the Masons in Freetown with whom I talked stressed the personal satisfaction which they derived from the regular, frequent and extensive rituals and ceremonies of the lodge. Some of these Masons said, in explanation, that after all they were Africans and thus fond of the type of drama that the movement provided. A particularly powerful sentiment in this respect is Freemasonic ceremonial connected with the death of a 'brother'. The Creoles are intensely concerned with death, and funerals are great public events, often attended by thousands of people, depending on the status of the deceased. Deaths and funerals are regularly announced on the national radio in special bulletins, and often the lodge or lodges connected with a deceased man are summoned to the funeral by a special announcement on the radio. Lodges under the English Masonic constitution are prohibited by special rules of the Grand Lodge of England from going out in regalia to attend a public funeral, although they are allowed by special permission to appear in regalia within the church for the funeral service of a brother. But this prohibition does not exist within the Scottish constitution to which the greater number of Freetown lodges belong. Many of the members of English lodges are however also affiliated within Scottish lodges, so that their funerals are often attended formally by their lodges of affiliation, in regalia. The deceased man is 'laid out' in his formal black suit, with his full Masonic regalia decorating him, for hours before the funeral service and large numbers of people file past. When the coffin is finally covered, the regalia is taken off the body and placed on top. Masons under the Scottish constitution proceed in their regalia to the burial ground and when the Christian burial service is over, the Masons perform a special service at the grave to send their deceased brother off to the 'Highest Lodge'. It is indeed the dream of many Creole men with whom I talked to be buried with all the pomp and colour of the Masonic ceremonial, and I have no doubt that this is an important source of satisfaction for members of the movement. Some of the obituaries in the newspapers also carry photographs of the deceased in their Masonic regalia.

A second body of intrinsic values that men find in Freemasonry is the 'system of morality' that it offers. A great deal of the organisation and ceremonial of the movement is concerned with the development and maintenance of a true brotherhood among its members. Members are asked specifically to 'fraternise' with one another, and a good deal of the time and resources of the lodges is devoted to this end. The regular ritual sessions of the lodge are followed by institutionalised, lavish banqueting and drinking. The Creoles generally drink heavily and many cynics in Freetown say that men take to Masonry primarily for 'boozing'. The lodge is indeed very much an exclusive club.

One important aspect of Freemasonry as a brotherhood is the elaborate organisation of mutual help which it develops, and there is no doubt that the welfare and social security benefits that it offers attract some to the movement. Freemason welfare services in Britain are indeed among the most lavish and efficient. Many of their benevolent institutions are patronised by members of the Royal Family. In the United States this aspect of the movement is even more pronounced. In Freetown, no formal benevolent institutions have been established yet. Such institutions take time to develop and nearly all Masons have a network of kin who are under customary obligations to help in the hour of need. Nevertheless, the lodges have provided help in many instances and their care for aged members is particularly pronounced. Every lodge has an almoner who attends to cases of need and has for the purpose a special welfare fund to which each member contributes regularly at a fixed rate. Thus, although a Creole may expect help in the time of need from his kin, he may still join in order to secure for himself and for his family an additional measure of support or security without the burden of kin obligations.

Some Masons mentioned also the importance of contacting brothers in foreign lands. The Creoles travel very frequently to Britain and the U.S.A. in the course of their educational and professional careers and they see in Freemasonry an organisation that enables them to find helping and welcoming brothers wherever they go. These brothers abroad tend to be at the same time people of means and influence and their help can be substantial. I met a young Creole on his way to Britain for the first time to study who told me that he was a member of a Scottish lodge but that shortly before he left he affiliated himself within one of the English Lodges in order to be able to make contacts with brothers in both England and Scotland.

Freemasons are required by special rules to harbour no enmity against one another and to settle any misunderstanding or tension between brothers promptly and amicably. This must be particularly significant for many Creole Masons who, in ordinary secular life, are caught by the tensions of competition for appointments and promotions and by the estrangement resulting from involvement in the hierarchical bureaucratic structures of the civil service or the professions.

One of the moral principles of the Freemasonic brotherhood which is particularly stressed by Creole Masons in Freetown is that no brother should flirt or commit adultery with the wife of another brother. This 'private' piece of morality is one of the mechanisms meant to reduce potential sources of tension and enmity between members, and is widely used in the organisation of many kinds of fraternities. Women are seen in many contexts as a source of tension between men. This is probably the main reason why Freemasonry and other secret societies of this kind are exclusively male organisations. Indeed one of the indirect consequences of Freemasonic membership among the Creoles is that it serves as a mechanism institutionalising the weaning of men from their wives. Wives and female relatives are invited only once a year to a Ladies' Night which each lodge holds. Even if a man belongs to only one lodge, he can spend two or three nights a week in ceremonial sessions, meetings of committees, or visiting other lodges, away from his wife. A substantial proportion of the members of a lodge are Office Bearers and their various duties necessitate frequent meetings. And, as many Creoles in Freetown are not only members in one lodge but are affiliated to one or more other lodges, their absence from their wives is indeed frequent and prolonged. Most Masonic meetings in Freetown start at about 6:30 p.m. and go on in ceremonial and in banqueting until about 2 a.m. While often sharing with their husbands some of the benefits of Freemasonry, wives are annoyed by it. Many wives think that their husbands use lodge meetings as an alibi for visiting other women.

The Creoles are devout Christians and pride themselves on being monogamous. Also, Creole marriage is governed by British law, so that while a Mende or a Temne can marry according to customary law more than one wife, a Creole man would be prosecuted for bigamy if he married another wife. But it is an established 'customary' institution that most Creole men take 'outside women', support them, and have children by them. One of the peculiarities of the demography of the Creoles is that within the age group of twenty-five to forty-five, women substantially outnumber men. The effect of this numerical imbalance between the sexes is aggravated by the fact that men marry late. As there is a very strong pressure on Creoles to marry Creoles, the result is that there are many more unmarried women than men, and hence the institution of the 'outside woman'. The wealthier and the more eminent a man is the more outside wives he has. This is true even of eminent clergymen within the Church hierarchy, and is certainly an integral part of Creole culture (see Fashole-Luke 1968). Its functioning has required a good deal of 'distance' or avoidance between man and wife and from my observation I can say that Freemasonry serves indirectly as a mechanism for bringing about this avoidance.

Apart from these ritual and moral values, some individual Creoles find in Freemasonry more 'practical' and mundane advantages. Non-Mason cynics in Freetown claim that men join in order to establish informal links with their superiors in the civil service or the professions, as the case may be. It must be remembered that many of the most eminent judges, lawyers, permanent secretaries, heads of departments, doctors, engineers and others are members of the Masonic lodges in Freetown. In a society where rank and patronage count for a great deal, this must indeed be an important factor attracting men to join. One often hears gossip in Freetown society to the effect that all appointments and promotions in certain establishments are 'cooked' in the lodges. Similar charges have also been made against Freemasonry in Britain, America and elsewhere. But one need not assume the validity of these charges in order to appreciate the fact that men should seek to establish primary relations with their superiors, irrespective of possible material gain. Many of the Masons are involved in bureaucratic hierarchies, as superiors and subordinates, outside the movement, and a great deal of tension arises between them in various situations. It is natural that they should welcome an institution which alleviates the effects of this tension.

Association with the 'high-ups' through Masonry leads many non-Masons in Freetown to complain that Masons are snobs and behave in a superior manner. Masonry is certainly synonymous with high class in Freetown for the simple reason that a man cannot become a Mason if he cannot afford to pay the high expenses of membership and of the very frequent and lavish banqueting. The annual cost of membership for an initiate into the Entered Apprentice degree is about £50, excluding the cost of a black suit, transport, and so on. At promotion to a second degree the cost will be higher. When he is eventually 'raised' to the Third degree, that of a Master Mason, the cost during the year when he is 'reigning' in the lodge is between £400 and £500. Although both kin and lodge brothers contribute towards this expense, the bulk of the cost will be borne by the man himself. The regular payments that members make annually include fees for registration, contribution to benevolent funds, and some other minor items. The regalia for the initiate costs over £25 and as the Mason rises in degrees so does the cost of his regalia. Most of the lodges in Freetown include the basic cost of banqueting for the whole year in their annual fees, so that whether a man attended a banquet or not he would have paid the costs. Quite apart from the expenses of membership, a man must also have the right connexions if he wants to join the order. Freemasons do not proselytise and candidates are nearly always introduced by kin and friends who are already members. There is an initial period of investigation by a Committee of Membership during which inquiries are made about the candidate, and the candidate himself is interviewed and questioned at length. When the Committee is satisfied, the candidate is proposed for election in a general meeting of the lodge. Election is by secret balloting. If more than one black-ball were cast the candidate would not be admitted. This means that only 'the right people', who are acceptable to nearly the whole lodge will be admitted. Membership is thus taken as a privilege and Masons are to a great extent proud of it.

Perhaps largely unconsciously, the Creoles generally see in Masonry a mechanism for the development and maintenance of a 'mystique' which marks and enhances their distinctiveness and superiority vis-à-vis the Natives. This is becoming increasingly necessary in recent years as native Sierra Leoneans, backed by the political power of their sheer numbers, which they have enjoyed since the early 1950's, are challenging the Creoles on their own grounds of claims to superiority—education. One myth which you hear over and over again in conversation with Creoles is that no matter how highly educated a Native may be, he will never have the same kind of 'mentality', 'civilisation' or cultural sophistication as the Creoles. These elite qualities, the Creoles maintain, are the outcome of centuries of 'civilisation' and can never be achieved by money or by formal education. There are various symbolic mechanisms for the development of this 'mystique' among the Creoles, and Freemasonry, through its association with Western civilisation, is seen as the hall-mark of superiority, in contrast to the 'bush' secret societies of the Mende, the Temne, and others. For the Creoles, Freemasonry is in this respect an organisation within which they share ritual and moral values with eminent Europeans on the bases of equality and 'brotherhood'. Freemasonry requires a good deal of literacy and education and of sophistication in dress and etiquette. Freemasonry probably serves the same kind of need in Britain and America for the development of a mystique of superiority which is created not so much to convince others as to convince the actors themselves.

STRUCTURAL CONSTRAINTS

But by far the most important factor driving Creole men to Freemasonry is pressure from kin, from friends, and from wider groupings. Indeed many of the benefits that individual Masons are said to gain from membership are elaborations or rationalisations developed after joining. A great deal of insight into the structural forces that constrain Creole men to join Freemasonry can be gained from talking to men who are not yet Masons.

Some men join because their fathers are or were Masons. A Mason regards it as a duty and a source of pride to bring his sons into membership, often within the same lodge. As sons reach the age of twenty-one their fathers begin to press them to join. I know of at least one case where a man who is eminent in both Freemasonry and in the political organisation of the state in Sierra Leone, took the trouble to ask the higher Masonic authorities in Britain for special permission to have his eighteen-year-old son admitted as a member. I talked to men in their twenties and a few in their thirties who told me they had been putting off joining the movement by telling their fathers or other related Masons that they were not yet 'really old enough' for it. Even when a father is dead, older brothers or other relatives urge their younger brothers that it was their father's wish that the sons should join. Pressure also comes from other kin who are already within the movement or who are not.

Most important of all is the pressure of friends. Friendship ties are significant among the Creoles. It must be remembered that we are discussing here a few thousand men who were born, brought up, had their schooling and most of their university education within a relatively small town. Men spend most of their leisure time in cliques of friends and when most of a man's peers join Masonry, one after the other and become absorbed within its activities, a great deal of pressure is exerted on him to join. If he does not, he is likely to lose his friends. A young engineer told me that his Masonic friends would sometimes request him to leave the room so that they could say something in the confidence of Masonic brothers. He was in fact not sure, as he was telling me this, that this was not done deliberately by his friends in order to induce him to join.

Although only about a third of Creole men are full members of the Masonic lodges, the other two-thirds are to a large extent structurally involved within the movement. The Creoles on the whole are the highest and most privileged status group in Sierra Leone. But they are themselves internally stratified. A few scores of households command a great deal of power derived from property and from professional standing and high prestige which they have held for many generations. Below these are the other professionals, and the senior civil servants. Below these are the clerks, the salesmen, teachers. At the bottom are the relatively poorer households whose members are mainly skilled and some unskilled workers. Only men from the two top sectors tend to be in the lodges. But the Creoles are organised in 'families' whose structure combines kinship relations and patronage. The Creoles are bilateral in their kinship organisation, and patrilateral, matrilateral as well as affinal kin and sometimes even friends, are included within what a Creole would call his 'family'. From this it is obvious that all the Creoles are potentially related to one another, and that what a person would call his 'family' tends to be an ego-centric entity. Nevertheless, a degree of permanence and discreteness is given to a set of kin through the system of patronage. Each eminent man becomes the patron of a large number of kinsmen some of whom will even adopt the name of the patron, whether they are related to him patrilaterally, matrilaterally or affinally. Even a preliminary study of the structure of these 'families' is sufficient to show that each includes men and women from all classes of Creoldom. Although there is at the same time a tendency for the wealthy and eminent to seek close social relations with their equals in status, there are strong economic, political, moral and ritual forces that link the members together.

Thus although only the relatively well-to-do are in the lodges, these are in fact the patrons of those who are not members. Patronage involves both privileges and obligations and it it difficult for a man to remain in this position without keeping in close relationship with the other patrons who occupy strategic positions in the society. Masonic membership is an important feature of the style of life of any Creole of importance. It is a collective representation without which a man will not be able to partake in the network of privilege. A patron is indeed under strong pressure to join if he does not want to forfeit his role and his power.

On deeper analysis, it will become evident that this pressure by relatives, friends, and status groups, operating on the individual, is itself a mechanism of constraint whose source is the wide cleavage between Creoles and non-Creoles within the Sierra Leone polity. To appreciate the nature of this structural constraint, we must view it developmentally. I have drawn for this purpose a list of the Freemasonic lodges in Freetown, each by name, year of consecration and constitution. The establishment, consecration, and continuity of a lodge are supervised and administered by the 'mother' Grand Lodge in Britain. No lodge can be formed unless it gets a special charter from the Grand Lodge to certify that the lodge is formed in accordance with all the regulations of the movement. This charter must be displayed in every lodge at every one of its meetings and without it the meeting is invalid. The charter must be renewed annually. Each lodge has a special serial number within the constitution and its name, address and other details are formally listed in the Year Book of the Mother Constitution (see table facing page).

The first point to be noticed from the list is that the proliferation of the lodges has not been a gradual process but has occurred in bouts. We can divide the development of Freemasonry in Freetown into three major periods. The first phase is from 1882 to 1914, when six lodges were formed, four under the English constitution and two under the Scottish constitution. Most of the members of those lodges were British officials. I am not concerned in this article with that period. For the following three decades, from 1914 to 1946, no new lodges were established. This was roughly the period of indirect rule in British West Africa, which came to an end in most British colonies shortly after the second world war.

Then in the course of four to five years, from 1947 to 1952, the number of lodges in Freetown doubled, from six to twelve. This was the beginning of new political developments leading to independence in 1961.

There followed a standstill period of about thirteen years which roughly coincided with the stable premiership of Sir Milton Margai, ending in 1964 with his death, and the succession to the premiership of

The Freemasonic Lodges in Freetown by Name, Year of Consecration, and Constitution.

English Constitution		Scottish Constitution	
Name	Year of Consecration	Name	Year of Constitution
Freetown	1882 *		
St George	1894 *		
Rokell	1899 *	S. L. Highland	1905 *
Loyal	1914	Academic	1914 *
ABOUT THIRTY YEARS WITH NO CHANGE			
Progressive	1947		
Wilberforce	1947		
		Tranquility	1949
		Harmony	1950 *
		Travellers	1950
Granville	1952		
ABOUT THIRTEEN YEARS WITH NO CHANGE			
		Mount Aureol	1949
		Sapiens	1966
		Delco	1966
		Leona	1968
		Earl of Eglington and Winton	1968

* Lodges with asterisk have been granted Royal Arch Status.

his brother, Sir Albert Margai. This ushered in a turbulent time which came to an end with the *coups d'état* of 1967 and 1968. In the course of less than three years the number of lodges leapt by nearly 50 per cent. from twelve to seventeen, with all the increase occurring within the Scottish constitution, the number of whose daughter lodges thus doubled.

We thus have two phases of concentrated and intensified 'freemasonisation', the 1947–52 period, and the 1965–68 period. What is significant in both periods is that each involved a direct and serious threat to Creoldom. This emerges clearly from the wealth of documentation of all sorts, and from the detailed studies of the politics of Sierra Leone since the second world war by political scientists and other scholars (see particularly Cartwright 1970; Kilsen 1966; Fisher 1969). I can here give only a brief outline of the relevant events.

The developments of the 1947–52 period still remain the most traumatic experience in the psychology of the Creoles. Until then the Creoles were securely entrenched in the Colony—despite the British policy of restraining them from dominating the natives from the Protectorate. Their ascendance in the civil service and in the professions was overwhelming. Even as late as 1950 there were at least seventy Creole doctors as against three from the Protectorate (Cartwright 1970:24). In 1953, 92 per cent. of the civil servants were Creoles. In 1947 the British government presented proposals for constitutional reform in Sierra Leone aiming at unifying the Colony and the Protectorate and setting the whole country on the path to independence. The proposals at that stage were not revolutionary for the country as a whole but they dramatically affected the balance of power between Colony and Protectorate. Among other things they stipulated that the fourteen African members of the new Legislative Council should be elected by the people. This virtually meant the beginning of the end of Creole political influence even within what they had hitherto regarded as their own home: the Colony.

Their reaction was frantic. In 1948 all the major Creole political groupings, including the Combined Rate Payers Association and the Sierra Leone Socialist Party presented a petition to the Secretary of State for the Colonies attacking the colonial government for intending to give power to illiterate 'foreigners'; i.e. the people of the Protectorate. The Creoles demanded that only the literate should be given the right to vote.

There were bitter exchanges across the deepening cleavage between the Creoles and the Natives. Dr. H. C. Bankole-Bright, the Creole political leader at the time, described the Creoles and the Natives as 'two mountains that can never meet'. In a letter published by the Creole *Sierra Leone Weekly News* (26 August, 1950) he recalled that the Protectorate had come into being 'after the massacre of some of our fathers and grandfathers . . . in Mendeland because they were described as "Black Englishmen"'. For the other camp, Milton Margai, who was soon to become the Prime Minister of Sierra Leone, described the Creoles (see Protectorate Assembly 1950:28–31) as a handful of foreigners to whom 'our forefathers' had given shelter and who imagined themselves to be superior because they aped Western modes of living but who had never breathed the true spirit of independence.

What is important to note here is that although the more conservative Creole elements fought a desperate battle for a long time and continue to do so still trying to put the clock back, most of the Creole moderates and intellectuals recognised the futility of this stand and tried to adjust to the times and make the most out of the new opportunities. They soon recognised that any attempt by the Creoles to organise politically on formal lines would be disastrous because of their hopeless numerical weaknesses. It should be emphasised that in their determination to leave Sierra Leone, the British pursued a consistent policy in the Africanisation of their administration. This entailed the replacement of British officials by Africans, and as few Natives were educated enough to qualify, it was inevitable that the bulk of the new recruits should come from among the Creoles. The British did their best to educate Africans particularly from the Protectorate for the new jobs, by giving them scholarships for study overseas. But even so and despite all pressure, 60 per cent. of the holders of these scholarships between 1951 and 1956 were Creoles (Cartwright 1970:24). Also, as holders of land property in the Colony, the Creoles began to reap the benefits of the impending independence by the rise in the value of their property. All this meant that the Creoles would lose everything if they stood as a formal solid political bloc within the new state structure, while, if they co-operated in the maintenance of a liberal regime on the basis of individual equality they would gain a great deal because of their superior education and cultural sophistication. The Creoles who were thinking along these lines, eventually co-operated with the Native-dominated Milton Margai government. Milton Margai, who was a shrewd politician, recognised that he could not establish a government without the Creoles and he also recognised the immense contribution that the Creoles had made and could still make to the country. He therefore included many Creoles in his Party's representation and retained Creole men in key administrative positions. Thus, despite the grumbling of some Creoles every now and then, a period of co-operation and stability prevailed throughout Milton Margai's regime, ending with his death in 1964.

His brother, Albert Margai who succeeded him, was different in character and in style of government. Within a short time he made a serious attempt to change the constitution in order to establish officially a one-party system. He could not do this without the close co-operation of the civil service, the judiciary as well as the legislature. But his attempt was immediately opposed by almost all the Creoles who now shifted their support to the opposition party. Opposition papers began to agitate against Albert and to expose his alleged corruption. The government brought the agitators to court. But the courts were presided over by Creole judges and verdicts were in the hands of juries who, because of the demand that they should be literate, were also Creole and most of the accused were acquitted. This outraged Albert Margai who began to attack ominously in his speeches the 'doctors, lawyers, and lecturers of Freetown' who were wilfully refusing to see the blessings of the one-party system.

Events during the following one or two years show what an influential small minority elite can do against an established government supported by a large section of the population. Creole heads of trade unions, clergymen, lawyers, doctors, teachers, and university students used every shred of influence they had to bring about the downfall of Albert Margai. An opportunity presented itself in the 1967 general elections when the majority of Creole men and women threw their influence and their organisational weight behind the opposition party. The governing party, the SLPP, was defeated though by a narrow majority (for details see Cartwright 1970; Fisher 1969).

Thus in both the 1947–52 and 1965–68 periods there was a sharp dramatic turn of events which brought about a serious threat to the continuity of Creole power and privilege. The very men whose power was most threatened in this way, mainly the civil servants and members of the professions, were those who filled the Freemasonic lodges in Freetown. Unless we assume that these men had split personalities, we can easily see that the two processes of change, i.e. the developing threat to Creole power and the increase in Freemasonic membership, are significantly interrelated. Nearly all the names of the Creoles who were involved in the struggle against Albert Margai in 1966 and 1967 are those of well-known Freemasons. The varied forms that Creole action took to bring about the downfall of Albert Margai showed a remarkable degree of overall co-ordination which no formal political party or association was at the time capable of achieving.

AN EXCLUSIVE ORGANISATION

Largely without any conscious policy or design, Freemasonic rituals and organisation helped to articulate an informal organisation, which helped the Creoles to protect their position in the face of increasing political threat. It did this in a number of ways, the most important being in providing an effective mechanism for regular communication, deliberation, decision-making, and for the development of an authority structure and of an integrated ideology. Although the members are divided into two constitutions and further, within each, into several lodges, there is a very great deal of intensive interaction between the whole membership. This is done through the manipulation of some of the institutions of Freemasonic organisation.

A Mason can become a Member in only one lodge, his 'lodge of birth', into which he is initiated. But he can seek 'affiliation' within other lodges, whether from his own constitution or from the other constitution. Many Masons are affiliated to one or more lodges, depending on their ability to meet the high expense in both time and money. Affiliation within a lodge costs only slightly less than membership. When you are affiliated within a lodge you enjoy the same privileges and share in the same activities as the members of that lodge. I know of some men who are affiliated within five lodges. On the individual level, men seek affiliation for the same reasons mentioned above in connexion with membership. They may want to associate with eminent men who are the members of other lodges, to interact socially, to enjoy eating and drinking more frequently. Other Masons seek affiliation within other lodges where they have better prospects for earlier promotion to the degree of Master Mason.

Another institution, which is probably even more important in establishing channels of communication between the lodges is that of visiting. A Mason can visit other lodges, where he may or may not have friends. All except the Royal Arch lodges are open to members from all degrees. Royal Arch lodges, however, are open to only reigning or past Master Masons. I understood from Masons in Freetown with whom I talked, that on average nearly a quarter to a third of those present in any lodge meeting are visitors from other lodges.

Sociologically, the most important feature of lodge ceremonials is not the formal rituals of the order but the banqueting following their performance. It is here, amidst heavy drinking and eating, that Masons are engaged in the process of true 'fraternising'. In my view this informal institution within Masonry, whose procedure is neither planned nor consciously pursued, is the most fundamental mechanism in welding the members of all the lodges into a single, highly interrelated organisation. It must be remembered that we are dealing here with a small and limited community of a few thousand men who were born and brought up within a relatively small town. Indeed, the seventeen lodges meet within less than one square mile. In some cases many lodges have their temples in the same building in the centre of the town. These are also the men who are related to one another as relatives, affines or friends, and who attend one another's weddings, funerals, and other family occasions.

It is obvious that the wealthier a man is the more mobile he becomes within the lodges, and this brings us to a second and a most fundamental structural function of Masonic organisation. This is that although there is emphasis in Masonry on equality and true brotherhood, Masonic organisation provides effective and efficient mechanisms for the establishment of a strong authority structure. Formally, this is achieved through the ritual promotion within the three degrees of the Craft, the Entered Apprentice, Fellow of the Craft, and Master Mason. These degrees are the same under both the English and the Scottish Constitutions. But the English Constitution has further degrees within what is known as the Royal Arch.

Initiation into the First Degree, and then promotion to the Second, 'raising' to the Third, and further promotion in the Royal Arch Degrees, are marked by very elaborate ritual dramas. Each stage is also marked by new regalia with additional signs of office. It is also marked by the acquisition of further secrets, by new duties and new privileges. Apart from these ritual degrees there is also in each lodge a large number of Office Bearers of all sorts, who are concerned with the running and organisation of the lodge. And at the top of the lodges within each Constitution there is a District Grand Lodge, headed by a District Grand Master, his Deputy and Secretary. A Master is always addressed as 'Worshipful Master'. A Grand Master is addressed as the 'Most Worshipful Master'. The higher a Mason's degree the greater his mobility within, and access to, the lodges. A Master Mason can enter, without permission or invitation, even the Royal Arch Lodges.

All promotions are formally on the basis of attainment in Freemasonic theology and ritual and require devotion to the movement in regular attendance. But as each promotion to a higher degree necessitates spending more money in fees, in regalia and, more especially in providing banquets, only those Masons who can meet these expenses and who have the necessary backing in the lodges will seek or accept promotion. Promotion usually takes time and sometimes it can take a man over ten years to become a Master Mason. But the process can be greatly speeded up, and there are cases in Freetown of men being raised to the Third Degree within three years.

In this respect, the Scottish Constitution is more helpful than the English. Promotion can be quicker. Masons from Scottish lodges in Freetown told me they thought the Scottish constitution was more democratic than the English, which they described as conservative. In a Scottish lodge it is the members of the lodge who decide on who will be raised to the position of Master and his Deputy while in English lodges the decision comes from above. On the whole, the Scottish constitution seems to be more easily adaptable to changing situations than the English one, and I believe that this is the main reason why, as the table above shows, it is now more predominant among the Creoles than the English one. In a rapidly changing situation it is important for a group to have a more flexible articulating ideology and organisation. For the Creoles, this is indeed crucial.

Within the hierarchy of degrees and offices in the Freemasonic organisation there is thus a close relationship between wealth and position in the non-Masonic sphere on the one hand, and ritual authority within the order on the other. The prominent men in the Masonic order are indeed the prominent men in Sierra Leone in general. There is a close relation between the two spheres.

Individual Masons often manipulate various factors to gain authority and power within the movement. A man who has just joined a lodge and who will probably have to take his place in the queue behind many other 'brothers' in order to be raised to the coveted status of Master Mason, will seek either affiliation to another lodge in which more opportunities exist, or will group with other members, who should include at least seven Masters, in order to drive an application through for the foundation of a new lodge. If he is a member of an English lodge he may discover that his chances are better in affiliation within a Scottish Lodge. And within the lodge he will try to gain the affection and support of various cliques of friends.

Even at the level of District Lodges, the two Masonic organisations are closely interrelated, and, taken together, they indeed merge in effect to articulate one unified Masonic hierarchy. The present District Grand Master of the Scottish constitution for example was originally initiated into an English constitution lodge, was then affiliated to other lodges from both constitutions, and became founding Master of a Scottish lodge. Other eminent Masons in Freetown had similar careers within the order.

This integrated hierarchy of authority is of immense significance for the Creoles as a corporate interest group. Like the middle classes in many countries, the Creoles are in general notoriously individualistic and no sooner does a leader begin to assume leadership than a number of other men begin to contest his claim in the spirit of 'why he, not me?'. It must be emphasized that during the Colonial period, while the Temne, Mende, and the other tribes of Sierra Leone had their own local and paramount chiefs whose authority was upheld by the Colonial administration, the Creoles were without traditional leadership. Up to the present, the Creoles are treated legally as non-Natives and their family and social life is regulated under British civil law, while the Natives are treated mainly according to customary law. The Creoles have for long identified strongly with the British and do not have any kind of tribal structure.

The difficulty in developing a unified leadership and a system of authority was further increased by the fact that, outside the formal political arena, the Creoles had several, often competing, hierarchies of authority within different groupings. One was the church hierarchy, the others were within each one of the major professions, including the teachers, as well as property holders. Furthermore, there was intensive strife within each grouping characterised by intense competition for promotion into higher positions and by perpetual tension between superior and subordinate within the bureaucratic structure. But when the members of all these groupings became incorporated within the Masonic lodges, they became integrated within an all-encompassing authority structure in which members from the higher positions of the different non-Masonic hierarchies were included. The different types and bases of power within those groupings were expressed in terms of the symbols and ideology of Freemasonry. A unified system of legitimation for a unified authority structure was thus created. This has been of course, not a once-and-for-all development, but a continuing process of interaction between the ritual authority within the order and the various authority systems outside it.

Freemasonry has thus provided the Creoles with the means for the articulation of the organisational functions of a political group. The organisation that has emerged is efficient and effective and is thus in sharp contrast with the loose and feeble political organisations in Sierra Leone generally. As Cartwright (1970) points out, the political parties of Sierra Leone are loose alliances between various groups, many of which shift their allegiance from one party to another unpredictably. But Freemasonic organisation is strictly supervised by the two Grand Lodges in Britain who enforce the same strict standards of organisation that have been evolved in an advanced and highly industrialised society. This is why, in my view, Freemasonic organisation in Sierra Leone today is one of the most efficient and effective organisations in the whole country. It has thus partly made up for Creole numerical weakness. A small group can indeed greatly enhance its power through rigorous organisation.

In adopting Freemasonry in this way, the Creoles are not making use of a novel kind of ideology and organisation in Sierra Leone politics. For it is well known that Sierra Leone and some of her neighbouring countries constitute an ethnographic area which is especially characterised by the variety and multiplicity of its secret societies. The role of the Poro secret society of the Mende in organising and staging the so-called Hut Tax War against the British and the Creoles in 1898 is well documented (see Chalmers 1899; Little 1965a; 1966; Scott 1960: 173–4). As Kilsen points out (1966: 256–8) the Poro has ever since been used in modern political contexts down to the present. Its symbols, ideology, and organisation have been used by the SLPP, the major, Mende-backed party of Milton Margai, to mobilise votes and support in elections. A similar use of the symbols and organisation of secret societies in the modern politics of neighbouring Liberia has also been reported (see Libenow 1969).

Although I have been discussing here the political functions of a ritual organisation, I am not implying any kind of reductionism which aims at explaining, or rather explaining away, the ritual in terms of political or economic relations. Nor am I imputing conscious and calculated political design on the part of men who observe the beliefs and the symbolic codes of such an organisation. Like many other ritual systems, Free-masonry is a phenomenon *sui generis*. It is a source of values in its own right, and individuals often look at it as an end in itself and not as a means to an end. A Creole Mason will be genuinely offended if he is told that he is joining the movement for political considerations. More funda-mentally, the Freemasonic movement is officially and formally opposed to the discussion of political issues in the course of its formal meetings. There is certainly no conscious and deliberate use of Freemasonry in political manoeuvring.

But all this does not mean that the movement has no political aspects or political consequences. Although man in contemporary society plays different roles in different fields of social life, these roles are nevertheless related to one another within one 'self', 'ego' or psyche. A normal man has his identity, his 'I', which is developed only through the integration of the disparate roles that he plays. To achieve selfhood at all, a man's role as a Mason must be brought into relation with his role as a profes-sional, a politician, a husband, a father.

The Creoles generally have been under severe pressure and strain during the past twenty-five years or so. During this period they have had to put up with threats of various sorts, in the street, in the courtroom, in parliament. These men are conscious of and worried about these prob-lems and they talk about them all the time. When they meet in the Masonic temples, they meet to perform the prescribed formal rituals. But when they adjourn to banqueting, or when they meet informally altogether outside the framework of Freemasonry, what do they discuss?

I addressed this question to several Masons. Almost invariably the reply was that they talk about 'the usual ordinary current problems', which people usually talk about. There is no doubt whatsoever that this is so. But it is not unreasonable to conjecture that these men do talk about their current problems and about their anxieties, hopes, and also deliberate about solutions. They do not even need to talk about these problems exclusively within the lodges or while banqueting. Through the sharing of the same sign language, the same system of beliefs, the same secret rituals, and the same organisation, and through frequent banqueting, strong moral bonds develop between them which often transcend, become stronger than, many other bonds, so that when they meet outside the lodge framework they talk together more confidentially and more intimately than if they were not brothers within the same movement. Attend any of the frequent ceremonials staged by the Creoles in their ordinary social life, such as weddings, christenings, or gradua-tion, and you will not fail to see that while the women are busy dancing on their own to the wild beat of the Gumbe band, the men sit quietly in cliques on the side drinking and talking. If you ask the women what their men were doing they will say 'they are talking lodge'. Indeed the phrase 'talking lodge' which is frequently heard in Freetown society, has the connotation of 'talking politics'.

Through these intimate and exclusive gatherings, within and outside the framework of the lodge, men pool their problems, deliberate about them, try to find solutions to them and eventually develop formulae for appropriate action. It is because of all this deliberation, communication, and co-ordination of decisional formulations, that there is a remarkable unanimity of opinion among the Creoles over major current problems. Talk about any public issue on any day with a number of Creoles in Freetown and you will most probably hear in comment the same statements, using almost the same phrases and words. Many expatriates in Sierra Leone have remarked on this uniformity of response to major issues on the part of the Creoles. In the course of a few months I followed a number of public issues, concentrating particularly on two of them. One issue was raised by three different men in different situations within two to four days of each other, including one article in a daily newspaper. On enquiry all three men turned out to be members of the same lodge. In a few days' time the statements about that issue became stereotyped, and truly became the 'collective representation', of a whole group of men and, later, of their women.

Freemasonry is, of course, not the only cultural institution which helps to articulate the corporate organisation of Creole interests. In my view, it is best to study an interest group in terms of two interconnected, though analytically separated, dimensions: the political and the symbolic. The symbolic consists of all the patterns of normative behaviour within a number of institutions such as the church, the family, friendship, art and literature. Most of these patterns of symbolic behaviour have consequences affecting the organisational functions of the group, although some will have more direct effects in articulating certain functions than others. A single institution, like Freemasonry, will contribute to the articulation of different organisational functions, such as communication and decision-making. On the other hand, a number of institutions will jointly help in the articulation of a single function such as that of distinctiveness (for details, see Cohen 1969:201–11). To study Creoldom in this way would require a complete monograph. What I have attempted here is simply to isolate the structural consequences of Freemasonry.

Throughout this discussion I have referred to the Creoles as if they were a discrete ethnic group. They indeed *are* such a group, having their own distinct culture and their own history. What is more, they are still regarded legally as 'non-Native'. They see themselves and are seen by others as a distinct culture group. But this is to some extent a false picture because it entails, among other things, the strict observance of a rigid principle of descent, and hence of recruitment. But the Creoles are bilateral and a man will often include within what he regards as his 'family' both patrilateral, matrilateral, and affinal relatives as well as friends. Throughout the history of the Creoles in Sierra Leone men and women of Native descent were Creolised through various processes (see Banton 1957; Porter 1963). By acquiring the symbols and style of life of Creoldom and by being incorporated within the Creole social network, these Natives became in effect Creole. On the other hand, there is evidence of an opposite process going on all the time whereby Creoles became Natives and came to identify themselves with different ethnic groups. More recently, some Creoles have publicly renounced their English names which they changed into African names and advocated complete integration with the Natives. Creole men today, and certainly almost all the Freemasons among them, declare publicly that they are opposed to 'tribalism', and play down their distinctive identity as Creoles.

Creoldom within the modern Sierra Leone polity is essentially a status group marked off from other social groups by a special style of life and by a dense network of relationships and co-operation. Although they are internally stratified, they stand as a group on their own within the wider society. There is no doubt that Freemasonry has helped them to co-ordinate their struggle to preserve their high status. It must be remembered that the Creoles are essentially professionals and wage earners. They are not exploiters. They have been the main factor in keeping the country's institutions liberal. Until very recently Sierra Leone was one of the few states in the Third World which was still democratic.[5] The Creoles want the country to remain liberal not only because of their ideological zeal, but also because they realise that as long as there is free competition for jobs in the civil service and the professions they, with their advanced schooling system, their Western style of life, and the advantages they have had over other groups in these fields for over a century and a half, are likely to win and to maintain their present high social status.

One of the sociological lessons we can learn from the study of a group like the Creoles for the understanding of Western industrial societies is the study of classes—particularly the higher classes—as groups which are informally organised for action through a variety of institutions like Freemasonry. The association between Freemasonry and the higher social classes in Britain and the U.S.A. has been known for a long time

[5] I left Freetown in September 1970. For some of the political developments since then, see Dalby 1971.

now. What I have tried to do in this article is to indicate how this cult operates in articulating a corporate organisation for a group of highly individualistic people. An analysis of this type can perhaps supplement that by, for example, Lupton and Wilson (1959) in their well-known study of decision-makers in Britain.

Freemasonry offers two major functions to its members: an exclusive organisation and a mechanism for the creation of a brotherhood. Through upholding the principle of secrecy, or rather of the monopoly of secrets, Freemasons are able to develop, maintain, and run a vast, intricate, efficient, and highly complex organisation, with its symbols of distinctiveness, channels of exclusive communication, structure of authority, ideology, and frequent socialisation through ceremonials. Through its networks of lodges, its ritual degrees and hierarchical structure, its institutions of affiliation and visiting, and the existence of three different constitutions, it is particularly suited to operate in the highly differentiated and complex structure of our industrial society. For it is capable of articulating the groupings of different occupational and social categories of people, allowing both unity and diversity.

As men join the organisation, the impersonal character of a social category like class gives way to the rapid development of moral bonds that link its individuals. Through the sharing of common secrets and of a common language of signs, passwords, and hand-clasps, through sharing the humilities of the ceremonials of initiation, through mutual aid, the frequent communion in worshipping and eating together, and the rules to settle disputes amicably between them, the members are transformed into a true brotherhood. This combination of strict, exclusive, organisation, with the primary bonds of a brotherhood, makes Freemasonry a powerful organisation in contemporary society.

Freemasonry has different structural functions under different social conditions, and in its history in Europe it has served to organise conservative as well as progressive movements. Its functions are determined neither by its doctrine nor by its formal organisation. But it is definitely an organisation especially suited for the well-to-do. What is more, because of its secrecy and its rules of recruitment, it is such that once it is captured or dominated by a strong interest group, or by a number of related interest groups, it tends to become the exclusive vehicle for promoting the interests of that group. Through secret balloting and the requirement of almost complete consensus for admitting new members, it can easily exclude the members of other groups from joining it. Sociologically, the question of whom it excludes becomes as significant as that of whom it includes.

14

Slum Clearance and
Family Life in Lagos

Peter Marris

Slums are amongst the most obtrusive of social evils. Physical squalor catches the eye; the degradation of human dignity shocks the social reformer, civic pride is outraged, the privileged are uncomfortably reminded of the circumstances in which their fellow countrymen must live. To people who do not live in slums, their demolition seems self-evidently desirable. Yet the slum dwellers themselves often bitterly resent being displaced. Where, as in South Africa, slum clearance is openly undertaken for the protection of the privileged, such a conflict of interests is not surprising. But the conflict also arises where the welfare of the people to be rehoused is the principal aim of policy.

In Africa, the initiative in slum clearance usually comes from public agencies, which are run by aliens, or the most privileged members of society. They tend to assume that physical squalor must be associated with moral degradation: the slums must be riven with crime, ill-health, a demoralized irresponsibility in family life. But this need not be so. The slum may be merely the longest-settled neighborhood, grown shabby with age, which yet enjoys the most integrated social life of any in the city. The people who live there are not necessarily all impoverished, or humiliated, by their surroundings. Even if they are, they probably cannot afford to live otherwise, and, unless the underlying causes of their poverty are first removed, the attempt to rehouse them at a standard beyond their means will only make them destitute. There is a danger, therefore, that slum clearance schemes will be based on arbitrary assumptions as to how slum-dwellers live, and ought to live; and that they will set standards related more to the social values of the leaders of society, than to the needs and resources of the people to be rehoused. But

SOURCE: *Human Organization*, 19, vol. 3 (1960): 123–28. Reprinted by permission of the Society for Applied Anthropology.

the more realistically the difficulties are assessed, the more intractable they are likely to appear.

I would like to illustrate the problem by the slum clearance scheme in Lagos, the federal capital of Nigeria, of which I made a study during 1958 and 1959—especially as to its effect on family life.[1] The figures quoted in the first section are based on a sample of the adult population of the area in Central Lagos scheduled for demolition as slums; and in the second, on two samples of heads of households, in four streets of the slum area and in the rehousing estate, respectively.[2]

THE PEOPLE OF CENTRAL LAGOS

The part of Central Lagos to be cleared as slums has been settled for two or more generations. The streets are shown in their present form on a map of 1885. The houses would have been built originally by families for their own use, although many have later been divided, or let to tenants. A few still standing follow the design of a traditional Yoruba compound, the rooms surrounding an open courtyard on four sides. But, in more recent building, the courtyard has dwindled to a passage leading from the street to a yard, often with rooms opening onto it from one or two sides, and lavatories and washplaces at the back. In these yards, or on a verandah overlooking the street, the women do most of their house-work. The rooms are sometimes so full of bed and baggage that there is hardly space to put a chair. In four streets of central Lagos which I investigated, there were 1.9 adults and 1.6 children to each room—3.5 people in all. But such cramped quarters are manageable because the occupants do little but sleep and make love there.

The houses are shabby—the walls patched, the roofs leaky, the ceilings blackened with smoke. But some have solid walls, well-made doors and windows, and a concrete floor raised above the ground. They have suffered as much from neglect as from dilapidation.

According to Yoruba custom,[3] the children of the founder of a family

[1] The material was collected during a visit to Lagos from July 1958 to August 1959. The study was financed by the Leverhulme Trust, and undertaken for the Institute of Community Studies, London.

[2] The sample of the adult population was drawn at random from a census made by the Lagos Executive Development Board, the Authority responsible for slum clearance. 372 men and women were interviewed. 110 households were intensively interviewed in the four streets of central Lagos. On the rehousing estate, 63 households were interviewed from addresses selected at random. Since the numbers in the latter samples are small, the percentages given in the second section can only be taken as a general indication of trends.

[3] The Yoruba account for seventy percent of the population of Lagos, and were the original settlers. Customary land-holding in Lagos is therefore according to tradi-

property occupy it, together with their wives and children, and their descendants after them. The daughters have much the same rights as the sons, except that they would be expected to live with their husband in his family house. In fact, there seem to be only a few family properties still occupied in this way in Lagos. Usually some rooms are let, some are occupied by the descendants of the founder, and others by more distant relatives, for whom those with rights in the house are responsible. For example, in the four streets I studied in detail, out of twenty-nine properties, eleven were occupied only by tenants, fourteen by both owners and tenants, and four entirely by the family which owned it. About sixty percent of the present residents are tenants.

The tenants in central Lagos, however, are long settled there. More than half of those interviewed had lived in Lagos for over twenty years, and nearly half had occupied the same rooms for more than ten years. Nine-tenths of the owners and their relatives were born in Lagos, half of them in the house in which they still lived. Even amongst the tenants who had taken their rooms most recently, the majority had occupied them for at least six years. The population is the most stable in Lagos.

The slum clearance area is at the heart of Lagos commercial life. It lies between the two main shopping streets; surrounded by the largest markets in cloth, vegetables, meat, and poultry, enamel and earthenware, herbs, fancy goods and fruit; and within a few minutes of the great importing houses. Much of the working population of Lagos passes every day by its narrow lanes. The people of the neighbourhood earn their living by the commerce of the city. The men are traders, importers and exporters, shopkeepers, dockers and market porters; drivers, watchmen, clerks or mechanics for the foreign firms; or craftsmen who often deal in goods on the side—bicycle repairers selling secondhand machines and tyres, spray painters selling paint, blacksmiths buying up used tins and making them into cheap oil lamps. The women nearly all trade.

Traders and many of the craftsmen work on their own account, and depend for their livelihood on attracting a group of regular customers to whom they are readily available. Some of the labourers, too, are only casually employed, and must be in easy reach of employers who may be hiring men for the day. So, more than half the working population are likely to earn less, at least for a while, if they are moved from the neighbourhood where they have established themselves.

Two-thirds of the men earn between £6 and £20 a month, the labourers earning least. Traders and craftsmen have the highest proportion of both the poorest and most prosperous. The women traders, however, usually make substantially less than the men: the majority have a

tional Yoruba practice. The Yoruba, a people of five millions, are the dominant tribal group of the Lagos hinterland.

profit of less than £10 a month, although there were still thirteen percent amongst those I interviewed with incomes over £20.

The people of central Lagos are, therefore, largely dependent upon their location at the centre of commerce for their livelihood. And because they have, on the whole, been long settled there, an integrated pattern of social and family life has grown up. The affection and sense of mutual obligation of the family group is the outstanding loyalty of Lagos social life.

Nigerians are brought up to regard the needs of their kinfolk as their first responsibility; they support their mothers and fathers in their old age, and often elderly aunts or cousins as well. They contribute to the marriage payment of a younger brother, bring up their nephews and nieces, help out their married sisters. More than half the people interviewed in central Lagos were spending at least a tenth of their income on help to their relatives. Without this family loyalty, there would be no one to care for the old, the sick, the widows and orphans, no one to set men on their feet when they were out of work, or to pass on to younger brothers and sisters the advantages of an education for which, as likely as not, the family has paid. For, as yet, public social services in Nigeria are few. The family group collects its dues, and distributes its funds to those in need; it gives its members at least an ultimate security against the misfortunes of life.

Besides these personal obligations, the family displays its unity in frequent celebrations—naming ceremonies for a newborn child, marriages, funerals, anniversaries, a sendoff for a brother going overseas—and to these each branch of the family will contribute its share. A group of relatives will often choose a costume for the occasion, and symbolise their unity by appearing in this uniform—a pretty but expensive custom. There are also regular meetings—sometimes weekly, or on a Sunday of each month—when the difficulties of members are discussed, disputes settled, and the progress of the family reviewed. Many meetings raise a small subscription, minutes are taken, and officers elected from time to time; they are, therefore, formal gatherings, comprising from half-a-dozen to fifty people or more. In some families, the subscription will be put aside toward the building or repair of the family house, or even the running of a corporate business in the name of the founder. Two-thirds of the men and women interviewed in central Lagos belonged to families which held such meetings regularly in the course of a year.

But the day-to-day visits exchanged by relatives strengthen the unity of the family group more than do these formal meetings. News is passed on, problems discussed as they arise, and the old people are able to live comfortably on the small presents of cash or kind brought for them by the kinsfolk who call during the day. Although it is less common now for all a man's descendants to be together in one house, the families of central Lagos live, for the most part, no more than ten or fifteen minutes walk from each other. Tenants tend to have fewer kin near them than owners, but the longer they have lived in Lagos, the more likely that they will have attracted other members of their family to the town. Amongst those interviewed in central Lagos, thirty-two percent of all those whose mother was still living shared the same house with her, thirty-eight percent had at least one of their brothers or sisters in the same house, twenty-three percent one of their half brothers or sisters. About two-thirds had one or more of their brothers or sisters, and of their parents, living on Lagos Island within a mile of them.

Most of the people in this part of Lagos, therefore, have many relatives nearby. They may also be members of mutual benefit societies, Bible study classes, Moslem organizations, or associations of people from their town or village of origin—all of which flourish. Everyone who belongs to such a group has a status, rights and obligations, and enjoys the sense of security which comes from these.

All Nigerians, I think, are very loyal to their family group—they regard their membership in it with pride and affection, and derive a deep sense of emotional security from it. I believe that some of the emotional security which a European would look for in marriage, a Nigerian expects to find rather in a more generalised relationship with his kin.

Because of this emotional and economic dependence upon the kin group, there is less emphasis on loyalty between husbands and wives. Marriage is more of a contract, with limited obligations. Husband and wife, recognising the attachment of the other to his own relatives, tend to trust each other less, and share less in common. Feelings are not deeply committed. The marriage may break down when money problems or the claims of other loyalties press upon it, especially in a polygamous household. When a man has to share his income amongst several wives, the place of any one of them is less secure. Jealousies and rivalries may lead to irreconcilable quarrels. A woman may prefer to return to her own people, rather than suffer the introduction of a new wife into the household—particularly if her husband did not consult her beforehand. Nearly a fifth of those interviewed in central Lagos had contracted a marriage which failed, some several times. These risks make a woman protect herself by a wariness in marriage, and she tends to look on it as a contract which must be exploited before it is dishonoured.

Even when there has been no quarrel, married couples do not always live together; a woman past child-bearing sometimes prefers to return to her own family. A third of the wives interviewed in central Lagos did not live with their husbands, a fifth of the husbands with none of their wives. Because of this, children may grow up apart from one of their parents, and sometimes from both; young children are sent for training to a brother, a sister, or a grandmother, where they will be expected to be useful about the house, and less spoilt. A quarter of the sample had some of their children under sixteen living elsewhere. Since the children spend more of their time outside their parents' household, they get used to regarding themselves as members of a family group. To protect themselves against the rivalries of a polygamous household, and the instability of the relationship between their parents, the children of the same mother tend to be drawn together with an enduring affection. As children grow up, therefore, it is natural for them to place their strongest affections and loyalties in the family group, rather than in a relationship with one man or woman. Thus, although most marriages are successful, there is less feeling of dependence on them. There is also less financial dependence.

A woman cannot allow her own and her children's welfare to rest only on what her husband can provide. Wages are low, employment insecure, traders are at the mercy of fluctuations in the market; illness, for lack of medical care, may be serious and protracted. There is no guarantee that her husband will always be able to support her. He may—with her consent or not—take other wives, and his resources will have to go all the further. So every woman tries to secure an independent income from a shop, or dressmaking, or, most commonly, from trade. Unless her parents have provided for her, she will expect a sum of money from her husband to buy a stock in trade, from which she may make anything from a few shillings to fifty pounds or more a month. Her profit is her own, an independent income which protects her against losing her husband, and enables her to fulfill her obligations to her own family. Her husband is saved responsibility for her personal expenses, and she may be able to help him out of her earnings if he finds himself in difficulties. The trading of women is, therefore, an essential part of the household economy and, but for it, she would be an unequal and vulnerable partner in marriage, and would have nothing to contribute to her own kin. A woman may be at her market stall from early morning until dusk, and this, rather than her home, gets her best attention.

THE CONSEQUENCES OF SLUM CLEARANCE

The slum clearance scheme requires the wholesale demolition of the neighbourhoods of central Lagos whose way of life has been described.

Families are offered tenancies in a rehousing estate, at Suru Lere in the suburbs, in terraced cottages of one to four rooms. The owners of the property are compensated and have the opportunity to repurchase plots in central Lagos as they are developed, but the price considerably exceeds the amount of compensation. At present, it seems unlikely that any of the owners formerly resident in central Lagos will be able to afford to return there. The population of central Lagos will probably be permanently dispersed by the scheme. Their rehabilitation presents serious difficulties, both for their family life and their livelihood.

The rehousing estate provides well-built and well-spaced houses, with gardens, quiet, running water, and proper sanitation. But it is five miles from the centre of Lagos, at the end of an uncomfortable sixpenny bus ride. So those who moved to the estate were much further from their relatives in central Lagos. Also many of those whose houses have been pulled down have not gone to the estate at all, preferring to rent cheaper accommodation on the outskirts of the town; or they have gone to stay with relatives, or have evicted tenants from other property which they own. A young clerk, who had been moved from a large family house, told me:

When we were about to come here, most of our people didn't want to come to this bush—they call this place bush—they think there are bad spirits here. So the proportion of us who came here, in short, was only two of us out of twenty. The rest went to rent places in E. B. or Idi Oro [suburbs of Lagos]. They think these houses here are not the kind of houses in which we Africans live— you know we live in groups, not one here, one there. So I have only one relative here. She is a woman selling cloth, and since she came here, the trade has flopped. This woman is too fat, she can't be going to Lagos every time on the bus, so she had to give up. She is even thinking of quitting because of the rent. They have a family house in E. B., and they have just quitted the tenant, who has been there a long time. Now she has to leave this place and go to live there. She has a brother too; that one did not come here. He could not afford the rentage in E. B., not to think of Lagos, and has to go to Agege [a town fifteen miles distant]. He is a pensioner, and if you see his condition now you will pity him.

A comparison of the two samples of households interviewed shows how much the family group had been disrupted. The proportion of householders at Suru Lere with their mother, a brother or sister living within a mile of them dropped by more than half. (See Table 1)

Because they live at a greater distance, the residents on the rehousing

Table 1

Lives Within a Mile	Central Lagos	Rehousing Estate
Mother	44%	15%
Brother	54	27
Sister	37	15
Half-brother or sister	59	35

estate also see their relatives less often. They pay fewer visits: leaving early and returning late, they make as many calls as they can on their way to and from work. Once home, they are usually too tired to go out again, even if they could afford it. And they receive fewer visitors. Many I interviewed explained that their relatives found Suru Lere too isolated: fares were too expensive, they lacked time for the journey, tired of waiting for the bus, or were even unable to find the address when they arrived.

> In Lagos you'd have your supper, and you'd think, I'd like to go and see my sister. And you'd come back in an hour's time and tell your wife, I've been to see my sister, see my aunt, see my brother . . . now sometimes for a month I don't see them.

> When I was in Lagos they were with me. We live in the same street. Old wife's family, new wife's family, we see each other every day. In Lagos you see everybody nearly every day. Do you see any of my family visiting me here?

> On Saturday I made 5 shillings gain, and I ran to see my mother. I've not seen her since Saturday and God knows when I shall see her again. She wept when I was to leave, because she didn't want to leave me, and she is afraid to come here. When I was in Lagos there was not a day I don't see her—if I couldn't go in the morning I go at night.

So the residents at Suru Lere could no longer maintain so easily the day-to-day contact with their families, and the proportion who saw them less often than once a month also rose sharply. (See Table 2)

The more formal cohesion of the family also suffered. Sixty-one percent of those interviewed in central Lagos were members of a regular family meeting, but only twenty-seven percent at Suru Lere—either because they no longer attended, or because the meetings had been abandoned with the demolition of the family property. Even where the meeting was still held, fewer came. One man remarked:

All these meetings I told you of were when we were in Lagos; when the slum came, it scattered us. [He was the most senior of his family, and the meeting was still held, at his home on the Estate. But it was now fortnightly instead of weekly, and attendance had dropped from thirty to five.] When we came here, you only get those of the same father. Last Saturday we had a meeting, there were only five. But before there would be my aunt, her children, my brother's children . . . This place is far, number one. Money to come, number two.

Slum clearance, therefore, means that family groups tend to be disrupted. This can be especially hard for old people who had lived in family property and been cared for by relatives around them. Their relatives elsewhere are no longer so aware of their needs, and they themselves cannot afford the fare to go and ask them for help. The system of mutual support begins to break down. Many of the people on the estate, who were used to giving regular help to their relatives, could no longer afford it. Although rents on the estate are subsidised, they are still, on the whole, more than was being paid before, partly because in central Lagos, where tenancies are of long standing, rents are exceptionally low; and partly because households occupy more space on the estate than they had before. The former owners are usually paying rent for the first time in their lives. In central Lagos the average rent of the accommodation occupied by the tenants interviewed was £2. 1s. 6d., on the rehousing estate £2. 7s. 9d. But the cost of transport worried them even more than the rent. It was the most universal complaint—fares to work, to get their children to school, their wives to market. It also raised their expenses indirectly: the men had to buy a midday meal at work, since they could not afford to come home, and prices in the local shops were higher because of transport charges. Apart from the shops, where prices were high, there was no market. Fifty-seven percent of those interviewed were

Table 2

	Seen Daily		Seen Less than Monthly	
	Central Lagos	Rehousing Estate	Central Lagos	Rehousing Estate
Mother	38%	21%	14%	24%
Brother	48	29	15	37
Sister	27	18	25	36
Son over 16	83	58	—	10
Daughter over 16	59	47	—	32

spending upwards of £1 a month on fares—a tenth of the income of over half the sample. Some of the men who worked late into the night, and had to depend on taxis, spent over £5 a month on fares.

To make ends meet, they could no longer be so generous in helping their kin. In central Lagos, thirty-five percent of the household heads made regular monthly allotments of at least £2 to relatives apart from their immediate family, but at Suru Lere only thirteen percent could do as much. Because they could no longer contribute, they were sometimes shy of visiting relatives whom they had been used to helping. One woman, for instance, told me she had an especially affectionate relationship with a young half-sister, who was still at school.

> She treats me like a father, she asks me for anything she wants—school books, money, clothes. I don't go to see her now—she's sure to ask me for something, and I can't afford it. Once in a month or two months perhaps I go, when I can scrape together five or ten shillings.

Their families apart, they also tended to give up entertainment and their membership of benefit societies, church groups and social clubs, because they could no longer afford either the fare or the subscription. One young man, a salesman who was earning a better income than most, remarked:

> I was a member of four clubs when I was in Lagos. I used to attend the functions regularly, almost every night. I've never been again since I came here. Even table tennis—I don't think I could hold a bat now. And cinema—I used to go to the cinema every night with my wife. But even if we could get transport, I don't think we have enough allowance for the pictures again. We used to attend dances in Lagos too, but we don't do it now. And I went to church every Sunday in Lagos too, every day in the Lenten season. Since we've been here, I don't think I've been to church more than twice.

The higher cost of living in the rehousing estate is much more difficult to meet, because so many of the households earn less as well. Traders and independent craftsmen lose most of their business when they move. Few if any of their former customers are willing to lose time and money on a long bus ride, when they can take their orders more conveniently elsewhere. The population of the estate itself is too small and too dispersed to support many traders or craftsmen, especially as most people go into central Lagos every day and continue to buy there, where the choice is wider and prices lower. The estate lies off the main roads and attracts few outsiders. Moreover, the people already established in the neighbourhood have pre-empted the best sites for market stalls along the road to the city centre. Even those on the estate who still work from a shop or stall in central Lagos find that business suffers. They are no longer accessible to customers at home; lose time in travelling and cannot supervise their apprentices so thoroughly; and since they cannot carry their stock home every night, have now expenses in storage or guards.

Most of the people interviewed on the estate who had been traders or independent craftsmen were therefore in real difficulties, some destitute. A shoemaker I went to interview greeted me with the comment,

> I am alone working. Alone "playing" I should say. When I was in Lagos I would reluctantly give you half an hour. Now, if you want five hours . . . Before I moved here, I was first class shoemaker having shoemaking machine. I had a shop—that was Broad Street —and if you see the condition of my shop in Lagos you will like to repair your shoes there. It was my father's occupation so I have sufficient tools. When I was there, I had a certain contract with the Police force, and another from the Elder Dempster Company for the crews' shoes. And the crews themselves when they came from England, they bring their shoe for repair. Broad Street is not far from the Customs. Murray Street [where he lived] is even nearer, only one street cross us. All now—nothing from there now. [He used to make £200 or £300 a year.] Since I came here, not sufficient money to rent a shop here, let alone work there. This is what I have since Monday—it is 4s.6d., and when I took it to the owner he said, "Didn't you know? This is not like Lagos, I will come for it when I have got to have money." From Monday now, I've got one threepence, this morning. If you look at the street now, you will not see a single man. They have all gone to Lagos, and take their shoes there for repair . . . This is not a place, but a punishment from God.

A butcher who had made 20s. to 30s. a day in Lagos, selling from a market stall, had used up all his capital on fares and meeting the higher cost of living, and his trade declined until he was virtually destitute.

> Everything has changed against me. I've never had anything like this happen to me since I was born. It seems like being taken from happiness to misery.

A dressmaker had been almost as unfortunate:

> I printed cards out and gave them, but they say they can't come the long journey, there are so many tailors in Lagos. All these peo-

ple here, they go to Lagos to buy, give all their business to traders in Lagos. They only come here to sleep. There's nothing at all here. They say we should take one of the shops here—but there's no one to patronise. I cut out paper patterns for the girls here sometimes, and that's all, except baby dresses occasionally—two or three shillings. Business is paralyzed.

Some of the skilled workers had given up working on their own account since they moved to the estate; and many of the traders and craftsmen probably avoided the estate in the first place. Nearly half the men interviewed in central Lagos were self-employed, but only a quarter at Suru Lere—and most of these were earning less. As a whole, the income of self-employed men had fallen by an average of £8 a month since their move to the estate. Since it is more difficult for a woman to find a paid job, they suffered even more; the income of the women interviewed fell by an average of £10.

The wives of the men interviewed were equally affected. A quarter had given up any attempt to trade, while as many had lost most of their business but still struggled, rather hopelessly, to scrape together a few shillings in the month. There were four times as many wives earning nothing on the estate, as in the households interviewed in central Lagos. They had to depend more on their husbands, and the men at Suru Lere did, in fact, give more substantial allowances to their wives—mostly at the expense of other family obligations.

The rehousing estate had, therefore, all the disadvantages to a trader that its isolation and dispersed population would suggest. Central Lagos is the hub of the city, alive from early morning until late at night: "It is Canaan to us," said a woman trader, "a land of milk and honey." Suru Lere is deserted for most of the day, and its only thoroughfare skirts rather than crosses the Estate. So there were fewer traders at Suru Lere, and more women not working at all, and those who still traded made much less by it. In central Lagos, the average profit of all the traders in the households interviewed was £11. 12s. 4d.: on the rehousing estate it was £4. 1s. 9d. As one old lady was driven to exclaim: "May God deliver me out of this place."

As a whole, therefore, the tenants on the Estate earned less and paid out more than before they were moved. The amenities of the estate, its gardens and peace, sanitation and piped water, were luxuries they could not appreciate. Many of the families had got into debt since they arrived, especially in arrears of rent, and were haunted by the fear of eviction. Harassed by financial worries, some households disintegrated.

Life on the estate, with fewer wives at work, husbands paying them more generous allowances, and interfering relatives at a distance, ought to have encouraged marriage: and there were several young couples who enjoyed their new independence and privacy. But more often, far from husband and wife drawing closer together, they were forced to separate. Unable to meet the expenses of suburban life some of the husbands sent their wives home to their families and distributed their children amongst relatives who could care for them. Wives, finding no opportunity for trade, left to live with their own relatives nearer the centre of the city; others simply deserted when their husbands could no longer support them. One man, who had been particularly unlucky, said of his junior wife, "I hadn't a penny to put down for her, so she had to desert me, she said she couldn't stay here to starve." Another man had sent his wife to her mother on Lagos Island. "I can't keep her here when I can't maintain her." He went to see her once a month. "It's no use going when you can only put your hand in an empty pocket." A van driver said:

> When I was in Lagos, I never pay for house, I had money. I could have financed my wife with something to sell. Now the house is pulled down it change everything. She is every time crying, fighting, worrying me for money. Even yesterday I told her to quit if she kept on worrying me for money. I can't steal.

Of the married men twenty-seven percent had been divorced at some time, an appreciably higher proportion than in the central Lagos sample, and at least in some cases the quarrel had arisen out of the difficulties they experienced since they were moved.

Even when there had been no quarrel, husbands and wives spent more time apart. In central Lagos eighty-one percent of the married people saw their husband or wife daily; at Suru Lere only sixty-four percent. More of the young children, too, were living outside the household. The more scattered the family group, the more difficult it is to fulfil obligations without absence from home. And the poorer people are, the greater the strain on the loyalty of husband or wife, and the competing claims of marriage and kin are less easily reconciled.

It would be wrong to imply, however, that all the families in the estate were either miserable, or in danger of disintegration. A third of those I interviewed preferred it on the whole to where they had lived before. They liked the houses, the quiet in which to study, it gave some of the young couples the chance of a private life out of reach of interfering neighbours and relatives. But those who were best pleased with their new surroundings were least characteristic of the people of central Lagos for whom the Estate was planned: they tended to be immigrants from distant parts of Nigeria, and in the more senior clerical posts. For the rest, the people of the Estate felt they had acquired the amenities of a modern house at a sacrifice of their family life and livelihood, a change which had been forced upon them and one which they would not have made from choice.

CONCLUSION

Slum clearance raises the fundamental problem: how can you destroy a neighbourhood physically, without destroying at the same time the livelihood and way of life of the people who have settled there? If these are destroyed, the clearance of slums is likely to do more harm than good.

If compulsory rehousing is to be just, and a benefit to those rehoused, it must, I believe, fulfil two conditions:

> 1) The people must be able to afford it. In Africa, this must mean that it will cost them no more to live in their new houses than their old, since very few people have money enough to pay for better housing. Those who can afford it and want to spend their money in this way will have already provided for themselves. If people are forced to pay for housing they cannot afford, their poverty will oblige them to restrict their participation in social life. Above all, it will withdraw them from their family, and this, in Africa especially, can cause great unhappiness.

> 2) They must be able to re-establish their pattern of life in the new surroundings. They must not be too far distant from their kin, nor their work, and the same range of economic activities must be open to them. And their new homes must be so designed that they can be adapted to their way of life. That is to say, if they have depended for their livelihood on being at the centre of trade, they must be rehoused where they have the same chances of custom, or where there are alternative ways of earning a living open to them.

These two conditions are likely to be very difficult to fulfil in practice. The second condition can most easily be realised by rehousing the people on the site which has been cleared, but if they are to be less crowded than before, the buildings will have to be of several storeys. In Lagos, at least, this would have been very expensive indeed and the cost could not have been recovered in rents. To provide for the people in the suburbs, as in Lagos, brings down the cost of housing only to increase the cost of fares, and makes it very much more difficult to prevent the disruption of family groups and economic relationships. New markets must be developed, new opportunities of employment provided; and the new estate must be able to absorb not only those removed from the slums, but relatives who wish to settle with them or near them.

Lastly, however the problem is tackled, it is likely to cost a lot of public money. The tendency is therefore to make the people who are rehoused pay for some of the cost themselves, on the grounds that they are, after all, enjoying a higher standard of housing, and the scheme is for their benefit. I believe this to be unjust: if they have to pay for it, it will not be to their benefit, for the reasons I have given. If their interests only are to be considered, it would be better not to rehouse them at all. If slums are to be cleared for reasons of national prestige, the cost is a fair charge on the public purse.[4]

But if slum clearance is costly, difficult to achieve without hardship and cannot fairly be charged to the people rehoused, then is it perhaps better to concentrate first on other equally urgent problems? Where the population of a town is growing so fast, overcrowding may well be more effectively stopped by building up new neighbourhoods as yet undeveloped, than by displacing those already settled. The worst housing can meanwhile be gradually improved and rebuilt as opportunity arises. After all, it will be some while before the people of Africa can afford what to us seems a minimum standard of housing. Meanwhile, I think they value more the social amenities of their lives.

[4] In a recent debate in the Federal Parliament, reasons of national prestige were in fact given by the minister responsible for Lagos affairs as the first justification of slum clearance.

SELECTED READINGS

ABLON, JOAN

1971 The Social Organization of an Urban Samoan Community. Southwestern Journal of Anthropology 27:75–96.

Focusing upon the set of relationships called into action after a community disaster, Ablon shows how the Samoan community in a west coast city has maintained its identity over time.

COHEN, ABNER

1969 Custom and Politics in Urban Africa: A Study of Hausa Migrants in Yoruba Towns. Berkeley: University of California Press.

Concentrating upon that part of the Hausa *diaspora* located in one city, Cohen describes the social structure of this group and the processes that maintain it as a separate entity. Of particular interest is his analysis of the adaptation of ideology to meet new political realities.

MANGIN, WILLIAM

1970 Peasants in Cities: Readings in the Anthropology of Urbanization. Boston: Houghton Mifflin.

This collection of articles dealing with migrant experiences and communities is an excellent representation of the anthropological search for the "folk in the city." The reader gains an intimate understanding of migrant adaptation in a number of cities in developing areas.

SPRADLEY, JAMES P.

1970 You Owe Yourself a Drunk: An Ethnography of Urban Nomads. Boston: Little, Brown.

In this ethnography of the inhabitants of Skid Road in Seattle, Washington, Spradley shows how the ethnoscience approach aids in understanding this complex and understudied group of Americans.

WADDELL, JACK O., and MICHAEL O. WATSON, EDS.

1971 The American Indian in Urban Society. Boston: Little, Brown.

A collection of articles dealing with the problems of migration and adaptation of American Indians, this book is of particular relevance to urban anthropologists in their attempt to make their findings applicable to the solution of contemporary social problems.

YOUNG, MICHAEL, and PETER WILLMOTT

1957 Family and Kinship in East London. Baltimore: Penguin Books.

This study of the pivotal role of the family in London's Bethnal Green is an excellent ethnography of the British working class. The significance of encapsulated community relationships to the individual is contrasted to the more single-family organization of a nearby housing estate. It may be read profitably with the Marris selection.

Part Five

URBAN ADJUSTMENT: THE CONTINUITY OF SOCIAL RELATIONSHIPS

For Wirth, urban social relationships were impersonal and segmental in most situations, urban dwellers being released from traditional social groups and their long-standing norms. In contrast to folk societies, the personal bonds of kinship, for example, might be less significant in the city because of conflicting pressures upon the individual. Perhaps because of the personal nature of anthropological field work and a continuing interest in such institutions as family and kinship, urban anthropologists have modified Wirth's initial conceptions. The articles in this part take up the problem of persistence and consistency in personal relationships in the city, each showing that traditions do not die in the city, but are adapted.

Lewis's classic response to the implications of the folk-urban continuum demonstrates that Tepoztecan migrants are not suddenly set adrift once they are in the new urban context of Mexico City. In fact, the kinship and *compadrazgo* systems continue as institutional means to personal social bonds. Little family disorganization was in evidence in Lewis's sample. The rural village of Tepoztlán was not simply transplanted, however. There were three waves of migrants, each of which varied from the other, as well as differences among the sample of Tepoztecan families in home type and goods, visiting patterns, religious participation, and food. Each family had adapted traditional patterns to new city ways.

In his reevaluation of previous American studies and contributions of new data from Africa, Jacobson suggests that seemingly transient relationships in the city may in fact be recurrent, thus indicating moral constraints upon participating individuals. He points out that kinship or occupational institutions, for example, provide for an expectation of future interaction, of social exchange, and of reciprocity among urban dwellers who are frequently spatially mobile. Neither the urban blacks on the eastern seaboard of the United States nor the civil servants of

Mbale, Uganda, are fully divorced from the kinds of social bonds usually associated with life in a settled community. Reflecting upon the difficulties of urban community research, Jacobson calls for a focus on social networks and their associated ideologies in order to understand not only the continuities of urban social life but also "the discontinuities between the multiplicity of social networks which comprise any city."

Continuity and adaptation in urban anthropology are typified by Mitchell's selection, in which he discusses the urban variant of African witchcraft, explicitly following Evans-Pritchard's classic analysis of misfortune and witchcraft among the Azande. Although witchcraft occurs in African urban areas (as well as in those of the United States), Mitchell "would expect the meaning which people read into their misfortunes to change when they become part of an industrial urban community." The changes described here correspond to the nature of the new social context of migrants: alternation in kinship, residential, and economic patterns. There is continuity of the African explanation of misfortune, but the personnel involved in both divining and accusation reflect the more complex urban environment. Mitchell notes that the meaning attached to misfortune by urban Africans "must be of a type which will allow them to take effective action."

Each of the three studies in this part, and numerous others in urban anthropology, discusses the effects of urban life upon traditional social relationships. However, the sum of their comments still does not approach the holistic conception of the city which Fox calls for in his article in Part One. Further theoretical work is necessary to merge the microcosmic and macrocosmic perspectives.

15

Urbanization without Breakdown:
A Case Study

Oscar Lewis

This is a preliminary work report on a research project on urbanization in Mexico City. The research is an outgrowth and continuation of my earlier work in the village of Tepoztlán. In brief, we attempted to learn what happened to individuals and families from the village of Tepoztlán who had gone to live in Mexico City.[1]

Before presenting some of the preliminary findings, I should like to indicate how our work is related to other studies in the same field. In the first place, it should be noted that there have been very few studies of the sociopsychological aspects of urbanization in Mexico or other Latin-American countries. Urban sociology in Mexico has lagged behind developments in some of the other social sciences. The data most nearly comparable to ours are to be found in the rural-urban migration studies done by rural sociologists in the United States. These studies have been primarily concerned with the causes, the rate and direction, and the amount of migration, factors of selectivity, and occupational accommodation.

To the extent to which they have dealt with the adjustment of migrants in the city, the findings have on the whole highlighted the negative aspects, such as personal maladjustment, breakdown of family life, decline of religion, and increase of delinquency. The total picture has been one of disorganization, sometimes referred to as culture shock incident upon city living. One common theoretical explanation of these findings has been in terms of the change from the primary group environment, which

SOURCE: *Scientific Monthly* 75 (July 1972): 31–41. Reprinted by permission.

[1] I am grateful to the Graduate Research Board of the University of Illinois for financial assistance on this project. The field research in Mexico City was carried out in the summer of 1951 with the aid of a group of students from the University of Illinois.

is generally characterized as warm, personal, moral, and intimate, to a secondary group environment, which is described as cold, impersonal, mechanistic, nonmoral, and unfriendly.[2]

The preliminary findings of the present study of urbanization in Mexico City indicate quite different trends and suggest the possibility of urbanization without breakdown. They also suggest that some of the hitherto unquestioned sociological generalizations about urbanization may be culture-bound and in need of re-examination in the light of comparative studies of urbanization in other areas.[3] Some of our generalizations about the differences between rural and urban life also need to be re-examined. It should be recalled that direct studies of the urbanization process itself are difficult, and most studies have been indirect and inferential. Sociological generalizations about the differences between rural and urban society have been based largely on comparative statistical data on the incidence of crime in rural and urban areas, on birth, fertility, and death rates, size of family, educational opportunities, and social participation. As Ralph Beals (1951:5) has recently pointed out, ". . . sociologists paid much more attention to urbanism than to urbanization." Moreover, we know very little about the psychological aspects of urbanization as it affects specific individuals and families.

Perhaps one of the difficulties in this field has been the inadequate methodology. There is not, to my knowledge, a single study that has followed up migrants from a rural community which had first been the subject of intensive analysis on the social, economic, political, and psy-

[2] The tendency to view the city as the source of all evil and to idealize rural life has been corrected somewhat by the work of rural sociologists in recent years. We are no longer certain that rural society per se is nearly as Rousseauan and anxiety-free as once thought. Studies by Mangus and his colleagues suggest just as high an incidence of psychosomatic illness among the farm population of portions of Ohio as in urban areas (Mangus and Seeley 1947). Moreover, a study by Goldhamer and Marshall suggests that there has been no increase in the psychoses (and, by inference, also in the neuroses) over the past hundred years in the state of Massachusetts, a state that has undergone considerable industrial development during this period (Goldhamer and Marshall 1949).

[3] Theodore Caplow's excellent article on "The Social Ecology of Guatemala City" (1949) suggests the provincialism of earlier sociological ideas about the nature of the city. Caplow writes, "The literature of urban geography and urban sociology has a tendency to project as universals those characteristics of urbanism with which European and American students are most familiar . . . there was until recently a tendency to ascribe to all cities characteristics which now appear to be specific to Chicago . . ." (p. 132). Caplow raises the question whether "much of the anarchic and unstable character attributed by many authorities to urban life in general is not merely a particular aspect of the urban history of the United States and Western Europe since the Renaissance" (p. 133).

chological levels. An adequate research design for the study of the socio-psychological aspects of urbanization would require a project consisting of three phases: a well-rounded study of a rural or peasant community, including intensive family and psychological studies; locating families from this community who have gone to live in the city; an intensive study of these families in the city.

The present research has attempted to conform to this design. The first phase was completed some time ago with a study of the village of Tepoztlán. The second and third phases were begun last summer in Mexico City.

The specific objectives of the research were conceived as follows: (1) to study the process of urbanization directly by analyzing the changes in custom, attitudes, and value systems of Tepoztecan individuals and families who had gone to live in Mexico City; (2) to compare family life and interpersonal relations of selected urban families of Tepoztecan origin with those of the rural community from which they had migrated; (3) to relate our findings to the more general theoretical findings and problems in the field of culture change.

The study was planned on two levels. First, we wanted to do a broad survey of all Tepoztecan families in Mexico City and obtain data for each family on such items as date of and reasons for leaving the village, size of family, kinship composition of the household, the extent of bilingualism (Spanish and Nahuatl), the general level of living, the religious life, the *compadre* system, curing practices, and the life cycle. For most of these items we had rather full data on the village of Tepoztlán; these data could therefore be used as a base line from which to analyze the nature and direction of change.

Second, we planned to do intensive studies of a few selected families representative of the different lengths of residence in the city and of different socioeconomic levels. Other variables that might become significant in the course of the study were also to be taken into consideration.

We located 100 Tepoztecan families in Mexico City and interviewed each family at least once. Sixty-nine families were interviewed twice, and 10 of these were interviewed ten times. The quantitative data in this paper are based on the 69 families for which we had the fullest data. The major factor in our inability to gather more information on the remainder of the families was lack of time. On the basis of the data obtained in the one interview with each of the 31 families, it appears probable that our total picture would not have been appreciably changed. The fact that the 69 families were distributed in many different sections of the city and that they represented distinct socioeconomic levels further insures against an inadvertently loaded sample.

The city families were located with the help of our informants in Tepoztlán, many of whom had friends and relatives in the city. But most of the families were located with the aid of officers of the now-defunct Colonia Tepozteco, an organization of Tepoztecans in Mexico City, which kept a list of the names and addresses of Tepoztecans living in the city. We have reason to believe that the 100 families we located represent approximately 10 per cent of all Tepoztecans living in the city.

It should be noted that field work in the city is in many ways more difficult, more costly, and more time-consuming than in the village. The Tepoztecan families were scattered in twenty-two different *colonias*, or neighborhoods, extending from one end of the city to the other. Much time was lost in traveling to and from the homes, in making appointments for interviews (only one of the families had a telephone), and in establishing rapport. Often we would spend an entire morning calling on two or three families, only to find people out or otherwise unavailable. Moreover, we did not have the advantage of working through community leaders, of becoming familiar and accepted figures in the community, or of utilizing neighbors—and village gossip—as sources of information.

The earliest contacts between Mexico City and Tepoztlán probably resulted from trade. A small number of Tepoztecan merchants regularly sold their products (mainly hog plums and corn) in the Merced, Lagunilla, and Tacubaya markets. Consequently, some of the earliest migrants of whom we have record settled near these markets, and to this day there are small concentrations of Tepoztecan families around the markets.

Our study revealed that the Tepoztecan families now living in Mexico City came in three distinct periods of migration. The first was prior to the Mexican Revolution of 1910; the second was during the Revolution, from about 1910 to 1920; the third since 1920. The motives for migration and the number and quality of migrants, as well as their social composition, show interesting differences for each of these periods.

During the first period only young men left, their primary motives being to get a higher education and to seek better employment opportunities. These early migrants were generally poor young men related to the best families in the village. We located 15 individuals who left during this period. In general these early migrants made good, economically speaking. Some became professionals and have achieved important positions in the city. Many became the intellectuals who later formed the core of the Colonia Tepozteca, which was to play such an important part in community affairs.

The second period was one of forced migration, when hundreds of

Tepoztecans left the village, generally as family units, to escape the ravages of the civil war. The earliest ones to leave during this period were the *cacique* families who fled before the threat of the Zapatista revolutionaries. Later, when the village became a battleground for opposing forces, people from all social levels fled. It is estimated that by 1918 there were approximately a thousand Tepoztecans in the city, and, according to our informants, approximately 700 attended one of the early meetings preceding the formation of the Colonia Tepozteco. Most of these migrants returned to the village after peace was established. Many of those who remained were the conservative, wealthier families who had been ruined by the Revolution. About 65 per cent of the families we studied came to the city during this period.

The striking thing about migration during the third period is the relatively small number of migrants. Only 25 per cent of our families came during 1920–50. We find a wider variety of motives for migration than formerly, but the two most important seem to be improved educational and economic opportunities. During the later twenties and early thirties, however, a number of men left because of the intense political strife which flared up in the village. Again we find that the young men predominated in the exodus, but now there were also young women, who came either to attend school or to serve as domestics. In all cases during this period, the migrants came to live with relatives or *compadres*. There was apparently a sharp increase in the number of migrants to the city toward the latter part of this period, particularly after the road was built in 1936.

The figures for Tepoztecans in Mexico City are not an accurate index of the total migration from the village. This was established by a study of all the cases that have left the village since 1943. Of 74 cases that left, only 41 went to live in Mexico City; the remainder went to other villages and towns. Of the 41 in Mexico City, there were 23 single males, 16 single females, and one married couple. Over 90 per cent were from two large barrios in the center of the village.

Tepoztecans in the city live in three types of housing: the *vecindad,* the apartment house, and the separate, privately owned dwelling. The *vecindad* represents some of the poorest housing conditions in the city. It consists of a series of one-story dwellings arranged around a courtyard. Often there is a communal water fountain in the center and one or two toilets for a settlement of 25 families. In a few cases there is piped water in each apartment. One of our families lived in a *vecindad* of 150 families —practically a small community in itself. The rentals varied from 25 to 65 pesos ($3–$8) a month. Forty-four per cent of Tepoztecan families live in *vecindades*. The dwellings are generally small, usually consisting of two rooms.

The apartment house provides much more privacy and represents a distinctly higher standard of living. Sixteen per cent of the families lived in apartment houses, at rentals ranging from 65 to 300 pesos a month. Professionals and skilled laborers live here—typical Mexican lower-middle-class families. The apartments are better constructed than the *vecindades* and have more and larger rooms.

Privately owned homes were dwellings for 28 per cent of the families. There was a wide range in the styles, size, and property value of these houses. Some were one- or two-room wooden shacks built on tiny lots on the outskirts of the city; others were modern eight- or ten-room buildings, with enclosed private gardens and patios, located in a thriving middle-class neighborhood. Home ownership is therefore not a good index of wealth or class position.

The average size of Tepoztecan households in the city was somewhat larger than in the village—5.8 as compared to about 5 (Table 1).

The composition of the household shows about the same pattern as in the village except that there is a slightly higher percentage of extended families living in the city (Table 2). In contrast to Tepoztlán there were no cases of persons living alone or of unrelated families living together. There is probably greater economic pressure for families to live together in the city than in the country. In Tepoztlán, if young couples do not get along well with the in-laws and wish to live alone, they can almost always find someone who has an empty house that can be used rent-free. The same is true of old people and widows, who manage to eke out a living with garden produce and by raising chickens or pigs.

We found very little evidence of family disorganization in the city. There were no cases of abandoned mothers and children among our 69 families studied nor was there a history of separation or divorce in more than a few families. Families remain strong; in fact, there is some evidence that family cohesiveness increases in the city in the face of the difficulties of city life. In Tepoztlán the extended family shows solidarity only in times of crisis or emergency. Although there is more freedom for young people in the city, the authority of parents shows little sign of weakening, and the phenomenon of rebellion against parental authority hardly exists. Nor are the second-generation children ashamed of their parents. Perhaps this can be explained by the general cultural emphasis upon respect for age, authority, and parenthood. Similarly, we found no sharp generation cleavage in values and general outlook on life.

As might be expected, the general standard of living of Tepoztecan families in Mexico City shows upward movement as compared with

Table 1. Number of Persons Per House Site, Tepoztlán and Mexico City

No. of Persons Per House Site	Percentage of House Sites, Tepoztlán	Percentage of House Sites, Mexico City
1–5	44.2	41
6–10	52.5	53
11 and over	3.3	6

Tepoztlán. Thus, 78 per cent of our city families had radios as compared to about 1 per cent in the village; 83 per cent had clocks as compared to about 20 per cent in the village; 54 per cent had sewing machines as compared to 25 per cent in Tepoztlán; 41 per cent reported buying a newspaper with some regularity as compared to 6 per cent; 3 of our 69 families owned cars in the city; there were no car owners at the time of our Tepoztlán study. In the city all slept in beds; in the village only 19 per cent slept in beds in 1940. However, there seemed to be more crowding in the city, especially among the poor families, than in the village. I found cases, in *vecindades*, of 10 people living in one room and sharing two beds. A similar situation holds in regard to toilet facilities. All Tepoztecan families in the city had some toilet facilities, but we found cases where 15 families shared a single toilet, and in other instances there was a semienclosed toilet in the kitchen. From the point of view of hygiene, it is doubtful whether this was an improvement over the orchards of Tepoztlán.

The diet of the city families is similar to that of the village except that there is greater variety, depending upon income. The city dwellers all enjoy Tepoztecan cooking and continue to make *mole* on festive occasions. They strongly prefer Tepoztecan *tortillas*, and many continue to prepare beans with *epazote*, as in Tepoztlán. About 80 per cent of the families continue to use the metate and *meclapil*, especially for preparing fiesta meals. A few buy corn and make *tortillas* at home; a larger number buy mill-ground corn or masa; a still larger number buy ready-made *tortillas*.

The Tepoztecan custom of having household pets continues in the city. Fifty-four per cent of the families owned a pet—dogs, cats, or pigeons, and 24 per cent owned either chickens or pigs or both. Most of these families lived in privately owned homes.

The religious life of Tepoztecans in Mexico City appears to be at least as vigorous as in Tepoztlán. Again, the evidence does not support the findings of rural sociologists in this country to the effect that there is a decline in church attendance and religious practices when farm people move to the city. In our study it is not so much a matter of becoming more or less religious, but rather of a change in the content and form of religious expression. Specifically, it is a matter of becoming more Catholic and less Indian.

In general, the city Tepoztecans follow the Roman Catholic tradition more closely. The village belief that El Tepozteco is the son of Mary is no longer held and is regarded as backward and superstitious in the city. Tepoztecans in the city tend to send their children more regularly to Sunday School to learn doctrine, to take first communion, and to attend mass. Confession is as unpopular among city Tepoztecans as in the village, but probably occurs more often.

Mexico City, as the center of the Catholic Church in Mexico, has better organized and better staffed associations, which carry on intensive programs of indoctrination. In many *vecindades* we found religious shrines, usually of the Virgin of Guadalupe, and all residents are expected to honor them as the protector of the *vecindad*, to lift the hat in passing, to cross themselves, and to partake in the collective prayers organized by some enterprising member of the *vecindad*. That social control is strong can be seen from this statement by an informant: "If one does not salute the Virgin, the janitor and all the old women of the *vecindad* begin to call one a heretic and throw dirty looks."

Such shrines are also found in some of the factories in which our informants worked. A few of our Tepoztecans who are bus drivers tell of the requirement to carry images of San Cristobal, the patron saint of their union. They also tell of religious pilgrimages organized by the unions. One Tepoztecan explained that he had never bothered about the Virgin of Guadalupe when he was in Tepoztlán, but since working in the city has

Table 2. Kinship Composition by Households—Tepoztlán, 1943, and Mexico City, 1951

Type	Families in Mexico City (69) (Percentage of all Families)	Families in Tepoztlán (662) (Percentage of all Families)
Simple biological family	66.6	70
Biological family with married children and grandchildren	17.2	13.5
Married siblings with their children	2.9	2.1
Persons living alone	0	6.7
Unrelated families living together	0	.7
Miscellaneous	13.3	7.5

gone on two union pilgrimages. This same informant, who as a child in the village had received no training in doctrine classes, had no first communion, and rarely was obliged to attend mass, now attends mass frequently, consults a priest about his economic and domestic problems, and, thanks to the perseverance of Acción Catolica, regularly sends his four children to Sunday School.

As another example of the increased activity of, and the greatest identification with, the church is the fact that several of our city informants draped their doors with black crepe to mourn the death of a bishop of the church. In Tepoztlán it is doubtful whether the death of the Pope himself would lead to such action.

There are some differences in church organization in the city which affect participation of Tepoztecans. Unlike the village, there are no barrio *mayordomos*. Many of the tasks connected with the care of the images and the church, which in the village are assigned to members of the community or to the specific barrio, are carried out by paid church personnel in the city. Since many of these jobs were the work of men in the village, the net result is that in the city the men play much smaller roles in the religious life. Another difference is that the Tepoztecans in the city contribute less money to the church than in the village.

The system of *compadrazgo* continues to function among Tepoztecans in the city. Each Tepoztecan interviewed in Mexico City had *compadres*, godparents, and godchildren. With one or two exceptions the changes that *compadrazgo* has undergone represent an adaptation to urban life rather than a breakdown or even a weakening of the system.

A major change in *compadrazgo* in the city is the disappearance of several types of godparents known in the village—namely, the godfather of *miscoton*, godfather of the ribbon, godfather of *evangelio*, godfather of the scapulary, godfather of the Child Jesus. There is also much less use of the godfather of confirmation and the godfather of communion. The *compadrazgo* system is largely limited to the godparents of baptism and of marriage, thereby resembling the original Catholic practice as introduced by the early Spaniards and as practiced to this day in Spain.

The decline in the role of the godfather of baptism is another important change. In the city he is no longer consulted in the selection of the godparent of confirmation in the cases where this occurs. Moreover, in the city there is no *sacamisa*, thereby eliminating the role of the godparent of baptism in this ritual. The absence of the *sacamisa* is probably due to the unwillingness of the mothers to remain at home for forty days after the birth of the child, as is required in Tepoztlán. Another adaptation to city life is the delayed baptism. In Tepoztlán babies are baptized as soon as possible, often when only a few days old, almost always before three months. In Mexico City baptisms in our families did not occur for 12 to 18 months and sometimes not for several years. This delay may be attributed in part to the lower death rate among infants born in the city and to a lessened anxiety about infant health.

Another interesting change in the city is the increased frequency with which relatives are selected as godparents. In Tepoztlán it is unusual to find relatives who are *compadres*. Most Tepoztecans consider this undesirable, for it conflicts with the basic notion of respect and social distance that should exist between *compadres*. In the city, where Tepoztecans find themselves without friends, they turn to relatives for godparents. Family ties are thereby reinforced by the ties of *compadrazgo*. But this changes the character of the *compadrazgo* relationship from a formal and ceremonial relationship to a more informal and personal one. The mode of address among *compadres* in the village is always of "Vd.–Ud." In the city it is frequently merely a continuation of the form of address used prior to becoming *compadres*. Thus, in the city we find *compadres* addressing each other as "*tu–tu*," "*Vd.–tu*," and "*Vd.–Vd*." The "*tu–tu*" is used between brothers or sisters who have become *compadres*. The "*Ud.–tu*" is used when an uncle and nephew become *compadres*. In rural Spain we found the *compadre* system to be practically identical with the urban forms in Mexico.

Still another change in the system in the city is the custom whereby a man or woman will offer to be a godparent before the child is born. In the village one always waits to be asked in a formal manner. Since it might be taken as an insult to turn down an offer of godparentage, the net effect is to reduce parental control in the matter of selection. The obligations of godparents to godchildren and of *compadres* to one another are more clearly and specifically defined in the village than in the city. In the city there is much more familiarity between *compadres,* and a *compadre* may ask for almost any kind of favor.

Many Tepoztecan families in the city still use herbs for cooking and curing. In almost all the privately owned homes and in some of the *vecindades* common herbs such as yerba buena, *santa maria,* and manzanilla are grown in gardens and flowerpots. Herbs are used to cure colds, headaches, stomachache, toothache, and so on, much the way they are in Tepoztlán; however, city families tend to rely more upon patent medicines than do village families. Illnesses such as evil eye, *los aires,* and *muina* ('illness of anger'), for which there are no patent medicines, necessarily are cured by native herbs. In these cases it is not uncommon for city people to return to the village to be cured. It should also be noted that, when other illnesses do not respond to patent medicines or to medical treatment, the sick person may be taken to the village for re-diagnosis and cure. One informant told of suffering a partial paralysis of the face and of being treated unsuccessfully by several doctors. Finally, a visitor from Tepoztlán diagnosed it as an attack of *los aires*, whereupon the patient went to the village and was promptly cured by means of appropriate herbs placed in a bag suspended around his neck. The daughter of another informant was stricken with poliomyelitis and despite hospital treatment remained paralyzed. Her father, in desperation, took her to Tepoztlán, where she was given a series of sweat baths in a *temazcal*. This treatment, according to her parent, brought about con-siderable improvement. Sometimes, in the hope that the local *curanderos* would "understand" the illness better, an incurably ill person may be taken from the city to the village, only to die there. Thus, not only do country people go to the city seeking cures, but the same process works the other way around.

In considering stability or change in the way of life of Tepoztecans in Mexico City it is important to realize that the ties between the city families and their relatives in the village remain strong and enduring for almost all the city families studied. They visit the village at least once a year on the occasion of the Carnaval. Many go much more often, to cele-brate their own Saint's Day, to attend their barrio fiesta, a funeral, or the inauguration of a new bridge or school, to act as godparent for some child, or to celebrate a wedding anniversary, or the Day of the Dead. The ties with the village do not seem to weaken with increase in years away from it. On the contrary, some of the most ardent and nostalgic villagers are those who have been away from it the longest. Many old people expressed a desire to return to the village to die. Some men, who have been living in the city for thirty years, still think of themselves as Tepoztecans first and Mexicans second. Fifty-six per cent of the families studied owned a house in the village, and 30 per cent owned their private milpas.

The proximity to Tepoztlán, and the bus line which now runs to the village, facilitate visiting. The young people enjoy spending a weekend or a Sunday in their village. There is also some visiting from Tepoztlán to friends and relatives in the city.

In the past few years Tepoztecans in the city have organized a soccer team and play against the village team. The organization of a team in the city means that Tepoztecans from distant *colonias* must get together; however, the cohesiveness of Tepoztecans with their village is much greater than among themselves in the city. The Colonia Tepozteco has not been functioning for many years, having broken up because of factionalism within the organization.

In summary, this study provides further evidence that urbanization is not a simple, unitary, universally similar process, but that it assumes different forms and meanings, depending upon the prevailing historic, economic, social, and cultural conditions. Generalizations concerning urbanization must take these conditions into consideration. From our study of Tepoztecans living in Mexico City, we find that peasants in Mexico adapt to city life with far greater ease than do American farm families. There is little evidence of disorganization and breakdown,[4] of culture conflict, or of irreconcilable differences between generations; many of the trends and characteristics found among these urbanized Tepoztecans are in direct opposition to those that occur among urbanized farm families in the United States. Family life remains strong in Mexico City. Family cohesiveness and extended family ties increase in the city, fewer cases of separation and divorce occur, no cases of abandoned mothers and children, no cases of persons living alone or of unrelated families living together. Household composition is similar to village patterns except that more extended families live together in the city. There is a general rise in the standard of living in the city, but dietary patterns do not change greatly. Religious life in the city becomes more Catholic and disciplined; however, men play a smaller religious role and contribute less money to the church in the city. The system of *compadrazgo* has undergone important changes, but remains strong. Although there is a greater reliance upon doctors and patent medicines to cure illness, city Tepoztecans still use village herbal cures and in cases of severe illness sometimes return to the village to be cured. Village ties remain strong, with much visiting back and forth.

In considering possible explanations for the above findings the following factors would seem to be most relevant: (1) Mexico City has been an important political, economic, and religious center for Tepoztecans since pre-Hispanic times. The contact with an urban, albeit Indian, culture was an old pattern, and has continued throughout recent history.

[4] There is the possibility of other kinds of disorganization which might be manifested on a "deeper" level. In this connection it will be interesting to compare the findings of the Rorschachs given to the Tepoztecan families living in the city, with the findings on the Rorschachs from the village of Tepoztlán. It should also be noted that our findings for Tepoztecan families in Mexico City do not mean that there is no "disorganization" in Mexico City as a whole. A comparison of the statistical indices on crime, delinquency, and divorce, between urban and rural populations in Mexico, shows a much higher incidence for urban areas (Iturriaga 1951).

(2) Mexico City is much more homogeneous than most large urban centers in the United States, both in terms of the predominance of Catholicism and of the cultural backgrounds of its people. Neither Mexico City nor Mexico as a whole has had much immigration from other parts of the world. The population of Mexico City therefore has very close ties with the rural hinterlands. (3) Mexico City is essentially conservative in tradition. In Mexico most of the revolutions have begun in the country. The city has been the refuge for the well-to-do rural families whose local positions were threatened. (4) Mexico City is not as highly industrialized as many American cities and does not present the same conditions of life. (5) Mexican farmers live in well-organized villages that are more like cities and towns than like the open-country settlement patterns of American farmers. (6) Finally, Tepoztlán is close to Mexico City, not only geographically but also culturally. The similarities between the value systems of working class and lower-middle-class families in Mexico City and those of Tepoztecans are probably much greater than those between, let us say, families from the hill country of Arkansas and working- and middle-class families from St. Louis or Detroit.

In conclusion, it must be emphasized that this study is still in its preliminary stage, and the findings are therefore tentative. The primary purpose has been to indicate a research design which might yield valid and reliable data for the understanding of the urbanization process.

It may be that Tepoztlán was not the best possible choice for this kind of study because of its proximity to Mexico City. It may also be that Tepoztlán is a special case from other points of view. Certainly we need other studies. We should have follow-up studies of migrants to the city from George Foster's Tarascan village of Tzintzuntzan, from Robert Redfield's and Villa Rojas' Maya village of Chan-Kom, from Julio de la Fuente's Zapotecan village of Yalalag, to determine to what extent the findings agree with those from Tepoztlán. It would also be important to have comparative studies of migrants to Mexico City, not from ancient and stable communities like Tepoztlán, but from plantation areas populated by poor and landless farm laborers.

16
Mobility, Continuity, and Urban Social Organisation

David Jacobson

Urban populations are typified by geographical mobility, which is often described as producing uncertainty and, potentially, social instability.[1] Social stability, by contrast, requires an expectation of future interaction or continuity.[2] One strategy, therefore, for coping with uncertainty in urban social life is to generate or confirm continuity in social relations, a process which requires the actors' social perception of factors and circumstances affecting their future interaction. This article, drawing on ethnographic data from American, English and African urban studies, examines variations in this strategy.

Evidence in support of the proposition that an expectation of future interaction is essential to the maintenance of social relationships comes from a wide range of sociological analyses.[3] The general argument that emerges from these studies is that a social relationship involves exchange,

SOURCE: *Man* 6, no. 4 (1971): 630–45. Reprinted by permission of the Royal Anthropological Institute, London.

I wish to thank Judy Blanc, Peter Hainer, Frederique Marglin, and Sally Merry for their comments on an earlier draft of this article.

My fieldwork in Uganda, in 1965–66, was supported by a research grant (MH 11477) from the National Institute of Mental Health, to which I am grateful. I have reported on the research in more detail elsewhere (1968; 1970).

[1] For example, Gans, in noting the importance of residential instability (or geographical mobility) in urban sociological theory, writes: 'The social features (anonymity, impersonality, and superficiality) of Wirth's concept of urbanism . . . seem to be a result of residential instability, rather than of number, density, or heterogeneity' (1967:311). See also Cloward & Ohlin (1960:172), and Keller (1968:61).

[2] My use of the term 'continuity' and the analysis built around it develop from Fortes's discussion of the time element in social structure, particularly his distinction of time as an 'index of forces and conditions' which determine social stability (or social instability) (Fortes 1949:54–5).

[3] See, for example, Firth (1951:194); Gouldner (1960:170, 174–5); McCall & Simmons (1966:156); Wolf (1966:16); and Goffman (1970:128 sqq.).

which implies a period of time over which the exchange is transacted. An exchange also implies that each party to the relationship has some confidence in the other's capacity and responsibility for meeting, at a future time, his obligation in the relationship. Anticipation of future interaction is, in this sense, one conditon for social exchange.

Studies of reciprocity emphasise the analytical significance of the actors' expectations of future interaction. Firth, for example, has suggested that an expectation of 'continuity of relations' is basic to, or in his terms a 'correlate' of, reciprocity (1951:194). Sahlins (1965) further elaborates Firth's hypothesis and develops a more complex model in which the solidarity of a relationship and its expected continuity are functionally related. Included in Sahlins's 'spectrum of reciprocities' are 'generalised reciprocity', 'balanced reciprocity', and 'negative reciprocity'. Each may be seen to have its place on a corresponding continuum of relationships with different expectations of continuity. Thus, in 'generalised reciprocity', the 'counter reciprocity is not stipulated by time' (1965:147), the implication being that the relationship is, and is expected to be, a long-term one. The example Sahlins suggests is a suckling child. It is not that the child does not reciprocate, but rather, as Firth has pointed out, that the exchange is delayed (Firth *et al.* 1970:397). 'Balanced reciprocity' connotes an exchange 'within limited time' (Firth 1965:148). Finally, 'negative reciprocity' is an example of a relationship with no expected future. It is 'the attempt to get something for nothing with impunity', a short-run relationship characterised, in its least sociable forms, as 'chicanery' and 'theft', and based on various degrees of 'cunning, guile, stealth, and violence . . .' (1965:148–9).

As Firth notes, the expectation of continuity is also expressed as 'confidence' or trust in a relationship.[4] A similar point is made by Eric Wolf (1966:13) when he writes of friendship that a 'charge of affect', real or feigned, in a relationship may be 'seen as a device for keeping the relationship a relation of open trust or open credit . . . a device to insure the continuity of the relationship. . .' . Even in the case of 'lopsided friendship' between patron and client, 'a minimal charge of affect invests the relation . . . to form that trust which underwrites the promise of future mutual support' (1966:16).

---

[4] Others have also noted the significance of a future orientation in the conception of trust and its importance for the maintenance of a social relationship. See Simmel (1950:318), and Isaacs *et al.* (1963:462). This conception of trust also extends its analysis as a property, quality, or image generated in and for a particular encounter or situation, although it is consistent with such a view, since the definition of a situation also connotes, through a variety of symbols, a future state of events (see Goffman 1959*a*:1–3).

Whereas trust sustains a relationship, distrust, and the lack of continuity it implies, undermines the solidarity of social relationships. Evidence for this correlative hypothesis comes from Nelkin's (1970) study of life styles in migrant labour camps. She argues that disorder in the camp life of migrant labourers is related to discontinuity in the membership of working crews:

> Relations between crew members reflect the non-permanent character of the crew; and crews with a large core of regular participants or with many kin differ considerably from those where the majority are strangers prior to the season. Most crews, however, contain many people who neither knew each other before the season nor expect to continue relations after the season is over. These relationships tend to exist only in the present with no reference in the past nor plans for the future (1970:482).

Among these strangers, relationships were characterised by distrust and those attributes associated with Sahlins's 'negative reciprocity': cunning, guile, stealth, and violence. At best, there was sometimes a tendency towards a form of 'balanced reciprocity': 'Friendships are maintained by extensive sharing, but the concept of reciprocity differs from that in more permanent groups . . . For the most striking aspect of exchange [among strangers] is the expectation that reciprocity will be prompt' (Nelkin 1970:484).

Whereas exchange theorists consider continuity in terms of the time during which an exchange takes place, and therefore as intrinsic to it, other analysts focus on its role in the social control process which structures but is external to social interaction. Uncertainty and discontinuity are seen as potentially disruptive of social order because they interfere with social control mechanisms. This is a central theme in Wirth's 'Urbanism as a way of life'. In that essay, Wirth was concerned with variations in the 'solidarity' of social relations under different conditions which he typified as 'urban' and 'rural'. The conditions which he labelled 'urban' and which he associated with disorder (1964:82) are not limited to and may occur elsewhere than in cities, as Wirth noted, and the conditions which he labelled 'rural' and which he associated with social solidarity (1964:70) occur elsewhere than in the countryside, as evidenced in his own study of ghetto social life.

The critical feature of Wirth's theory is its emphasis on a system of social control as the foundation of social solidarity. A system of social control involves two related components: identity—in contrast to anonymity—and continuity. In other words, a system of social control depends not only on the availability of sanctions but also on the ability to enforce them.[5] Enforcement requires that individuals be located and subjected to sanctions, and it is in locating a person that identity and continuity are crucial factors. Together they imply knowledge of an individual's future whereabouts, which is essential for the implementation of sanctions for his past or present behaviour.

In contrast to the discontinuity and disorder of urban life, rural society, in Wirth's theory, is characterised by social solidarity which is based on conditions which facilitate social control. Under rural conditions, individuals are known and can be located by virtue of their membership in kin groups (1964:81), often localised and corporate, and by their places of residence and livelihood, neither of which is likely to change or at least to change rapidly and unpredictably.

Although Wirth associated urbanism with potential disorder, he also analysed the means by which order is introduced into urban life. Whereas the social solidarity of rural life is based on a system of social control exercised through kin and residential groups, in urban life it is achieved through voluntary associations (1964:82). Wirth hypothesised that urbanities participate in voluntary groups by means of which they acquire identity and through which control is implemented. Group membership is critical in Wirth's theory. Social control and social solidarity are problematic only in the case of 'detached' individuals (Wirth 1964:76). It is not problematic for those individuals incorporated in and identified with 'formal' (corporate) groups, regardless of their geographical mobility, a point which Wirth stressed, but which has been systematically ignored by later writers who have uncritically assumed a position regarding the disruptive consequences of geographical mobility.

Although Wirth emphasised group membership, there are other structural arrangements by which individuals may be located and through which sanctions can be enforced. For example, Henslin's analysis of the 'fleeting' relationship between cab-drivers and their passengers illustrates the way in which 'strangers' seek to locate one another in a social network, in order to gain control over the relationship. Henslin describes the process of thus locating an individual in terms of his 'trackability' (1968:144). Drivers assume greater trackability, Henslin suggests, on the part of a potential passenger when he calls from a residentially stable neighbourhood, in the belief that there is a link between the caller and others residing at his point of departure. The argument also holds for passengers: a passenger is said to be able to track a cab-driver in so far

[5] Pitts suggests a similar argument in a more general discussion of social control (1968:388).

as he 'is someone who has an identity with others in the community, is someone who ordinarily cannot simply appear from nowhere and then disappear into nothingness, but is a man who is traceable to an organization that is easily found' (Henslin 1968:154).

In other contexts, as well, trackability is produced by knowledge of a person's network of family or friends. 'Who do you know,' (i.e., where are you from, what do you do, and, by implication, who knows you) is a game often played by people who have just met one another and, in part, represents their attempt to locate themselves and others in social space. Being part of the same 'small world' implies responsiveness to a relationship's norms because a person can be traced and can be sanctioned, often by others (mutual friends, kin, employers) as well as by those directly involved in the relationship.[6] Knowledge of an individual's associates, and of his place in different kinds of networks, then, is another way in which an expectation of continuity is generated, uncertainty reduced, and social control is secured in urban situations.

The question of the conditions under which social relations are stable is also raised in social network studies, although it is approached from another perspective and is couched in a different terminology. As Mitchell (1969:26) has remarked:

> A network exists in the recognition of people of the sets of obligations and rights in respect of certain other identified people . . . The recognized rights and obligations are thus potential links . . . [Moreover] not all of the potential links that a person may have with another need be activated at any particular moment. The relationship an individual has with some person may be dormant or latent until it becomes the basis of some social action.

The problem, from the viewpoint of network analysis, is to account for the maintenance, or, in Mitchell's terms, the 'durability', of a network during periods of latency in the social relationships which define it.

To summarise, the hypothesis to be examined is that expected interaction, or continuity, is one of the factors essential to the stability and solidarity of a social relationship and to the maintenance of a network of which it is a constituent element. Expected continuity implies the time necessary for the completion of the transaction which constitutes the relationship, and it implies that the individual in a relationship can be located and sanctioned and will therefore be responsive to its normative regulations. Furthermore, it is based on the actors' social perception of conditions which make future interaction probable. One strategy, there-

6 For an interesting analysis of the dimensions of a 'small world', see Milgram (1967), and Travers & Milgram (1969).

fore, for coping with the uncertainty of urban life is to limit interaction to those with whom association at a future time is expected. This strategy requires an actor to analyse and to evaluate his and others' present and future circumstances which will result in their recurrent interaction.

A sense of continuity is not problematic among those urban dwellers who are geographically immobile, and their social relationships with one another are typically characterised by solidarity, a pattern which has prompted their being described as 'urban villagers'.[7] Their solidarity, however, is not simply a product of past association, but is also based on the implication of future interaction. As Suttles, for example, points out, in his analysis of social order among residentially stable slum inhabitants, the actors' anticipation of their future interaction is critical for their mutual trust and social solidarity (1968:34–5, 98–110).

In contrast to the solidarity among residentially stable populations, social relations among geographically mobile individuals are often described as uncertain and unstable. This argument is presented, for example, in Liebow's study of transient streetcorner men: the instability of their current friendships is directly related to their uncertainty about their future association (1967:64–71, 204–7). Analytically, Liebow's hypothesis is inversely consistent with the proposition that social solidarity is based on expectations of future interaction. Empirically, however, the facts of Liebow's case do not support his interpretation, and this discrepancy invites a reconsideration of both Liebow's conclusions and of the relationship between geographical mobility and social solidarity.

The subjects of *Tally's corner* are geographically mobile. They are characterised as a 'shifting collection of anchorless adult Negro males' (1967:vii), men who, for various reasons, moved into and out of the locality which Liebow studied. Mobility, moreover, characterises not only the population of the street-corner on which Liebow focused, but also its wider setting: Liebow notes that Washington, D.C. has long been one of the principal stopping-off places for Negroes moving up the Eastern seaboard out of Alabama, Georgia, the Carolinas, and Virginia (1967: 17n.). That Liebow considers the geographical mobility of the street-corner men to be a critical factor in their social organisation is evident from his reference to W. F. Whyte's differentiation of 'relatively stable slum communities . . . and unstable slum districts' (1967:204n.). The implication is that Whyte's *Street corner society* concerns slum residents who are geographically stable and 'highly organised and integrated', and

[7] See Gans (1962). Other examples include those of Young & Willmott (1957), and Suttles (1968).

that *Tally's corner* concerns those who are geographically mobile and disorganised.[8]

The argument that geographical mobility produces social instability is made often and explicitly in *Tally's corner*. In Liebow's own words, 'transience is perhaps the most striking and pervasive characteristic of the street-corner world' (1967:218); '. . . a constant readiness to leave . . . discourages the man from sinking roots into the world he lives in . . . [and] it discourages him from deep and lasting commitments to family and friends . . .' (1967:70). His conclusion, however, is open to criticism on logical and empirical grounds.

In *Tally's corner*, the concept of social instability is not explicitly defined, but implicitly means the termination of frequent, face-to-face contact.[9] This is clear from Liebow's discussion of the properties of personal networks, which he describes in terms of concentric circles: 'in toward the center . . . are people in more or less daily, face-to-face contact', and at the edges of the network are those whose relationships are characterised by low frequency of contact and 'avoidance' (1967:162–3). Liebow's reliance on the criteria of the 'frequency and duration' of face-to-face contact is also evident in his analysis of the range of father-child relationships: at the 'low end of the spectrum' there is 'no contact with mother or child' (1967:74), and at the 'high end of the spectrum are those relationships where father and child are regular members of the same household . . . [and] are in more or less continuous contact' (1967: 78). Given the geographical mobility of the street-corner men, it would be difficult, using Liebow's conceptualisation, to consider their relationships anything but unstable. In contrast, an analytical framework which includes a concept of latent or suspended relationships would not neces-

[8] Incidentally, the distinction between stable and unstable slum-located systems of social relations raises the interesting possibility that the most apparent condition of slum residence, that is, poverty, is not the critical factor in ordering urban social relations, a hypothesis which would counteract Liebow's primary and intended argument.

[9] Liebow's identification of instability with short-run interaction is common in anthropological studies and is based, in many cases, on theoretical biases and fieldwork practices rather than on empirical evidence. See Nadel's discussion and criticism of this tendency (1957:141–7). In Liebow's case, his particular conception of social instability does appear to derive from his analytical and methodological framework. He focuses on the street-corner men and their relationships with others 'at a particular time and place' (1967:16), specifically when they appeared on the street-corner where he did most of his fieldwork. Latent relationships, or relationships in which interaction was intermittent or which occurred elsewhere than in the 'immediate neighbourhood' of the focal street-corner, or which occurred other than during the time of fieldwork were not systematically studied by Liebow and do not occupy a significant place in his analysis and interpretation.

sarily reach Liebow's conclusion. Rather, the relationships of street-corner men, and of any other geographically mobile urban dwellers, might be regarded as enduring but intermittently activated.

Some evidence in *Tally's corner* supports this alternative view, although the data necessary to confirm either interpretation are scanty. There is, for example, the case (1967:192 sqq.) of two men who first met one another away from the place Liebow studied and who were in frequent face-to-face contact until one of them moved away. Two years later they met again and re-established their friendship for several months before drifting apart again. Such constancy is not limited to friendships; kin and affines also continue to see each other sporadically, even though they are dispersed between the rural south and the urban north-east. Finally, there is the example of Liebow himself: he notes his 'ongoing' relationships with various street-corner men four years after he left the field (1967:11n.).

Although data supporting an interpretation of stability of social relations among geographically mobile men are not ample in Liebow's monograph, there is more evidence in at least two other works: Claude Brown's *Manchild in the Promised Land* (1965) and Ulf Hannerz' *Soulside* (1969). Claude Brown's account of ghetto street life describes young men growing up in Harlem who are constantly moving from one part of New York to another, from one city to another, and from street life to prison life. Necessarily, they periodically lose contact with one another. Yet their friendships persist for years, being renewed as they cross paths both in and out of jail (1965:252, 255, 375 sqq.). Even when these men do not meet face-to-face, they keep track of one another in street-corner gossip (1965:202, 212, 304, 418–25).

A similar account is contained in *Soulside*. Hannerz's study is particularly interesting since it is based on observations made among ghetto residents in Washington, D.C., the site of Liebow's fieldwork. Hannerz describes a category of men who resemble those dealt with by Liebow: that is, regularly unemployed men who are sometimes in the neighbourhood, sometimes out of it (1969:26). Although these men are transients, their social relationships are not unstable: they keep up, Hannerz claims, with friends and kinsmen who are not in their own neighbourhood by getting together with them more or less frequently (1969:27). He also describes 'Southern migrants' who keep in touch with people back home by visiting relatives during holidays or sending children to spend part of the summer vacation with their cousins (1969:24–5); non-migrant 'main-streamers' who live in one neighbourhood, but who have most of their friends and kin scattered over town, as well as in other cities, and with whom they maintain contact by visiting (1969:40); and 'swingers' who are highly mobile residentially and who participate in widely dispersed networks, the links of which are renewed at dances and picnics and through gossip between mutual friends (1969:42–5).[10]

In contrast to time-specific and place-specific descriptions, other studies of geographically mobile populations also indicate that their social relationships are stable, although not marked by frequent face-to-face interaction. Two examples are Whyte's *The organization man* (1956) and Bell's *Middle class families* (1968). Whyte describes the middle-class transients he studied as being 'rootless in the old sense of the term', but suggests that 'through a sort of national, floating, co-operative, they are developing a new kind of roots', and that 'they find as much stability in the new kind of roots as in the old geographical ones . . .' (1956:319–20, 329). This conclusion of Whyte's provides an interesting comparison with Liebow's, quoted earlier: 'a constant readiness to leave . . . discourages the man from sinking roots into the world he lives in. . .' . The differences in their interpretations correspond to the scope of their perspectives.

Bell's *Middle class families* is a more detailed case study which confirms the general impression created by Whyte. Bell identifies as 'spiralists' those whom Whyte would describe as 'organization men'. They are residentially mobile, their movement from town to town being determined by job opportunities. Bell contrasts these 'spiralists' with middle-class families who are local residents and whom he labels 'burgesses'. Other differences between spiralists and burgesses are reflected in their social patterns. For example, 'none of the locals had best friends over 100 miles away, but almost 50 per cent. of the transients did' (1968:63). Bell also gives examples of what he terms the 'long distance friendships' of the spiralists, described also as 'suspended relationships', which can be reactivated either at very short notice or with a change in location of friends (1968:66).

The stability of relationships among the geographically mobile middle-class is based on expected continuity, which is implied in the concept of a 'career'. For transient organisation men, their careers offer them the likelihood of continuing social relationships, despite their geographical mobility. As they move from one locality to another, 'there are,' as Whyte observes, 'almost bound to be some fellow transients nearby and the chances are good that some of them will be [people] that the most recent arrivals have run into somewhere else . . .' (1956:305). The chances are also good of running into one another in still another place, and the

---

[10] Extra-ghetto systems of social relations are described by both Hannerz and his informants as networks (Hannerz 1969:34, 44). The role of gossip as one mechanism of network maintenance is more explicitly analyzed by Hannerz elsewhere (1967:56).

transients conceptualise this probability, and their expectation of continuity in their social relations, in their view that they live in a 'small world' (1956:306).[11]

Although the career concept seems especially appropriate to the idea of continuity among middle-class transients, it may also be applicable to mobile ghetto residents. The significance of the term 'career' is not merely in its implication of a particular kind of employment, but in its suggestion of a life style which has a predictable developmental sequence.[12] In this sense, it holds for the young Blacks growing up in Harlem, described by Claude Brown, as well as for Bell's spiralists. For Brown and his friends, the prospects were those of moving between street life and prison, a pattern of circulation which can be seen to underlie the persistence of their relationships, since they expect to see each other again and again both in and out of jail (Brown 1965:23, 65, 140–6).

Network analyses, or similar methods without that title, are not common in American studies of urban social organisation, but they are prominent in African urban studies. Moreover, with the use of network concepts, analysis has focused on African townsmen's expectations of continuity in their social relations and on stability in African urban life. The descriptions of African urbanism are especially striking, since African townsmen are very much geographically mobile, yet their mobility has *not* led to an interpretation of urban life as impersonal, anomic, or disorganised.[13]

African townsmen are typically on the move. As uneducated and unskilled workers, they circulate between urban-located wage labour and rural-based cash-cropping or subsistence farming. Given their poverty and a lack of or insufficient provision for 'social security' in most African towns, they are often forced to return periodically to their land, and their kinsmen on it, for the security it and they provide. Alternatively, as educated and wealthy 'new elite' bureaucrats, they are moved between towns which are the centres of government administration and commercial management, to the work 'posts' found in them. In both cases, their movement separates them from kin, friends, and co-workers who are

11 Recent research confirms the existence among geographically mobile professional workers of 'contact networks', which are sustained by the expectation and occurrence of intermittent interaction associated with occupationally related geographical mobility (Ladinsky 1967).

12 This interpretation of the concept of a career draws on the work of Goffman (1959b) and Wilensky (1961).

13 See Epstein's discussion of African urbanism and its interpretation by social anthropologists (1969:77–80).

dispersed between cities and towns and over the countryside. This migratory existence of most African townsmen has led many students of African urban life to focus their attention not on descriptive units such as a city or an urban locality, but on the networks of African townsmen which are urban-located but which stretch beyond any one town to other urban centres or to diverse hinterlands.

One of the earlier and most notable efforts to deal with these problems in African urban studies was Philip Mayer's work with migrant labourers in East London, South Africa. As he has stated, migrancy studies require a shift of focus from the study of towns to the study of networks (1962: 576–7). Furthermore, the extra-town ties of an individual migrant, which in part comprise his network, 'require that, during his stay in town, he should maintain certain relationships in a latent state . . .' (Mayer 1962: 578), and these latent relationships, in turn, directed Mayer's attention to a study of the 'mechanisms' whereby these relationships are maintained.

Mayer found that these latent relationships were maintained in two ways: the home-visiting of migrants and their association, in town, with home fellows. It was, however, not only the practice of periodically returning home which renewed and sustained these relationships, thereby keeping the migrants encapsulated in their networks, but also their expectation of doing so. This comes out clearly in Mayer's discussion of the differences between those migrants who maintain their relationships—the 'home-visitors'—and those who let them lapse—the 'absconders' (1961: 95, 96). For the migrant who expects to return home, his behaviour with his home-fellows in town is regulated by his anticipation of returning home and the future sanctions on his present behaviour. For example, the principle of mutual responsibility among 'home-bound' home fellows is supported by their orientation to the 'people at home'; as Mayer writes, they reprimand one another by saying 'If anything did happen to you, what could we have said to the elders at home? The blame would fall on us' (1961:104). On the other hand, for the absconders who do not expect to return home, threats of future sanctions by the people at home are meaningless (Mayer 1961:132–3). For migrant labourers in East London, then, the anticipation and realisation of their occupationally-based geographical mobility—in the form of circular migration—sustained their urban networks and maintained their latent ties with kinsmen at home.

A similar pattern, but one with important variations, characterises the networks of African townsmen in Uganda. To describe these variations, I draw on Parkin's study (1969) of Kenyan migrants living in Kampala, Uganda's capital, and on my fieldwork among Africans living in Mbale, an administrative and commercial regional centre. The Kenyan migrants (mostly Luo and Luhya) residing in the two housing estates studied by Parkin live there for varying lengths of time, but ultimately, for reasons of security, are tied to their land, homes, and kinsmen in Kenya (Parkin 1969:85, 189). Moreover, as access to land among Luo and Luhya in Kenya is controlled by local descent groups, there is good reason for maintaining links with kin, and, 'by way of reinforcing these links, for adhering to customary expectations in urban domestic life' (Parkin 1969: 189). These customary expectations are primarily intra-tribal marriage (Parkin 1969:98, 111). The situation among Kenya migrants, then, is structurally similar to that among the Xhosa migrants in East London described by Mayer. The Kenyans, however, do not visit home as often as do the Xhosa, and they maintain their relationships by conforming to tribal custom, thereby expressing their loyalty and their intention of returning home. Deviation from tribal ideals of proper behaviour is sanctioned by withholding friendship and unwillingness to 'recommend' a man for proper tribal marriage (1969:109). Intra-tribal marriage is so much taken as a sign of a man's expectation of returning home that the few cases of inter-tribal marriage which do occur happen among men and women who are 'of high educational and occupational status and [who] do not envisage settling in either of their rural homes' (Parkin 1969:100).

The migrants' 'tribalism' in town, with its implication of continuity of social relationships, also appears in differing degrees in the friendship networks of African townsmen in Mbale. The Africans in Mbale generally fall into two major socio-economic categories of either senior civil servants and other high-ranking bureaucrats or skilled and unskilled labourers, categories which I describe as 'elite' and 'non-elite'. The separation between these two categories is interactional as well as attributive. The elite and non-elite Africans participate in different friendship networks, the elite in a unified, urban-based, and tribally heterogeneous network, and the non-elite in several discrete tribally homogeneous networks, a pattern which is consistent with both their ideas about friendship and their occupationally-related patterns of geographical mobility.

Both the elite and the non-elite Africans are transients in the town. The elite work for organisations which transfer their senior employees regularly and frequently, and most of them live in Mbale for only a few years. Moreover, and related to the frequency of their transfers, most of the elite had worked and lived in more than three different towns in Uganda. The non-elite are also mobile, but they have a different pattern of movement. Because of occupational and other economic constraints, including the absence of a social security system in town, the non-elite must circulate between town and countryside in order to supplement their incomes with subsistence farming and cash-cropping, a basic pattern for most African townsmen in Uganda and elsewhere. When they move into and out of Mbale, they go back and forth from their natal homes, rather than to other towns. Therefore, most of the non-elite have worked only in Mbale or one other town, although they live there for only a short period. The circulation of non-elite Africans is primarily between town and tribal home and contrasts with the movement of elite Africans which is primarily from town to town.

The elite's work-based geographical mobility is conducive to the fulfilment of the reciprocity expected in their friendships. The elite's movement from town to town, through the same circuit, sustains their friendships. Evidence of this is the 70 per cent. of elite friendships in Mbale which were first established elsewhere, usually through work contacts in other Ugandan towns. They expect to and do see again friends they have met before. They are aware of continuing relationships among the elite. By giving them a sense of confidence in the continuity of their relationships, the elite's mobility encourages their participation in the system despite their limited stay in any one town.

Non-elite friendships also involve reciprocity, which again is facilitated for them by their pattern of movement. Non-elite Africans live in a dual system, shuttling back and forth between town and tribal area. Their security derives from the land, which is controlled by and administered through traditional tribal authorities. Over time, non-elite Africans have to return to their land and their fellow tribesmen. This movement underlies a sense of continuity in the relationships between non-elite fellow tribesmen which maintains their ties just as the probability of renewed acquaintance in different towns supports the friendships of the elite.

The differing significance of 'tribalism' in the friendship of elite and non-elite Africans reflects the differences between them in their occupations, in their work-related patterns of geographical mobility, and in the varying degrees of freedom from retiring to tribal land which their incomes allow them. Elite Africans in Mbale choose their friends primarily from among colleagues, and tribal identity is not an important factor in their choices: just over 80 per cent. of elite friendship sets are tribally mixed and just less than 10 per cent. of the elite verbally attach primary significance to tribal homogeneity in their friendships. Moreover, in situations in which both fellow tribesmen and others are available as friends, they are just as likely to choose colleagues from different tribes as to choose fellow tribesmen. In contrast, tribal homogeneity is a major factor in the non-elite friendship choices. They verbally stress its importance: almost half of them say that being of the same tribe is the most important factor in their friendships in the town. It is also expressed interactionally: most non-elite Africans choose their fellow tribesmen not only as friends but as neighbours in Mbale, thereby forming distinct tribal enclaves in the town. Urban tribalism, among both Kenyans in Kampala and migrants in Mbale, is not merely an expression of primordial sentiment, but is an idiom for recognised continuity in social relationships and for the largely economic conditions which underlie such continuity.

In west Africa, too, the study of townsmen reveals stability in social relationships despite geographical mobility and the disruptions it causes. Krapf-Askari (1969) demonstrates that continuity in the lives of Yoruba townsmen is related to their inclusion in different kinds of corporate groupings which give them a place and an identity in urban society regardless of their movement into and out of various urban centres.

Yoruba urbanism is typified by the presence of descent groups which hold rights in town land and the fact that citizenship in a Yoruba town is normally acquired through birth in one of these descent groups. Yoruba towns contrast with most urban centres in that they include not only a nucleated residential area but also outlying farm lands owned and worked by the townsmen. That is, Yoruba townsmen live in a kind of 'inner-city' and commute to work on their farms in the 'suburbs' although these are legally within city limits. The Yoruba term for such an urban settlement is *ìlú* and they conceptually identify townsmen as *ará ìlú*, 'those who are by birthright members of an *ìlú*' (Krapf-Askari 1969:25). As with other kinship identities, this birthright lasts a lifetime, whether or not a person resides in his hometown (Krapf-Askari 1969:26, 30–1, 33, 36, 63, 75). This custom has two interesting social consequences. First, there are few Yoruba 'strangers' in a Yoruba town, in the sense that individuals cannot easily settle down away from their home town and in the sense that men are identified by particular facial scars or other diacritical marks associated with membership in their descent groups. Secondly, since home-town identities are not affected by prolonged absences and individuals retain land rights in their home towns, rights which are difficult to acquire elsewhere, there exists a kind of tribalism similar to that found among rural-based migrants elsewhere in African towns, except that it is based on participation in a politico-economic system which has urban, and not rural, roots.

Craft organisation in Yoruba towns also lends trackability to Yoruba townsmen. Where a craft is not controlled by kinship relationships, it is organised in 'guilds'. Furthermore, membership of these 'guilds is both unrestricted and compulsory: all practitioners of a craft within a given town must join the appropriate guild' (Krapf-Askari 1969:93). Not only is a craftsman trackable, but, like Henslin's cabdrivers, he works within an organisation which is well-known and which assumes responsibility for his behaviour (Krapf-Askari 1969:93–6).

Progressive Unions provide another context in which Yoruba townsmen acquire trackability as well as expressing their expectation of returning home, thereby maintaining their networks. These civic organisations provide a means for Yoruba townsmen to demonstrate interest in the improvement of their home towns as well as to show a 'sentiment of solidarity' as home-fellows (Krapf-Askari 1969:124). Yoruba Progressive Unions thus resemble the *amakhaya* among East London Xhosa; they furnish migrants with 'a group with which they can identify', in which they spend their leisure time, and through which they symbolise their intention of returning home (1969:124–6, 150).

Comparison of these African urban studies indicates that African townsmen participate in enduring but intermittently activated systems of social relationships. Although their relationships are interrupted by geographical mobility, they are maintained by the expectation of their continuity, i.e., through the social perception by the actors involved of conditions which support and stabilise their social relationships and which remain more or less constant over time. The idiom of this continuity for most African townsmen is that of 'tribalism', a term that summarises conditions under which individuals seek to control economic and/or political resources whether these are land in rural areas, trade in urban centres, or both. Among elite Africans who are not subject to the same economic constraints on returning home, urban tribalism is relatively unimportant and is not used as a mechanism for maintaining relationships. Rather, their relationships with one another are maintained, like their American and English 'organisation man' counterparts, in terms of career concepts which express the economic conditions underlying continuity in their lives.

This analysis of social stability and network durability in urban situations suggests three conclusions. First, geographical mobility does not necessarily produce social instability, when those who are mobile are also encapsulated in a system of social relations. This point was made by Wirth in his classic essay on urbanism (1964), but has often been overlooked in sociological and anthropological interpretations of urban social organisation. The reasons for this oversight are not clear, although there are several possible factors. Wirth perceived encapsulation (and the reduction of urban anonymity and anomie) primarily in terms of individuals' attachments to, or membership in corporate groups, which, in his theory, were essential for social order. In part, this reflected Wirth's

attempt to identify in the urban context social units which were structurally similar and functionally analogous to those which he believed
were the bases of social order in 'rural society'. Most urban dwellers,
however, do not belong to or participate in voluntary associations; and
for those who do, membership does not seem too critical to the organisation of their social relationships. Thus, Wirth's emphasis on corporate
group membership as the primary mode of encapsulation, in conjunction
with the relative insignificance of voluntary associations in the lives of
urban residents, may have misled researchers into discounting Wirth's
differentiation of the types of geographical mobility and their different
social consequences.

The other reasons appear to derive from methodological inadequacies
in urban studies. Most studies of urban social organisation, at least in
the United States, have been 'community' studies, in which the boundaries of a 'community' have been assumed to be congruous with a specific
locality. Concepts and methods of research appropriate for the study of a
locality, however, often preclude the adequate interpretation of the social
relations of geographically mobile, non-localised populations. An alternative to the locality approach is the study of non-localised systems of
social relations, usually conceptualised as social networks.

Secondly, particularly with the advent of network-type analyses, a significant problem in urban research is to account for the maintenance of
social relations between individuals who are geographically mobile or
who are otherwise not localised or in frequent face-to-face contact. One
solution, as suggested in this article, is that social relations are characterised by stability, and networks by durability, when individuals in them
expect to interact recurrently with one another, an expectation based
on their perception of the factors and circumstances which make their
future interaction probable. In the cases examined, this expectation was
based on the actors' analysis and evaluation of their economic and occupational opportunities, expressed as a concern with their careers or tribal
identities. There seem to be, however, other possible bases for expected
continuity in social relations which appear to reflect normative rather
than pragmatic constraints.

Kinship ideology, for example, often provides an idiom for, and may
be the basis of, continuity in social relations. Liebow suggests that when,
among the transient street-corner men he knew, friends said they were
'going for brothers', they were borrowing from the 'bony structure of
kinship' to lend structural support to their relationship, to attribute to it
the durability of kinship (1967:207, 218). This happens, Liebow argues,
because a man 'wants to believe that his friendships reach back into the

distant past and have an unlimited future' (1967:176). Kinship is presumed by both Liebow and his informants to imply continuity in a relationship despite interruptions to it.

Not only has kinship as an idiom of continuity been noted ethnographically, but the rationale for its selection as a measure of permanence has been the subject of recent analyses. Schneider, for example, argues that kinship in American culture is conceptualised as a relationship of substance ('blood'), denoting incorporation, and thought to be permanent (1968:23–9, 91). The relationship cannot be broken, although its obligations may be avoided, its rights withheld, and its affectivity neutralised. No one, as Schneider points out, speaks of an ex-mother, an ex-father, or an ex-child. In this sense, the use of a kinship idiom to provide a framework for, or a reflection of, continuity is culturally sound.[14]

Finally, this analysis suggests some possible guidelines for further research. One is to analyse, much more systematically than previously, the nature of 'fleeting' relationships in urban situations. There is little doubt that for urban dwellers many contacts with others are in transient relationships. One question, however, is to determine just how fleeting such relationships are. Certainly, there are relationships which are entered into and pass quickly. But there are also others, which, although activated only intermittently, continue over long periods of time. From the point of view of the time at which they actually take place, they may appear as fleeting as other short-run terminal interactions. However, as Denzin has argued (1970:125–31), they differ precisely because they do persist. A second research strategy is to focus not on place phenomena— an enclave, a ghetto, the city—but on questions dealing with systems of social relations defined interactionally, which are urban-based but which are not, or may not be, confined to a single place. Such research would analyse not only the structural properties of social networks, but also their normative and pragmatic foundations, in order to determine the extent to which ideologies, such as those associated with career, tribalism, and kinship, and the conditions which they reflect, provide a basis for social stability and network durability. The third problem is one which is not examined at all in this article, but which is implicit in it. It has been suggested that social relations within networks are continuing and orderly, and that it is useful to analyse the processes which maintain such

[14] A similar argument is presented in a recent monograph on English kinship patterns, the companion study to Schneider's analysis. Firth and his colleagues write of kinship relations among middle class Londoners that there is 'the recognition of the kinship bond as one marked by continuity (1970:387). Fortes, making cross-cultural comparisons, has analysed the implication of expected continuity in kinship relations. See his *Kinship and the social order* (1969), especially chapters 12 and 13.

networks. It is necessary, however, to examine not only continuity in urban life, but also discontinuity and its social consequences. It may well be that the most significant social, if not sociological, problems follow not from social order within networks but from the discontinuities between the multiplicity of social networks which comprise any city. How these relatively discrete networks articulate with one another is then a further problem in urban social organisation.

17
The Meaning in Misfortune for Urban Africans

J. Clyde Mitchell

Evans-Pritchard's (1937) classical study of witchcraft among the Azande showed, among other things, how the Azande are able to relate their misfortunes to the hostilities and fears that arise in the communities in which they live. The Azande blame witches for unusual or capricious events and then seek the witches among those whom they suspect bear them malice. The crucial link between witchcraft as the abstract causative element behind misfortune a man experiences and the network of social relationships out of which the witchcraft arises, is the divining seance. Evans-Pritchard was able to show that the victim deliberately tests the names for witchcraft of those whom he knows bear him malice. The divining seance then merely uncovers the hostilities and fears of which the victim himself was already secretly aware.

Marwick (1952), utilizing the rationale of the divining situation, has been able to extend Evans-Pritchard's argument and to show that witchcraft accusations are particularly likely to fall between persons who are in competition with each other and who are unable in terms of the mores to express their hostility openly. The accusations of witchcraft bring tensions into the open which previously lay hidden and give kinsmen a justifiable cause to attack their rivals who, as kinsmen, in other circumstances should rather be protected. Accusations of witchcraft, therefore, act as a catalyst in the process of segmentation. For Marwick then, the meaning which tribesmen read into misfortunes derives from latent strains in the positions they occupy in the social structure. My own studies among the Yao of Nyasaland lend support to this view (Mitchell 1952, 1956b).

SOURCE: Meyer Fortes and G. Dieterlen, eds., *African Systems of Thought* (London: Oxford University Press, 1965), pp. 192–202. Reprinted by permission of the International African Institute, London.

These observations refer to tribal systems where the social structure has been studied in detail and where the consequences and circumstances of accusations of witchcraft can be easily traced. We are able here to interpret the meaning people attribute to misfortunes in terms of the set of social relationships in which they are personally involved.

If this hypothesis is valid we would expect the meaning which people read into their misfortunes to change when they become part of an industrial urban community. These urban communities in Southern Africa are phenomena which have appeared in the last seventy-five years. In the Rhodesias they are even more recent—the Copperbelt having come into being only in 1927. The African populations in these towns are characterized by a set of particular social and demographic features. The most striking difference between the rural and urban communities is the heterogeneity of the towns. The labour required for industrial enterprises is drawn from a wide hinterland so that the people of many different tribes and language groups are thrown higgledy-piggledy together in the African townships. Since the demand is predominantly for able-bodied manual workers young men tend to be attracted to the towns more than women or older men. These men seldom sever relationships completely with the rural communities out of which they come but continue to consider themselves part of them. There is thus a great deal of mobility between town and tribal area. This mobility of the African population underlies and is further encouraged by the form of administration which has developed in industrial towns. Since the African workers were considered to be temporary residents only, the control of law and order and of housing and amenities have rested in the hands of various municipal and Central Government officials. In a population so heterogeneous and so unstable residentially few institutions of social control have arisen spontaneously. Instead differences which arise must be ironed out informally by friends or kinsmen or formally by the agents of municipal or central Government.

Migrants who move into a town such as Salisbury, therefore, move into a community which is composed overwhelmingly of strangers. The migrant almost certainly knows a few kinsmen in the town and possibly a few other tribesmen. Among the others he gradually builds up a network of connexion—among those employed at the same place, in the various Burial Societies which have developed to meet the needs such as his own, among members of the congregation of the church at which he worships, and among his neighbours. This then is the social context in which the African townsman has to interpret his misfortunes.

The first point to note is that, as in rural areas, Africans in towns interpret misfortunes in direct and personal terms. They are likely to see in a motor accident not 'bad luck' or an unfortunate misadventure but rather the machinations of some witch who owes the victim a personal grudge, or the action of some aggrieved ancestor spirit who has chosen this way to express his displeasure to his descendants. This explanation is specific to the individual concerned: it explains why the accident should befall that particular person and not his workmate who was perhaps travelling next to him. It explains, as Gluckman puts it, the *why* of the event, rather than the *how* (1955:84).

This 'egocentric' interpretation of misfortune leads us to seek its meaning in the network of relationships in which the victim or his representative is involved. Consider, for example, this case history: [1]

> Two African families in Salisbury were neighbours. The husbands in both families and the wife in Family B were from the Cewa tribe in Northern Rhodesia. The wife in Family A was an Ngoni also from Northern Rhodesia. Both wives were accustomed to brew and sell beer illicitly to supplement their family incomes. Illicit liquor brewing is very common in Southern African townships where the combined effects of poverty, the restrictions on the sale of liquor to Africans, and the unbalanced sex ratio leading to a keen demand from bored and unattached young men, drive many women into this lucrative trade. Each of these 'shebeen queens' in time builds up a 'name' and a regular clientele. Competition for trade between them for customers is thus likely to be sharp. The two wives in these families were able to compete amicably until a lodger came to live with Family B. This lodger soon started to have an affair with wife B. Since the two women were well known to each other, the lodger eventually began to take an interest in wife A also. The latent hostility between the two women arising out of their economic competition had thus far been held in check by the bonds of a common tribal and territorial unity since the number of peoples from Northern Rhodesian tribes in Salisbury is very small. But when the additional competition over a lover arose the hostility became overt. The two women quarrelled openly in a beerhall one night and the friendship between the two husbands also began to cool now.

> Soon after this quarrel wife A decided to brew beer and to obscure her activities from the authorities she took out a permit to buy beer from the Municipal Beerhall. Wife B, however, familiar with the tricks of the trade, recognized the import of the purchase of beer from the Beerhall and reported to the police that wife A was brewing beer illegally. The police duly raided the home of wife A and found her in possession of liquor. Unfortunately for

[1] I am indebted to Mr. B. Lukhero for this case history.

wife B, however, the policeman who conducted the raid was one of wife A's previous lovers. He not only released her before a charge was laid but also told her how the police had become informed. The relationships between the women were now so tense that wife B openly threatened to knife wife A when she had the opportunity.

Very shortly afterwards a teacher brought a pubescent daughter from family A home from school. He reported that the girl had fainted there. A week later the girl was well enough to go back to school but she collapsed once again as soon as she got to the classroom. The teacher now confessed his fear that there was some 'foul play' afoot. The father of the girl consulted a fellow-tribesman who was a diviner and was told that an enemy of the family in the neighbourhood was 'throwing witchcraft' at the family but that since there was no blood relationship between the parties the witchcraft was not very powerful. The 'doctor' then buried an egg wrapped in black cloth with a piece of root attached to it at each of the three entrances to the house. He explained that when the witch came to the house to do harm he would find the house like the eggs —without doors and in darkness. Both families withdrew from the shebeen trade and the lodger sought another landlady. The friendship of the two men has completely ended!

This is a straightforward account of the deterioration of relationships arising out of competition in both the sexual and economic fields, and the interpretation of misfortune in terms of these relationships. In contrast to what might have been the course of events in a rural area there are two specific points of interest. The first is that the witch was sought not in the family, as would almost certainly have happened among rural Cewa (Marwick 1952:216-217). The fact that the girl had survived, however, was still explained in terms of belief that normally only kinsmen bewitch one another. The significant point is that while the family is the locus of much competition and hostility in Cewa rural life, in a town like Salisbury, where not only kinsmen but even tribesmen hold together and support one another in the face of a large majority of foreigners, the family is essentially a tightly integrated co-operative group. Tensions intrude, rather, from the larger society. Hostility and jealousy are likely to arise in those situations where individuals are linked in close personal relationships but who nevertheless compete with each other for advancement and success. This is likely to occur, particularly in the economic field.

Employment looms large in the life of Africans in towns. Most of them are in the town in the first instance as wage-earners. While they are able to find succour with some kinsmen for a spell if they lose their employment, in the end if they do not find work they must return to their rural homes. The control of employment, however, is largely in the hands of the Europeans who appear to behave capriciously and unpredictably. Whether a workman is engaged or discharged it seems, and indeed often is, so much a matter of luck that becoming and remaining a wage-earner is fraught with as much uncertainty as hunting dangerous animals, embarking on a long journey, or similar activities in which magic and ritual figure prominently. It is difficult to secure accurate information on the degree to which African work-seekers make use of charms in their search for employment. Of thirty-five men who visited a 'doctor' in Harare, fifteen of them sought treatment primarily for a straightforward medical complaint such as a headache, constipation, or something similar. Of the remaining twenty no less than ten sought charms to help them to secure employment or to stay in it. The remaining ten were seeking advice about sexual virility, love potions, gambling charms, or straightforward anti-witchcraft medicine.

The uncertainty of employment falls unequally on different occupational strata. A shrewd research assistant remarked that the clerks in a large tobacco firm feared witchcraft, while the unskilled workers did not. The clerks compete for a few highly paid permanent posts in which there are opportunities for personal advancement. There are not many of them and they work constantly together and know each other relatively well. The unskilled workers on the other hand work for a fixed wage which is the same for them all, there are several hundreds of them and they are seasonal workers. Their security lies in their tribal areas rather than in employment. Of thirteen unskilled workers who consulted the 'doctor' in Harare only two sought charms to get work or to keep them in it. Of the fifteen skilled and white-collar workers no less than eight sought work charms.

Among women the emphasis is likely to be on economic competition only if they happen to be traders or beer-brewers operating in the same neighbourhood and are thus known to each other. I have recorded several cases of accusations of witchcraft between 'shebeen queens' who were close neighbours. A more likely foundation to personal animosity is sexual jealousy where women compete for the attentions of the same man.

In the case history we have quoted we have seen that Family A interpreted the misfortune they suffered immediately in terms of the tensions which arose in the network of personal relationships in which they were involved and that they protected themselves with magic and avoided contact with Family B.

We have seen that in tribal areas lineage oppositions are likely to find vent in accusations of witchcraft. On these grounds kinsmen are able to appeal to the tribal authorities and demand punishment. In the towns, however, Europeans exercise authority and to them witchcraft beliefs are unreal. African women dare not make an accusation of witchcraft arising indirectly out of illicit liquor brewing to the authorities. Not only is liquor brewing illegal but to accuse another of witchcraft by Southern Rhodesian law is a criminal offence. The interpretation of misfortune in terms of witchcraft, therefore, does not lead naturally to a solution of personal difficulties as it may in rural areas. Casting the interpretation of misfortune in terms of witchcraft although likely to be initially the most natural to townsmen is unsatisfactory because they are unable to take action which they believe will be effective in removing the basic cause of the witchcraft. They must therefore seek an alternative explanation which will allow them an effective course of action. This is shown in the following case history.[2]

> A Shona man who worked as a wine-steward in a Salisbury hotel for nine years earning a salary of £8 a month and a considerable income from tips, was relieved by another African to enable him to go home on leave. When he returned he found that his employers had decided to retain the substitute in his place. The displaced man consulted a diviner and he was told that his rival had obtained a charm to make the employers prefer him to the original wine-steward. The diviner warned the displaced man not to resort to vengeance magic for this would be likely to bring death or disaster upon himself.

> Dissatisfied, the man consulted another diviner. Now he was told that his misfortunes could be traced to the action of the angered spirit (*ngozi*) of his father's brother's wife. It appeared that before he was born his mother had taken his elder sister then aged three to her home. There the child had died. The man's father had then forced his brother's wife, unwilling as she was, to return to the father's village with the body of the child on her back. When the man's father's brother's wife died misfortunes started to attend the family, and it was her spirit which had caused the man (and also his younger brother) to lose his employment. To overcome these misfortunes the diviner advised the man to give a heifer or £10 to the brothers of the man's father's brother's wife, so they could lay the angered spirit.

There are some similarities between this case and that of the two 'shebeen queens'. Once again the misfortune is interpreted initially in the

2 I am indebted to Mr. M. Bganya for this case history.

light of economic competition, but once again the victim is helpless to take any direct action against the suspected witch. But there is a further development: the misfortune is later traced through the action of the ancestor spirits to the man's relationships with his rural kinsmen. This re-interpretation of the misfortune is particularly significant in the light of the administrative system in the towns. The victim is unable to take positive measures against his rival; measures which would enable him to redefine his relationships with his rival. The victim therefore seeks a new meaning in the misfortune and finds one which accords with tribal belief and one for which there is a recognized and customary remedial action. This double interpretation of misfortune may be seen as successive attempts to handle personal conflicts within a social framework which contains no institutionalized mechanism to achieve this.

Exactly the same sequence of events arises in a more complicated case history.[3]

> The case concerns the misfortunes that befell a family raised in Salisbury by a Nyasaland man who had married a Shona wife. This man, a staunch Christian, died towards the end of 1959. His widow and her six children visited a diviner to find out the cause of death. All these children it should be noted were relatively well educated, two of the sons having achieved University entrance standard, one of the others being a teacher and both daughters being trained nurses. The diviner indicated that three people were responsible for the death of the man. Two were church leaders who were rivals with the dead man for a position in the church organization. The other was a co-worker. The widow confessed later that she had always suspected the church leaders but being a staunch Christian she could herself take no action against them.

> But the diviner noticed also that when the man's father had died in Nyasaland some time previously no one from the family had gone to take part in the mortuary rites. Again when the man's mother and other relatives in Nyasaland had died no one from this family had visited them: the widow, a Shona woman, in fact had never been to Nyasaland at all. The diviner suggested that the members of this family ought to buy a goat and sacrifice it at an expiatory feast to which all their kinsmen should come.

> The feast was not held immediately, and before it was, the eldest son of the family took ill. In April he and his younger brother went to consult a 'doctor" about this illness some eleven miles outside Salisbury. Here, at a cost of £1 10s. 0d. the 'doctor' sucked some worms out of the sick man's body. Who was responsible for plant-

[3] I am indebted to Mr. G. Chavunduka for this case history.

ing these worms in the man's body was obscure. The sick man returned to Salisbury and continued to be treated at the Harare General Hospital.

In May the man had not improved much and sought aid from another 'doctor' who lived, once again, some miles outside Salisbury. This 'doctor' runs his practice along the lines of a modern clinic. He wears a white dust coat, keeps a register of his patients and keeps his herbs in stoppered bottles. The sick man and his wife went in to see the herbalist. The herbalist used a mirror to look into the sick man's body. After some time he removed a piece of rotten meat from the man's body, and a large dead worm which he said was a human kidney. After some additional treatment the sick man was allowed to return to Salisbury. The fee was £2 5s. 0d. Before the man left, however, he asked the 'doctor' who was bewitching him. The 'doctor' refused to tell him, saying that he was too weak to stand the shock of the revelation. He said that the sick man should return at a specified date later on when he would reveal the names of the man's enemies.

In the meantime the man's condition had not improved. He therefore sought out a third 'doctor', one who lived this time in Harare. The 'doctor' proceeded in much the same way as the others, finally removing several objects which looked like childrens' teeth and several worms. When the sick man asked the 'doctor' who had caused all this trouble the 'doctor' said that there were some rivals at his place of employment who were jealous of his social standing, and of the trust which the employer had placed in the sick man. When the sick man pressed the doctor to mention the names of the miscreants the doctor refused saying that he had been warned by a judge of the High Court not to mention the names of people in his treatments. He did, however, offer some vengeance magic for £5, but the sick man refused this. The doctor went on to assure the sick man that if he listened carefully to what people said to him he would not find it difficult to identify the guilty people. Later on the sick man noticed that two of his co-workers had greeted him by saying 'Hallo, Big Boss' when he first came to work, and he thought that this was strange. He would, however, not commit himself to saying that these were indeed the witches who were troubling him.

The man's health improved for a while and he was then convinced that the first two 'doctors' he had consulted were incompetent and that the third had in fact removed the objects which were causing his illness. Three days before he was due to return to the second 'doctor' to learn the names of the witches, the man fell seriously ill again and was admitted to hospital. As his condition seemed to be worsening his family hastily procured two black goats from a

European farmer some 39 miles away at a cost of £2 each. Beer worth fifteen shillings was purchased from the beerhall, though not much of this was actually drunk by the family since they are staunch Methodists. However, all other members of the family including the sick man's brothers-in-law attended the rite. The sick man's father's sister from Nyasaland made the invocation to the ancestor spirits. The feast was held in Old Highfields Township and people who were there said that it was not held under ideal conditions. The sick man was obviously getting worse and this cloud hung over the gathering. Also curious visitors from the neighbourhood kept interrupting the proceedings.

Immediately after the feast a diviner was consulted to find out whether the spirits had accepted the sacrifice. This diviner said that the feast had been conducted satisfactorily but that he could not guarantee that the sick man would recover. He pointed out that while everything possible had been done to appease the spirits on the father's side, nothing had been done for the spirits on the mother's side. Those at the feast had all been Nyasas; the man's mother was the only Shona person there. Sources of dissatisfaction on the mother's side were said to be:

(a) The man's Nyasa father who had recently died had not paid the 'mother's cow' which is part of the traditional Shona marriage payment.
(b) The man's mother's mother had brought up two of the children of this family but had never been thanked by having some clothing bought for her. The sick man was in fact one of these children.

Two days after the feast, after several blood transfusions, the sick man died in hospital. The death certificate showed that the man died from leukemia. The family are now faced with the duty of appeasing the ancestor spirits on the mother's side.

This case history shows the dual interpretation of misfortune very clearly. The sick man's father was thought to have been bewitched by his rivals for a church position or by a jealous fellow workman. But ostensibly because this was a Christian family his widow could take no action against them. Instead she found the ultimate explanation in the relationship between this urban family and their patrilateral kinsmen in Nyasaland whom they had never seen. Their immediate and feasible action therefore was to appease these spirits. The tragic history of the dead man's son follows exactly the same pattern. He has foreign objects removed by a number of 'doctors'. These 'doctors' were all extremely reluctant to indicate the names of his tormentors, possibly because of the law which makes it an offence to do so. Eventually when the sick man does persuade a 'doctor' to reveal who the witches are he points to the jealousy of the sick man's co-workers. Yet the victim is unable to take action against them and once again his kinsmen interpret the misfortune in terms of the ancestor cult for which there are specific and definite procedures.

I argue then that town Africans in the main continue to interpret their misfortunes in 'personal' terms but the final meaning they attach to the misfortune must be of a type which will allow them to take effective action. There are institutionalized means of dealing directly with believed witches in rural societies, devices which assist the normal social processes of division and reintegration to take place. In the towns, however, there is a preponderance of strangers who are not intimately and emotionally linked to each other as kinsmen are in a tribal society. Hostility and opposition may be openly expressed towards strangers so that there is no need for accusations of witchcraft. Social separation is a feature of urban societies so that the tensions that arise in the towns do not call for a catalytic agent such as witchcraft accusations to provide a justification for segmentations. Where townsfolk are linked in co-operative enterprises, however, in which competition is nevertheless an essential element, such as in work groups in factories or as rival brewers in a neighbourhood, the hostility is likely to be expressed in terms of accusations of witchcraft. If hostilties are phrased in terms of witchcraft accusations, however, this is the end of the matter, for the accuser cannot use these beliefs to bring the opposition into the open as he would do for example among the Yao. The judicial processes in the town are part of an administrative system which does not countenance witchcraft beliefs. To see the hand of witchcraft in misfortunes may be the first reaction of a townsman, but it is an interpretation which in terms of the social and administrative structure of the urban community allows him no direct retributive action. He tends to see misfortunes ultimately then in terms of the action of the angered spirits of a deceased kinsman. There are, after all, time-honoured methods of adjusting the relationships of a man to his ancestor spirits, but none of dealing with a witch in the alien circumstances of the town. A man takes his ancestor spirits to town with him and if he sees their hand in the misfortunes that befall him he has the satisfaction of knowing that at least there is something he can do about it.

SELECTED READINGS

BANTON, MICHAEL

1957 West African City. A Study of Tribal Life in Freetown. London: Oxford University Press.

An analysis of three problems connected with urbanization: the causes and character of migration to the town; the provision of an effective administrative structure regulating immigrant life in a town with a mixed population; and adaptation of immigrant social institutions to the new environment.

BEALS, RALPH

1951 Urbanism, Urbanization and Acculturation. American Anthropologist 53:1–10.

Criticizes sociologists for studying the nature of urbanism (order) rather than the processes of urbanism or the adaptation of men to urban life (change).

DOUGHTY, PAUL

1972 Peruvian Migrant Identity in the Urban Milieu. *In* The Anthropology of Urban Environments. Thomas Weaver and Douglas White, Eds. Society for Applied Anthropology, Monograph Series, No. 11, pp. 39–50.

Doughty examines the continuity and meaning of rural origins for Peruvian urban dwellers in this article. His use of the content of radio programs is particularly suggestive for further urban research.

IANNI, FRANCIS A. J.

1972 A Family Business: Kinship and Social Control in Organized Crime. New York: Russell Sage Foundation.

Suggesting a continuity of tradition from the Sicilian Mafia to Italian immigrant adaptation to New York City, Ianni examines the kin and business relationships of a contemporary Italian-American "family." In his criticism of the claims of criminologists and others, the author demonstrates the role of kinship in the capitalistic expansion of the family business.

JACOBSON, DAVID

1973 Itinerant Townsmen: Friendship and Social Order in Urban Uganda. Menlo Park, Ca: Cummings Publishing Co.

In this study of urban relationships in Mbale, Uganda, Jacobson expands upon his discussion in Selection 16 above.

LITTLE, KENNETH

1965 West African Urbanization: A Study of Voluntary Associations in Social Change. Cambridge: Cambridge University Press.

This major source of information on African voluntary associations clearly presents the important issues in the role of such associations in the process of migrant adaptation to the city. Defining various sorts of associations, Little shows how each fills the needs of urban Africans.

MITCHELL, J. CLYDE

1968 The Kalela Dance: Aspects of Social Relationships among Urban Africans in Northern Rhodesia. Rhodes-Livingstone Institute Papers, No. 27.

A fascinating study of the organization and presentation of a favorite urban African dance, through it the reader will gain insight into intertribal and interracial relationships in Southern Africa.

Part Six
THE CULTURE
OF POVERTY

One of the most popular, and popularized, concepts to emerge from
the work of urban anthropologists has been that of the "culture of
poverty." Introduced by Oscar Lewis and based upon his investigations
of urban Latin Americans, this notion has been adopted by politicians,
administrators, and social scientists. One of its attractive aspects is its
seeming ability to capture a life style or a subcultural way of life.
In addition, according to Lewis, individuals living within a culture
of poverty may be found in numerous cities, including large American
metropolitan areas.

The culture of poverty is located in urban slums; yet all slum
dwellers are not part of the subculture. In Selection 18, Lewis lists a
set of traits characterizing the poverty subculture. But because these
traits are distributed unevenly throughout a slum population, it is
difficult to identify a cultural *group* whose way of life can be called
the culture of poverty. Leeds (1971) has pointed out that Lewis
presented a static description of traits and not a dynamic concept
explaining coherence. Although Lewis has captured something of the
quality of slum life in his ethnographic statements, more dynamic
descriptions relating to groups larger than the family may be found in
Tally's Corner (Liebow 1967) and *Soulside* (Hannerz 1969). Critical
discussions of the notion of the culture of poverty appear in Valentine
(1968) and Leacock (1971), particularly the Leeds contribution in
the latter.

One of the most important aspects of culture-of-poverty discussions
is that poor populations must be seen as part of a larger national society.
Lewis, for example, hypothesizes that the culture of poverty is more
likely to exist in an exploitative capitalist society than one with a
socialist economic system. In Selection 19, Glazer considers the varying

responses of poor populations to political and economic policies in New York City. Pointing out that all urban poor do not have a culture of poverty and that some nonpoor do, Glazer calls for more research among urban subcultural groups in order to determine the cultural characteristics that lead to adoption or rejection of culture-of-poverty traits. Dependence upon urban support institutions seems to be critical to developing a culture of poverty in Glazer's view. Thus, groups able to maintain a sense of internal cohesiveness, increasing the possibility of interfamilial integration, may be poor but will not be included in the culture of poverty. We might speculate, on the basis of his sample of "successful" groups, that possession of an integrating ideology—a Great Tradition—is the critical factor.

The relationship of a relatively poor community to its outside patrons is also the topic of Spicer's (Selection 20) contribution to this volume. In this discussion of a particular conflict situation and its meaning to participating groups, Spicer identifies the rationale for each position and the consequences of these for the community. Although this southwestern minority community remained relatively well integrated under its native leadership, "the operation of competing clienteles headed by outside patrons" tended to erode this condition. In many ways, this article marks a step in the process within anthropology which has deemphasized the unitary and isolated notion of culture, concentrating instead upon interrelations among various tribes, ethnic groups, and other societal groupings.

18
The Culture of Poverty
Oscar Lewis

Poverty and the so-called war against it provide a principal theme for the domestic program of the present Administration. In the midst of a population that enjoys unexampled material well-being—with the average annual family income exceeding $7,000—it is officially acknowledged that some 18 million families, numbering more than 50 million individuals, live below the $3,000 "poverty line." Toward the improvement of the lot of these people some $1,600 million of Federal funds are directly allocated through the Office of Economic Opportunity, and many hundreds of millions of additional dollars flow indirectly through expanded Federal expenditures in the fields of health, education, welfare and urban affairs.

Along with the increase in activity on behalf of the poor indicated by these figures there has come a parallel expansion of publication in the social sciences on the subject of poverty. The new writings advance the same two opposed evaluations of the poor that are to be found in literature, in proverbs and in popular sayings throughout recorded history. Just as the poor have been pronounced blessed, virtuous, upright, serene, independent, honest, kind and happy, so contemporary students stress their great and neglected capacity for self-help, leadership and community organization. Conversely, as the poor have been characterized as shiftless, mean, sordid, violent, evil and criminal, so other students point to the irreversibly destructive effects of poverty on individual character and emphasize the corresponding need to keep guidance and control of poverty projects in the hands of duly constituted authorities. This clash of viewpoints reflects in part the infighting for political control of the program between Federal and local officials. The confusion results also from the tendency to focus study and attention on the personality of the in-

source: Oscar Lewis, *La Vida* (New York: Random House, 1966). Copyright © 1965, 1966 by Oscar Lewis. Reprinted by permission of Random House, Inc. This article originally appeared in *Scientific American* 215, no. 4, October 1966: 19–25.

dividual victim of poverty rather than on the slum community and family and from the consequent failure to distinguish between poverty and what I have called the culture of poverty.

The phrase is a catchy one and is used and misused with some frequency in the current literature. In my writings it is the label for a specific conceptual model that describes in positive terms a subculture of Western society with its own structure and rationale, a way of life handed on from generation to generation along family lines. The culture of poverty is not just a matter of deprivation or disorganization, a term signifying the absence of something. It is a culture in the traditional anthropological sense in that it provides human beings with a design for living, with a ready-made set of solutions for human problems, and so serves a significant adaptive function. This style of life transcends national boundaries and regional and rural-urban differences within nations. Wherever it occurs, its practitioners exhibit remarkable similarity in the structure of their families, in interpersonal relations, in spending habits, in their value systems and in their orientation in time.

Not nearly enough is known about this important complex of human behavior. My own concept of it has evolved as my work has progressed and remains subject to amendment by my own further work and that of others. The scarcity of literature on the culture of poverty is a measure of the gap in communication that exists between the very poor and the middle-class personnel—social scientists, social workers, teachers, physicians, priests and others—who bear the major responsibility for carrying out the antipoverty programs. Much of the behavior accepted in the culture of poverty goes counter to cherished ideals of the larger society. In writing about "multiproblem" families social scientists thus often stress their instability, their lack of order, direction and organization. Yet, as I have observed them, their behavior seems clearly patterned and reasonably predictable. I am more often struck by the inexorable repetitiousness and the iron entrenchment of their lifeways.

The concept of the culture of poverty may help to correct misapprehensions that have ascribed some behavior patterns of ethnic, national or regional groups as distinctive characteristics. For example, a high incidence of common-law marriage and of households headed by women has been thought to be distinctive of Negro family life in this country and has been attributed to the Negro's historical experience of slavery. In actuality it turns out that such households express essential traits of the culture of poverty and are found among diverse peoples in many parts of the world and among peoples that have had no history of slavery. Although it is now possible to assert such generalizations, there is still much to be learned about this difficult and affecting subject. The absence of intensive anthropological studies of poor families in a wide variety of national contexts—particularly the lack of such studies in socialist countries—remains a serious handicap to the formulation of dependable cross-cultural constants of the culture of poverty.

My studies of poverty and family life have centered largely in Mexico. On occasion some of my Mexican friends have suggested delicately that I turn to a study of poverty in my own country. As a first step in this direction I am currently engaged in a study of Puerto Rican families. Over the past three years my staff and I have been assembling data on 100 representative families in four slums of Greater San Juan and some 50 families of their relatives in New York City.

Our methods combine the traditional techniques of sociology, anthropology and psychology. This includes a battery of 19 questionnaires, the administration of which requires 12 hours per informant. They cover the residence and employment history of each adult; family relations; income and expenditures; complete inventory of household and personal possessions; friendship patterns, particularly the *compadrazgo*, or godparent, relationship that serves as a kind of informal social security for the children of these families and establishes special obligations among the adults; recreational patterns; health and medical history; politics; religion; world view and "cosmopolitanism." Open-end interviews and psychological tests (such as the thematic apperception test, the Rorschach test and the sentence-completion test) are administered to a sampling of this population.

All this work serves to establish the context for close-range study of a selected few families. Because the family is a small social system, it lends itself to the holistic approach of anthropology. Whole-family studies bridge the gap between the conceptual extremes of the culture at one pole and of the individual at the other, making possible observation of both culture and personality as they are interrelated in real life. In a large metropolis such as San Juan or New York the family is the natural unit of study.

Ideally our objective is the naturalistic observation of the life of "our" families, with a minimum of intervention. Such intensive study, however, necessarily involves the establishment of deep personal ties. My assistants include two Mexicans whose families I had studied; their "Mexican's-eye view" of the Puerto Rican slum has helped to point up the similarities and differences between the Mexican and Puerto Rican subcultures. We have spent many hours attending family parties, wakes and baptisms, responding to emergency calls, taking people to the hospital, getting them out of jail, filling out applications for them, hunting apartments with them, helping them to get jobs or to get on relief. With each member of these families we conduct tape-recorded interviews, taking down their life stories and their answers to questions on a wide variety of topics. For the ordering of our material we undertake to reconstruct, by close interrogation, the history of a week or more of consecutive days in the lives of each family, and we observe and record complete days as they unfold. The first volume to issue from this study is to be published next month under the title of *La Vida, a Puerto Rican Family in the Culture of Poverty—San Juan and New York* (Random House).

There are many poor people in the world. Indeed, the poverty of the two-thirds of the world's population who live in the underdeveloped countries has been rightly called "the problem of problems." But not all of them by any means live in the culture of poverty. For this way of life to come into being and flourish it seems clear that certain preconditions must be met.

The setting is a cash economy, with wage labor and production for profit and with a persistently high rate of unemployment and underemployment, at low wages, for unskilled labor. The society fails to provide social, political and economic organization, on either a voluntary basis or by government imposition, for the low-income population. There is a bilateral kinship system centered on the nuclear progenitive family, as distinguished from the unilateral extended kinship system of lineage and clan. The dominant class asserts a set of values that prizes thrift and the accumulation of wealth and property, stresses the possibility of upward mobility and explains low economic status as the result of individual personal inadequacy and inferiority.

Where these conditions prevail the way of life that develops among some of the poor is the culture of poverty. That is why I have described it as a subculture of the Western social order. It is both an adaptation and a reaction of the poor to their marginal position in a class-stratified, highly individuated, capitalistic society. It represents an effort to cope with feelings of hopelessness and despair that arise from the realization by the members of the marginal communities in these societies of the improbability of their achieving success in terms of the prevailing values and goals. Many of the traits of the culture of poverty can be viewed as local, spontaneous attempts to meet needs not served in the case of the poor by the institutions and agencies of the larger society because the poor are not eligible for such service, cannot afford it or are ignorant and suspicious.

Once the culture of poverty has come into existence it tends to perpetuate itself. By the time slum children are six or seven they have usually absorbed the basic attitudes and values of their subculture. Thereafter they are psychologically unready to take full advantage of changing conditions or improving opportunities that may develop in their lifetime.

My studies have identified some 70 traits that characterize the culture of poverty. The principal ones may be described in four dimensions of the system: the relationship between the subculture and the larger society; the nature of the slum community; the nature of the family, and the attitudes, values and character structure of the individual.

The disengagement, the nonintegration, of the poor with respect to the major institutions of society is a crucial element in the culture of poverty. It reflects the combined effect of a variety of factors including poverty, to begin with, but also segregation and discrimination, fear, suspicion and apathy and the development of alternative institutions and procedures in the slum community. The people do not belong to labor unions or political parties and make little use of banks, hospitals, department stores or museums. Such involvement as there is in the institutions of the larger society—in the jails, the army and the public welfare system—does little to suppress the traits of the culture of poverty. A relief system that barely keeps people alive perpetuates rather than eliminates poverty and the pervading sense of hopelessness.

People in a culture of poverty produce little wealth and receive little in return. Chronic unemployment and underemployment, low wages, lack of property, lack of savings, absence of food reserves in the home and chronic shortage of cash imprison the family and the individual in a vicious circle. Thus for lack of cash the slum householder makes frequent purchases of small quantities of food at higher prices. The slum economy turns inward; it shows a high incidence of pawning of personal goods, borrowing at usurious rates of interest, informal credit arrangements among neighbors, use of secondhand clothing and furniture.

There is awareness of middle-class values. People talk about them and even claim some of them as their own. On the whole, however, they do not live by them. They will declare that marriage by law, by the church or by both is the ideal form of marriage, but few will marry. For men who have no steady jobs, no property and no prospect of wealth to pass on to their children, who live in the present without expectations of the future, who want to avoid the expense and legal difficulties involved in marriage and divorce, a free union or consensual marriage makes good sense. The women, for their part, will turn down offers of marriage from men who are likely to be immature, punishing and generally unreliable. They feel that a consensual union gives them some of the freedom and flexibility men have. By not giving the fathers of their children legal status as husbands, the women have a stronger claim on the children. They also maintain exclusive rights to their own property.

Along with disengagement from the larger society, there is a hostility to the basic institutions of what are regarded as the dominant classes. There is hatred of the police, mistrust of government and of those in high positions and a cynicism that extends to the church. The culture of poverty thus holds a certain potential for protest and for entrainment in political movements aimed against the existing order.

With its poor housing and overcrowding, the community of the culture of poverty is high in gregariousness, but it has a minimum of organization beyond the nuclear and extended family. Occasionally slum dwellers come together in temporary informal groupings; neighborhood gangs that cut across slum settlements represent a considerable advance beyond the zero point of the continuum I have in mind. It is the low level of organization that gives the culture of poverty its marginal and anomalous quality in our highly organized society. Most primitive peoples have achieved a higher degree of sociocultural organization than contemporary urban slum dwellers. This is not to say that there may not be a sense of community and *esprit de corps* in a slum neighborhood. In fact, where slums are isolated from their surroundings by enclosing walls or other physical barriers, where rents are low and residence is stable and where the population constitutes a distinct ethnic, racial or language group, the sense of community may approach that of a village. In Mexico City and San Juan such territoriality is engendered by the scarcity of low-cost housing outside of established slum areas. In South Africa it is actively enforced by the *apartheid* that confines rural migrants to prescribed locations.

The family in the culture of poverty does not cherish childhood as a specially prolonged and protected stage in the life cycle. Initiation into sex comes early. With the instability of consensual marriage the family tends to be mother-centered and tied more closely to the mother's extended family. The female head of the house is given to authoritarian rule. In spite of much verbal emphasis on family solidarity, sibling rivalry for the limited supply of goods and maternal affection is intense. There is little privacy.

The individual who grows up in this culture has a strong feeling of fatalism, helplessness, dependence and inferiority. These traits, so often remarked in the current literature as characteristic of the American Negro, I found equally strong in slum dwellers of Mexico City and San Juan, who are not segregated or discriminated against as a distinct ethnic or racial group. Other traits include a high incidence of weak ego structure, orality and confusion of sexual identification, all reflecting maternal deprivation; a strong present-time orientation with relatively little disposition to defer gratification and plan for the future, and a high tolerance for psychological pathology of all kinds. There is widespread belief in male superiority and among the men a strong preoccupation with *machismo,* their masculinity.

Provincial and local in outlook, with little sense of history, these people know only their own neighborhood and their own way of life. Usually they do not have the knowledge, the vision or the ideology to see the similarities between their troubles and those of their counterparts elsewhere in the world. They are not class-conscious, although they are sensitive indeed to symbols of status.

The distinction between poverty and the culture of poverty is basic to the model described here. There are numerous examples of poor people whose way of life I would not characterize as belonging to this subculture. Many primitive and preliterate peoples that have been studied by anthropologists suffer dire poverty attributable to low technology or thin resources or both. Yet even the simplest of these peoples have a high degree of social organization and a relatively integrated, satisfying and self-sufficient culture.

In India the destitute lower-caste peoples—such as the Chamars, the leatherworkers, and the Bhangis, the sweepers—remain integrated in the larger society and have their own panchayat institutions of self-government. Their panchayats and either extended unilateral kinship systems, or clans, cut across village lines, giving them a strong sense of identity and continuity. In my studies of these peoples I found no culture of poverty to go with their poverty.

The Jews of eastern Europe were a poor urban people, often confined to ghettos. Yet they did not have many traits of the culture of poverty. They had a tradition of literacy that placed great value on learning; they formed many voluntary associations and adhered with devotion to the central community organization around the rabbi, and they had a religion that taught them they were the chosen people.

I would cite also a fourth, somewhat speculative example of poverty dissociated from the culture of poverty. On the basis of limited direct observation in one country—Cuba—and from indirect evidence, I am inclined to believe the culture of poverty does not exist in socialist countries. In 1947 I undertook a study of a slum in Havana. Recently I had an opportunity to revisit the same slum and some of the same families. The physical aspect of the place had changed little, except for a beautiful new nursery school. The people were as poor as before, but I was impressed to find much less of the feelings of despair and apathy, so symptomatic of the culture of poverty in the urban slums of the U.S. The slum was now highly organized, with block committees, educational committees, party committees. The people had found a new sense of power and importance in a doctrine that glorified the lower class as the hope of humanity, and they were armed. I was told by one Cuban official that the Castro government had practically eliminated delinquency by giving arms to the delinquents!

Evidently the Castro regime—revising Marx and Engels—did not write off the so-called *lumpenproletariat* as an inherently reactionary and anti-revolutionary force but rather found in them a revolutionary potential and utilized it. Frantz Fanon, in his book *The Wretched of the Earth,* makes a similar evaluation of their role in the Algerian revolution: "It is within this mass of humanity, this people of the shantytowns, at the core of the *lumpenproletariat,* that the rebellion will find its urban spearhead. For the *lumpenproletariat,* that horde of starving men, uprooted from their tribe and from their clan, constitutes one of the most spontaneous and most radically revolutionary forces of a colonized people."

It is true that I have found little revolutionary spirit or radical ideology among low-income Puerto Ricans. Most of the families I studied were politically conservative, about half of them favoring the Statehood Republican Party, which provides opposition on the right to the Popular Democratic Party that dominates the politics of the commonwealth. It seems to me, therefore, that disposition for protest among people living in the culture of poverty will vary considerably according to the national context and historical circumstances. In contrast to Algeria, the independence movement in Puerto Rico has found little popular support. In Mexico, where the cause of independence carried long ago, there is no longer any such movement to stir the dwellers in the new and old slums of the capital city.

Yet it would seem that any movement—be it religious, pacifist or revolutionary—that organizes and gives hope to the poor and effectively promotes a sense of solidarity with larger groups must effectively destroy the psychological and social core of the culture of poverty. In this connection, I suspect that the civil rights movement among American Negroes has of itself done more to improve their self-image and self-respect than such economic gains as it has won although, without doubt, the two kinds of progress are mutually reinforcing. In the culture of poverty of the American Negro the additional disadvantage of racial discrimination has generated a potential for revolutionary protest and organization that is absent in the slums of San Juan and Mexico City and, for that matter, among the poor whites in the South.

If it is true, as I suspect, that the culture of poverty flourishes and is endemic to the free-enterprise, pre-welfare-state stage of capitalism, then it is also endemic in colonial societies. The most likely candidates for the culture of poverty would be the people who come from the lower strata of a rapidly changing society and who are already partially alienated from it. Accordingly the subculture is likely to be found where imperial conquest has smashed the native social and economic structure and held the natives, perhaps for generations, in servile status, or where feudalism is yielding to capitalism in the later evolution of a colonial economy. Landless rural workers who migrate to the cities, as in Latin America, can be expected to fall into this way of life more readily than migrants from stable peasant villages with a well-organized traditional culture, as in India. It remains to be seen, however, whether the culture of poverty has not already begun to develop in the slums of Bombay and Calcutta. Compared with Latin America also, the strong corporate nature of many African tribal societies may tend to inhibit or delay the formation of a full-blown culture of poverty in the new towns and cities of that continent. In South Africa the institutionalization of repression and discrimination under *apartheid* may also have begun to promote an immunizing sense of identity and group consciousness among the African Negroes.

One must therefore keep the dynamic aspects of human institutions forward in observing and assessing the evidence for the presence, the waxing or the waning of this subculture. Measured on the dimension of relationship to the larger society, some slum dwellers may have a warmer identification with their national tradition even though they suffer deeper poverty than members of a similar community in another country. In Mexico City a high percentage of our respondents, including those with little or no formal schooling, knew of Cuauhtémoc Hidalgo, Father Morelos, Juárez, Díaz, Zapata, Carranza and Cardenas. In San Juan the names of Rámon Power, José de Diego, Baldorioty de Castro, Rámon Betances, Nemesio Canales, Lloréns Torres rang no bell; a few could tell about the late Albizu Campos. For the lower income Puerto Rican, however, history begins with Muñoz Rivera and ends with his son Muñoz Marin.

The national context can make a big difference in the play of the crucial traits of fatalism and hopelessness. Given the advanced technology, the high level of literacy, the all-pervasive reach of the media of mass communications and the relatively high aspirations of all sectors of the population, even the poorest and most marginal communities of the U.S. must aspire to a larger future than the slum dwellers of Ecuador and Peru, where the actual possibilities are more limited and where an authoritarian social order persists in city and country. Among the 50 million U.S. citizens now more or less officially certified as poor, I would guess that about 20 percent live in a culture of poverty. The largest members in this group are made up of Negroes, Puerto Ricans, Mexicans, American Indians and Southern poor whites. In these figures there is some reassurance for those concerned, because it is much more difficult to undo the culture of poverty than to cure poverty itself.

Middle class people—this would certainly include most social scientists—tend to concentrate on the negative aspects of the culture of poverty. They attach a minus sign to such traits as present-time orientation and readiness to indulge impulses. I do not intend to idealize or romanticize the culture of poverty—"it is easier to praise poverty than to live in it." Yet the positive aspects of these traits must not be overlooked. Living in the present may develop a capacity for spontaneity, for the enjoyment of the sensual, which is often blunted in the middle-class, future-oriented man. Indeed, I am often struck by the analogies that can be drawn between the mores of the very rich—of the "jet set" and "café society"—and the culture of the very poor. Yet it is, on the whole, a comparatively superficial culture. There is in it much pathos, suffering and emptiness. It does not provide much support or satisfaction; its pervading mistrust magnifies individual helplessness and isolation. Indeed, poverty of culture is one of the crucial traits of the culture of poverty.

The concept of the culture of poverty provides a generalization that may help to unify and explain a number of phenomena hitherto viewed as peculiar to certain racial, national or regional groups. Problems we think of as being distinctively our own or distinctively Negro (or as typifying any other ethnic group) prove to be endemic in countries where there are no segregated ethnic minority groups. If it follows that the elimination of physical poverty may not by itself eliminate the culture of poverty, then an understanding of the subculture may contribute to the design of measures specific to that purpose.

What is the future of the culture of poverty? In considering this question one must distinguish between those countries in which it represents a relatively small segment of the population and those in which it constitutes a large one. In the U.S. the major solution proposed by social workers dealing with the "hard core" poor has been slowly to raise their level of living and incorporate them in the middle class. Wherever possible psychiatric treatment is prescribed.

In underdeveloped countries where great masses of people live in the culture of poverty, such a social-work solution does not seem feasible. The local psychiatrists have all they can do to care for their own growing middle class. In those countries the people with a culture of poverty may seek a more revolutionary solution. By creating basic structural changes in society, by redistributing wealth, by organizing the poor and giving them a sense of belonging, of power and of leadership, revolutions frequently succeed in abolishing some of the basic characteristics of the culture of poverty even when they do not succeed in curing poverty itself.

19

The Culture of Poverty:
The View from New York City

Nathan Glazer

Oscar Lewis' most valuable contribution to the concept of the culture of poverty was to make it clear—or clearer—that there are various ways of being poor and that some are better than others. On the basis of his experiences with the poor in India, Mexico, Puerto Rico and New York, Lewis argued that the material realities of poverty in various settings—overcrowding, few capital goods, private or public, insufficient and unvaried food, difficulty of access to consumption goods, medical aid, and education—have varied consequences in varied social settings.

In India, for example, the lower castes and the untouchables lived at a level of material deprivation unmatched in the slums of Mexico City, and certainly not equaled in the slums of San Juan. The expected social consequences did not follow. Indeed, the whole point of the culture of poverty hypothesis was that there are no inevitable social consequences of a level of deprivation. The lower castes in India were organized into social units—families, kin groups, castes—that maintained a certain degree of solidarity, and in doing so they could exercise, even at that deprived material level, some degree of power to assist the members of their group. In addition, these social forms made up part of a whole complex of forms that gave each group its legitimacy, its role, its modicum of power in the society, and even, if one lived as part of the system, some degree of respect. If one had the official place of sweeper of the village's offal, since it was a place that had come down by inheritance and was justified and explained in the common religion and beliefs, it gave one a position, even though the formal attitude toward it did involve formal disrespect. The sweeper thus also had his dignity.

SOURCE: J. Alan Winter, ed., *The Poor: A Culture of Poverty or a Poverty of Culture?* (Grand Rapids, Mich.: Wm. B. Eerdmans Publishing Co., 1969), pp. 29–48. Reprinted by permission.

This may be excessively romantic: but there are things in traditional India that a high-caste Hindu can and cannot do to an untouchable.

I emphasize India because there poverty may be seen at its worst, but the culture of poverty as Lewis has described it is fragmentary in India; indeed, it is questionable whether it exists there at all. On the streets of Calcutta, where hundreds of thousands of people sleep and live and wash and eat, a culture may be seen in process, and it is oddly enough not the culture of poverty. Each fragment of that humanity has important social ties—to a village, a caste, a family—and even if none of these ties is physically evident when one walks down those awful streets, they are present in the mind of each of those individuals, guiding and controlling behavior. So work is sought, money is saved, remittances are sent back to the village, children are raised and married off.

Once again, this is perhaps idealized and romanticized. There are family breakdown, prostitution, vagrancy, abandoned children, and the like in India. But these are all viewed by those in and outside the culture of the streets as exceptional and deplorable. No one justifies illegitimacy, family abandonment, prostitution, robbery. Hard as it may be to believe, there is something middle class, from our perspective, about the way the Indian pavement dweller prepares himself for the night. The mat is spread out, the ablutions are ceremonially performed, prayers are said, the passersby are ignored.

Oscar Lewis gives two other examples of poverty that display less of the culture of poverty or lack it entirely. One is the African town, where the tribe and ethnic group still make their presence felt and organize the social life of the impoverished town-dweller, in ways not much different from the role of caste and village in India. A second example Lewis is fond of is the Jews of Eastern Europe. A third case is well recorded: the Chinese of Hong Kong, who live under conditions of crowding and deprivation far worse than found in any American big city. One estimate suggests that the amount of space an individual in a Hong Kong resettlement block has is one-tenth that available to the poor in the most crowded American cities. Families of seven and ten and fifteen live in relatively small rooms, where the only visible possessions are some clothing, a chest or two, some cooking utensils and dishes. Certainly the poor in Mexico City live under no worse physical circumstances, except that concrete blocks with water and sanitary disposal facilities are made available by the Hong Kong government. One writer points out that the level of juvenile delinquency, illegitimacy, family break-up, mental illness, and various other consequences that result from this incredible crowding are really quite moderate compared to what we might expect (Schmitt 1963: 210–217).

In all these cases, city-dwellers manage to maintain a cultural orientation distinct from the culture of poverty. We find patriarchalism, male authority, control of children's sexual lives, fixed roles for family members that lead to some degree of confidence in how they will behave in crisis, long-range planning, both in the area of work and production and in the area of consumption, foresight in the acquisition and care of material goods.

In contrast, the culture of poverty as Oscar Lewis describes it has its own characteristics that distinguish it from poverty *per se:* the ease with which the marriage tie breaks up, or is not formed to begin with; the uncertain degree of male responsibility for children; female responsibility for children; the early induction of children into sexuality; the emphasis on present time—or limited long-range planning; mistrust between family members; mistrust of others; a feeling of helplessness and inferiority.

I have pointed out that there is poverty without the culture of poverty —Lewis gives the examples of India, East European Jews, and, more briefly, African towns. I have added Hong Kong. In addition Lewis points out that preliterate societies, despite their poverty, form no part of the "culture of poverty." Finally, the culture of poverty, he suggests, has been overcome in revolutionary Communist societies (Eastern Europe, Cuba), and in advanced welfare states. What then *is* the setting of the culture of poverty?

> In effect, we find that in primitive societies and in caste societies the culture of poverty does not develop. In socialist, fascist, and highly developed capitalist societies with a welfare state, the culture of poverty tends to decline. I suspect that the culture of poverty flourishes in, and is generic to, the early free-enterprise stage of capitalism and it is also endemic to colonialism. (Lewis 1969: 195)

In other words, for Lewis it is free enterprise capitalism in its earlier and more brutal stages that provides the setting for the culture of poverty. The conditions in which it flourishes are societies with

> (1) a cash economy, wage labor, and production for profit; (2) a persistently high rate of unemployment and underemployment for unskilled labor; (3) low wages; (4) the failure to provide social, political and economic organization, either on a voluntary basis or by government imposition, for the low-income population; (5) the existence of a bilateral kinship system rather than a unilateral one; and finally, (6) the existence in the dominant class of a set of

values that stresses the accumulation of wealth and property, the possibility of upward mobility, and thrift, and that explains low economic status as the result of personal inadequacy or inferiority. (Lewis 1969:188)

And yet all these features (except for number five, the bilateral kinship system, which may in any case be better seen as a characteristic of the culture of poverty rather than a cause) may be found in the exceptional areas too—Indian cities, African cities, East European Jews, Hong Kong Chinese, and we might add East European peasants.

The United States forms another problem for Lewis. It is not in the early stages of capitalism, when we might expect the culture of poverty to be epidemic. The material level at which its poor live tends to be quite high, at least in the cities, as measured simply by consumption of food, housing, clothing, and other consumer goods. Yet what Lewis has described as the culture of poverty characterizes the poor of our cities— and in particular the welfare poor—as well as it characterizes the poor of Mexico City or San Juan. Thus while Lewis has been at pains to emphasize that we can have poverty without the culture of poverty, the case of American cities raises another paradox: can we have the culture of poverty without poverty? My argument is that we can, and indeed do, have it. And if we analyze the reasons for it, we must come to somewhat different conclusions as to the origins of the culture of poverty and the reasons it persists.

Do we truly have a culture of poverty without poverty in large American cities? Most of my evidence for the contention that we do is drawn from New York City.

Obviously, the term poverty may be relative as well as absolute (Miller 1969). In Oscar Lewis' usage, the emphasis has been on the absolute character of poverty, which is why he speaks of the residents of Mexico City slums, Indian cities and villages, Eastern European villages, and the preliterates everywhere, as candidates for the culture of poverty. All these groups suffer from absolute poverty. Whatever the cultural riches that may exist together with absolute poverty, absolute poverty means a primary concern with the immediate necessities of life: food, shelter, and clothing. The traditional image of the possessions of Gandhi, who took a vow of poverty, at his death is a picture of absolute poverty: some scraps of clothing, a bowl for eating, sandals, a pair of eyeglasses. Such poverty characterizes hundreds of millions in the world today. Food for the absolutely poor consists of a staple cereal, perhaps occasional vegetables. Meat, milk, and fish for the absolutely poor are rare luxuries. The culture of absolute poverty is recorded in the folklore of the very poor.

"When a Jew eats chicken," an old Jewish joke runs, "one of the two is sick." Clothes are rags and shelters are shacks. The expensive public capital goods that serve even poor city-dwellers in advanced and wealthy countries—clean water supplies piped into every home, systems of sewage and garbage removal, electricity—are unknown or rare.

Having pointed all this out, we can see that there is hardly any absolute poverty in New York. Those who are ill-clothed or ill-fed—and we see many on the streets of New York—are more commonly victims of mental illness than of poverty in the absolute sense. Even if we consider the worst aspect of the life of the poor in New York—housing—we find that almost no units in the city are without hot and cold running water, fully equipped kitchens, flush toilets and baths for individual units. Very few of the poor in New York live in units in which they must double up with other families. Yet New York's housing for the poor is worse than that of other large cities. But in contrast to Mexico City, San Juan, Hong Kong, Eastern Europe and immigrants in the city itself fifty years ago, lavish and modern housing accommodations are available to the poor. If we consider food or clothing, we are even more hard put to argue that a level of absolute deprivation prevails in the city.

For a statistical picture, consider the following. In 1960 only 5 percent of white households and 10 percent of black households with incomes under $4,000 in large cities lacked "adequate" housing (that is, housing with hot and cold piped water, private kitchen, private flush toilet and bath, less than one person per room), telephone and television.[1]

Is it relevant, one may ask, to inquire into the level of absolute poverty in such a city as New York, the wealthiest in the world by some measures? I would argue that it is if we are to talk about the culture of poverty, because some of its key aspects, as presented by Lewis, must derive in large measure from absolute conditions of poverty. Thus, the terrible overcrowding facilitates early sexual experience. The difficulty of acquiring the necessities of life encourages competition, double-dealing and mistrust in the family. The insecurity of life encourages an emphasis on the present and hedonism. All these themselves encourage the breakup of families and the abandonment of children. If, then, the culture of poverty is the result of conditions of absolute poverty, it is relevant to inquire into its extent in exploring the relationship between poverty and the culture of poverty.

Of course we know there is poverty in New York City, but it is poverty relative to a standard of living defined as necessary to a decent life

[1] Task Force on Economic Growth and Opportunity, *The Concept of Poverty*, 2, Washington, 1967, pp. 122–123, as reported in Irving H. Welfeld, "A New Framework for Federal Housing Aids," *Columbia Law Review*, LXIX (1969), 1367.

by individuals, groups, and the mass media. The problem with using measures of relative poverty to explore the relationship between the culture of poverty and poverty itself is twofold. First, as we have already pointed out, it is the conditions of absolute poverty that we expect will lead—in some cases if not all—to "the culture of poverty." Thus, if as certain analysts confidently expect, families with an income of $15,000 by present standards will be considered poor by the turn of the century, we would certainly not expect them to show any features of "the culture of poverty." Second, we have another problem in using relative measures of poverty, and that is, relative to whom?

Jason Epstein some years ago asserted in the *New York Review of Books* that it took $50,000 a year to live in New York City. *New York* magazine, more recently, demonstrated how one can be poor in New York on $80,000 a year. On that basis, just about everyone in New York is poor. Dropping from this ridiculous level to define "relative" poverty, the Bureau of Labor Statistics defined in 1967 a "modest but adequate standard of living" in New York City as requiring $9,400 for a family of four. Sixty-three percent of New York's population falls below that line, and thus presumably maintained an "inadequate" standard of living. Poor families, using the Social Security Administration's poverty line of $3,500 for a family of four, include 15.3 percent of the population, which brings us closer to a reasonable definition of relative poverty.

It seems obvious that one should be able to define a meaningful measure of relative poverty in New York City, which would enable one to focus on a target population and suggest policies that may be undertaken by a modern welfare society to alleviate and overcome poverty. But the matter is not that simple. It is very hard to draw a line that differentiates the "poor" from the "not poor" and yet does not encompass within the poor a large part of the population of this most affluent society, including many who are working and in no way candidates for the "culture of poverty" and many who do not deem themselves, if we take account of their behavior, poor. The social scientists Richard A. Cloward and Frances Fox Piven have become well known for pointing to the discrepancy between those eligible for welfare and those who apply for it. Cloward and Piven helped launch a campaign to teach those eligible and not on welfare to apply—to teach them, in other words, that they were "poor," at least in the sense that they were eligible for welfare. Recently they demonstrated in an article entitled "The Poor Against Themselves" that a good part of the working population of New York City is eligible for welfare on the basis of economic criteria; that is, they earned less than a family on welfare would get and by the laws of New York State were eligible for wage supplements (Cloward and Piven 1969).

To give an example, a family with three children, the oldest in college, would be eligible under welfare for $4,916. But if someone in the family worked and they received wage supplements, their maximum income could be $5,736. On the wage supplement (which if there was one worker employed at the minimum wage, would be $2,616), they would pay no federal, state, or local income tax. They would also be eligible for completely free medical care. Cloward and Piven urged those in such circumstances to apply for welfare, in the form of wage supplement. They estimated that 150,000 to 300,000 working families in New York City were eligible for such supplements, and that only 12,000 applied for them. Because of ignorance, embarrassment, or because they did not consider themselves poor, this huge population, perhaps ten to twenty percent of the population of the city, did not apply for welfare.

To consider another example, David Gordon has estimated that about 60 percent of those in New York City eligible for welfare (on the basis of economic criteria) apply (Gordon 1969:84). Once again, we find that 40 percent of the eligible population do not apply for welfare.

What can we conclude? Only that the welfare payment levels in New York City are such that it is a voluntary act for many families whether they apply or not. We do not know why those who do not apply engage in this act of self-denial. Ignorance, perhaps, although the Welfare Rights Organization has done its best to enlighten them. Shame (in their own eyes or in those of others) in defining themselves as a welfare case. Cultural standards, perhaps, which define their income as adequate, even though it is not considered so by the welfare authorities. I do not know how those not on welfare and earning less than welfare would give them define their situation, but I would guess that many of them do not consider themselves desperately poor.[2]

It would thus be a travesty to expect to find a "culture of poverty" among the so-called "working poor," who are the subject of much recent discussion. Many of them, after all, have regular union-protected jobs and children in school, some expecting to go to college. Many own their own homes, worry about inflation and taxes, discipline their children, and are concerned about the sexual revolution. If these are the poor, they do not show the characteristics of the culture of poverty—along with Lewis' examples of Indians, Jews, and preliterates.

My point is that in New York City the culture of poverty has become divorced from the conditions of poverty themselves. We have the poor who do not show the culture of poverty, as Lewis pointed out. But more significantly, we have the nonpoor—at least in terms of absolute measures

[2] On the question of whether the poor consider themselves poor, or workers, or poor but honest, or some other category that is not simply "poor," see Schensul et al. 1968.

of poverty—who do. One of the most striking examples of the divorce of conditions of poverty from the culture of poverty may be seen in the enormous increase in the welfare population of the city in recent years. During the past ten years in New York City, the number of the poor, by any measure, has grown at most only slightly. But the number of those on welfare has increased enormously, almost tripling.

Now the number on welfare may be taken as a crude measure of the population subject to the culture of poverty. For by far the greatest part of those on welfare are women and children who have been abandoned by husbands, male friends, and fathers. If one sees the weakness of the marital and parental ties—as I see it—as *the* key characteristic of the culture of poverty, the welfare population can be seen as a crude approximation of those subject to this culture. Admittedly there are those on welfare whose husbands have been killed or hurt as well as some whose husbands have joined them on welfare as complete families under the provisions of various programs that permit welfare aid to complete families with unemployed earners. But these are few. A study of a sample of families on the various family programs of the New York City Department of Welfare (Aid to Dependent Children, Temporary Aid to Dependent Children, and Home Relief) bears out my general characterization. Husbands were in residence in only one-quarter of the households, and the overwhelming majority of mothers who were without husbands were separated (40 percent of the sample) or unmarried (20 percent of the sample). Divorce was responsible for a mother without a husband in 5 percent of the families; widowhood in only 5 percent (Podell 1968:1). Thus, if welfare aid is a measure, as it seems to be, of abandonment and illegitimacy, this has increased enormously in recent years despite the fact that we find no increase in the number of the poor.

This is not a new observation. Daniel P. Moynihan pointed out in his famous report on the Negro family that ADC cases no longer moved together with unemployment figures, but rose independently of them. Other measures also support the general argument that poverty has become divorced from the culture of poverty—for example, the steady increase in the number of families headed by women in Northern cities, particularly among blacks, and the steady if slower increase in illegitimacy, which characteristically means the fiscal abandonment of the child to state care.[3]

But if all this is so, what are we to make of it? Certainly Oscar Lewis'

[3] Black female-headed families in metropolitan areas of 1,000,000 or more increased 83 percent between 1960 and 1968: white, 16 percent. See "Trends in Social and Economic Conditions in Metropolitan Areas," U.S. Bureau of the Census, Current Population Reports, February 7, 1969.

general characterization of the causes of the culture of poverty will not hold. To Lewis, it is the conditions of early and rampant capitalism that explain the culture of poverty—wages close to the survival line, the reserve army of the unemployed, the grim necessity to work at any menial or casual labor to exist, the absence of organization among the poor. And yet, those who live in and study Hong Kong view it as the sole survivor of a Victorian level of pure laissez-faire capitalism in the world. There is almost no social legislation, no free education, no requirement that children go to school, no child labor laws, no minimum wages. If one wants to find the conditions that Oscar Lewis feels lead to capitalism, go to Hong Kong. It is not only an example of the unmoderatedly fierce early stage of capitalism, but it remains one of the few existing examples in the world of an unmoderated, classic colonialism—the other feature that by Lewis' account leads to the culture of poverty. For in Hong Kong, the overwhelming majority of the population has no political rights—it does not vote—and in any case all power is held by the crown. We might extend these observations. India was and is the seat of early capitalism, somewhat stifled by efforts at central controls, social legislation, and central planning. It was the classic case of colonialism. Yet the culture of poverty is found there only in moderation.

On the other hand, in New York City we find the culture of poverty proceeding apace with the rapid development of the welfare state—higher levels of welfare, broader social insurance coverage, reduced unemployment, growing means of state assistance in seeking employment and preparing oneself for employment, and even (and this is hardly a characteristic of all welfare states, but one in which the United States has pioneered) growing organization among the welfare poor to demand higher benefits and greater power.

Certainly this phenomenon of the increase of the culture of poverty along with the decline of poverty deserves research—research that relatively few social scientists have carried out. I would list as two notable exceptions Elliot Liebow and Walter B. Miller. It will be of no help in illuminating this paradox to insist rather blindly and ahistorically that there is no paradox. There are two broad examples of the way this is done by contemporary researchers and analysts. On the one hand, there are those who insist that poverty in the United States is rampant and not declining. This is done not only by political leaders. One can also find examples of this insistence on the denial of the best facts and information we have among the social scientists. Those who dismiss the paradox by asserting that the number of the poor remains as large as it has always been and their conditions as deplorable have an obligation to analyze the Census and Bureau of Labor statistics and demonstrate that these figures are misleading or wrong. Such an approach would contribute more than simple assertions, which may testify to their sympathy and morality but not to their ability as social scientists.[4]

There is a second and to my mind sadder means of dismissing the paradox: to deny that what we have is a culture of poverty in the pejorative sense of that term at all. If there are families headed by women, it testifies to their strength. If there are more illegitimate children, it testifies to greater honesty and greater love of children. If there is a greater rate of abandonment, it is owing only to the agony of being unable to provide adequate support. If there is mistrust, it is an accurate reaction to the nature of the environment. Indeed, there is no culture of poverty at all. There is simply sensible, strong, and adequate response to environment. Here too we find more assertion of the case than demonstration. We find little research to demonstrate that within this culture there is greater love of children, more accurate perceptions of the world, greater honesty, and all the rest.

I say this is a sad way of dismissing the paradox because to my mind it refuses to recognize grave and lacerating problems. Indeed, this kind of denial often shows a class blindness. The well-to-do hedonist and bohemian can, to be sure, through choice and with fewer long-range consequences lead a life of casual alliances. But he leaves fewer children behind to be raised by abandoned and despairing and angry women; or if he does, he can generally provide monetary support for them. There has been a lot of loose talk about the strength of the culture of poverty. There is strength, but those who exercise it would, it is my impression, gladly exchange the test that calls it forth for a stabler and more dependable existence.

But if we cannot deny the paradox, what can we make of it? Here I become more speculative. I return to Lewis' distinction between the cultures that, in poverty, develop a culture of poverty, and those that seem capable of maintaining, simply, a culture. One cannot help being impressed by the variations with which certain groups resort to welfare. Thus, in New York City, two-fifths of the Puerto Rican population is on welfare, and, somewhat further behind, one-third of the black. A study of a sample of the population of the West Side of New York, which includes a substantial number of Cubans and Haitians and other Caribbean and Latin American groups, shows a strikingly low proportion of welfare cases among them, only 10 percent, compared to 21 percent of those raised in New York City, 44 percent of those raised in Puerto Rico, 26 percent of those raised in the southern United States, 10 percent of

4 On this general point, see Stephen Thernstrom's excellent article, "Poverty in Historical Perspective," in Moynihan, op. cit.

those raised in the northeastern United States, and only 8 percent of those raised elsewhere, presumably European and Asian immigrants. What is the cause of these differences? Gross observation suggests that it cannot be explained simply by differences in literacy, occupation, skill, and the like, though these certainly play a role. It does seem that certain cultures resist dependency, as others accept it. It would be important to understand these phenomena better, for we are saying very little by merely asserting that one culture "resists" dependency and another "accepts" it.

If we understood these differences better, could we do much about them? After all, we are hardly likely to become social engineers of culture. Nevertheless, I believe this could be a fruitful line of investigation. Just as the investigations into ethnic and racial differences in educational achievement begin to give us certain glimmers of lines of action that might perhaps improve achievement, so research into culture differences in behavior in connection with dependency could give us some insight into policy measures that might be successful there. Of course it is hardly likely that we could agree on policy measures if we fail to agree that the culture of poverty demands some intervention or amelioration, or that dependence is worse than independence. And unfortunately many do not agree on these points.

A second highly hypothetical line of investigation is suggested to me by the odd fact that the culture of poverty and dependency seems to expand—at least in this country—along with the policy measures designed to deal with it. Thus our steady tinkering with welfare has been accompanied by a steady increase in the welfare population. Even the proposals of President Nixon, the most radical since the adoption of federal support for public assistance in 1937, begin with another huge increase in the population to be aided. Other aspects of these revolutionary changes are designed to transform the stigma of welfare into the positively valued new program of family assistance, but one must cross one's fingers as to whether such a radical change in identity can be accomplished easily, or at all. I am impressed by the observation of Tocqueville, 135 years ago, in his "Memoir on Pauperism," that the most prosperous nation in Europe (England) had a much higher rate of dependency than the poorest states (Spain and Portugal), and that the most prosperous parts of France had much higher rates of dependency than the least prosperous. Tocqueville did not resort to any differences in culture in explaining this, but insisted that dependency would have to increase with prosperity and enlightenment. Education would lead to new tastes and new desires, the expansion of transportation and communication would permit new invidious comparisons, inevitably prosperity would mean dependency.

> We should not delude ourselves [he wrote]. . . . As long as the present movement of civilization continues, the standard of living of the greatest number will rise: the society will become more perfected, better informed; existence will be easier, milder, more embellished, and longer. But at the same time we must look forward to an increase of those who will need to resort to the support of all their fellow men to obtain a small part of these benefits. It will be possible to moderate this double movement; special national circumstances will precipitate or suspend its course; but no one can stop it. (Drescher 1968:11)

Tocqueville went on to analyze, correctly I think, the inevitable effects of public charity, which could only be degrading. He did not envisage that it could be turned into a right, so that it could be stripped of its degrading character. This is a hope we now cling to. We speak of redefining dependencies into something ennobling. We have not sufficiently analyzed how complex such an operation must be. Once again to quote Tocqueville:

> There is something great and virile in the idea of right which removes from any bequest its suppliant character, and places the one who claims it on the same level as the one who grants it. But the right of the poor to obtain society's help is unique in that instead of elevating the heart of the man who exercises it, it lowers him.
> . . . From the moment that an indigent is inscribed on the poor list of his parish he can certainly demand relief, but what is the achievement of this right if not a notarized manifestation of misery, of weakness, of misconduct on the part of its recipient? Ordinary rights are conferred on men by reason of some personal advantage acquired by them over their fellow men. This other kind is accorded by reason of a recognized inferiority. The first is a clear statement of superiority; the second publicizes inferiority and legalizes it. The more extensive and secure ordinary rights are, the more honor they confer; the more permanent and extended the right to relief is, the more it degrades.

We can suggest then two hypotheses—that cultures show a variable resistance to features of the culture of poverty and to the dependency that is its consequence in advanced welfare states; and that social policy itself must increase the number of those who become dependent, not only by simply providing for relief, but by mechanisms of eligibility, provision, and administration that have various side effects leading to features of the culture of poverty and dependency. Now it is possible that in certain ways the culture of modern society itself, of welfare state society, takes on features that encourage the culture of poverty. Here I cannot do better than quote from Thernstrom:

> A . . . change which demands attention is the steady erosion of the subcultures which defined the expectations of working men in the past. There were once working-class-enclaves—often, but not necessarily—with ethnic boundaries—within which the mobility values of the society were redefined in more attainable terms. The workingmen of nineteenth-century America toiled with remarkable dedication to accumulate the funds to pay for tiny cottages of their own and were amazingly successful at it. . . . But everything about contemporary American society conspires to make . . . having lower aspirations than others more difficult. . . . Many of the poor today expect more and put up with less from others in order to get it, precisely because the enclaves of old have been levelled, with all the docility and deference which they fostered. Of course one can always say this represents a weakening of the moral fibre of the common man, . . . but the point is that this weakening of the moral fibre, if you wish to call it that, is no accident; it is not a mere passing whim, but the result of some large and irreversible changes in society.
>
> It is obvious that this line of argument applies with special force to the Negro. His objective grievances are real enough, . . . but they are by no means new. . . . (Thernstrom 1969:180)

Thernstrom then points to the startling changes in the levels of demand by the dependent, for example, the demands of the Welfare Rights organizations, and points out they were unimaginable in the past but must continue to rise in the future. And he concludes: "The American Negro has never lived in the thrift-oriented subculture of the classic European immigrant. . . . This is no longer the nineteenth century and there is no way of isolating the ghetto from the mass media and inundating it with McGuffey's readers. . . ." (Thernstrom 1969:180)

In effect, changes in modern society itself—the downgrading of thrift, foresight, hard work, family responsibility—combine with certain features of existing subcultures, and give them greater legitimacy and greater general acceptance, and those who carry its features therefore show a new self-confidence in asserting that their ways, too, have virtue —perhaps exceptional virtue—and demand support.

If then, as Tocqueville wrote, public charity grows with the increase of prosperity, of education, of knowledge, all of which raise desires and expectations; if it has degrading consequences, despite its origin in the virtuous desire to alleviate distress, what are our alternatives? To let people starve is impossible; even to allow them to exist on, or fall to a standard of living that all our laws and regulations condemn and even ban, is quite out of the question. Our most useful alternatives are to try to expand the measures that might prevent a resort to public charity as a right. If more of those who might fall subject to the culture of poverty could be induced to remain on the farms and in the small towns through proper rewards; if more could be assisted to higher paying jobs, which themselves carried various insurances, that is, "rights"—health, unemployment, sick leaves, and the like; if more of the costs of raising a family could be shifted to funds that could indeed be granted as of right, rather than on the basis of special appeal, a means test, and a special determination; then perhaps the inevitably increasing demand of the poor—and the nonpoor too—to a higher measure of public insurance and support could be met in ways that were not degrading. In short, our task is to translate demeaning charity into rights. But it is not to be done as simply as many now think, by fiat and renaming. It can only be done by subtle and close attention to what most people understand by right and what most people understand as unworthy privilege. It will involve hard and close work to expand the realm of right, and narrow as much as we can the domain defined as charity.

20
Patrons of the Poor

Edward H. Spicer

In industrialized societies no less than in feudal landlord societies there are extreme differences in wealth. There has been no clear trend toward leveling the extremes in those Western industrialized societies in which the private sector of the economy has maintained an important controlling role. Extreme poverty is clearly a persistent accompaniment of industrialization in such societies. The current great concern in the United States with this phenomenon, in the sense of its being conceived as a problem condition to be changed, may or may not be indicative that change is incipient. Fundamental change would of course involve new ideological orientations and new social structure—in short, a different kind of social system. Symptoms of such change are perhaps to be seen in the new orientations embodied in the Economic Opportunity Act and in what has been labeled civil disorder. The legislation proposes new forms of social structure for linking people in poverty areas directly with the national political organization. Civil disorder, too, may be symptomatic of new forms of internal social organization stimulated both by the new legislation and by other conditions.

The importance of Oscar Lewis' (1966) conception of the "culture of poverty" is that it calls attention to the social organization of the poor in industrialized societies. The work of Lewis and of others makes it clear that there are forms of family organization distinctive of the extremely poor and that the cultural interests of the poor find only very limited expression, if any at all, in voluntary and political organizations.[2] On the other hand, the relations between the social organization characteristic of the poor and the structures which link them with the societies of

SOURCE: *Human Organization* 29, no. 1 (1970): 12–20. Reprinted by permission of the Society for Applied Anthropology.

[1] This paper is based on research financed by the Office of Economic Opportunity.

[2] See, for example, Stone and Schlamp 1966: ch. 4 and 5; Safa 1968:335–351.

which they are a part require more attention than they have received.

It is the purpose of this paper to present an analysis of the structural linkages of one segment of the poor with the United States society and to indicate some of the ways these linkages affect the internal organization of poor people. The data are drawn from a study of one ethnic group in a Southwestern city of 250,000 which has been undergoing industrialization over the past forty years. The group consists of some 400 descendants of immigrants from Mexico who have maintained a sense of identity as Indians during this period. They live in a *barrio,* or district of the city, which we shall call Navidad.

The case can be viewed as an instance of the general phenomenon of differentially organized segments of industrialized societies as correlated with wealth differentials. If one is concerned with changing in any fundamental way the wealth differential, it seems essential first to understand clearly the social correlates. The instance chosen has, of course, its unique qualities; but it shares certain features, especially regarding wider linkages, with the situations of poor people throughout the United States.

The common general features may be viewed as a network of clienteles through which individuals and families of lower income are linked with individuals of higher income. The individual about whom each set of clients focuses is a person who does not participate in the community life of the low-income segment. Nevertheless, although not participating, he or she has important indirect influences on the internal organization of the poor group. I shall call such individuals "patrons." There are many different varieties of patrons, but they have so many behavioral features in common that it seems justified to speak of a single role type. The people of Navidad recognize this and sometimes use the general Spanish term *patrón* for all such persons despite their different occupations and other varying characteristics.

SOCIAL BACKGROUND OF NAVIDAD NEIGHBORHOOD

The people of the Navidad neighborhood by 1965 were at an advanced stage in the process of entry into urban-industrial society. For some fifty years, their chief reliance had been on agricultural labor; but the techniques they had learned were becoming obsolete as a result of mechanization and because nearby ranches where they had worked were swallowed up by the expanding city which now surrounded their settlement. After a rapid doubling of their population during the 1920's and early 1930's, the population stabilized in the following thirty years. The males were employed irregularly (only a few months of the year) in the usual casual labor pattern, and a third or more of the men were chronically drunk or under the influence of drugs. Those households which maintained any degree of stability achieved it in terms of female-dominance. These were of course the familiar symptoms of the conditions of urban poverty. There was, however, another condition at odds with the dominant trend: the existence of a community organization oriented to religious interests which produced a considerable degree of solidarity within the group and *vis-à-vis* other segments of the poor in the city. Its activities focused on the maintenance of an annual round of ceremony based on a modified Catholic calendar, but these interests and the organization operated independently of the Roman Catholic Church.

The organization constituted a continuity with the cultural tradition which had developed among the group in Mexico before migration. In the United States, the religious orientations were to some extent encouraged by attitudes and actions of the dominant Anglo society. For example, for forty years the Chamber of Commerce had made small contributions for the annual Easter ceremony. Various persons, including anthropologists, had written about the ceremonies, which gave them publicity and encouraged their development as a tourist attraction. The community organization also had certain social insurance functions which continued as other aspects of ceremonial life altered in response to economic demands. The ceremonial life was a focus of interest and concern for nearly all the different kinds of patrons; for some it was something to be exploited, for others something to be eliminated as an undesirable form of superstition.

Navidad had what members of the surrounding society called a chief. The office had been filled by a succession of individuals during the forty-five years since the people first settled in their location several miles outside the city. What distinguished the office in the 1960's was that the native of Navidad who occupied it was also the highest official in the community's religious organization. Prior to the 1950's, Anglos had, in effect, appointed a Navidader to deal with them in matters of law and order and other affairs which interested the Anglo (white American) society. Thus, persons who held the chiefly office rarely had any influence that derived from status within the Navidad community itself. They performed services which met the occasional needs of Anglo officials and, by virtue of their relations with Anglos, were sometimes able to perform services desired by citizens of Navidad. The chief in the 1960's, however, had strong influence within Navidad by virtue of his traditional role as head of the ceremonial organization. He accepted the title of "chief" as conferred by Anglos, but he also held an office known by the traditional title. He was effective in dealing with both Anglos and Mexican-Americans in the social agencies and political parties and thus was able to get various benefits for people in Navidad. This combination of an important internal role and an effective role in external relations led many to rely on him more than they had on former chiefs, but it also led to smoldering opposition.

THE PATRONAGE NETWORK

A remarkable concert of effort developed rapidly among the various patrons of Navidad during the five-month period from August through December 1966, in response to what was felt quite correctly to be a threat to the relations they had built up with the people over many years. What happened during this period made it possible to see with great clarity how the patronage network operated. The event which sparked the patrons to action and to public declarations of their positions was the funding of a housing improvement program by the Office of Economic Opportunity. The funds became available in August and an office for the project was set up in a Navidad house in September. Members of the Navidad group were hired as laborers for the housing operation and also as community workers. Most of the patrons promptly became active in opposition to the program.

One of the most vigorous opponents was a minister of a lower class church who had been proselytizing for several years in the neighborhood. He was the current representative of a long line of Protestant missionaries who have sought to convert this ethnic group from their native Catholicism. Almost from the beginning of the settlement, Jehovah's Witnesses, Baptists, Methodists, members of the Assembly of God, and others appeared in the community on proselytizing missions. Some entered people's homes with phonographs to play evangelizing records. Some distributed literature in Spanish about the Second Coming. Others were subsidized by the wealthy in the city to set up a community center, and still others established themselves in nearby buildings where they held meetings and invited people from Navidad to attend. The effort through the years was intensive, but not more than a half dozen persons were converted. And nearly all of those who were converted at the same time continued activities in the Navidad religious community.

The minister who took action in September 1966 lived on the edge of the community and had access to a building established by a charitable foundation within the neighborhood. Some Navidad young people attended his services intermittently, and two had become fairly regular in their attendance. One of these felt that he had benefited by a service provided by the minister's church, namely, a short residence in a "dry-out" resort for chronic drinkers. The minister also provided other services, such as giving out old clothing and other castoff articles and giving free rides on weekends to other churches and to picnics sponsored by the denomination. Sporadically, some members of the community made use of these services, and as many as twenty-five or thirty persons sometimes attended meetings. There was curiosity on the part of younger people who were interested in what the various denominations in the city had to offer. The minister made efforts to build a following by visiting all families who would allow him to enter their houses. He had worked hard for many months, but could be said to have developed a regular Navidad clientele of only two families, and not all members of those families were regular participants in the church activities. The overwhelming majority held aloof, although they tolerated the minister's presence at the edge of the community and utilized his services when it was advantageous.

The minister's immediate reaction when the new project was announced was to ask the Navidad chief for an assignment of land in the location set aside for the improved housing. It was pointed out that the land was for residences, and his oral application was turned down. Since the chief, whose devotion to the Navidad religious organization was very strong, had been in opposition to the minister many times before, the refusal of the land assignment was interpreted by the minister as religious discrimination.

There was immediate reaction also from another patron, the principal of the public school located in the midst of the community. She was backed by the assistant superintendent of the school district, a number of teachers in her school, some teachers who had formerly taught there, and the principal of a junior high in which Navidad children were enrolled. Like the missionary contacts, school contacts with the Navidad community were longstanding. A year after the settlement was founded in 1921, a retired schoolteacher of great energy persuaded the district to set up a special one-room school for the immigrant children. A school had thus operated for more than forty years in Navidad and had, several years prior to 1966, become a first-rate modern elementary school serving not only Navidad but the whole area of the city which had expanded around the original settlement. The principal developed a deep personal interest in Navidad families, especially those whose children attended the school. The principal spent a good deal of time visiting the families and, like the minister, was a well-known figure in the community. The benefits that she brought were more acceptable than those offered by the clergyman. She, too, obtained clothing and other commodities, and some of these were more or less eagerly accepted. Moreover, acceptance did not involve pressure to change religious beliefs and practices. The principal therefore, had a larger and more permanent clientele by far than did the minister. She was a welcome visitor in a dozen or more homes and had built up friendships over a number of years. Some teachers followed suit, but the principal was the most important patron.

It was true also, however, that she had antagonized some parents, most notably the chief, who had broken with her over what he considered undue strictness regarding children's behavior and had transferred his children to another school. Clearly, there was rivalry between her and the chief with respect to influence in the community. This was in part based on competition regarding services to people of Navidad and partly on the principal's low regard for the religious organization the chief headed. Unlike the minister, though, she did not come into direct conflict with the religious beliefs and practices since her basic position was one of tolerance. She encouraged the Navidad children in the school to make colored pictures of the Easter ceremonies and write short essays about their meaning. The view implicit in her activities was that the parents could not be diverted from their colorful ceremonies, but the children could be expected to lose interest and eventually be weaned away and enter the "mainstream of American life." This, in her view, was the objective of sound schooling.

The view was shared by the assistant Superintendent of Schools who held an additional view obviously directly related to his position as superintendent of physical facilities. He expressed himself in meetings to the effect that because the people of Navidad had been provided with a school facility in their own neighborhood, nothing should be done that would result in families withdrawing their children from that school. In other words, the school district had an investment that should be protected. An immediate reaction of the school authorities was to conduct a survey among the children attending the Navidad school to get some indication of the feelings about the new project. The results were not very conclusive, but one or more statements made by pupils were interpreted by the principal and her staff to mean that families in Navidad were being forced into the program whether they wanted or not.

A third variety of patron consists of workers in various county offices who as bureaucratic administrators of law and order, welfare, health, and other services have frequent contacts with the people of Navidad. The most concerned of these in September 1966 were functionaries in the juvenile probation office. Some of them had many contacts with parents of juveniles who had been classed as delinquents; and one at least, herself formerly associated with the Navidad community as a nearby resident, made a special effort to discuss the housing project with the young people she knew best. Her clientele was perhaps more devoted than either of the others, but it was smaller and confined mostly to teenage girls. The values and orientations which characterized the probation officer came out later and will be described below. It is sufficient here to emphasize that there were many small and inconstant clienteles forming and falling apart as different specialists were required by their jobs to make contacts in Navidad. Sometimes their assignments were reinforced by personal interest stimulated in doing their jobs. The official worker of this sort was a common figure in the community. Some persons in Navidad were on the lookout for advantages that might be obtained through such officials, but others were annoyed and tried to seclude themselves from the changing succession of outsiders bent on giving various kinds of assistance.

BELIEFS AND VALUES OF THE PATRONS

Two events in the fall of 1966, following the beginning of the OEO project, led to rather full statements by the three varieties of patrons just described regarding their conceptions of their roles and their understanding of the Navidad neighborhood. The first event was a general meeting in the plaza of the Navidad church, called by the chief for the purpose of explaining the new project which he strongly supported. Several hundred neighborhood residents attended. Also in the crowd which stood in front of the chapel were representatives of the clienteles of the minister, the school principal, the juvenile probation office, and a scattering of others. During the general discussion following the chief's announcement questions were raised and charges made. The two major charges in opposition were: (1) that the people of Navidad were being coerced to become involved in the project against their real desires, and (2) that the project was discriminatory on the basis of religious belief. The contradictory nature of the charges did not at first seem to be recognized by the opponents. The newspapers of the city reported the meeting, thus throwing the matter into the arena of public discussion. As the newspapers printed the views of the patrons, it became apparent during the following month that the underlying viewpoints were very much in accord with the view of the Navidad community which prevailed in the city at large.

Three basic assumptions of this prevailing view can be summarized. In the first place, it became widely apparent that those persons in the higher income levels who became interested at all took it for granted that the people of Navidad were incapable of doing anything for themselves. The idea that they might have initiated efforts to improve their housing seemed incredible. It was even less believable that they might have taken part in initiating and planning a full-scale improvement project. Evidence showing that they had indeed participated over a period of many months prior to the OEO funding was too incredible to be accepted.

A corollary of the first basic assumption was that if something was actually happening it must be the work of behind-the-scene manipulators. One newspaper gave banner headlines to a story concocted by the minister, charging that anthropologists were carrying out a scheme for putting the Navidad people in a museum situation where they could be studied at leisure. The essence of the story was that Navidaders were pawns in the hands of others. Only such an interpretation could make sense to the patrons who were accustomed in their professional operations to manipulate the people in accordance with their own ends. The third assumption which became clear was that the proposal in the improvement plan for removal to the suburbs was highly offensive. The view was deep-rooted that somehow the destiny of the people was inextricably linked with their existing slum neighborhood. These fundamental beliefs of the patrons were obviously part of a more general belief system prevailing widely in the city.

It was in the atmosphere of public statement and restatement of these and related conceptions that the patrons called for an investigation by the Mayor's Committee on Human Relations. A special subcommittee was appointed which carried out a brief preliminary investigation and then called for a hearing. Patrons of the three varieties described attended, along with three representatives of the OEO project, the chief, a Navidad community worker, and an anthropologist who had assumed an administrative role in the new program. The hearing was called specifically to consider the charges of coercion and religious discrimination. However, when no cases were offered, the meeting became a forum in which the views of the patrons occupied most of the time.

These viewpoints reveal the values and cultural orientations of the patron system very clearly. The spokesman for the school authorities was the least coherent and obviously least acquainted with the nature of the Navidad community. He focused his opposition to the housing project on the label "ghetto." He thought that a concerted effort by people of Navidad to improve their housing in a new location would create a ghetto. Although the hearing uncovered information demonstrating that the program was entirely voluntary, he insisted that it would bring about segregation. This spokesman had earlier held that the school district's investment in the Navidad school required that the people stay in its vicinity. When pressed, he said that he did believe that the Navidad area was one of the worst slums in the city; but he seemed to believe that the school held the solution to bettering conditions, that it would equip children to leave the slum. When he was reminded that the school had been located in the midst of Navidad for forty years, he replied that in another forty years it would bring about the solution.

The views of the probation officials were considerably more reasoned. They were explicit in their belief that it was the "culture" of the Navidaders which caused the delinquency of their children. An Indian member of the subcommittee insisted that people should have the right to choose their culture; and in the discussion that followed, the chief probation officer said that he had not really meant that they should not. But it was clear that until that moment he had regarded the organized community ceremonials as the cause of his problems and thought their eradication was necessary for solving them. His assistant based her position on interviews with young persons. She was convinced that the girls especially were deeply unhappy as a result of their parents being "different" from other inhabitants of the city. She herself had become marginal to the Navidad community and had been working in terms of extruding others from it. She seemed to feel that the children's desires should be the central consideration and that the children should somehow be separated from identification with their parents.

Like the other patrons, the missionary's viewpoint was based on his own professional interests and included conceptions growing out of his efforts to further those interests. Like the others, he held that the persons in the community who were most "advanced" were those who had disassociated themselves from the community religious life and had progressed farthest in school. Like the others, in short, he was deeply hostile to Navidad interests which were not organized in terms of his own cultural orientations. Yet only he among this group of patrons offered any sort of alternative model of community life: this was of course his kind of Protestant congregation. He had added to this during the previous month a plan for a democratically organized improvement committee to be centered at his church but under local leadership.

The views which became defined so sharply during the crisis in patron influence had much in common, primarily their attack on the existing community structure. Nevertheless, it proved impossible to coordinate the patrons' approaches. Efforts at unity were inaugurated, but they promptly failed. It became increasingly apparent that school, lower class church, and county officialdom had too many institutionalized oppositions among themselves to be brought together. Each in its own way continued to oppose the OEO project; but, although they succeeded in seriously confusing the Navidaders for several months and thus threatening the continuation of the program, their respective attacks steadily disintegrated.

DISCUSSION

I have examined only three of the many varieties of patron. Nevertheless, it seems possible to regard all patrons as belonging to three major types.

In the first place there are the large number of patrons with their clienteles that are characteristic of all levels of life in industrial societies. These are the shopkeepers, employers of labor, physicians, other professionals, and many others whose operations are primarily intraclass and whose benefits are not managed specifically with reference to the wealth and cultural differentials between lower and upper income groups.

Second, there are the patrons who are clearly *exploitative,* whose operations are specifically adapted to the differentials in terms of maximum advantage to the higher income patron. These are familiar as business operators of various kinds, ranging from installment sellers of insurance schemes to dope pushers. Perhaps we should include in this category social scientists such as anthropologists. Navidad, during its long existence, has had its share of such patrons. Anthropologists from the university in the city have derived a supply of information from Navidad for theses and publications which were used for their own professional advancement, which provided no return to the Navidaders, and which resulted in the establishment of small clienteles of "informants" who were the recipients of small gifts.

The third type of patron is that with which we have been primarily concerned in this paper. Looking at their operations with respect to their function in the poor community, we might label these *disruptive* patrons. They build up clienteles like the other kinds of patrons, through dispensing goods and services; but this is not done to gain economic advantage. There may be an economic effect, but it is not in the charter of the institution. The economic effect is indeed sometimes the other way—advantage for the client. The distinctive quality of these clienteles is that they involve competitive influence statuses and that the processes of competition are disruptive with respect to the poor community.

They are disruptive in two ways. On the one hand the structure of the clientele network organizes individuals in the poor community into segments which cut vertically through other social units, whether they be kin, ritual kin, sodality, or community-wide units. The basis of a clientele is a dyadic relationship between patron and client. The patron, as an outsider differentiated by wealth and way of life from members of the community, and nonparticipant in the community, is the instrument of power and authority in the relationship. Clients who enter into the relationship are to some extent oriented in the direction of the cultural values of the patron. Thus each clientele constitutes a segmental organization independent of the internal authority system of the community and in some degree of the interest system of the clients. If a community organization exists among the poor group, a clientele affiliation therefore tends to disrupt it. Similarly, if a community organization is breaking down—or if none exists—the clientele unit tends to inhibit growth towards community organization.

Moreover, when several clienteles are in competition, the disruptive or inhibitive influences are intensified, not only because of the structural characteristics of each clientele but also because of the competition for clients. The advantages obtainable through affiliation with patrons orient individuals toward these segmental structures rather than toward any internal associations. Even the growth of leadership on a basis of the development of patrons within the poor group is interfered with, as was clear in the case under review. The chief, who had begun to know his way around in the surrounding society, gained followers on very much the same basis as other patrons—by obtaining advantages for individuals in the community. But the growth of a communitywide clientele affiliated with the chief was obstructed at point after point by the operation of competing clienteles headed by outside patrons. The result was continued growth of the clientele system with polarization of Navidad residents around outside patrons, the chief, and a few Navidaders who sought intermittently to compete with the chief. In this case, the segmental structure of shifting loyalties according to immediate advantages obtainable through one affiliation or another had begun to affect the community organization by reducing its solidarity. The social clusters based on personal loyalty between individual client and patron seemed to mark a stage in the development of a culture of poverty, the final stage of chronic internal disorganization which accompanies incorporation into the industrial society.

The clienteles were disruptive also in another way. The patrons were characterized by an ideology which was consistent with the structural effects of the clienteles. They were all (with the exception of the native patron, the chief) deeply hostile to the existing community organization in Navidad. In this, they were influenced not only by the practical consideration that the internal organization necessarily limited their patronage power, but also by strongly-held value orientations which viewed the Navidad way of life negatively. Given such an orientation the patrons did all in their power to undermine the authority system of the community religious organization and to influence as many persons as they could to value it negatively. Thus we find them concentrating their efforts on children and young men and women. Evidently their common view was that older adults probably could not be influenced, and any hope for increasing their own power lay in orienting the young people away from community life. Apparently all entertained as a model for the future a Navidad without any community organization. Their goal was to channel young people out of the Navidad social system. They furthermore believed that this approach was supported by the ideal of "integration" in the dominant society. The United States as a society with a formal legal adherence to integrationist policy seemed to them to sanction positively their individual operations as patrons in Navidad.

CONCLUSION

I see the implications of this case study in the following terms. First, disruptive clienteles seem to be widespread in the United States, and I would venture that they are also to be found in other highly industrialized societies. Moreover, in the United States the three varieties of the disruptive type analyzed here constitute a very widespread combination. The school, the religious denomination, and the governmental bureau with their clienteles are found everywhere operating in ways similar to those described. However unusual the internal social system of Navidad, the clientele system affecting its people is a generally recurrent one.

Second, such clientele systems operate effectively to destroy, to inhibit, or to subvert internal organization in communities of the poor only so long as those communities are relatively small and the individuals in them are reachable by the patrons. When the poor population expands greatly and rapidly—as has happened in our cities—the patronage system of control becomes less and less effective in breaking the poor down into clientele segments at odds with one another. Moreover, if ethnic groups among the poor are rejected or become culturally unintelligible to potential disruptive patrons, the clientele system does not develop. This of course has been happening especially with respect to blacks in our cities. This means that a large proportion of the poor cannot be kept chronically disorganized with respect to their own cultural interests.

Third, what is called civil disorder tends to appear among those poor whom the patron system fails to reach. Such disorder, though not the only symptom, is actually symptomatic of a developing community organization. It heralds a phase in industrial society in which the patron system as a control in the relations between lowest income and other groups in the society ceases to function as an important maintenance mechanism.

SELECTED READINGS

BANFIELD, EDWARD C.

1968 The Unheavenly City: The Nature and Future of Our Urban Crisis. Boston: Little, Brown.

A controversial study of urban poverty which has been sharply attacked for its views on the self-perpetuating nature of an urban poverty culture.

CURRENT ANTHROPOLOGY

1969 A CA Book Review: Culture and Poverty: Critique and Counter-Proposals. Current Anthropology 10:2–3:181–202.

A number of anthropologists, including Valentine and Lewis, comment on the issues raised in Valentine's book.

LEACOCK, ELEANOR BURKE, ED.

1971 The Culture of Poverty: A Critique. New York: Simon and Schuster.

This collection of articles explores the relationship between education and poor people. In addition, the concept of the culture of poverty is critically examined by a number of social scientists.

LEWIS, OSCAR

1965 La Vida: A Puerto Rican Family in the Culture of Poverty—San Juan and New York. New York: Random House.

In addition to his detailed discussion of the culture of poverty in the introduction, Lewis provides the reader with a full and detailed description of the daily lives of Puerto Rican family members in two urban settings.

VALENTINE, CHARLES A.

1968 Culture and Poverty: Critique and Counterproposals. Chicago: University of Chicago Press.

Valentine examines a number of views of lower-class life in cities, including Lewis' culture of poverty. In addition, he presents an outline of further research, a section which may be compared with his article included in Part Two of this volume.

WINTER, J. ALAN, ED.

1971 The Poor: A Culture of Poverty or a Poverty of Culture? Grand Rapids, Mich.: W. B. Eerdmans.

A collection of articles, including Glazer's paper reprinted in this part, critically examining the notion of the culture of poverty.

Bibliographical References

ADAMS, ROBERT M.
1960 The Origin of Cities. Scientific American 2033:153–172.

ALEXANDER, CHRISTOPHER
1966 A City Is Not a Tree. Design 206:46–55.

AMYOT, J.
1960 The Chinese Community of Manila. Thesis, University of Chicago.

ANANT, SANTOKH S.
1970 Self- and Mutual Perception of Salient Personality Traits of Different Caste Groups. Journal of Cross-Cultural Psychology 1:1:41–52.

n.d.a "Stereotyped" Character Traits of Various Religious Groups in India as Seen by Hindus. Ms.

n.d.b Provincial and Regional Stereotypes in India. Ms.

ARENSBERG, CONRAD M.
1961 The Community as Object and as Sample. American Anthropologist 63:241–264.

1968 The Urban in Crosscultural Perspective. *In* Urban Anthropology: Research Perspectives and Strategies. Elizabeth M. Eddy, Ed. Southern Anthropological Society Proceedings, No. 2. Athens: University of Georgia Press, pp. 3–15.

AXELROD, MORRIS
1956 Urban Structure and Social Participation. American Sociological Review 21:13–18.

BALANDIER, G.
1952 Approche sociologique des "Brazzavilles noires": étude préliminaire. Africa 22:23–24.

BANNISTER, P., and J. M. M. MAIR
1968 Evaluation of Personal Constructs. London: Academic Press.

BANTON, MICHAEL

1957 West African City. A Study of Tribal Life in Freetown. London: Oxford University Press.

BARNES, J. A.

1954 Class and Committees in a Norwegian Island Parish. Human Relations 7:1:39–58.

BARTH, FREDRIK, ED.

1969 Ethnic Groups and Boundaries. Boston: Little, Brown.

BASCOM, WILLIAM

1952 The Esusu: A Credit Institution of the Yoruba. Journal of the Royal Anthropological Institute 82:63–69.

1955 Urbanization among the Yoruba. In World Urbanism. Philip M. Hauser, Ed. American Journal of Sociology 60:446–454. Reprinted in Cultures and Societies of Africa. S. and P. Ottenberg, Eds. New York: Random House, 1960, pp. 255–267.

1958 Yoruba Urbanism: A Summary. Man 58:190–191.

1959a Urbanism as a Traditional African Pattern. In Urbanism in West Africa. Kenneth Little, Ed. The Sociological Review 7:29–43.

1959b Les premiers fondements historiques de l'urbanisme yoruba. Présence Africaine 23:22–40.

1960 Lander's Routes through Yoruba Country. Nigerian Field 25:12–22.

BASTIDE, R.

1964 Ethnologie des capitales latino-americaines. D. G. Epstein, Trans. Caravelle 3:73–89.

BEALS, RALPH L.

1951 Urbanism, Urbanization and Acculturation. American Anthropologist 53:1–10.

BEALS, RALPH L., and HARRY HOIJER

1971 An Introduction to Anthropology. Fourth Edition. New York: Macmillan.

BELL, COLIN R.

1968 Middle Class Families. New York: Humanities Press.

BELL, WENDELL

1958 Social Choice, Life Styles and Suburban Residence. In The Suburban Community. William M. Dobriner, Ed. New York: G. P. Putnam's Sons, pp. 225–247.

BELL, WENDELL, and MARYANNE T. FORCE

1956 Urban Neighborhood Types and Participation in Formal Associations. American Sociological Review 21:25–34.

BERGER, BENNETT

1960 Working Class Suburb: A Study of Auto Workers in Suburbia. Berkeley: University of California Press.

BERLIN, BRENT, PAUL KAY, D. E. BREEDLOVE, and P. H. RAVEN

1968 Covert Categories and Folk Taxonomies. American Anthropologist 70: 290–299.

BERREMAN, GERALD D.

1960 Cultural Variability and Drift in the Himalayan Hills. American Anthropologist 62:774–794.

1962 Behind Many Masks: Ethnography and Impression Management in a Himalayan Village. Monograph No. 4. Ithaca: Society for Applied Anthropology.

1964 Aleut Reference Group Alienation, Mobility and Acculturation. American Anthropologist 66:231–250.

1966a Caste in Cross-Cultural Perspective. In Japan's Invisible Race: Caste in Culture and Personality. G. DeVos and H. Wagatsuma, Eds. Berkeley: University of California Press, pp. 275–324.

1966b Anemic and Emetic Analyses in Social Anthropology. American Anthropologist 68:346–354.

1967 Caste as Social Process. Southwestern Journal of Anthropology 23:351–370.

1972a Hindus of the Himalayas: Ethnography and Change. Berkeley: University of California Press (First Edition 1963).

1972b Race, Caste and Other Invidious Distinctions in Social Stratification. Race 13, April (In press).

BÉTEILLE, ANDRÉ

1969 Castes: Old and New. Bombay: Asia Publishing House.

BHATT, G. S.

1960 Urban Impact and the Trends of Intra-Caste Solidarity and Dissociability as Measures of Status Mobility Among the Chamar. Paper presented at the Indian Sociological Conference, Saugar, India.

BLACK, CYRIL E.

1966 The Dynamics of Modernization. New York: Harper and Row.

BLACK, MARY, and DUANE METZGER

1965 Ethnographic Description and the Study of Law. *In* Anthropological Study of Law. Laura Nader, Ed. American Anthropologist 67:6 (pt. 2):141–165.

BLUMER, HERBERT

1969 Symbolic Interactionism. Englewood Cliffs: Prentice-Hall.

BLUNT, E. A. H.

1931 The Caste System of Northern India. London: H. Milford, Oxford University Press.

BONILLA, FRANK

1962 The Favelas of Rio: The Rundown Rural Barrio in the City. Dissent 9:383–386.

BOURRICARD, F.

1964 Lima en la vida política peruana. America Latina October–December: 89–96.

BROOM, LEONARD, and JOHN I. KITSUSE

1955 The Validation of Acculturation: A Condition to Ethnic Assimilation. American Anthropologist 57:44–48.

BROWN, CLAUDE

1965 Manchild in the Promised Land. New York: Signet.

BRUNER, EDWARD M.

1961 Urbanization and Ethnic Identity in North Sumatra. American Anthropologist 63:508–521.

1967 Comments on A. L. Epstein's "Urbanization and Social Change in Africa." Current Anthropology 8:297.

n.d. The Expression of Ethnicity in Indonesia. Ms.

BRUNER, J. S., J. J. GOODNOW, and G. A. AUSTIN

1956 A Study of Thinking. New York: John Wiley and Sons.

BUSIA, K. A.

1950 Report on a Social Survey of Sekondi-Takoradi. London: Crown Agents.

CAPLOW, THEODORE

1949 The Social Ecology of Guatemala City. Social Forces 28:113.

CARTWRIGHT, JOHN R.

1970 Politics in Sierra Leone 1947–1967. Toronto: University of Toronto Press.

CENTRAL STATISTICS OFFICE, FREETOWN

1965 1963 Population Census of Sierra Leone, vol. 2. Freetown: Central Statistics Office.

CHALMERS, DAVID

1899 Report by Her Majesty's Commissioner and Correspondence on the Subject of the Insurrection in the Sierra Leone Protectorate 1898. I–II Cmd. 9388, 9391. London: H.M.S.O.

CHANG, P.

1958 The Distribution and Relative Strength of the Provincial Merchant Groups in China. Thesis, University of Washington. Ann Arbor: University Microfilms 58-2134.

CHAUDHURI, NIRAD

1967 The Continent of Circe. London: Chatto and Windus.

CHENG, H.

1950 The Network of Singapore Societies. Journal of South Seas Societies 6:10–12.

CHHIBBAR, Y. P.

1968 From Caste to Class: A Study of the Indian Middle Classes. New Delhi: Associated Publishing House.

CICOUREL, AARON V.

1964 Method and Measurement in Sociology. Glencoe: The Free Press.

1968 Preliminary Issues of Theory and Method. In The Social Organization of Juvenile Justice. New York: John Wiley, pp. 1–21.

CLOWARD, RICHARD A., and L. E. OHLIN

1960 Delinquency and Opportunity: A Theory of Delinquent Gangs. Glencoe: The Free Press.

CLOWARD, RICHARD A., and FRANCIS F. PIVEN

1969 The Poor Against Themselves. Nation, November 25.

COHEN, ABNER

1969 Custom and Politics in Urban Africa. A Study of Hausa Migrants in Yoruba Towns. Berkeley: University of California Press.

COMBER, L. F.

1957 An Introduction to Chinese Societies. Singapore: Straits Times Press.

1959 Chinese Secret Societies in Malaya. Monograph of the Association of Asian Studies. Locust Valley, N.Y.: J. J. Augustin Inc.

CONKLIN, HAROLD C.

1962 Lexicographical Treatment of Folk Taxonomies. International Journal of American Linguistics 28(2, part IV):119–141.

1964 Ethnogenealogical Method. In Exploration in Cultural Anthropology. Ward Goodenough, Ed. New York: McGraw-Hill.

COOK, SCOTT

1968 The Obsolete Anti-Market Mentality. In Readings in Anthropology, Vol. II, Second Edition. Morton Fried, Ed. New York: Crowell.

COSTA, LUCIA

1957 Relatorio do plano pilôto. Revista Brasileira de Municípos Vol. 10.

COUGHLIN, R. J.

1955 The Chinese in Bangkok. American Sociological Review 20: 311–316.

1960 Double Identity, the Chinese in Modern Thailand. Hong Kong: Hong Kong University Press.

CURLE, ADAM, and E. L. TRIST

1947 Transitional Communities and Social Reconnection. Human Relations 1:42–68, 240–288

DALBY, DAVID

1971 Africa in a New Era of Intervention. New Society April 22: 670–671.

DAVIS, KINGSLEY, and ANA CASIS

1946 Urbanization in Latin America. Milbank Memorial Fund Quarterly 24: 186–207. [Reprinted in Reader in Urban Sociology. P. K. Hatt and A. J. Reiss, Eds. Glencoe: The Free Press, 1951, pp. 150–165.]

DENZIN, NORMAN K.

1970 Rules of Conduct and the Study of Deviant Behavior: Some Notes on the Social Relationship. In Deviance and Respectability. J. D. Douglas, Ed. New York: Basic Books.

DEWAR, JAMES

1966 The Unlocked Secret: Freemasonry Examined. London: William Kimber.

DEWEY, RICHARD

1960 The Rural-Urban Continuum: Real but Relatively Unimportant. American Journal of Sociology 66:60–66.

DICKINSON, W. V., et al.

1966 Report of the Working Party on Local Administration. Hong Kong: The Government Press.

DOBRINER, WILLIAM M.

1958 Introduction: Theory and Research in the Sociology of the Suburbs. *In* The Surburban Community. William M. Dobriner, Ed. New York: G. P. Putnam's Sons, pp. xiii–xxviii.

DRESCHER, SEYMOUR

1968 Tocqueville and Beaumont on Social Reform. New York: Harper.

DUBE, S. C.

1955 A Deccan Village. *In* India's Villages. Calcutta: West Bengal Government Press, pp. 180–191.

DUHL, LEONARD J.

1956 Mental Health and Community Planning. *In* Planning 1955. Chicago: American Society of Planning Officials, pp. 31–39.

DUNCAN, OTIS DUDLEY, and ALBERT J. REISS, JR.

1956 Social Characteristics of Rural and Urban Communities, 1950. New York: John Wiley and Sons.

DUNCAN, OTIS DUDLEY, and LEO F. SCHNORE

1959 Cultural, Behavioral and Ecological Perspectives in the Study of Social Organization. American Journal of Sociology 65:132–155.

DURKHEIM, ÉMILE

1912 The Elementary Forms of Religious Life. London: Allen and Unwin.

1932 [1893] De la Division du Travail Social. Paris: F. Alcan.

ENDERS, JOHN

n.d. Profile of the Theater Market. New York: Playbill, undated and unpaged.

ENGLISH, PAUL WARD

1966 City and Village in Iran: Settlement and Economy in the Kerman Basin. Madison: University of Wisconsin Press.

EPSTEIN, A. L.

1958 Politics in an Urban African Community. Manchester: Manchester University Press.

1967 Urbanization and Social Change in Africa. Current Anthropology 8:275–296.

1969 The Network and Urban Social Organization. *In* Social Networks in Urban Situations. Analyses of Personal Relationships in Central African Towns. J. Clyde Mitchell, Ed. Manchester: Manchester University Press.

EPSTEIN, DAVID G.

1969 Planned and Spontaneous Urban Settlement in Brasilia. Ann Arbor: University Microfilms.

EVANS-PRITCHARD, E. E.

1937 Witchcraft, Oracles and Magic among the Azande. Oxford: Clarendon Press.

FARIS, ELLSWORTH

1932 The Primary Group, Essence and Accident. American Journal of Sociology 38:41–50.

FASHOLE-LUKE, E. W.

1968 Religion in Freetown. In Freetown: A Symposium. C. Fyfe and E. Jones, Eds. Freetown: Sierra Leone University Press.

FAVA, SYLVIA FLEIS

1958 Contrasts in Neighboring: New York City and a Suburban Community. In The Suburban Community. William M. Dobriner, Ed. New York: G. P. Putnam's Sons, pp. 122–131.

FIRTH, RAYMOND

1951 Elements of Social Organization. Boston: Beacon Press.

FIRTH, RAYMOND, J. HUBERT, and A. FORGE

1970 Families and Their Relatives. London: Routledge and Kegan Paul.

FISHER, HUMPHREY J.

1969 Elections and Coups in Sierra Leone, 1967. Journal of Modern African Studies 7:611–636.

FOLEY, DONALD L.

1957 The Use of Local Facilities in a Metropolis. In Cities and Society. Paul Hatt and Albert J. Reiss, Jr., Eds. Glencoe: The Free Press, pp. 237–247.

FORDE, C. DARYLL, ED.

1956 Social Implications of Industrialization and Urbanization in Africa South of the Sahara. Paris: UNESCO.

FORM, WILLIAM H., et al.

1954 The Compatibility of Alternative Approaches to the Delimitation of Urban Sub-areas. American Sociological Review 19:434–440.

FORTES, MEYER

1948 Time and Social Structure. In Social Structure. Meyer Fortes, Ed. New York: Russell & Russell.

1969 Kinship and the Social Order. Chicago: Aldine.

FOX, RICHARD G.

1969a Professional Primitives: Hunters and Gatherers of Nuclear South Asia. Man in India 49:13–27.

1969b From Zamindar to Ballot Box: Community Change in a North Indian Market Town. Ithaca: Cornell University Press.

1971 Rajput Clans and Rurban Settlements in Northern India. *In* Urban India: Society, Space, and Image. Richard G. Fox, Ed. Program in Comparative Studies on Southern Asia. Durham: Duke University.

FRAKE, CHARLES O.

1961 The Diagnosis of Disease among the Subanun of Mindinao. American Anthropologist 63:113–132.

1962a Cultural Ecology and Ethnography. American Anthropologist 64:53–59.

1962b The Ethnographic Study of Cognitive Systems. *In* Anthropology and Human Behavior. T. Gladwin and W. C. Sturtevant, Eds. Washington, D.C.: Anthropological Society of Washington.

1964 Notes and Queries in Ethnography. American Anthropologist 66:1 (pt. 2):132–145.

FRANK, ANDRE GUNDER

1967a Capitalism and Underdevelopment in Latin America. New York: Monthly Review Press.

1967b Sociology of Development and Underdevelopment of Sociology. Catalyst Summer:20–73.

FREEDMAN, M.

1950 Colonial Law and Chinese Society. Journal of the Royal Anthropological Institute 89:97–126.

1956 Kinship, Local Grouping and Migration: A Study in Social Realignment among the Chinese Overseas. Thesis, University of London.

1957 Chinese Family and Marriage in Singapore. London: Her Majesty's Stationery Office.

1958 Lineage Organization in Southeastern China. London School of Economics Monographs in Social Anthropology 18. London: Athlone Press.

1959 The Handling of Money. Man 59:64–65.

1961a Immigrants and Associations: Chinese in 19th Century Singapore. Comparative Studies in Society and History 3:25–48.

1961b Overseas Chinese Associations: A Comment. Comparative Studies in Society and History 3:478–480.

FROMM, ERICH

1955 The Sane Society. New York: Rinehart & Co., Inc.

FYFE, CHRISTOPHER

1962 A History of Sierra Leone. London: Oxford University Press.

1964 Sierra Leone Inheritance. London: Oxford University Press.

GANS, HERBERT J.

1959 The Urban Villagers: A Study of the Second Generation Italians in the West End of Boston. Boston: Center for Community Studies (Mimeo).

1961 Planning and Social Life: An Evaluation of Friendship and Neighbor Relations in Suburban Communities. Journal of the American Institute of Planners 27:134–140.

1962 The Urban Villagers: Group and Class in the Life of Italian-Americans. New York: The Free Press.

1967 Urbanism and Suburbanism as Ways of Life: A Re-evaluation of Definitions. In The Study of Society. P. I. Rose, Ed. New York: Random House. [Reprinted from Human Behavior and Social Process. Arnold P. Rose, Ed. 1962.]

GARFINKEL, HAROLD

1967 Studies in Ethnomethodology. Englewood Cliffs: Prentice-Hall.

GEERTZ, CLIFFORD

1963 The Integrative Revolution: Primordial Sentiments and Civil Politics in the New States. In Old Societies and New States. Clifford Geertz, Ed. New York: The Free Press, pp. 105–157.

1965 Social History of an Indonesian Town. Cambridge: MIT Press.

GERTH, H. H., and C. WRIGHT MILLS, TRANS. and EDS.

1947 From Max Weber: Essays in Sociology. London: Kegan Paul, Trench, Trubner.

GLUCKMAN, MAX

1955 Custom and Conflict in Africa. Oxford: Basil Blackwell.

1961 Anthropological Problems Arising from the African Industrial Revolution. In Social Change in Modern Africa. Aidan Southall, Ed. London: Oxford University Press, pp. 67–82.

GOFFMAN, ERVING

1959a The Presentation of Self in Everyday Life. New York: Doubleday.

1959b The Moral Career of the Mental Patient. Psychiatry 22:2:123–142.

1963 Behavior in Public Places. Glencoe: The Free Press.

1967 Interaction Ritual: Essays on Face-To-Face Behavior. Garden City, N.Y.: Doubleday.

1970 Strategic Interaction. Philadelphia: University of Pennsylvania Press.

GOLDHAMER, HERBERT, and ANDREW W. MARSHALL

1949 The Frequency of Mental Disease: Long-Term Trends and Present Status. The Rand Corp.

GOODENOUGH, WARD H.

1956 Componential Analysis and the Study of Meaning. Language 32:195–216.

1957 Cultural Anthropology and Linguistics. Georgetown University Monograph Series on Language and Linguistics 9:173.

1965 Yankee Kinship Terminology: A Problem in Componential Analysis. American Anthropologist 67:259–287.

GORDON, DAVID

1969 Income and Welfare in New York City. The Public Interest Summer: 84.

GOUGH, KATHLEEN

1968 Anthropology and Imperialism. Monthy Review 19:12–27.

GOULDNER, ALVIN

1960 The Norm of Reciprocity: A Preliminary Statement. American Sociological Review 25:161–178.

GRANT, CHARLES S.

1970 Democracy in the Connecticut Frontier Town of Kent. New York: AMS Press.

GRANT, JAMES

1960 A Geography of Western Nigeria. Cambridge: Cambridge University Press.

GREER, SCOTT

1956 Urbanism Reconsidered: A Comparative Study of Local Areas in a Metropolis. American Sociological Review 21:19–25.

1960 The Social Structure and Political Process of Suburbia. American Sociological Review 25:514–526.

1962 The Emerging City: Myth and Reality. New York: The Free Press.

GREER, SCOTT, and ELLA KUBE

1959 Urbanism and Social Structure: A Los Angeles Study. In Community

Structure and Analysis. Marvin B. Sussman, Ed. New York: Thomas Y. Crowell Company, pp. 93–112.

GULICK, JOHN

1963 Urban Anthropology: Its Present and Future. *In* Readings in Anthropology, Vol. II: Cultural Anthropology. Morton H. Fried, Ed. Second Edition. New York: Crowell.

1967 Tripoli: A Modern Arab City. Cambridge: Harvard University Press.

1968 The Outlook, Research Strategies, and Relevance of Urban Anthropology: A Commentary. *In* Urban Anthropology: Research Perspectives and Strategies. Elizabeth M. Eddy, Ed. Southern Anthropological Society Proceedings No. 2. Athens: University of Georgia Press, pp. 93–98.

GUMPERZ, JOHN J.

1962 Hindi-Punjabi Code-Switching in Delhi. Proceedings of the Ninth International Congress of Linguists. The Hague: Mouton.

1964 Linguistic and Social Interaction in Two Communities. American Anthropologist 66(pt. 2):137–153.

GUTKIND, E. A.

1964 International History of City Development. New York: The Free Press.

GUTKIND, PETER C. W.

1969 African Urban Life and the Urban System. *In* Urbanism, Urbanization, and Change: Comparative Perspectives. Paul Meadows and Ephraim H. Mizruchi, Eds. Reading, Mass: Addison-Wesley.

HAGE, PER

1968 A Structural Analysis of Muncherian Beer Terms and Beer Drinking. Unpublished ms.

HALPERIN, E.

1963 The Decline of Communism in Latin America. Atlantic Monthly May: 65–70.

HANNERZ, ULF

1967 Gossip, Networks, and Culture in a Black American Ghetto. Ethnos 1:4: 35–60.

1969 Soulside: Inquiries Into Ghetto Culture. New York: Columbia University Press.

HARRIS, MARVIN

1956 Town and Country in Brazil. New York: Columbia University Press.

HELLMAN, ELLEN

1948 Rooiyard. A Sociological Survey of an Urban Native Slum Yard. The Rhodes-Livingstone Papers No. 13.

HENSLIN, JAMES

1968 Trust and the Cab Driver. *In* Sociology and Everyday Life. M. Truzzi, Ed. Englewood Cliffs: Prentice-Hall.

HERRICK, B. A.

1966 Urban Migration and Economic Development in Chile. Cambridge: Harvard University Press.

HEYER, V.

1953 Patterns of Social Organization in New York City's Chinatown. Thesis, Columbia University. Ann Arbor: University Microfilms 19-099.

HUDDLESTON, TREVOR

1956 Naught For Your Comfort. New York: Doubleday & Company.

HUTCHINSON, H. W.

1968 Social Anthropology and Urban Studies. *In* Urban Anthropology: Research Perspectives and Strategies. Elizabeth M. Eddy, Ed. Southern Anthropological Society Proceedings, No. 2. Athens: University of Georgia Press, pp. 24–30.

ISAACS, HAROLD

1964 India's Ex-Untouchables. New York: John Day.

ISAACS, K. S., J. M. ALEXANDER, and E. A. HAGGARD

1963 Faith, Trust and Gullibility. International Journal of Psychoanalysis 44:461–469.

ITURRIAGA, JOSE E.

1951 La Estructura Social y Cultural de Mexico. Mexico: Fundo de Cultura Económica.

JACOBSON, DAVID

1968 Friendship and Mobility in the Development of an Urban Elite African Social System. Southwestern Journal of Anthropology 24:123–138.

1970 Culture and Stratification among Urban Africans. Journal of Asian and African Studies 3:176–183.

JANOWITZ, MORRIS

1952 The Community Press in an Urban Setting. Glencoe: The Free Press.

JEFFERSON, MARK

1909 The Anthropogeography of Some Great Cities. Bulletin of the American Geographical Society 41:537–566.

1939 The Law of the Primate City. Geographical Review 29:226–232.

JONASSEN, CHRISTEN T.

1955 The Shopping Center Versus Downtown. Columbus, Ohio: Bureau of Business Research, Ohio State University.

KARIM, A. K. NAZMUL

1956 Changing Society in India and Pakistan. Dacca, Pakistan: Geoffrey Cumberlege, Oxford University Press.

KAY, PAUL

1966 Comment. Current Anthropology 7:20–23.

1969 Some Theoretical Implications of Ethnographic Semantics. Working Paper No. 24. Language-Behavior Research Laboratory, University of California, Berkeley.

KEISER, R. LINCOLN

1969 The Vice Lords: Warriors of the Streets. New York: Holt, Rinehart and Winston.

KELLER, SUZANNE

1968 The Urban Neighbourhood. New York: Random House.

KELLY, GEORGE

1955 The Psychology of Personal Constructs. New York: W. W. Norton.

KEYFITZ, NATHAN

1967 Urbanization in South and Southeast Asia. In The Study of Urbanization. Philip M. Hauser and Leo F. Schnore, Eds. New York: John Wiley and Sons, pp. 265–309.

KILSEN, MARTIN

1967 Political Change in a West African State. Cambridge: Harvard University Press.

KLAPP, ORRIN E.

1962 Heroes, Villains, and Fools. Englewood Cliffs: Prentice-Hall.

KRAPF-ASKARI, EVA

1969 Yoruba Towns and Cities. London: Oxford University Press.

KTSANES, THOMAS, and LEONARD REISSMAN

1959 Suburbia: New Homes for Old Values. Social Problems 7:187–194.

KUPER, HILDA, ED.

1965 Urbanization and Migration in West Africa. Los Angeles: University of California Press.

KUTNER, B., C. WILKINS, and P. R. YARROW

1952 Verbal Attitudes and Overt Behavior Involving Racial Prejudice. Journal of Abnormal and Social Psychology 47:649–652.

KWOK, S.

1954 An Account of the Sources of Benevolent Assistance Which are Asian in Origin and Organization. Research Paper, University of Malaya.

LADINSKY, JACK

1967 Occupational Determinants of Geographic Mobility among Professional Workers. American Sociological Review 32:257–264.

LAMBERT, JACQUES

1959 Os dois brasis. Rio de Janeiro: Centro Brasileiro de Pesquisas Educacionais.

1967 Conclusáes, Seminario sobre a Politôca de Integracao de uma Populacão Marginalizada. Brasilia.

LAMPARD, ERIC E.

1967 Historical Aspects of Urbanization. *In* The Study of Urbanization. Philip M. Hauser and Leo F. Schnore, Eds. New York: John Wiley and Sons, pp. 519–554.

LAPIDUS, IRA MARVIN

1967 Muslim Cities in the Later Middle Ages. Cambridge: Harvard University Press.

LA PIERE, RICHARD T.

1934 Attitudes Versus Actions. Social Forces 13:230–237.

LAUDON, K. P.

1941 The Chinese in Thailand. London: Oxford University Press.

LEACH, EDMUND

1954 Political Systems of Highland Burma, 1965 Edition. Boston: Beacon Press.

LEACOCK, ELEANOR B., ED.

1971 The Culture of Poverty: A Critique. New York: Simon and Schuster.

LEEDS, ANTHONY

1968a The Anthropology of Cities: Some Methodological Issues. *In* Urban

Anthropology: Research Perspectives and Strategies. Elizabeth M. Eddy, Ed. Southern Anthropological Society Proceedings No. 2. Athens: University of Georgia Press, pp. 31–47.

1968b Brazilian Careers and Social Structure: An Evolutionary Model and Case History. American Anthropologist 70: 1321–1347.

1971 The Concept of the "Culture of Poverty": Conceptual, Logical, and Empirical Problems, with Perspectives from Brazil and Peru. *In* The Culture of Poverty: A Critique. Eleanor Burke Leacock, Ed. New York: Simon and Schuster, pp. 226–284.

LEEDS, ANTHONY, and ELIZABETH LEEDS

1967 Brazil and the Myth of Urban Rurality: Urban Experience, Work and Values in "Squatments" of Rio de Janeiro and Lima. Paper presented at the Conference on Work and Urbanization in Modernizing Societies, St. Thomas, Virgin Islands.

LEWIS, OSCAR

1952 Urbanization without Breakdown: A Case Study. Scientific Monthly 75:31–41.

1959 Five Families: Mexican Case Studies in the Culture of Poverty. New York: Basic Books, Inc.

1961 The Children of Sanchez: Autobiography of a Mexican Family. New York: Random House.

1965 La Vida: A Puerto Rican Family in the Culture of Poverty—San Juan and New York. New York: Random House.

1966 The Culture of Poverty. Scientific American 215:4:19–25.

1967 Further Observations on the Folk-Urban Continuum and Urbanization with Special Reference to Mexico City. *In* The Study of Urbanization. Philip M. Hauser and Leo F. Schnore, Eds. New York: John Wiley and Sons, pp. 491–502.

1969 The Culture of Poverty. *In* On Understanding Poverty. Daniel P. Moynihan, Ed. New York: Basic Books, pp. 187–200.

LIBENOW, J. GUS

1969 Liberia: The Evolution of Privilege. Ithaca: Cornell University Press.

LIEBOW, ELLIOT

1967 Tally's Corner. A Study of Negro Streetcorner Men. Boston: Little, Brown and Company.

LIM, M.

1958 The Hainanese of Singapore. Research Paper, University of Malaya.

LITTLE, KENNETH

1957   The Role of Voluntary Associations in West African Urbanization. American Anthropologist 59:579–596.

1965a The Political Functions of the Poro, I. Africa 35:349–365.

1965b West African Urbanization: A Study of Voluntary Associations in Social Change. New York: Cambridge University Press.

1966   The Political Functions of the Poro, II. Africa 36:62–72.

LOCKRIDGE, KENNETH A.

1970 A New England Town, The First Hundred Years. New York: Norton.

LUPTON, T., and S. WILSON

1959 Background and Connections of Top Decision-Makers. Manchester School 30–51.

LYNCH, OWEN

1967 Rural Cities in India, Continuities and Discontinuities. *In* India and Ceylon: Unity and Diversity. Philip Mason, Ed. London: Oxford University Press, pp. 142–158.

MCCALL, GEORGE, and J. L. SIMMONS

1966 Identities and Interactions. New York: The Free Press.

MACIVER, R. M.

1917 Community, a Sociological Study. London: Macmillan.

MANGIN, WILLIAM P.

1963 Urbanization Case History in Peru. Architectural Design August:365–370.

1964 Sociological, Cultural and Political Characteristics of Some Rural Indians and Urban Migrants in Peru. Paper presented at Wenner-Gren Symposium on Cross-Cultural Similarities in the Urbanization Process (Mimeo).

1965 The Role of Social Organization in Improving the Environment. *In* Environmental Determinants of Community Well-Being. Pan American Health Organization.

1967 Latin America Squatter Settlements: A Problem and a Solution. Latin American Research Review 2:65–98.

MANGIN, WILLIAM P., ED.

1970 Peasants in Cities: Readings in the Anthropology of Urbanization. Boston: Houghton Mifflin.

MANGUS, A. R., and JOHN R. SEELEY

1947 Mental Health Needs in a Rural and Semirural Area of Ohio. Bulletin No. 1951. Columbus: The Ohio State University (Mimeo).

MARRIS, PETER

1962 Family and Social Change in an African City. A Study of Rehousing in Lagos. Chicago: Northwestern University Press.

MARTINDALE, DON

1966 Prefatory Remarks: The Theory of the City. *In* The City, by Max Weber. Don Martindale and Gertrud Neuwirth, Trans. and Eds. New York: The Free Press, pp. 9–62.

MARWICK, M.

1952 The Social Context of Cewa Witch Beliefs. Africa 22:120–135, 215–233.

MAYER, PHILIP

1961 Townsmen or Tribesmen: Conservatism and the Process of Urbanization in a South African City. Cape Town: Oxford University Press.

1962 Migrancy and the Study of Africans in Towns. American Anthropologist 64:576–592.

MEHTA, VED

1971 Letter from West Bengal. New Yorker December 11:166–176.

METZGER, DUANE, and GERALD E. WILLIAMS

1963 A Formal Ethnographic Analysis of Tenejapa Indino Weddings. American Anthropologist 65:1076–1101.

1966 Some Procedures and Results in the Study of Native Categories: Tzeltal "Firewood." American Anthropologist 68:389–407.

MILGRAM, S.

1967 The Small World Problem. Psychology Today 1:61–67.

MILLER, WALTER

1969 The Elimination of the American Lower Class as National Policy. *In* On Understanding Poverty: A Critique of the Ideology of the Poverty Movement of the 1960's, Daniel P. Moynihan, Ed. New York: Basic Books, pp. 260–315.

MINER, HORACE

1953 The Primitive City of Timbuctoo. Princeton: Princeton University Press. Published for the American Philosophical Society, Memoirs vol. 32 [Revised Edition 1965].

1967 The City and Modernization: An Introduction. *In* The City in Modern Africa. Horace Miner, Ed. London: Frederick A. Praeger.

MITCHELL, J. CLYDE

1952 A Note on the African Conception of Causality. The Nyasaland Journal 5:51–58.

1956a Urbanization, Detribalization, and Stabilization in Southern Africa: A Problem of Definition and Measurement. *In* Social Implications of Industrialization and Urbanization in Africa South of the Sahara. C. Daryll Forde, Ed. Paris: UNESCO, pp. 693–711.

1956b The Yao Village. Manchester: Manchester University Press for Rhodes-Livingston Institute.

1966 Theoretical Orientations in African Urban Studies. *In* The Social Anthropology of Complex Societies. Michael Banton, Ed. London: Tavistock Publications, pp. 37–61.

1969a The Concept and Use of Social Networks. *In* Social Networks in Urban Situations. J. Clyde Mitchell, Ed. New York: Humanities Press.

1969b Social Networks in Urban Situations. Analyses of Personal Relationships in Central African Towns. Manchester: Manchester University Press.

MORENO, J. L.

1934 Who Shall Survive? Washington: Nervous and Mental Disease Publishing Co., pp. 256–265.

NADEL, S. F.

1957 The Theory of Social Structure. Glencoe: The Free Press.

NATIONAL RESOURCES COMMITTEE

1937 Our Cities: Their Role in the National Economy. Washington: Government Printing Office.

NELKIN, DOROTHY

1970 Unpredictability and Life Style in a Migrant Labor Camp. Social Problems 17:472–486.

NICHOLAUS, MARTIN

1968 Radicals in the Professions. Newsletter of the American Anthropological Association November:9–10.

OPLER, MORRIS E.

1968 The Themal Approach in Cultural Anthropology and Its Application to North Indian Data. Southwestern Journal of Anthropology 24:215–227.

ORANS, MARTIN

1965 The Santal: A Tribe in Search of a Great Tradition. Detroit: Wayne University Press.

PARKIN, DAVID

1969 Neighbors and Nationals in an African City Ward. Berkeley: University of California Press.

PARK, ROBERT E., ERNEST W. BURGESS, et al.

1925 The City. Chicago: University of Chicago Press.

PASTORE, J.

1968 Satisfaction among Migrants to Brasilia, Brazil: A Sociological Interpretation. Dissertation, University of Wisconsin.

PATON, ALAN

1951 Cry, the Beloved Country. New York: Charles Scribners.

PEARSON, S. VERE

1935 The Growth and Distribution of Population. New York: J. Wiley and Sons, Inc.

PEATTIE, L.

n.d. Social Issues in Housing. Joint Center for Urban Studies. Unpublished ms.

PERCHONOCK, NORMA, and OSWALD WERNER

1969 Navaho Systems of Classification: Some Implications for Ethnoscience. Ethnology 8:229–242.

PETERSON, JOHN

1969 Province of Freedom. London: Faber & Faber.

PETRAS, J.

1969 The New Revolutionary Politics in Latin America. Monthly Review 20: 34–39.

PHILLIPS, RAY EDMUND

1938 The Bantu in the City. A Study of Cultural Adjustment in the Witwatersrand. Lovedale: The Lovedale Press.

PITTS, JESSE R.

1968 Social Control. In International Encyclopedia of the Social Sciences 14:381–396.

PLOTNICOV, LEONARD

1967 Strangers to the City. Urban Man in Jos, Nigeria. Pittsburgh: University of Pittsburgh Press.

POCOCK, DAVID F.

1960 Sociologies—Rural and Urban. Contributions to Indian Sociology 4:63–81.

PODELL, LAWRENCE

1968 Families on Welfare in New York City. Center for the Study of Urban Problems, Bernard M. Baruch College, the City University of New York, part 1.

PORTER, ARTHUR

1963 Creoldom: A Study of the Development of Freetown Society. London: Oxford University Press.

PRICE, JOHN A.

1968 The Migration and Adaptation of American Indians to Los Angeles. Human Organization 27:168–175.

1971 Cultural Divergence Related to Urban Proximity on American Indian Reservations. Community Training Program, University of Minnesota, Minneapolis.

PROTECTORATE ASSEMBLY

1950 Proceedings of the Seventh Meeting. 26 September 1950.

PURCELL, V. W.

1965 The Chinese in Southeast Asia. Second Edition. London: Oxford University Press.

PYE, LUCIEN W.

1963 The Political Implications of Urbanization and the Development Process. *In* Social Problems of Development and Urbanization. Science, Technology and Development Vol. 7. Washington: Government Printing Office.

RADCLIFFE-BROWN, A. R.

1940 On Social Structure. Journal of the Royal Anthropological Institute 70:1–12.

RATH, R., and N. D. SIRCAR

1960 The Mental Pictures of Six Hindu Caste Groups About Each Other as Reflected in Verbal Stereotypes. Journal of Social Psychology 51:277–293.

REDFIELD, M. P., ED.

1962 Human Nature and the Study of Society, the Papers of Robert Redfield. Chicago: University of Chicago Press.

REDFIELD, ROBERT

1941 The Folk Culture of Yucatan. Chicago: University of Chicago Press.

1956 Peasant Society and Culture. Chicago: University of Chicago Press.

REDFIELD, ROBERT, and MILTON B. SINGER

1954 The Cultural Role of Cities. Economic Development and Culture Change 3:53–73.

REISS, ALBERT J., JR.

1955 An Analysis of Urban Phenomena. *In* The Metropolis in Modern Life. Robert M. Fisher, Ed. Garden City, N.Y.: Doubleday and Company, Inc., pp. 41–49.

1959 Rural-Urban and Status Differences in Interpersonal Contacts. American Journal of Sociology 65:182–195.

RESEK, CARL

1960 Lewis Henry Morgan: American Scholar. Chicago: University of Chicago Press.

RIESMAN, DAVID

1958 The Suburban Sadness. *In* The Suburban Community. William M. Dobriner, Ed. New York: G. P. Putnam's Sons, pp. 375–408.

ROBB, J. H.

1953 Experiences with Ordinary Families. British Journal of Medical Psychology 26:215–221.

1955 Working-Class Anti-Semite. London: Tavistock Publications Ltd.

RODGERS, GEORGE C.

1962 Evolution of a Federalist: William Loughton Smith of Charleston (1758–1812). Columbia: University of South Carolina Press.

RODWIN, L.

n.d. Urban Planning in Developing Countries. Washington, D.C.: Department of Housing and Urban Development.

ROMNEY, A. K., and R. G. D'ANDRADE

1964 Cognitive Aspects of English Kin Terms. American Anthropologist 66 (3, part 2):146–170.

ROSE, ARNOLD M.

1947 Living Arrangements of Unattached Persons. American Sociological Review 12:429–435.

ROSTOW, WALTER W.

1960 The Stages of Economic Growth: A Non-Communist Manifesto. Cambridge: Cambridge University Press.

RUBEL, ARTHUR J.

1966 Across the Tracks. Mexican-Americans in a Texas City. Austin: University of Texas Press.

RUDOLPH, LLOYD I., and SUSAN H. RUDOLPH

1960 The Political Role of India's Caste Associations. Pacific Affairs 33:5–22.

SACHS, WULF

1937 Black Hamlet. The Mind of an African Negro Revealed by Psychoanalysis. London: Geoffrey Bles.

SAFA, HELEN ICKEN

1964 From Shantytown to Public Housing: A Comparison of Family Structure in Two Urban Neighborhoods in Puerto Rico. Caribbean Studies 4.

1968 The Social Isolation of the Urban Poor. In Among the People: Encounters with the Poor. Irwin Deutscher and Elizabeth J. Thompson, Eds. New York: Basic Books, Inc., pp. 335–351.

SAHLINS, MARSHALL

1965 On the Sociology of Primitive Exchange. In The Relevance of Models for Social Anthropology. Michael Banton, Ed. A.S.A. Monographs No. 1. London: Tavistock Publications.

SALMEN, L.

1969 A Perspective on the Resettlement of Squatters in Brazil. America Latina 12:73–95.

SCHENSUL, STEPHEN J., J. ANTHONY PAREDES, and PERTTI J. PELTO

1968 The Twilight Zone of Poverty: A New Perspective on a Financially Depressed Area. Human Organization 27:30–40.

SCHMITT, ROBERT C.

1963 Implications of Density in Hong Kong. Journal of the American Institute of Planners August: 210–217.

SCHNEIDER, DAVID

1968 American Kinship: A Cultural Account. Englewood Cliffs: Prentice-Hall.

SCHUTZ, ALFRED

1962 Collected Papers, I: The Problem of Social Reality. M. Natanson, Ed. The Hague: M. Nijhoff.

SCHWAB, WILLIAM

n.d. Urbanization and Acculturation. Ms.

SCOTT, D. J. R.

1960 The Sierra Leone Election, May 1957. *In* Five Elections in Africa. W. J. M. Mackenzie and K. Robinson, Eds. London: Oxford University Press.

SEBRING, JAMES M.

1968 Caste Ranking and Caste Interaction in a North India Village. Unpublished dissertation, University of California, Berkeley.

1969 Caste Indicators and Caste Identification of Strangers. Human Organization 28:199–207.

SEELEY, JOHN R.

1959 The Slum: Its Nature, Use and Users. Journal of the American Institute of Planners 25:7–14.

SHARMA, K. N.

1969 Resource Networks and Resource Groups in the Social Structure. The Eastern Anthropologist 22:1:13–27.

SILVERBERG, JAMES

1968 Colloquium and Interpretive Conclusions. *In* Social Mobility in the Caste System of India. James Silverberg, Ed. Comparative Studies in Society and History, Supplement III. The Hague: Mouton, pp. 115–138.

SIMMEL, GEORG

1903 Die Grosstädte und das Geistesleben. *In* Die Grosstadt. Theodor Petermann, Ed. Dresden, pp. 187–206.

1950 The Sociology of Georg Simmel. K. H. Wolf, Trans., Ed. New York: The Free Press.

SIMMS, RUTH P.

1965 Urbanization in West Africa: A Review of Current Literature. Evanston: Northwestern University Press.

SINGER, MILTON

1960 The Expansion of Society and its Cultural Implications. *In* City Invincible: A Symposium on Urbanization and Cultural Development in Ancient Near East. Carl H. Kraeling and Robert M. Adams, Eds. Chicago: University of Chicago Press.

SINHA, G. S., and R. C. SINHA

1967 Exploration in Caste Stereotypes. Social Forces 46:42–47.

SJOBERG, GIDEON

1960 The Preindustrial City, Past and Present. Glencoe: The Free Press.

SKINNER, G. W.

1957 Chinese Society in Thailand: An Analytical History. Ithaca: Cornell University Press.

1958 Leadership and Power in the Chinese Community of Thailand. Ithaca: Cornell University Press.

SLATER, E., and M. WOODSIDE

1951 Patterns of Marriage. London: Cassell and Co. Ltd.

SMITH, JOEL, WILLIAM FORM, and GREGORY STONE

1954 Local Intimacy in a Middle-Sized City. American Journal of Sociology 60:276–284.

SOLOMON, P.

1966 Psychiatric Treatment of the Alcoholic Patient. In Alcoholism. J. H. Mendelson, Ed. Boston: Little, Brown and Company.

SOMBART, WERNER

1931 Städtische Siedlung, Stadt. In Handwörterbuch der Soziologie. Alfred Vierkandt, Ed. Stuttgart: F. Enke, pp. 527–533.

SONG, O. S.

1923 One Hundred Years of the Chinese in Singapore. London: John Murray.

SOUTHALL, AIDAN, ED.

1961 Social Change in Modern Africa. London: Oxford University Press.

SPECTORSKY, A. C.

1955 The Exurbanites. Philadelphia: J. B. Lippincott Co.

SPRADLEY, JAMES G.

1968 A Cognitive Analysis of Tramp Behavior. In Proceedings of the Eighth International Congress of Anthropological and Ethnological Sciences, Japan.

1970 You Owe Yourself a Drunk: An Ethnography of Urban Nomads. Boston: Little, Brown and Company.

SRINIVAS, M. N.

1966 Social Change in Modern India. Berkeley: University of California Press.

STERN, BERNHARD J.

1931 Lewis Henry Morgan: Social Evolutionist. Chicago: University of Chicago Press.

STONE, GREGORY P.

1954 City Shoppers and Urban Identification: Observations on the Social Psychology of City Life. American Journal of Sociology 60:36–45.

STONE, ROBERT C., and FREDERIC SCHLAMP

1966 Family Life Styles Below the Poverty Line. San Francisco: The Institute for Social Science Research, San Francisco State College.

SUMNER, WILLIAM GRAHAM

1906 Folkways; A Study of the Sociological Importance of Usages, Manners, Customs, Mores and Morals. Boston: Ginn and Company.

SUTTLES, GERALD

1968 The Social Order of the Slum. Chicago: University of Chicago Press.

SYCIP, F. C.

1957 Chinese Buddhism in Manila: A Case Study of the Social Structure of the Seng Guan Temple Congregation. Thesis, University of the Philippines.

TAN, G.

1963 The Chinese of Sukabumi. Monograph Series Cornell Modern Indonesian Project. Ithaca: Cornell University Press.

TAN, K. S.

1962 A Study of Kongsi Houses in Singapore Housing Immigrant Men. Research Paper, University of Singapore.

THERNSTROM, STEPHEN

1969 Poverty in Historical Perspective. In On Understanding Poverty: A Critique of the Ideology of the Poverty Movement of the 1960's. Daniel P. Moynihan, Ed. New York: Basic Books, pp. 160–186.

THRUPP, SYLVIA

1961 The Creativity of Cities. Comparative Studies in Society and History 4:53–64.

T'IEN, J-K.

1953 The Chinese of Sarawak: A Study of Social Structure. London School of Economics Monographs in Social Anthropology 12. London: Lund Humphries.

TIGER, LIONEL

1967 Bureaucracy and Urban Symbol Systems. In The City in Modern Africa. Horace Miner, Ed. London: Frederick A. Praeger.

TOOTH, G.

1956 Survey of Juvenile Delinquency in the Gold Coast. *In* C. Daryll Forde, Ed. Social Implications of Industrialization and Urbanization in Africa South of the Sahara. Paris: UNESCO, pp. 86–91.

TOPLEY, M.

1961 The Emergence and Social Function of Chinese Religious Associations in Singapore. Comparative Studies in Society and History 3:289–314.

TRAVERS, J., and S. MILGRAM

1969 An Experimental Study of the Small World Problems. Sociometry 32:425–443.

TURNER, J.

1963 Dwelling Resources in South America. Architectural Design August: 389–393.

U.S. BUREAU OF THE CENSUS

1969 Trends in Social and Economic Conditions in Metropolitan Areas. Current Population Reports, February 7, 1969.

VALENTINE, CHARLES A.

1968 Culture and Poverty. Critique and Counter-Proposal. Chicago: University of Chicago Press.

VALENTINE, CHARLES A., and BETTY LOU VALENTINE

1970 Making the Scene, Digging the Action, and Telling It Like It Is: Anthropologists at Work in a Dark Ghetto. *In* Afro-American Anthropology. Norman Whitten and J. F. Szwed, Eds. New York: The Free Press.

VAN DER BERGHE, PIERRE L., with EDNA MILLER

1964 Caneville. The Social Structure of a South African Town. Middletown, Conn.: Wesleyan University Press.

VAUGHAN, J. D.

1879 The Manners and Customs of the Chinese of the Straits Settlements. Singapore: Mission Press.

VERNON, RAYMOND

1959 The Changing Economic Function of the Central City. New York: Committee on Economic Development, Supplementary Paper No. 1.

VIDICH, ARTHUR J., and JOSEPH BENSMAN

1958 Small Town in Mass Society: Class, Power and Religion in a Rural Community. Princeton: Princeton University Press. [Revised Edition 1968].

WALLACE, ANTHONY F. C.

1961 Culture and Personality. New York: Random House.

1962 Culture and Cognition. Science 135:351.

WALLACE, ANTHONY F. C., and J. ATKINS

1960 The Meaning of Kinship Terms. American Anthropologist 62:58–80.

WALLACE, S. E.

1965 Skid Row as a Way of Life. Totowa, N.J.: The Bedminister Press.

WALLER, WILLARD

1938 The Family: A Dynamic Interpretation. New York: Dryden Press.

WALSH, RICHARD

1959 Charleston's Sons of Liberty. A Study of the Artisans, 1763–1789. Columbia: University of South Carolina Press.

WANG, G.

1959 A Short History of the Nan Yang Chinese. Singapore: Eastern University Press.

WARNER, SAM B.

1968 The Private City. Philadelphia in Three Periods of Growth. Philadelphia: University of Pennsylvania Press.

WARNER, W. LLOYD, and P. S. LUNT

1941 The Social Life of a Modern Community. New Haven: Yale University Press.

WATTELL, HAROLD

1958 Levittown: A Suburban Community. *In* The Suburban Community. William M. Dobriner, Ed. New York: G. P. Putnam's Sons, pp. 287–313.

WEAVER, THOMAS, and DOUGLAS WHITE

1972 Anthropological Approaches to Urban and Complex Society. *In* The Anthropology of Urban Environments. Thomas Weaver and Douglas White, Eds. Society for Applied Anthropology Monograph Series, Number 11, pp. 109–125.

WEBER, MAX

1925 Wirtschaft und Gesellschaft. Tübingen.

1927 General Economic History. Glencoe: The Free Press.

1966 The City. Don Martindale and Gertrud Neuwirth, Trans. and Eds. Introduction by Don Martindale. New York: The Free Press.

WEIGHTMAN, G. W.

1954 Community Organization of Chinese Living in Manila. Philippines Social Science and Humanities Review 19:25–39.

1960 The Philippine Chinese: A Culture History of a Marginal Trading Community. Thesis, Cornell University.

WHITE, DOUGLAS, and THOMAS WEAVER

1972 Sociological Contributions to an Urban Anthropology. In The Anthropology of Urban Environments. Thomas Weaver and Douglas White, Eds. Society for Applied Anthropology Monograph Series, Number 11, pp. 97–107.

WHITTEN, NORMAN E., and JAMES F. SZWED

1968 Negroes in the New World: Anthropologists Look at Afro-Americans. Transaction 5:49–56.

WHITTEN, NORMAN E., and JAMES F. SZWED, EDS.

1970 Preface. In Afro-American Anthropology. New York: The Free Press.

WHYTE, WILLIAM FOOTE

1955 Street Corner Society: The Social Structure of an Italian Slum. Second Edition. Chicago: University of Chicago Press. [First publication 1943. Paperback edition 1967].

WHYTE, WILLIAM H., JR.

1956 The Organization Man. New York: Simon and Schuster.

WILENSKY, HAROLD L.

1961 Orderly Careers and Social Participation: The Impact of Work History and Social Integration in the Middle Mass. American Sociological Review 26:521–539.

WILENSKY, HAROLD L., and CHARLES LEBEAUX

1958 Industrial Society and Social Welfare. New York: Russell Sage Foundation.

WILLCOX, WALTER F.

1926 A Definition of "City" in Terms of Density. In The Urban Community. E. W. Burgess, Ed. Chicago: University of Chicago Press, pp. 115–121.

WILLMOTT, D. E.

1960 The Chinese of Semarang: A Changing Minority Community in Indonesia. Ithaca: Cornell University Press.

WILLMOTT, PETER, and MICHAEL YOUNG

1957 Family and Kinship in East London. Baltimore: Penguin Books.

WILLMOTT, W. W.

1964 Chinese Society in Cambodia, with Special Reference to the System of Congregations in Phnom-Penh. Thesis, London University.

WIRTH, LOUIS

1928 The Ghetto. Chicago: The University of Chicago Press.

1938 Urbanism as a Way of Life. American Journal of Sociology 44: 1–24. [Reprinted in Cities and Society. Paul Hatt and Albert J. Reiss, Jr., Eds. Glencoe: The Free Press, pp. 46–64, 1957. Reprinted in On Cities and Social Life. A. J. Reiss, Jr., Ed. Chicago: The University of Chicago Press, 1964].

WOLF, ERIC

1966 Kinship, Friendship and Patron-Client Relations in Complex Societies. In The Social Anthropology of Complex Societies. Michael Banton, Ed. A.S.A. Monographs No. 4. London: Tavistock Publications.

WONG, C. S.

1963 A Gallery of Chinese Kapitans. Signapore: Government Printing Office.

YOUNG, MICHAEL

1954a Kinship and Family in East London. Man 54:137–139.

1954b The Planners and the Planned—The Family. Journal of the Town Planning Institute 40(6).

YOUNG, MICHAEL, and PETER WILLMOTT

1957 Family and Kinship in East London. London: Routledge & Kegan Paul, Ltd.

ZORBAUGH, HARVEY WARREN

1929 The Gold Coast and the Slum. A Sociological Study of Chicago's Near North Side. Chicago: University of Chicago Press.

Printer and Binder: The Murray Printing Compa
80 81 82 83 84 10 9 8 7 6 5 4 3